Colorado Museums and Historic Sites

Colorado Museums and Historic Sites

Victor J. Danilov

University Press of Colorado

Copyright © 2000 by the University Press of Colorado

Published by the University Press of Colorado
5589 Arapahoe Avenue, Suite 206C
Boulder, Colorado 80303

The University Press of Colorado is a cooperative publishing enterprise supported, in part, by Adams State College, Colorado State University, Fort Lewis College, Mesa State College, Metropolitan State College of Denver, University of Colorado, University of Northern Colorado, University of Southern Colorado, and Western State College of Colorado.

The paper used in this publication meets the minimum requirements of the American National Standard for Information Sciences—Permanence of Paper for Printed Library Materials. ANSI Z39.48-1984

Library of Congress Cataloging-in-Publication Data

Danilov, Victor J.
  Colorado museums and historic sites / Victor J. Danilov.
    p. cm.
  Includes bibliographical references (p.) and index.
  ISBN 0-87081-572-5 (cloth : acid-free paper) — ISBN 0-87081-573-3 (paper : acid-free paper)
    1. Museums—Colorado—Guidebooks. 2. Historic sites—Colorado—Guidebooks. 3.
  Colorado—Guidebooks. 4. Colorado—History, Local. I. Title.

  F773.D36 2000
  917.8804'34—dc21   00-027175

Designed by Laura Furney
Typeset by Daniel Pratt

09 08 07 06 05 04 03 02 01 00   10 9 8 7 6 5 4 3 2 1

Contents

Preface

This publication brings together for the first time a guide to Colorado's many museums, historic sites, and related facilities open to the public.

Information on more than 600 institutions, sites, and facilities in 90 categories is provided to help Colorado residents and visitors learn about—and hopefully visit—these cultural and historical places.

Sights include art, history, science, and specialized museums; art galleries, aquariums, botanic gardens, planetariums, and zoos; visitor centers of many varieties; and historic buildings, districts, parks, monuments, homesteads, farms, ranches, hotels, cemeteries, and ghost towns.

The introductory section provides an overview of Colorado's offerings; the second section describes the various entries and gives their addresses, hours, and admission prices. The appendices list cities and sites by geographic region, and museums, historic sites, and other facilities by category of interest. A select bibliography supplies additional information.

The author wishes to thank the representatives of the museums, historic sites, and other facilities listed for their assistance, as well as the authors of prior studies of historic places in Colorado.

Colorado Museums and Historic Sites

Colorado Museums and Historic Sites

Colorado has much to offer both resident and visitor alike—snow-capped mountains, spectacular views, abundant and diverse wildlife, sweeping farms and ranches, booming industry and economy, expanding cities, friendly people, and especially its fascinating cultural and historic sites.

This guidebook describes more than 600 of the state's museums, historic sites, and related facilities, almost equally divided between historic places and museums/museumlike institutions in 210 cities, towns, and other locations.

The Front Range—particularly the Denver metropolitan area—has the highest concentrations, but museums and historic sites can be found throughout the state. Colorado's museums, historic sites, and related facilities fall into 90 categories, the greatest number representing history museums (156), followed by art galleries (53), historic districts (52), historic ghost towns (50), visitor centers (40), and historic houses (32). Many of these institutions and sites are located on college campuses (52) and in national parks, monuments, and wildlife areas (31).

Colorado has 46 types of museums, ranging from art, history, and science museums to those devoted to such diverse topics as bells, boxing, buttons, cable television, carousels, dolls, ethnic history and culture, farming, figure skating, firefighting, jails, mental health, mining, money, pewter, racing cars, railroads, skiing, transportation, and western heritage.

Colorado also has a considerable number of other institutions usually classified as museums, including art galleries, aquariums, arboretums, botanic gardens, herbariums, observatories, planetariums, science centers, sculpture gardens, and zoos. Almost as numerous are other museumlike facilities, such as butterfly and insect centers, nature centers, environmental centers, interpretive centers, visitor centers, and wildlife parks and refuges.

Most of the museums and related facilities have opened since World War II. Some, however, were established in the late nineteenth century, such as the Carter Museum in Breckenridge and the Denver Art Museum.

The Colorado Historical Society was founded in 1879 but did not open its Colorado History Museum (and 11 other regional museums) until later in the twentieth century.

New museums and museumlike facilities open each year. Among the newest institutions are Colorado's Ocean Journey aquarium in Denver, the Brush Area Museum and Cultural Center in Brush, the Vilar Center for the Arts at the Beaver Creek Resort in Avon, and the U.S. Military Historical Museum in Fort Morgan.

The 295 historic places described in this book represent 20 types of historic sites. In addition to historic districts, ghost towns, and houses, Colorado has historic cemeteries, churches, farms, forts, homesteads, hotels, mines, opera houses, railroads, and schoolhouses. Many are National Historic Landmarks.

Among these sites are the Central City–Black Hawk Historic District, Rock Ledge Ranch Historic Site in Colorado Springs, Bent's Old Fort National Historic Site near La Junta, the Strater Hotel in Durango, Baca House and Bloom House in Trinidad, the Matchless Mine in Leadville, and Ashcroft and Independence ghost towns near Aspen.

GEOGRAPHIC DISTRIBUTION

Museums, historic sites, and related facilities can be seen in virtually every part of the state. However, slightly more than half of the 210 communities and places listed are in the north-central region, dominated by the Denver metropolitan area, and the south-central region, where Colorado Springs and many of the historic ghost towns are located.

NORTH-CENTRAL REGION

Of the more than 600 entries in this guidebook, 188 are in the six counties—Adams, Arapahoe, Boulder, Denver, Douglas, and Jefferson—constituting the Denver metropolitan area. This is where the largest and best-attended museums and museumlike institutions—with some of the most comprehensive collections—are found. Two of the most popular are the Denver Museum of Natural History and the Denver Zoological Gardens, each attracting nearly 2 million visitors annually. Other major sites are the Denver Art Museum, Colorado History Museum, Children's Museum of Denver, Denver Botanic Gardens, and the newly opened Colorado's Ocean Journey.

Denver offers a wide assortment of other museums, galleries, and historic sites, including the Forney Transportation Museum; Wings Over the Rockies Air & Space Museum; Black American West Museum & Heritage Center; Denver Firefighters Museum; Denver Museum of Miniatures, Dolls, and Toys; Molly Brown House Museum; Byers-Evans House and Denver History Museum; and Larimer Square and Lower Downtown (LoDo) historic districts.

Some of the metropolitan suburbs also boast a considerable number of museums and historic sites. Boulder features 26 facilities, 9 of which are on the University of Colorado campus, and Golden weighs in with 17 offerings, among them the Colorado Railroad Museum, Buffalo Bill Memorial Museum and Grave, and Astor House Museum. Littleton has 10 facilities, the prime attraction being the outdoor Littleton Historical Museum.

Numerous other museums, historic sites, and related facilities are located elsewhere in the north-central region. Fort Collins and Estes Park each have 13 offerings, including museums, galleries, visitor centers, and historic sites. Fort Collins is home to the Fort Collins Museum, the Discovery Center Science Museum, Avery House, and four galleries at Colorado State University. Estes Park features the Estes Park Area Historical Museum and the Lula W. Dorsey Museum of the YMCA of the Rockies, as well as a natural history museum and four visitor centers at Rocky Mountain National Park. In Greeley, the city operates four historical museums—Greeley Municipal Museum, Meeker Home Museum, Centennial Village Museum, and Plum Farm Museum—and the University of Northern Colorado has an art gallery.

SOUTH-CENTRAL REGION

Colorado Springs alone has 32 offerings, including museums, galleries, visitor centers, and historic sites, but many of the south-central region's 60 attractions are historic museums and ghost towns in the valleys and mountains of central Colorado.

Among the major institutions in Colorado Springs are the Colorado Springs Museum, Colorado Springs Fine Arts Center, ProRodeo Hall of Fame and Museum of the American Cowboy, and Cheyenne Mountain Zoo. Other popular facilities include the Peterson Air and Space Museum, the World Figure Skating Museum and Hall of Fame, the Western Museum of Mining and Industry, the Museum of the American Numismatic Association, the May Natural History Museum, Will Rogers Shrine of the Sun, the McAllister House Museum, Rock Ledge Ranch Historic Site, and Garden of the Gods Visitor Center.

Other cities in the region also have numerous offerings, including Leadville (12), Manitou Springs (8), and Cañon City (8). Leadville is home to the National Mining Hall of Fame and Museum, Heritage Museum and Gallery, and Tabor Opera House, as well as historic buildings, a historic mine, and a historic railroad. In Manitou Springs, visitors can see such sights as the Pikes Peak Hill Climb Museum, Miramont Castle Museum, Manitou Cliff Dwellings and Museums, and Pikes Peak Cog Railway. Cañon City's attractions include the Cañon City Municipal Museum, Museum of Colorado Prisons, Dinosaur Depot, Buckskin Joe Park and Railway, and Royal Gorge Bridge.

Many of Colorado's historic ghost towns, such as Bachelor, Buckskin Joe, St. Elmo, Sts. John, Spar City, Turret, Vicksburg, and Winfield, are in the middle of the state and are accessible (usually) by four-wheel-drive vehicle. Unfortunately, little remains of many of these once bustling nineteenth-century mining communities.

Various other sites of interest include the Cripple Creek District Museum and Victor/Lowell Thomas Museum in the old gold-mining towns of Cripple Creek and Victor; historic Fort Garland, a military fort opened in 1858 in the San Luis Valley; Florissant Fossil Beds National Monument Visitor Center, with its petrified redwood stumps and fossils, in Florissant; Jack Dempsey Museum in the boxer's birthplace, Manassa; South Park City Museum, a reconstructed late-nineteenth-century mining village in Fairplay; and the historic Cumbres & Toltec Scenic Railroad, built in the 1880s, which now carries tourists between Antonito, Colorado, and Chama, New Mexico.

NORTHEAST REGION

History museums predominate in Colorado's northeastern plains. But visitors also can see historic sites, a farming ghost town, a 65-foot view tower and museum, and even an animal refuge.

Fort Morgan has three history museums—the Fort Morgan Museum, which traces the history of the area; the Oasis on the Plains Museum, which contains a diverse collection of historical materials; and the U.S. Military Historical Museum, which features military uniforms, accoutrements, and weapons from the American Revolution to the present.

The Fort Sedgwick Historical Society operates two museums in Julesburg, an important Overland Trail crossroads that once had a historic military fort and was home to Colorado's only Pony Express station. The Fort Sedgwick Depot Museum, located in a 1930s-era railroad station, was joined in 1998 by the Fort Sedgwick Museum, which focuses on the old fort and functions as an interpretive center.

Among the region's other history museums are Sterling's Overland Trail Museum, originally built to replicate early fur-trading forts on the plains; Old Town, a living-history museum in Burlington with a collection of more than 20 historic and re-created buildings, 40 vintage wagons, and other artifacts of the Old West; Old Cheyenne County Jail Museum in Cheyenne Wells; Fleming Heritage Museum Park, a 10-acre historically oriented park in Fleming; Limon Heritage Museum, a complex of historical buildings, objects, and exhibits along a six-block railroad track in Limon; and Wray Museum in Wray, which features a comprehensive exhibit on paleo-Indians and one of the oldest and largest communal bison-kill sites from the Stone Age.

The region is also the site of the Battle of Beecher Island, fought south of Wray between the U.S. Army and the Sioux, Cheyenne, and Arapaho Indians on a small island in the Arikaree River in 1868; Heartstrong, an agricultural ghost town southeast of Yuma; the Wonder View Tower and Museum, a 65-foot view tower and 22-room museum in Genoa; and Prairie Wind Animal Refuge near Agate, with approximately 70 lions, tigers, bears, cougars, wolves, and other wild animals.

NORTHWEST REGION

Colorado's northwest region is home to farms, ranches, mines, forests, mountain resorts, skiing centers, and ghost towns and has many varied points of interest.

The old mining town of Breckenridge, now a major ski resort, has nine attractions, among them museums, historic structures, and mines. The Summit Historical Society oversees 13 historical properties in Summit County, 7 of which are open to the public in Breckenridge. These include the Carter Museum and Barn, two historic houses, two mines, and a gold dredge. Breckenridge also has a 12-block historic district and another hard-rock mine open to tours.

The Museum of Western Colorado, a regional and natural history museum, is the principal cultural attraction in Grand Junction, which has eight offerings. The Museum of Western Colorado consists of three facilities—the Regional History Museum; the Dinosaur Valley Museum, featuring dinosaur fossils; and Cross Orchards Historic Farm Site, a living-history museum re-creating the early twentieth century. In addition, the museum manages three nearby natural resource areas. Grand Junction also boasts a children's museum, an arts center, an art gallery, a botanic garden, and a historic district.

Aspen and Redstone each have five entries. Aspen's facilities include the Aspen Art Museum, the Wheeler/Stallard House Museum, and the historic Wheeler Opera House, Sardy House, and Hotel Jerome. The Aspen Historical Society also administers two of the more accessible nearby ghost towns—Ashcroft and Independence. Redstone is the site of the Redstone Museum, the historic Redstone Castle and Redstone Inn, and two historic districts.

Among the region's other sights are three historical facilities in Glenwood Springs—the Frontier Historical Society Museum, Glenwood Hot Springs Pool, and Hotel Colorado; two dinosaur visitor centers in Dinosaur National Monument, one in Dinosaur and the other across the state line in Utah; the White River Museum, historic Meeker Hotel, and the site of an infamous massacre, all in Meeker; the Colorado Ski Museum–Ski Hall of Fame and Betty Ford Alpine Gardens in Vail; Grand County Museum, which occupies six historic buildings in Hot Sulphur Springs and operates a historic ranch house, stage stop, and post office near Winter Park; the Tread of Pioneers Museum and the Eleanor Bliss Center for the Arts at the Depot in Steamboat Springs; and the Vilar Center for the Arts and its May Gallery at the Beaver Creek Resort in Avon.

SOUTHEAST REGION

Pueblo and Trinidad are home to more than half of the museums and historic sites in the sparsely settled southeastern plains of Colorado, yet interesting museums and historic sites can be found in other communities as well.

The El Pueblo Museum, which features a full-sized replica of an 1842 adobe fur-trading post, is one of 15 attractions in Pueblo. Other principal institutions are the Sangre de Cristo Arts and Conference Center, which includes the Buell Children's Museum; the Fred E. Weisbrod/B-24 International Museum, which displays 25 military aircraft; and the Pueblo Zoo, which houses more than 300 animals. Pueblo is also the site of the Rosemount Museum, the Pueblo Historical Society Museum, Hose Co. No. 3-A Fire Museum, and the Greenway and Nature Center of Pueblo.

Trinidad has four museums, two historic houses, a historic garden, and a historic district. The Trinidad History Museum operates half of these facilities. It is the umbrella name for a complex that includes the Santa Fe Trail Museum, the Baca and Bloom historic houses, and their adjoining gardens. The other museums are the A. R. Mitchell Memorial Museum of Western Art, the Louden-Henritze Archaeology Museum, and the Children's Museum. The Corazón de Trinidad (Heart of Trinidad) Historic District includes the city's historic old downtown, with its Victorian structures.

The Otero Museum, Koshare Indian Museum, and Bent's Old Fort National Historic Site can be seen in La Junta. The Otero Museum has seven buildings filled with collections and exhibits on local life from the 1870s to the present. The Koshare Indian Museum is devoted primarily to the art and artifacts of Southwest and Plains Indians and is home to the Koshare Indian Dancers. Bent's Old Fort is a reconstruction of the 1833 adobe trading post built by William and Charles Bent and Ceran St. Vrain along the Arkansas River.

The region's other sites include history museums in Eads, Lamar, Las Animas, Rocky Ford, and Springfield; the Walsenburg Mining Museum in Walsenburg and Fort Francisco Museum in La Veta, both operated by the Huerfano County Historical Society; the historic sites of Ludlow, where the Ludlow Massacre took place during the 1913–1914 coal strike, and Hastings, where a coal mine explosion killed 121 men in 1917; the Cokedale Historic District, which is the best-preserved early-twentieth-century coal/coke camp and boasts the largest surviving coke ovens in the state; and the historic ghost towns of Badito, Boggsville, and Maxey.

SOUTHWEST REGION

Southwestern Colorado is best known for its farming, ranching, mining, skiing, mountains, and such historic sights as its ghost towns, the Mesa Verde cliff dwellings, and the Durango & Silverton Narrow Gauge Railroad.

Durango is the center for many of these activities. It has nine attractions, including the historic Durango & Silverton Narrow Gauge Railroad, which takes tourists through the San Juan Mountains to and from the old mining town of Silverton. Durango's two museums are the Animas Museum, which focuses on area history, and the new Durango & Silverton Narrow Gauge Railroad Museum, devoted to the railroad's history. Fort Lewis College has an art gallery and the Center of Southwest Studies, which serves as a museum and research facility. Durango also boasts two historic Victorian hotels—the Strater and the General Palmer—and two historic districts, one preserving the late-nineteenth-century downtown area, the other a street with imposing Victorian homes.

Six museums and historic sites can be visited in Silverton. They include the San Juan County Historical Society Museum, housed in a 1902 county jail building; the Silverton Freight Yard Museum, opened in 1999 by the Durango & Silverton Narrow Gauge Railroad; a historic gold mine and gold mill, both offering tours; a historic hotel; and a historic district that encompasses all of Silverton and some nearby mining-related facilities.

Two other southwestern cities—Gunnison and Ouray—have five attractions each. In addition to the Gunnison Pioneer Museum, Gunnison is headquarters for the Curecanti National Recreation Area's four visitor centers. Ouray is the site of the Ouray County Historical Museum, the

Bachelor-Syracuse Mine, the historic St. Elmo Hotel and Beaumont Hotel, and a historic district that includes almost the entire downtown.

The region is pockmarked with abandoned mines and ghost towns, most of them near Gunnison, Lake City, Ouray, Telluride, and Silverton. The ghost towns, usually little more than the ruins of old buildings and mines, include Alta, Animas Forks, Carson, Crystal, Eureka, Gothic, Ironton, Ophir, Pandora, Red Mountain, and Tincup. In some cases, a number of the old structures have been restored as summer cabins.

The region's prime attraction is Mesa Verde National Park near Cortez, where the Anasazi lived in cliff dwellings before disappearing around A.D. 1300. The story of these early dwellers is told at the park's Far View Visitor Center and Chapin Mesa Archeological Museum. Nearby are Hovenweep National Monument, with six groups of towers, pueblos, and cliff dwellings west of Cortez; Ute Mountain Tribal Park, which contains cliff houses, kivas, storage rooms, and rock art at Towac; and the Anasazi Heritage Center, a museum and interpretive center near Dolores. Two Ute cultural museums also are located in the region—the Ute Indian Museum in Montrose and the Southern Ute Indian Cultural Center in Ignacio.

TYPES of MUSEUMS, HISTORIC SITES, AND RELATED FACILITIES

Many types of museums, historic sites, and related facilities can be found in Colorado. A description of some of the principal varieties follows.

HISTORY MUSEUMS

History museums are the most common museums in Colorado, numbering 156 (even more when some of the specialized museums are included). They are found everywhere. In most cases they are small, focus on local and/or area history, and are operated by volunteers, frequently through historical societies. But some facilities are quite large, with extensive staffs, collections, and exhibits. Many are open only in summer and are free or charge nominal admission. A number are outdoor museum parks or villages with historic structures and costumed interpreters. Others are even more specialized.

The largest historical museum in the state is the Colorado History Museum in Denver. It is operated by the Colorado Historical Society, which maintains 11 other branch museums and historic houses and has amassed the state's the most extensive collection of historical materials relating to Colorado and the American West. The collection includes

140,000 artifacts; more than 600,000 historic photographs, moving images, and negatives; and approximately 14 million documents, microfilms, and publications. The museum's exhibits trace the lives, history, and diversity of Colorado's people.

Virtually every sizable city—and many smaller ones—has a history museum devoted to the area. Many are located in old railroad depots, historic houses, retired schoolhouses, and other public buildings. Among the best examples are the Boulder Museum of History, Fort Collins Museum, Cripple Creek District Museum, Golden Pioneer Museum, Fort Sedgwick Depot Museum in Julesburg, Hinsdale County Museum in Lake City, and Tread of Pioneers Museum in Steamboat Springs.

Some historical museums are quite focused, dealing primarily with a specific building, person, or field of endeavor. Examples include the Museum of Colorado Prisons in Cañon City, Miramont Castle Museum in Manitou Springs, Victor/Lowell Thomas Museum in Victor, Buffalo Bill Memorial Museum and Grave in Golden, Lafayette Miners Museum, and Ute Indian Museum in Montrose.

Many of the more specialized museums, such as Wings Over the Rockies Air & Space Museum in Denver and the Western Museum of Mining and Industry near Colorado Springs, also are history-based. The same can be said for several other types of museums—hall of fame museums, such as the World Figure Skating Museum and Hall of Fame in Colorado Springs and the National Mining Hall of Fame and Museum in Leadville; western heritage museums, including the Black American West Museum & Heritage Center in Denver and the ProRodeo Hall of Fame and Museum of the American Cowboy in Colorado Springs; and ethnic history and cultural museums like the Mizel Museum of Judaica and Museo de las Americas in Denver.

Most historic houses, farms, ranches, forts, and schoolhouses are essentially historical museums, though usually limited in scope. They include such places as the Molly Brown House Museum in Denver, Rosemount Museum in Pueblo, Farm Heritage Museum in Fort Collins, Wyman Elk Ranch and Western Museum near Craig, Fort Vasquez Museum in Platteville, and Bowie Schoolhouse Museum in Paonia.

A few museums that are primarily historical in nature also feature art, natural history, and other subjects. They sometimes are known as general museums. The Colorado Springs Museum, Fort Collins Museum, and Luther E. Bean Museum at Adams State College in Alamosa fall into this category.

A number of history museums have several locations or branches. Among these are the Aurora History Museum, which operates the

DeLaney Farm, Gully Homestead, Centennial House, and Coal Creek Schoolhouse; the Museum of Western Colorado in Grand Junction, which includes the Regional History Museum, Dinosaur Valley Museum, and Cross Orchards Historic Farm Site; Grand County Museum in Hot Sulphur Springs, whose Cozens Ranch Museum branch is located near Winter Park; and the Trinidad History Museum, a city block containing the Santa Fe Trail Museum and the Baca and Bloom historic houses and gardens.

Colorado has 21 outdoor history museums and villages. Typically, these consist of a number of buildings, artifacts, and, sometimes, costumed interpreters performing tasks from the period represented. In most cases, the log cabins, schoolhouses, barns, and other buildings have been relocated from elsewhere in the area. Outdoor history museums include McGraw Park in Bailey, Fleming Heritage Museum Park, Rangely Outdoor Museum, Limon Heritage Museum, Comanche Crossing Museum in Strasburg, Wheat Ridge Historic Park, and Lakeview Pioneer Village in Windsor. Living-history museums (representative outdoor history museums with historic buildings and costumed interpreters) include South Park City Museum, a 34-building historic village re-creating the late nineteenth century in Fairplay; Centennial Village Museum, 28 historic buildings illustrating the 1860–1920 settlement history of Greeley and Weld County; Littleton Historical Museum, featuring two living-history farms and a number of other early buildings representative of pioneer life in the late nineteenth and early twentieth centuries; Four Mile Historic Park, an 11-acre site containing Denver's oldest building—an 1859 structure that served as a stage stop, wayside inn, and farmhouse—plus its outbuildings and equipment; and Fort Uncompahgre Living History Museum, a reconstructed mid-nineteenth-century fur-trading post in Delta.

ART MUSEUMS, GALLERIES, AND CENTERS

Colorado's art museums have the most extensive art collections and exhibits in the state. But art museums are far outnumbered by art galleries and arts centers, which mount changing exhibitions but generally do not have permanent collections.

The largest and most important of the state's eight art museums is the Denver Art Museum, which has more than 40,000 artworks. Its extensive galleries feature American, European, Asian, Spanish colonial, and Native American art, as well as art of the American West and works from the Modern and Contemporary and the Architecture, Design, and Graphics collections. On display are such leading American artists as

Albert Bierstadt, Thomas Moran, Homer Winslow, and Georgia O'Keeffe, as well as European masters, among them Renoir, Degas, Monet, Matisse, Rodin, and Picasso.

Other art museums include the Colorado Springs Fine Arts Center, boasting a museum, art school, performing arts theater, and art library; the Aspen Art Museum, featuring contemporary art and changing exhibitions; the Boulder Museum of Contemporary Art, emphasizing new art forms in the work of emerging and established contemporary artists; the A. R. Mitchell Memorial Museum of Western Art in Trinidad, presenting the work of Arthur Roy Mitchell and other western artists; the Fred Harman Art Museum in Pagosa Springs, holding more than 300 of the cartoon artist's major oils and pen-and-ink works; the Vance Kirkland Foundation and Museum in Denver, containing more than 500 of the diverse works of this early Colorado modernist painter; and the Trianon Museum and Art Gallery, a privately operated Denver facility displaying eighteenth- and nineteenth-century European art and furnishings.

Colorado has more than 50 nonprofit art galleries, 17 arts centers with galleries, and two outdoor sculpture parks. Almost half of the galleries are at colleges and universities. The University of Colorado has five art galleries (three on the Boulder campus and one each at the Denver and Colorado Springs branches), Colorado State University in Fort Collins has three, and Regis University in Denver has two. Galleries are also found at Colorado College in Colorado Springs, Metropolitan State College of Denver, University of Denver, Fort Lewis College in Durango, Mesa State College in Grand Junction, University of Northern Colorado in Greeley, Red Rocks Community College in Lakewood, Arapahoe Community College in Littleton, and University of Southern Colorado in Pueblo. The Auraria Higher Education Center in Denver has the Emmanuel Gallery, which is shared by Community College of Denver, Metropolitan State College of Denver, and the University of Colorado at Denver.

Denver visitors may view the Vida Ellison and Western History galleries at the Denver Public Library's Central Library, the Philip J. Steele Gallery and the Fine Arts Center Exhibition Space at the Rocky Mountain College of Art and Design, and the Harriet Howe Kelly Gallery at the Art Students League of Denver.

A few arts centers, such as the Foothills Art Center, which has six galleries in Golden, present only art exhibitions, but most offer a variety of arts programming in theater, music, dance, arts and crafts, and visual arts. Examples include the Dairy Center for the Arts in Boulder, Western Colorado Center for the Arts in Grand Junction, Town Hall Arts

Center in Littleton, Sangre de Cristo Arts and Conference Center in Pueblo, Lincoln Center in Fort Collins, and Eleanor Bliss Center for the Arts at the Depot in Steamboat Springs. Two other facilities—the Arvada Center for the Arts and Humanities and the Curtis Arts and Humanities Center in Greenwood Village—have arts and humanities offerings.

Colorado's two sculpture parks are the Museum of Outdoor Arts, which displays more than 50 sculptures and other works in a Greenwood Village business park, and the Swetsville Zoo, a collection of more than 150 outdoor sculptures made of old farm equipment and car parts, located near Fort Collins.

NATURAL HISTORY MUSEUMS AND OTHER SCIENCE FACILITIES

Colorado has a wide variety of scientific attractions, including museums devoted to natural history, anthropology, archaeology, dinosaurs, entomology, and geology and minerals; science centers; institutions such as aquariums, arboretums, botanic gardens, herbariums, observatories, planetariums, and zoos; and other science-based facilities with museumlike aspects, including nature centers, environmental centers, butterfly and insect centers, and wildlife parks, refuges, visitor centers, and repositories.

The most numerous and comprehensive museums are the natural history museums, which generally encompass anthropology, archaeology, astronomy, entomology, geology, mineralogy, paleontology, and zoology. Some—including the Denver Museum of Natural History, the largest and most popular museum in Colorado—even cross over into applied science and technology.

The Denver Museum of Natural History, one of the largest natural history museums in the nation, has more than 500,000 specimens and artifacts pertaining to the natural and cultural history of the Rocky Mountain region. It is best known for its 95 world-renowned dioramas of animals and habitats; extensive collections of gems, minerals, fossils, and other materials; exhibits on dinosaurs, Native American culture, and health; planetarium and IMAX large-screen theater; and education and research activities.

Among the other broad-based natural history museums are the University of Colorado Museum in Boulder and the Museum of Western Colorado in Grand Junction. The Boulder museum has more than 4 million objects, ranging from dinosaur fossils and spiders to rare plants and Navajo rugs, and presents exhibits, public programs, and educational services that emphasize the natural history and native cultures of the region. The Grand Junction museum consists of three sites. Historical, archaeological, ethnological, botanical, zoological, and other materials are displayed in its Regional History Museum; paleontology, fossil specimens, and animated dinosaur models are featured in the Dinosaur Valley Museum; and the early-twentieth-century lifeways and agricultural traditions of western Colorado are re-created at the Cross Orchards Historic Farm Site, a living-history museum.

Most of the other natural history museums are more specialized, focusing primarily on one aspect of the discipline—for example, the Museum of Anthropology at the University of Denver, Chapin Mesa Archeological Museum at Mesa Verde National Park, Louden-Henritze Archaeology Museum at Trinidad State Junior College, Dinosaur Depot in Cañon City, May Natural History Museum (of entomology) near Colorado Springs, and Colorado School of Mines Geology Museum in Golden.

Colorado has two science centers that emphasize applied science and hands-on activities (the Denver Museum of Natural History is also moving in this direction)—the Discovery Center Science Museum in Fort Collins, with 90 interactive exhibits on scientific principles and technological applications, and the Fiske Planetarium and Science Center at the University of Colorado in Boulder, which mounts lobby exhibits on telescopes, the solar system, and optics.

Although they are not called museums, a number of science-oriented institutions—aquariums, arboretums, botanic gardens, herbariums, zoological parks, planetariums, and observatories—are included in this category because their collections and exhibits focus on the natural world.

The newest splash in aquariums is Colorado's Ocean Journey, a $93-million facility that opened in Denver in 1999. The aquarium takes visitors on two journeys—one from the Continental Divide to Mexico's Sea of Cortez and the other from an Indonesian rain forest to the Pacific Ocean. It also provides exhibits, dedicated focus areas, and interactive stations. Approximately 15,000 specimens, representing more than 300 species of fish, birds, and mammals, are featured. A second aquarium is the small EPOB Aquarium in the Department of Environmental, Population, and Organismic Biology at the University of Colorado at Boulder.

The Denver Botanic Gardens, the most extensive of Colorado's five botanic gardens, has more than 14,000 species of plants, covers 23 acres, and is internationally recognized for its water-lily, Japanese, xeriscape, plains, and rock alpine gardens. The Denver Botanic Gardens also operates the 700-acre Chatfield Arboretum near Littleton. The other four gardens are the Western Colorado Botanical Gardens in Grand Junction, Betty Ford Alpine Gardens in Vail, Hudson Gardens in Littleton, and Baca House and Bloom House gardens, part of the Trinidad History Museum. Colorado's arboretums include the Rocky Mountain Arboretum, containing native plants of the region, at the Rock Ledge Ranch Historic Site in Colorado Springs, and the newly opened Chester M. Alter Arboretum at the University of Denver.

Colorado has three zoos—the Denver Zoological Gardens, Cheyenne Mountain Zoo in Colorado Springs, and Pueblo Zoo. The Denver Zoo is the oldest, largest, and best attended of the three, housing nearly 3,500 animals of more than 660 species on an 80-acre site adjacent to the Denver Museum of Natural History in City Park. The animals—among them 144 endangered species—are some of the most exotic and beautiful on the planet and include amur leopards, king cobras, black rhinos, elephants, zebras, gorillas, and many others. The Cheyenne Mountain Zoo, built on 75 acres on the eastern slope of Cheyenne Mountain, is this country's only mountain zoo and has more than 500 animals representing 150 species. It is known for its diverse collection of exotic wildlife, such as reticulated giraffes, okapis, bongos, Siberian tigers, Mexican gray wolves, and orangutans. The Pueblo Zoo has more than 300 animals on 25 acres in City Park.

Sky shows are presented by six planetariums, some of which also have exhibits and observatories. The oldest and largest is the Charles C. Gates Planetarium at the Denver Museum of Natural History; the astronomical shows are now included in museum admission. Other planetariums are the Fiske Planetarium and Science Center on the University of Colorado campus in Boulder, Zacheis Planetarium/Observatory at Adams State College in Alamosa, the Center for Educational Multimedia at the U.S. Air Force Academy, the Robert H. Johnson Planetarium of the Jefferson County School District in Lakewood, and a Starlab inflatable planetarium at the Discovery Center Science Museum in Fort Collins.

Observatories are used mostly for instruction and research, but the telescopes sometimes are available to the public for limited periods. One of the oldest and most active is the Chamberlain Observatory, which opened in 1890 at the University of Denver and is now a National Historic Landmark. People may also visit the Sommers-Bausch Observatory at the University of Colorado at Boulder, Zacheis Planetarium/Observatory at Adams State College in Alamosa, and the Little Thompson Observatory at Berthoud High School.

Nature centers are the most numerous of the facilities that offer museumlike exhibits but are not museums. Colorado has many nature centers in parks and preserves; 10 of these centers are listed in this guidebook. They include the Barr Lake Nature Center in Brighton, Bear Creek

Nature Center in Colorado Springs, Lookout Mountain Nature Center near Golden, and Polly Steele Nature Center at the Chatfield Arboretum near Littleton. The Butterfly and Insect Center in Westminster is a relatively new specialized nature center that has attracted large crowds.

Closely related to nature centers are environmental centers (sometimes called by other names), which focus on geology, wildlife, and ecosystems. Among Colorado's attractions are the Aiken Canyon Preserve Field Station and Beidleman Environmental Center in Colorado Springs, Castlewood Canyon State Park Visitor Center near Franktown, Max Watts Interpretive Center in Pueblo, and Golden Gate Canyon State Park Visitors Center near Golden.

At wildlife parks, refuges, and centers, it is possible to see animals, birds, reptiles, and other creatures. Sometimes, exhibits and education programs are offered as well. Live and mounted native animals of the region are displayed at the Rocky Mountain Wildlife Park (which also has a wildlife art gallery) near Pagosa Springs. Tours are available at a number of privately operated wildlife refuges, such as Prairie Wind Animal Refuge near Agate, Big Cats of Serenity Springs at Calhan, Colorado Alligator Farm near Alamosa, and the Mission: Wolf Refuge near Silver Cliff.

Wildlife can be observed near several public centers as well, among them the Alamosa–Monte Vista National Wildlife Refuge Complex Visitor Center, Rocky Mountain Arsenal Wildlife Refuge Visitor's Center in Commerce City, the Leadville National Fish Hatchery Visitor Center, and the Raptor Center of Pueblo. The National Eagle and Wildlife Property Repository at the wildlife refuge in Commerce City, where eagle feathers and contraband wildlife parts and products seized in illegal interstate and international trade are kept, also is open to the public.

SPECIALIZED MUSEUMS

Colorado has an abundance of specialty museums, ranging from children's museums, hall of fame museums, and ethnic history and cultural museums to museums devoted to such fields as mining, aviation and space, railroads, western heritage, transportation, jails and prisons, firefighting, religion, racing cars, quilts, dolls, miniatures, bells, figure skating, biking, boxing, carousels, horses, skiing, model railroads, pewter, money, mountaineering, toys, street railways, cable television, recycling, and mental health. Among the most numerous are ethnic history and cultural museums and centers, of which there are nine, including the Southern Ute Indian Cultural Center in Ignacio, the San Luis Museum and Cultural Center in San Luis, the Cortez Center in Cortez, the Koshare

Indian Museum in La Junta, and Denver's Mizel Museum of Judaica, Museo de las Americas, and Black American West Museum & Heritage Center.

Colorado also has nine mining museums, crowned by the National Mining Hall of Fame and Museum in Leadville. People may also visit the Walsenburg Mining Museum, Western Museum of Mining and Industry near Colorado Springs, Creede Underground Mining Museum, and Clear Creek Historic Mining and Milling Museum in Idaho Springs.

In addition to historic military forts, Colorado has eight military-oriented museums and centers, including the 3rd Calvary Museum at Fort Carson, U.S. Military Historical Museum in Fort Morgan, and two facilities at the U.S. Air Force Academy.

Seven cities have children's museums; the largest and most popular is the Children's Museum of Denver. Others include the Collage Children's Museum in Boulder, Children's Museum of Colorado Springs, Doo Zoo Children's Museum in Grand Junction, World of Wonder! Children's Museum in Louisville, The Children's Museum in Trinidad, and the new Buell Children's Museum at the Sangre de Cristo Arts and Conference Center in Pueblo.

In Colorado, three types of specialized museums—hall of fame museums, western heritage museums, and jail and prison museums—are represented by five sites each. The hall of fame museums include the ProRodeo Hall of Fame and Museum of the American Cowboy, and the World Figure Skating Museum and Hall of Fame in Colorado Springs; the Mountain Bike Hall of Fame and Museum in Crested Butte; the National Mining Hall of Fame and Museum in Leadville; and the Colorado Ski Museum–Ski Hall of Fame in Vail. Western heritage museums range from the Buffalo Bill Memorial Museum and Grave near Golden to the Black American West Museum & Heritage Center in Denver. Among the jail and prison museums are the Museum of Colorado Prisons in Cañon City, Saguache County Museum in Saguache, and San Juan County Historical Society Museum in Silverton.

The state's aviation and space museums include the Peterson Air and Space Museum in Colorado Springs and the Fred E. Weisbrod/B-24 International Museum in Pueblo. Railroad museums are represented by the Colorado Railroad Museum in Golden and the newly opened Durango & Silverton Narrow Gauge Railroad Museum in Durango. Those intrigued by firefighting can visit the Alma Firehouse and Mining Museum, Denver Firefighters Museum, and Hose Co. No. 3-A Fire Museum in Pueblo. The history-based Georgetown Energy Museum and two museumlike visitor centers—the Dan Schaefer Visitors Center at the National Renewable Energy Laboratory in Golden and the Mt. Elbert Power Plant Visitor's Center at Twin Lakes—will interest energy buffs. The Forney Transportation Museum in Denver is the larger of Colorado's two transportation museums; racing car aficionados will enjoy the Pikes Peak Hill Climb Museum in Manitou Springs. Costumes and textiles may be viewed in the Gustafson Gallery at Colorado State University in Fort Collins, and miniatures and dolls are on display at the Denver Museum of Miniatures, Dolls, and Toys.

Among the many other specialized museums are the International Bell Museum in Evergreen, Kit Carson County Carousel Museum in Burlington, Arabian Horse Trust Museum in Westminster, Museum of the American Numismatic Association in Colorado Springs, Michael Ricker Pewter Museum and Gallery in Estes Park, Jack Dempsey Museum in Manassa, JHB Button Museum in Denver, Colorado Mental Health Institute at Pueblo Museum, American Mountaineering Museum and Rocky Mountain Quilt Museum in Golden, and the National Cable Television Center and Museum, scheduled to open in Denver in 2001.

VISITOR CENTERS AND EXHIBIT SPACES

Visitor centers and exhibit spaces usually are not considered museums, though they have museumlike qualities. Visitor centers presenting exhibits on the facility's history and the natural world most often are found at parks, monuments, preserves, wildlife refuges, and company plants, frequently in connection with tours. Exhibit spaces generally are located in libraries, laboratories, and office buildings.

Colorado has at least 40 visitor centers. More than half are in national parks, monuments, forests, refuges, and recreation areas. Rocky Mountain National Park in Estes Park and Curecanti National Recreation Area near Gunnison each have four visitor centers. Grand Mesa National Forest has two, as does Dinosaur National Monument (one of them is across the state line in Utah). Mesa Verde National Park provides both a visitor center and a museum.

Among the other federal facilities with visitor centers are Colorado National Monument near Fruita, Hovenweep National Monument near Cortez, Florissant Fossil Beds National Monument at Florissant, Black Canyon of the Gunnison National Park near Montrose, Great Sand Dunes National Monument near Mosca, Chimney Rock Archaeological Area near Pagosa Springs, the Army Corps of Engineers' South Platte basin facility near Littleton, Alamosa–Monte Vista National Wildlife Refuge Complex near Alamosa, Rocky Mountain Arsenal Wildlife Refuge in Commerce City, National Renewable Energy Laboratory in Golden, and

Leadville National Fish Hatchery near Leadville. The Anasazi Heritage Center near Dolores is a museum and interpretive center.

The United States Mint in Denver and the U.S. Air Force Academy near Colorado Springs have visitor centers and organized tours, as do a number of companies, such as Coors Brewery in Golden, Van Briggle Art Pottery in Colorado Springs, Celestial Seasonings in Boulder, Anheuser-Busch Brewery in Fort Collins, Mt. Elbert Power Plant in Twin Lakes, and JHB International in Denver.

Most other visitor centers are found at local or state parks. Examples include Garden of the Gods and Helen Hunt Falls in Colorado Springs, Castlewood Canyon State Park near Franktown, Lookout Mountain near Golden, and Roxborough State Park near Littleton. Visitor centers also are located on Dinosaur Ridge near Morrison and at the Ute Mountain Tribal Park at Towac.

Some libraries feature exhibits in galleries; others use rooms, lobbies, and hallways to present changing exhibitions on a variety of subjects. The latter category includes the Boulder Public Library, the University of Colorado at Boulder's Norlin Library, and Regis University's Dayton Memorial Library in Denver. Exhibits also are mounted in the entrance and balcony areas of the National Center for Atmospheric Research in Boulder, the lobby and concourse areas of Republic Plaza in Denver, and throughout the Geological Society of America's headquarters in Boulder.

HISTORIC SITES

Historic sites range from places where significant historical events took place to old buildings, mines, and railroads of historical value. Twenty categories of historic sites, with 295 listings, are described in this guidebook. The most numerous are historic districts (52), historic ghost towns (50), historic houses (32), and historic hotels (25). Other categories include historic homesteads, farms, ranches, forts, mines, opera houses, churches, cemeteries, and schoolhouses.

More than 20 places are cited because important historical incidents transpired there. For example, monuments mark the Battle of Beecher Island, where a small band of soldiers fought off nearly 1,000 Indians south of Wray in 1868; the Meeker Massacre, where Indian Agent Nathan C. Meeker and 10 others were killed during a Ute uprising; Colorado's greatest coal mine disaster, in which 121 men were killed by an explosion in Hastings in 1917; and the Ludlow Massacre, where 21 people died during the 1913–1914 Colorado coal strike that became a virtual civil war. Other historic sites include Mesa Verde National Park, with its ancient cliff dwellings; Four Corners Monument, where four states converge near Cortez; Will Rogers Shrine of the Sun, a memorial to the cowboy humorist and political commentator in Colorado Springs; and the Royal Gorge Bridge, the world's highest suspension bridge, which spans the Arkansas River near Cañon City.

Colorado also has many historic districts. Of the 52 listed, 18 are in Denver, including Civic Center, Larimer Square, Lower Downtown, and many preserved neighborhoods. Historic districts are also found in 30 other cities and towns and include the Central City–Blackhawk Historic District, Downtown Boulder Historic District, Old Town Historic District in Fort Collins, Georgetown–Silver Plume Historic District, Redstone Coke Oven Historic District, and Plaza de San Luis de la Rio Culebra Historic District in San Luis.

Fifty of the hundreds of deserted old mining and farming towns—those with remaining buildings or ruins to see—are described in this guidebook. Among them are such former thriving mining towns as Animas Forks, Ashcroft, Buckskin Joe, Caribou, Independence, Goldfield, and Waldorf, as well as farming and ranching communities like Badito, Boggsville, Dearfield, and Heartstrong. Some of the structures have been rebuilt (and, in some cases, new cabins added); these are used as summer homes in ghost towns including Alice, Crystal, Nevadaville, St. Elmo, Spar City, Tincup, and Vicksburg. Other ghost-town buildings have been moved to create historic museum parks and villages and commercial historic town attractions—for example, Ghost Town Museum at Colorado Springs and Buckskin Joe Park and Railway near Cañon City.

Of all the historic sites, the most museumlike tend to be the historic houses, some of which are actually called museums. Among the latter are the Wheeler/Stallard House Museum in Aspen, McAllister House Museum in Colorado Springs, Molly Brown House Museum in Denver, Hiwan Homestead Museum in Evergreen, Hamill House Museum in Georgetown, Astor House Museum in Golden, Meeker Home Museum in Greeley, Miramont Castle Museum in Manitou Springs, and Rosemount Museum in Pueblo. Other historic houses include the Lace House in Black Hawk, Governor's Mansion and Byers-Evans House in Denver, Avery House in Fort Collins, Boettcher Mansion in Golden, Healy House and Dexter Cabin in Leadville, Hoverhome in Longmont, Baca House and Bloom House in Trinidad, and Sod House in Wheat Ridge.

Some historic houses have been converted to bed-and-breakfasts, such as the Sardy House in Aspen, Hearthstone Inn in Colorado Springs, Redstone Castle in Redstone, Ice Palace Inn in Leadville, and Castle Marne and Queen Anne Inn in Denver.

Historic hotels, many of which originally opened in the late nineteenth century, are scattered throughout the state. Some of the best known and best preserved are The Brown Palace and the Oxford Hotel in Denver, The Broadmoor in Colorado Springs, Hotel Jerome in Aspen, Teller House in Central City, Strater Hotel and General Palmer Hotel in Durango, Hotel Boulderado in Boulder, Hotel Colorado in Glenwood Springs, and Stanley Hotel and Conference Center in Estes Park. However, there are many others, such as the Imperial Hotel and Casino in Cripple Creek, Peck House in Empire, Delaware Hotel in Leadville, Redstone Inn in Redstone, Grand Imperial Hotel in Silverton, and New Sheridan Hotel in Telluride. One early hotel, the Hotel de Paris in Georgetown, has become a museum and no longer accepts guests.

Colorado has six early trading or military posts that are now historic forts—some with costumed interpreters—open to the public. They include what remains of the 1858 Fort Garland in the San Luis Valley, the reconstructed Fort Uncompahgre Living History Museum in Delta, Bent's Old Fort National Historic Site near La Junta, Fort Francisco Museum in La Veta, Fort Vasquez Museum in Platteville, and Pike's Stockade near Sanford. In addition, two national cemeteries are located at the site of old forts—Fort Logan in Denver and Fort Lyon near Las Animas.

Historic homesteads, farms, and ranches trace pioneer settlement and development of the state. Among the homesteads are the Gully Homestead in Aurora, Koenig-Ramsey Homestead and Ranch in Bellvue, Carpenter Ranch in Hayden, Horbek Homestead near Florissant, and Hildebrand Homestead near Littleton. Historic farms and ranches include the Farm Heritage Museum in Fort Collins, Plum Farm Museum in Greeley, Rock Ledge Ranch Historic Site in Colorado Springs, Wyman Elk Ranch and Western Museum near Craig, MacGregor Ranch near Estes Park, Cross Orchards Historic Farm Site near Grand Junction, Zapata Ranch near Mosca, and Cozens Ranch Museum near Winter Park. The Plains Conservation Center in Aurora features a homestead farmhouse, schoolhouse, blacksmith's shop, three sod-house replicas, and plant and wildlife species of eastern Colorado's native grasslands.

Many other buildings have been declared historic landmarks, including opera houses, schoolhouses, and churches. Frequently visited opera houses, some of which are still in operation, include the Wheeler Opera House in Aspen, Central City Opera House, and Tabor Opera House in Leadville. Numerous old schoolhouses have been restored, and sometimes relocated and made part of museum parks and villages. Among these are the Melvin Schoolhouse Museum-Library in Aurora, Cherry Creek Schoolhouse, Second Central School Building in Flagler, Bowie

Schoolhouse Museum in Paonia, and George Rowe Museum in Silver Plume. Historic churches include four in Denver—Trinity United Methodist Church and three buildings on the Auraria Higher Education Center campus that once served as places of worship (Emmanuel Chapel, St. Cajetan's Church, and St. Elizabeth's Church). Other historic structures are the Colorado State Capitol and the Buckhorn Exchange restaurant in Denver, Old Georgetown Station in Georgetown, Glenwood Hot Springs Pool in Glenwood Springs, and Redstone Castle and Redstone Inn in Redstone.

Colorado is known for its historic gold and silver mines, many of which can be toured. Among those open to the public are the Country Boy Mine near Breckenridge, Molly Kathleen Mine near Cripple Creek, Edgar Experimental Mine in Idaho Springs, Bachelor-Syracuse Mine near Ouray, Lebanon Mine near Silver Plume, and Old Hundred Gold Mine near Silverton. It also is possible to visit the grounds of the famed Matchless Mine near Leadville and the Mayflower Gold Mill near Silverton. Popular historic railroads include the Cripple Creek & Victor Narrow-Gauge Railroad, the Durango & Silverton Narrow Gauge Railroad, the Georgetown Loop Railroad, the Cumbres & Toltec Scenic Railroad in Antonito, and the Leadville, Colorado & Southern Railroad. The Pikes Peak Cog Railway in Manitou Springs also takes tourists to the summit of the 14,110-foot mountain.

A CHANGING SCENE

The number and types of museums, historic sites, and related facilities have changed considerably in recent years and will continue to do so in the future. Some museums and museumlike institutions fail for lack of public interest, funds, or adequate offerings. Among those that have closed are the Museum of Western Art, Turner Museum, and Metropolitan Science Center in Denver; the Military Heritage Command Museum in Watkins; the *Herald Democrat* Newspaper Museum and the House with the Eye Museum in Leadville; the Fruita Museum in Fruita; the Wildlife World Art Museum in Monument; and the Nikola Tesla Museum of Science and Technology in Colorado Springs.

During the same period, however, many new facilities have opened, including the Museo de las Americas and Colorado's Ocean Journey in Denver, the Brush Area Museum and Cultural Center, the U.S. Military Historical Museum in Fort Morgan, Dinosaur Depot in Cañon City, Buell Children's Museum in Pueblo, the Vilar Center for the Arts in Avon, the Little Thompson Observatory in Berthoud, and the Plum Farm Museum in Greeley.

Other institutions are in development, such as the National Cable Television Center and Museum, Museum of Contemporary Art, and the Women of the West Museum in Denver; Harmson Museum in Golden; Wise Homestead Museum in Erie; Colorado Museum of the High Plains in Greeley; and a natural history museum in Lamar.

Some of the collapsing buildings and fragmentary ruins at historic ghost towns are disappearing due to weather, vandalism, and souvenir-hunting. Other historic sites are not open to the public, such as the Lindenmeir archaeological site near Fort Collins, where discoveries established human habitation in North America much earlier than previously known, and the scene of the Sand Creek Massacre near Chivington, where Colorado militia killed an estimated 163 Native Americans in response to attacks on white settlers. Yet new sites are being added to the National Register of Historic Places, and more historic houses and other buildings are being restored each year.

Much can be seen in the way of museums, historic sites, and related facilities in Colorado, and it appears that even more will be available in the years ahead.

Guide to Museums, Historic Sites, and Related Facilities

AGATE

Wildlife refuge

PRAIRIE WIND ANIMAL REFUGE

The Prairie Wind Animal Refuge near Agate in Elbert County was created by retired cement-truck driver Michael Jurich. In about 1980, Jurich began caring for animals such as cougars, wolves, coyotes, bobcats—and even an African lion—that people no longer wanted. In 1990, he bought 42 acres of land to provide more space for his growing menagerie. It wasn't long before people from around the nation began offering him unwanted and abused animals.

Today, he cares for approximately 70 lions, tigers, bears, jaguars, cougars, wolves, lynxes, coyotes, bobcats, and raccoons. The animals, many of which have become quite tame, live in cages and fenced-in areas with insulated shelters and can be seen on free guided tours.

Sue Cranston, volunteer coordinator and wildlife photographer, also arranges photo safaris under the auspices of Colorado Free University to raise funds for the refuge. Through this program, amateur and professional photographers can photograph tame wolves, lion cubs, and other animals roaming the grounds in controlled situations.

Prairie Wind Animal Refuge, 2211 County Rd. 150, Agate, CO 80101. Phone: 303/763-6130. Hours: guided tours at 11, 1, and 3 Sat.–Sun. year-round; also at 11, 1, and 3 Wed.–Thurs. in summer. Admission: free, but contributions accepted. Photo safaris: $50.

AKRON

History museum

WASHINGTON COUNTY MUSEUM

The Washington County Museum in Akron comprises four buildings—a 1911 railroad depot, a 1911 dormitory, a 1917 schoolhouse, and a stone building containing artifacts and memorabilia from the area. Founded in 1958, the museum contains collections of late-nineteenth- and early-twentieth-century clothes, tools, farm machinery, horse-drawn vehicles, and other historical materials.

Washington County Museum, 225 E. 1st St., Akron, CO 80720. Phone: 970/ 345-6446. Hours: 2–5 Sun. Admission: free.

ALAMOSA

General museum

LUTHER E. BEAN MUSEUM AT ADAMS STATE COLLEGE

The Luther E. Bean Museum at Adams State College in Alamosa was founded as an anthropology/ethnology museum in 1968 but evolved into a general museum as its scope was expanded to include western art and historical objects. The museum now occupies nearly 5,000 square feet on the second floor of renovated Richardson Hall, the first building on campus and formerly the library.

Native American artifacts represent the core of the museum's original collection. These have been supplemented by western paintings, bronze sculptures, antique furniture, and other materials from Europe and Asia, and pottery and *santos* of the early 1800s from southern Colorado and northern New Mexico.

A full-size statue of a cowboy with horse by Bill Moyers, cowboy artist and Adams State alumnus, stands in front of the building. The western paintings and sculptures inside are also the work of Moyers.

Luther E. Bean Museum, Richardson Hall, 208 Edgemont Blvd., Alamosa, CO 81101. Phone: 719/587-7122. Fax: 719/587-7522. Hours: 1–4:30 Mon.–Fri.; other times by appointment; closed national holidays and Dec. 23–Jan. 1. Admission: free.

Planetarium/observatory

ZACHEIS PLANETARIUM/OBSERVATORY AT ADAMS STATE COLLEGE

The Zacheis Planetarium/Observatory at Adams State College in Alamosa provides instructional programs for students and offers other programs to the public. Opened in 1964, the facility is operated by the Science Department, which presents free public sky shows and celestial viewing, as well as hands-on science activities for schoolchildren. Scheduling varies.

Zacheis Planetarium/Observatory, Adams State College, Alamosa, CO 81102. Phone: 719/587-7616. Hours: vary. Admission: free.

Wildlife refuge/visitor center

ALAMOSA–MONTE VISTA NATIONAL WILDLIFE REFUGE COMPLEX VISITOR CENTER

The Alamosa–Monte Vista National Wildlife Refuge Complex comprises two large tracts of land—mostly wetlands—rich in wildfowl habitats, especially for migratory birds.

Dabbler ducks, greater sandhill cranes, black-crowned night herons, whooping cranes, ibis, avocets, snowy egrets, hawks, and bald and golden eagles are just a few of the wildfowl species that stop or nest at the refuges near the Rio Grande River in the San Luis Valley.

The U.S. Fish and Wildlife Service opened the 14,189-acre Monte Vista refuge, located six miles south of Monte Vista along Colorado Highway 15, in 1953 and the 11,168-acre Alamosa refuge, three miles east of Alamosa on U.S. Highway 160 and two miles south on El Rancho Lane, in 1962.

Self-guided tours can be taken year-round. The headquarters and a visitor center are located at the Alamosa refuge. The visitor center features mounted specimens and exhibits on the history and wildlife of the refuges.

Alamosa–Monte Vista National Wildlife Refuge Complex Visitor Center, 9383 El Rancho Lane, Alamosa, CO 81101. Phone: 719/589-4021. Fax: 719/587-0595. Hours: 7–4:30 Mon.–Fri.; closed major holidays. Admission: free.

Wildlife farm/park

COLORADO ALLIGATOR FARM

Erwin and Lynne Young moved from Florida to Colorado in 1987 to start a fish farm and brought along some alligators to dispose of the fish remains. People began dropping in to see the alligators, and thus was born the Colorado Alligator Farm, just north of Alamosa. The Youngs now have approximately 120 alligators in a large fenced lagoon, as well as other reptiles and a petting zoo. Tours of the fish tanks are offered. Visitors can picnic on the grounds, enjoy boating and fishing, and purchase fish and gator meat.

Colorado Alligator Farm, Colo. Hwy. 17, Lane 9 North, P.O. Box 1052, Alamosa, CO 81101. Phone and fax: 719/589-3032. Hours: Memorial Day–Labor Day, 7–7 daily; Sept.–Oct. and Apr.–May, 9–5 daily; remainder of the year, 10–3 daily; closed Thanksgiving and Christmas. Admission: adults, $5; children 6–12, $2.50; children under 6, free.

ALICE

Historic ghost town

ALICE GHOST TOWN

With the discovery of the Alice Mine in 1868, the name of this mining camp on the Fall River below St. Mary's Glacier was changed from Yorktown to Alice. The mine, the richest in the area, was initially worked as a placer until hydraulic equipment located a large body of ore. A stamp mill was built and lode mining intensified as the mining camp, 10 miles northwest of Idaho Springs, became an established town.

In 1897, the Alice Mine was sold for $250,000. The new owner planned to use large air drills and enlarge the mill but gave up on development after several years. Little mining has taken place since.

The ruins of some old mining cabins remain, as do the 1915 schoolhouse, the teacher's house, and the Alice glory hole, which is 100 feet wide and 50 feet deep. Recently, a number of old structures have been renovated into summer cabins, and the area has even attracted a few year-round residents.

Alice Ghost Town, 10 miles northwest of Idaho Springs. Contact: Historical Society of Idaho Springs, 1416 Miner St., P.O. Box 1318, Idaho Springs, CO 80452. Phone: 303/567-4709. Fax: 303/567-4605.

ALMA

Firefighting/mining museum

ALMA FIREHOUSE AND MINING MUSEUM

In 1937, a huge fire destroyed the business district of Alma, a mining town in Park County. The disaster is documented at the Alma Firehouse and Mining Museum, which contains firefighting equipment, gold-mining equipment, and historical photographs.

Alma, five miles northwest of Fairplay, was founded in 1872 and became an important smelting center with the discovery of silver at nearby mines, including the Dolly Varden, Hiawatha, Moose, Eagle, True Blue, and Gertrude, in about 1880. Many of the mines have closed, but considerable mining still is carried out in the area.

Alma Firehouse and Mining Museum, 1 W. Buckskin Rd., P.O. Box 246, Alma, CO 80420-0336. Phones: 719/836-3413 and 719/836-3117. Hours: by appointment. Admission: free.

ALPINE STATION

Historic site/historic district

ALPINE TUNNEL HISTORIC DISTRICT

When it opened in 1881, the 1,771-foot Alpine Tunnel, which spanned the Continental Divide, was an engineering marvel. Bored through the Sawatch Range southwest of Buena Vista, it provided railroad service to the Gunnison area.

The historic tunnel—the highest railway bore in North America and Europe and the first linking Colorado's eastern and western slopes through the main range of the Rocky Mountains—was constructed at 11,523 feet by the Denver, South Park & Pacific Railroad in a desperate race to be the first to reach Gunnison (and eventually, it was hoped, the West Coast). The Denver & Rio Grande Railroad, however, beat its competitor by almost a year, accessing Gunnison via Marshall Pass south of Poncha Springs. The Denver, South Park & Pacific was extremely expensive to maintain because of deep snows and snowslides on its steep mountain grades, and it later suffered with the decline of mining. The tunnel finally was abandoned in 1910.

The tunnel, which was instrumental in development of the St. Elmo, Romley, and Hancock mining areas, still exists, although the entrances have caved in. The railroad station–relay building has been reconstructed, and ruins of a huge stone engine shed, coal bin, water tank, bunkhouse, store, and other structures remain near the western portal. The Alpine Tunnel Historic District was listed on the National Register of Historic Places in 1996.

Alpine Tunnel Historic District, 9 miles northeast of Pitkin. Contact: Gunnison County Chamber of Commerce, 500 E. Tomichi Ave., P.O. Box 36, Gunnison, CO 81230. Phones: 970/641-1501 and 800/323-2453. Fax: 970/641-3467.

ALTA

Historic ghost town

ALTA GHOST TOWN

Because mining did not cease there until the 1940s, many buildings still survive in the Gold King Mine company town of Alta, perched above Ophir and located 14 miles south of Telluride.

Gold was discovered at the mine in 1878. Ore from the Gold King and other Alta mines was transported by aerial tram to the Ophir Loop rail hub two miles down the mountain. Because of the high cost of hauling coal up the mountain, the Gold King was one of the first mines in the nation to experiment with electric generators. The Alta mines were later sold to the Silver Mountain Mining Company, which continued limited operations through World War II.

The Alta mill burned in 1948. Vandals and the weather have taken their toll on the remaining structures, which include the manager's house, a boardinghouse, and a number of miners' dwellings.

Alta Ghost Town, 14 miles south of Telluride. Contact: Telluride Visitors Center, 666 W. Colorado Ave., P.O. Box 653, Telluride, CO 81435. Phones: 970/728-4431 and 800/525-1455. Fax: 970/728-6475.

ALTMAN

Historic ghost town

ALTMAN GHOST TOWN

The gold-mining town of Altman, located on top of Bull Hill three miles north of Victor in the Cripple Creek Mining District, was the center of bloody strikes and much violence during the 1890s and 1900s. Labor disputes with mine owners became so intense that union leader John Calderwood announced that Altman was seceding from the United States and "passports" would be required to enter the union-dominated town.

An army of 1,200 men was recruited by mine owners to attack the mountain stronghold during the 1893–1894 strike. When the raid did not materialize, the miners went on the offensive and took control of the Strong Mine near Victor. A number of miners were killed and many injured in the fighting, which prompted the governor to call out the militia and declare martial law in the mining district.

A reluctant truce ensued, followed by a settlement in which mine owners agreed to continue the eight-hour work day instead of increasing it to nine hours for the same rate of pay, and to grant amnesty to strike leaders. It was the first major victory for the Western Federation of Miners.

The remains of the American Eagle Mine, which dominated the hilltop, are now open to visitors, as are a few of the miners' cabins and the foundations of various buildings. Among other nearby turn-of-the-twentieth-century mines are the Buena Vista, Victor, and Pharmacist.

Altman Ghost Town, 3 miles north of Victor. Contact: Victor Chamber of Commerce, P.O. Box 83, Victor, CO 80860. Phone: 719/689-3553.

AMERICAN CITY

Historic ghost town

AMERICAN CITY GHOST TOWN

American City, on the wind-swept Continental Divide seven miles northwest of Central City, thrived briefly as a gold-mining camp in the 1890s, then served as a filming location during the early days of the motion picture industry. Little remains of the town today.

American City once had a number of mines, including those of the Boston-Occidental Mining Company and the American Mining Company, as well as a mill, a hotel, a school, and a number of houses for its approximately 100 residents. Only a few of the structures remain; most of these have been converted to summer cabins.

American City Ghost Town, 7 miles northwest of Central City. Contact: Gilpin County Chamber of Commerce, P.O. Box 488, Central City, CO 80427. Phone and fax: 303/582-5077.

ANIMAS FORKS

Historic ghost town

ANIMAS FORKS GHOST TOWN

Animas Forks—once the highest incorporated town in Colorado, at an elevation of 11,584 feet—is a mining ghost town with about a dozen crumbling houses, a mill, and a jail.

Gold was discovered in the area in 1875, and Animas Forks prospered until the early 1890s. The town was nearly deserted after the Gold Prince Mill moved to Eureka in 1917, though a small amount of mining continued through the 1930s.

Snow and avalanches were an ongoing problem for Animas Forks, located 12 miles northeast of Silverton. Winter snows frequently drifted up to 25 feet deep. However, the remote mining town did have telephone service, which came over the 12,500-foot Continental Divide from Lake City, and a railroad spur, built up the four-mile grade from Eureka by Otto Mears, creator of the Million Dollar Highway, linking Silverton and Ouray.

Animas Forks Ghost Town, 12 miles northeast of Silverton. Contact: Silverton Area Chamber of Commerce, 414 Greene St., P.O. Box 56, Silverton, CO 81433. Phones: 970/387-5654 and 800/752-4494. Fax: 970/387-0282.

ANTONITO

Historic railroad

CUMBRES & TOLTEC SCENIC RAILROAD

Built in the 1880s to serve mining camps in the San Juan Mountains, the Cumbres & Toltec Scenic Railroad now carries tourists between Antonito, Colorado, and Chama, New Mexico, during the summer and early fall.

The steam-powered narrow-gauge railroad—a National Historic Site—operates two trains daily from mid-May to mid-October on a 64-

The historic Cumbres & Toltec Scenic Railroad carries tourists between Antonito, Colorado, and Chama, New Mexico. Courtesy Cumbres & Toltec Scenic Railroad.

mile track that runs over trestles and through mountain meadows, forested slopes, rock formations, and tunnels. It spans the Toltec Gorge of the Los Pinos River and crosses the 10,015-foot Cumbres Pass (the highest pass crossed by any scheduled passenger train in the United States). Passengers have seven different ride options.

North America's longest narrow-gauge railroad crosses the Colorado–New Mexico border 11 times as it winds through the mountains, using two locomotives to pull trains up the steep (4 percent grade) western slope of Cumbres Pass on busy days.

The railroad has 10 steam locomotives—6 of which are in operation—all built by the Baldwin Locomotive Works in Philadelphia. It owns the largest collection of narrow-gauge rolling stock on the continent, ranging from replicas of traditional passenger coaches of the 1880s to open-air gondola cars and vintage freight cars.

Historic structures dating back to the 1880s are located along the tracks, including log bunkhouses for track maintenance crews, a wooden coal tipple (loading tower), and a partially razed brick roundhouse, which still houses some of the locomotives and repair facilities. Five old wooden water tanks are visible along the line.

Originally the San Juan extension of the Denver & Rio Grande Railroad, the Cumbres & Toltec is now jointly owned by the states of Colorado and New Mexico and is operated on a contract basis. It began operations as a tourist attraction in 1971 and now serves 60,000 passengers a year.

Cumbres & Toltec Scenic Railroad, P.O. Box 668, Antonito, CO 81120, or P.O. Box 789, Chama, NM 87520. Phones: Antonito, 719/276-5483; Chama, 505/756-2151. Fax: 505/756-2694. Hours: Trains leave Antonito from 8 to 10:30 A.M. and arrive back in Antonito from 4 to 6:05 P.M. daily from mid-May to mid-October; closed remainder of the year. Prices: adults, $38–$58; children 3–11, $19–$29; children under 3, free; groups, 10 percent discount.

APEX

Historic ghost town

APEX GHOST TOWN

The ghost town of Apex, seven miles northwest of Central City in Gilpin County, was the center of the Pine Creek Mining District, which had its heyday in the 1890s. Gold was discovered in the area in the 1870s by Richard Mackey, who founded the Mackey Mine. The mine was sold several times before being acquired by a man named Mountz, who uncovered a rich lode when he blew up the unproductive mine in disgust. Among the area's other producing mines were the Schultz Wonder, Wetstein, Jersey City, Rooster, Evergreen, and Tip Top.

Although the population of Apex never much exceeded 1,000, it was one of the most sophisticated towns in the region. The Apex Hotel was one of the best in the county, the Palace Dancehall among the busiest, and *The Apex Pine Cone* one of the most popular newspapers in the state. The mining town also had a school, several churches, and approximately 100 businesses.

The remains of the Palace Dancehall still stand, as do a number of cabins, some of which have been improved by summer residents.

Apex Ghost Town, 7 miles northwest of Central City. Contact: Gilpin County Chamber of Commerce, P.O. Box 488, Central City, CO 80427. Phone and fax: 303/582-5077.

ARVADA

Arts center/history museum/art gallery

ARVADA CENTER FOR THE ARTS AND HUMANITIES

The Arvada Center for the Arts and Humanities is a 105,000-square-foot arts complex offering a range of programs and facilities, including a historical museum, two art galleries, theater and performing arts events, and extensive arts education programs for children and adults.

The multidisciplinary nature of the city-operated center encourages integrating aspects of theater, music, visual arts, and education into frequently innovative and comprehensive programs on a single subject, issue, or theme.

The center emphasizes education throughout its disciplines. The museum/gallery program, for example, offers master tours by artists and/or the curator, docent-led tours of the exhibit halls, and various lectures relating to exhibitions.

The museum focuses on the history of Arvada and the American West; the two changing exhibition galleries promote understanding of the visual arts through imaginative presentations of regional contemporary art and historical photographs. The museum has a large collection of regional history artifacts, among them the restored Haines Log Cabin, the first log home in the area.

More than 225,000 people take advantage of the center's programming each year. The center offers more than 600 education classes and workshops in drama, ceramics, humanities, music, photography, visual arts, and dance. The Arts Day program for school groups features a play, a museum/gallery tour, and a hands-on workshop. Other activities include resident and traveling theater programs, summer pops concerts, a children's theater, and various music, choral, and dance offerings.

Arvada Center for the Arts and Humanities, 6901 Wadsworth Blvd., Arvada, CO 80003. Phone: 303/431-3080. Fax: 303/431-3083. E-mail: kathy-a@arvadacenter.org. Website: www.arvadacenter.org. Museum/gallery hours: 9–5 Mon.–Sat., 1–5 Sun.; closed New Year's Day, Martin Luther King Day, Memorial Day, Fourth of July, Labor Day, Thanksgiving, and Christmas. Admission: free (fees for the center's special events vary).

Visitor center

STEPHANY'S CHOCOLATES VISITOR CENTER

Stephany's Chocolates offers tours of its new factory in Arvada twice daily on weekdays. The retail store serves as the visitor center and meeting point for the 45-minute tours of the chocolate-making plant.

Stephany's Chocolates Visitor Center, 6670 W. 52nd Ave., Arvada, CO 80002. Phone: 303/421-7229, ext. 111. Fax: 303/421-7256. Tour hours: 10 and 1 Mon.–Fri.; closed major holidays. Admission: free.

Historic site

ARVADA FLOUR MILL

The Arvada Historical Society has been conducting tours of the 1926 Arvada Flour Mill, which is listed on the National Register of Historic Places, since acquiring the property in the mid-1950s. The historic four-floor structure was built by Eugene Benjamin and sold to the Tiller family in 1944. It still retains much of its original rolling equipment, which ground grain into flour.

The historical society also offers tours of historic downtown Arvada.

Arvada Flour Mill, Arvada Historical Society, 5590 Old Wadsworth Blvd., P.O. Box 419, Arvada, CO 80001. Phone: 303/431-1261. Hours: tours by appointment. Tour fees: adults, $1; children under 12, $.50.

ASHCROFT

Historic ghost town

ASHCROFT GHOST TOWN

Like many early western mining camps, Ashcroft in Pitkin County boomed in the early 1880s. In 1883, three years after its founding, it boasted a courthouse, two newspapers, a school, sawmills, a small smelter, 20 saloons, and perhaps 2,000 residents, surpassing Aspen 14 miles to the north.

The silver ore deposits turned out to be shallow, the promised rail links to Crested Butte failed to materialize, and major silver strikes in Aspen lured away capital investment and workers. By 1885, there were just 100 summer residents; by the turn of the twentieth century only a handful of aging miners remained. The last original Ashcroft resident, Jack Leahy, died in 1939.

In the late 1930s, a European-style ski resort was planned for the site but never developed. In the summer of 1942, the 10th Mountain Division and its ski troops, who trained at Camp Hale near Leadville, used Ashcroft for mountaineering training. After the war, the land was deeded to the U.S. Forest Service.

In 1948, Stuart Mace, a veteran of the 10th Mountain Division and commander of the canine section, brought his family and dogsled operation to the ghost town and devoted the rest of his life to protecting the area from development and restoring the ecology. In 1974, the Aspen Historical Society joined in the effort. Ashcroft became a National Register Historic Site, and the Aspen Historical Society received the first Forest Service permit issued to a historical society to preserve and interpret a ghost town.

The remains of approximately 15 buildings from the mining days— the jail, school, hotel, mercantile store, gambling hall, post office, livery stable, two saloons, and a number of cabins—are scattered on the site. A few later structures also survive, including several from the 1950s, when scenes for the *Sgt. Preston of the Yukon* television series were shot.

Ashcroft Ghost Town, 14 miles south of Aspen on Castle Creek Rd. Contact: Aspen Historical Society, 620 W. Bleeker St., Aspen, CO 81611. Phone: 970/925-3721. Fax: 970/925-5347. E-mail: ahistory@rof.net. Hours: summer tours at 11, 1, and 3 daily. Admission: free, but suggested donation of $2 for adults and $1 for children.

ASPEN

Art museum

ASPEN ART MUSEUM

The Aspen Art Museum is housed in a historic 1885 hydroelectric plant, one of the first such plants west of the Mississippi River. Opened in 1979 as the Center for Visual Arts, the museum emphasizes changing exhibitions. It also offers lectures, classes, and special events for adults and children.

Many of the exhibitions and programs focus on leading artists. Recent shows have featured the works of Georgia O'Keeffe, William Wegman, Andy Warhol, Ana Mendieta, Peter Saul, Nancy Rubins, and Tony Oursler. A 1998 exhibition, "Old Masters from Colorado Collections," presented a selection of largely European paintings and drawings created before 1800 by such masters as François Boucher, Gaspard Dughet, and Thomas Gainsborough.

Aspen Art Museum, 590 N. Mill St., Aspen, CO 81611. Phone: 970/925-8050. Fax: 970/925-8054. E-mail: aam@rof.net. Website: www.aspen.com/aam. Hours: 10–6 Tues.–Sat. (with free reception 6–8 Thurs.); closed New Year's Day, Fourth of July, Thanksgiving, and Christmas. Admission: adults, $3; seniors and students, $2; children under 12, free; admission is free on Sat.

Historic house museum

WHEELER/STALLARD HOUSE MUSEUM

The Wheeler/Stallard House Museum, operated by the Aspen Historical Society, is located in an 1888 Queen Anne–style house in the former mining town of Aspen, now a major resort.

Jerome B. Wheeler built the house, but his wife, Harriet Macy Valentine Wheeler, refused to leave Manitou Springs, so the family never lived in the dwelling. Edgar and Mary Ella Stallard moved into the house in 1905 and stayed for 40 years. The historical society purchased it in 1968.

This elegant Victorian home has seven rooms open to the public—the front parlor, with Renaissance Revival furniture popular in the late 1880s; dining room, featuring a period-pattern china known as Moss Rose and a light fixture from the old Castle Creek hydroelectric plant; modernized kitchen, with a display of early utensils and appliances; music room, which reflects Aspen's musical heritage; front bedroom, containing clothing and accessories from the World War II era; back bedroom, with furniture that could have been found in the house in the 1880s; and children's room, displaying memorabilia of children raised in Aspen.

The Aspen Historical Society, whose offices are in the Wheeler/ Stallard House Museum, is also responsible for two nearby ghost towns— Independence and Ashcroft—both National Register Historic Sites (see separate listings).

Wheeler/Stallard House, Aspen Historical Society, 620 W. Bleeker St., Aspen, CO 81611. Phone: 970/925-3721. Fax: 970/925-5347. E-mail: ahistory@rof.net. Hours: Dec.–Mar. and June–Sept., 1–4 Tues.–Fri.; closed remainder of the year and major holidays. Admission: adults, $3; children, $.50.

Historic house/bed-and-breakfast

SARDY HOUSE

This beautifully restored 1892 Queen Anne Victorian mansion, now an upscale Aspen bed-and-breakfast, has gables, turrets, a balcony, a winding staircase, and vaulted ceilings. The well-appointed facility, which opened in 1985, offers such amenities as cherry armoires, feather comforters, heated towel racks, whirlpool tubs, sauna, hot tub, swimming pool, and gourmet restaurant.

Sardy House has 14 rooms and six suites in the former residence and its connecting wing, the Carriage House, added when the bed-and-breakfast opened.

Sardy House, 128 E. Main St., Aspen, CO 81611. Phones: 970/920-2525 and 800/321-3457. Fax: 970/920-4478. Hours: open 24 hours. Rates: vary with room and season.

Historic opera house

WHEELER OPERA HOUSE

Aspen's Wheeler Opera House was built by Jerome B. Wheeler in 1889, saved from a fire by devoted residents in 1912, resurrected as a working theater by Walter and Elizabeth Paepcke in the 1940s, and restored and opened as an architectural and performing arts landmark by the City of Aspen in 1984.

The 38,000-square-foot structure now offers a year-round events schedule that includes local and traveling plays, dance programs, musical concerts, a film series, photography shows, lectures, and changing exhibitions. The lobby, where intimate performances, discussions, and readings often are presented, serves as a gallery for the

Tracy Keenan Wynn family collection of nineteenth-century theater posters and for changing exhibitions of art, photography, and design.

Wheeler Opera House, 320 E. Hyman Ave., Aspen, CO 81611. Phone: 970/920-5770. Fax: 970/920-5780. Hours: 10–5 Mon.–Sat.; closed major holidays. Admission: varies with event.

Historic hotel

HOTEL JEROME

The four-star Hotel Jerome in Aspen opened in 1889 during the height of Colorado's silver boom and was restored to its original Victorian splendor in 1985 at a cost of $20 million. The hotel was built by silver-mine owner Jerome B. Wheeler as a rival to another grand hotel of the day, The Ritz in Paris. Wheeler also opened the Wheeler Opera House a few blocks away (see previous listing).

The Jerome, which is listed on the National Register of Historic Places, pays tribute to the elegance and charm of a bygone era. The exterior was constructed of rich terra-cotta bricks and sandstone from nearby kilns and quarries; the interior features antique brass light fixtures, cut silver, etched cranberry glass, and copper and brass door latches and striker plates, all restored to their original luster. The main lobby is dominated by a fireplace relief carved in oak with a silver-dust mirror mantel. The hotel's 93 guest rooms and suites are individually decorated in the Victorian style. Meeting and conference space is also available. One of the best restaurants in Aspen is the hotel's Century Room.

Hotel Jerome, 330 E. Main St., Aspen, CO 81611. Phones: 970/920-1000 and 800/331-7213. Fax: 970/925-2784. E-mail: hjerome@aol.com. Hours: open 24 hours. Rates: vary with room and season.

AURORA

History museum

AURORA HISTORY MUSEUM

The story of Aurora from prehistoric Native American times to the present is told at the Aurora History Museum, a city-operated facility that also administers four historic sites.

Founded in 1979, the museum has a permanent exhibit called "Portrait of Aurora" and presents changing exhibitions on a variety of topics, such as local archaeology, women's history, art, water resource development, farming, Native American history, and life on the Great Plains.

The museum also offers gallery tours, school programs, hands-on activities, classes, field trips, lectures, children's programs, special events, and historical research resources.

The museum operates four historic sites—the DeLaney Farm, Gully Homestead, and Centennial House (all historic landmarks) and Coal Creek Schoolhouse (see separate listings). Aurora has 12 historic landmarks, ranging from historic houses and schools to an art deco theater that now serves as a community cultural center (Aurora Fox Arts Center). Some are privately owned and others are not regularly open to the public.

Aurora History Museum, 15001 E. Alameda Dr., Aurora, CO 80012-1547. Phone: 303/739-6660. Fax: 303/739-6657. E-mail: amain@ci.aurora.co.us. Hours: 11– 4 Tues.–Sun.; closed city holidays. Admission: adults, $2; children 6–17, $1; children under 6, free; free on Sundays.

Historic homestead

PLAINS CONSERVATION CENTER

The Plains Conservation Center in Aurora reveals how pioneers changed the Great Plains with sod houses, barbed wire, and deep plows. It also is a sanctuary for plants and wildlife native to the grasslands of eastern Colorado.

The center, owned by the West Arapahoe Soil Conservation District, was created in 1949 from surplus federal property. It opened to the public in 1950. No other large remnant of native grassland has been so readily accessible to a growing urban population.

Until recently, the Plains Conservation Center occupied 1,920 acres. Its size was reduced when an express highway was built through approximately 300 acres. The City of Aurora bought the remaining land, designating nearly 1,200 acres for the center's use.

The center's operations now are concentrated in an 80-acre area, where three 1890s sod houses were replicated for educational program purposes—a homestead farmhouse, a one-room schoolhouse, and a blacksmith's shop. Each has an assortment of period artifacts. Outside are examples of early agricultural machines used to work the plains, such as plows, balers, binders, harrowers, and threshers.

The Plains Conservation Center offers a variety of educational programs, including school-group and public tours; a two-mile wagon ride; day camps; Scout overnights in tipis; Native American and pioneer storytelling; Cheyenne tipi encampments with games, beadwork, and storytelling; and nature walks and hikes.

Plains Conservation Center, 21901 E. Hampden Ave., Aurora, CO 80013. Phone: 303/693-3621. E-mail: plainscc@dnvr.uswest.net. Website: www.ci.aurora.co.us/ parks/plainscenter.htm. Hours: reservation office, 8–3 Mon.–Fri.; program, varies by type and requires advance reservation; closed major holidays. Admission: varies with program, but sod-house visit is $1 and moon walk is $4; school groups pay $3 per student for a 2-hour tour and $4.50 for a 3-hour program.

Historic homestead

DeLaney Farm

A large round barn is the featured attraction at historic DeLaney Farm, originally homesteaded in the 1880s and now a historic landmark.

The barn was constructed as a grain storage silo, then converted into a two-story cow barn around 1912. It now houses an exhibit on agriculture in the Aurora area. It is considered to be the only surviving perfectly round barn in Colorado.

The John DeLaney family homesteaded the 168-acre farm, lived in a small house across Toll Gate Creek, and raised livestock. The restored complex now consists of the DeLaney farmhouse, the Gully Homestead (see separate listing), and 11 outbuildings. It is located on Aurora open space and operated by the Aurora History Museum, which offers tours.

Educational programs and special events are presented at DeLaney Farm. An annual event sponsored by the Aurora Museum Foundation is "Homestead City," a three-day event over Labor Day weekend during which nearly 100 costumed adults and children re-create pioneer life in the 1890s. Among the attractions are a tent city where visitors can purchase food, refreshments, and other items representative of the period, and a collection of farm animals.

DeLaney Farm, 170 S. Chambers Rd., Aurora, CO 80012. (Contact: Aurora History Museum, 15001 E. Alameda Dr., Aurora, CO 80012. Phone: 303/739-6660. Fax: 303/739-6657. E-mail: amain@ci.aurora.co.us.) Hours: vary with programs and events. Admission: May–Aug., weekends are free; other times, varies by program or event.

Historic homestead

GULLY HOMESTEAD

Aurora's oldest surviving house is the Gully Homestead, built in 1870–1871 by Irish immigrants John and Elizabeth Gully, who raised cattle and horses. The house was initially a one-room structure, but a front section containing a parlor, bedchamber, and children's sleeping loft was added later.

The house, stables, and corrals originally were located on the homestead property at Mississippi Avenue and Chambers Road. Recently, they were moved to the DeLaney Farm, where visitors can tour them as part of educational programs and during special events. Both DeLaney Farm and Gully Homestead are operated as historic landmarks by the Aurora History Museum.

Gully Homestead, 200 S. Chambers Rd., Aurora, CO 80012. (Contact: Aurora History Museum, 15001 E. Alameda Dr., Aurora, CO 80012. Phone: 303/739-6660. Fax: 303/739-6657. E-mail: amain@ci.aurora.co.us.). Hours: vary with programs and events. Admission: varies by program or event.

Historic house

CENTENNIAL HOUSE

The Blanche A. Wilson House, known as the Centennial House, is the oldest of nine remaining Queen Anne Victorian houses that Aurora founder Donald Fletcher built for his speculative community east of Denver. This historic landmark house was constructed in 1890 and restored in 1991.

Like all Fletcher houses, it has indoor plumbing and an upstairs bathroom—luxuries at the time. The City of Aurora purchased the house in 1990, and community volunteers restored it for the city's centennial observance.

Educational programs and special events are presented at this historic site, one of four operated by the Aurora History Museum.

Centennial House, 1671 Galena St., Aurora, CO 80010. (Contact: Aurora History Museum, 15001 E. Alameda Dr., Aurora, CO 80012. Phone: 303/739-6660. Fax: 303/739-6657. E-mail: amain@ci.aurora.co.us.). Hours: vary with programs and events. Admission: donation requested.

Historic schoolhouse

MELVIN SCHOOLHOUSE MUSEUM-LIBRARY

The Melvin Schoolhouse Museum-Library on the campus of the Smoky Hill High School in Aurora is one of two historic schoolhouses operated by Cherry Creek School District 5 (the other is the Cherry Creek Schoolhouse on the grounds of Cherry Creek High School in Greenwood Village [see separate listing]).

The two-room Melvin Schoolhouse, which is listed on the National Register of Historic Places, operated as a school and community center from 1922 to 1949, when it was moved to make way for the Cherry Creek Dam. The schoolhouse was relocated, remodeled, and operated as a tavern at Parker Road and Quincy Avenue for many years.

In 1976, the newly formed Cherry Creek Valley Historical Society joined forces with the Cherry Creek School District to move the Melvin Schoolhouse to the Smoky Hill High School–Laredo Middle School grounds. It was gradually restored and reopened in 1982. Today, the schoolhouse is used primarily to demonstrate to school classes how school conditions and education have changed since the early twentieth century. The school and its library are also open to the public for browsing and library study on an appointment basis.

Melvin Schoolhouse Museum-Library, Smoky Hill High School, 16100 E. Smoky Hill Rd., Aurora, CO 80015. Phones: 303/693-1500, ext. 5258, and 303/690-5005. Fax: 303/693-1700. Hours: by appointment. Admission: free.

Historic schoolhouse

COAL CREEK SCHOOLHOUSE

The Coal Creek Schoolhouse, built in 1920, is a one-room structure that was used for classes until the 1960s. The historic building was moved from its location along Coal Creek in eastern Aurora as part of the nation's bicentennial celebration. It is now operated by the Aurora History Museum and used for educational programs and special events.

Coal Creek Schoolhouse, 800 Telluride St., Aurora, CO 80011. (Contact: Aurora History Museum, 15001 E. Alameda Dr., Aurora, CO 80012. Phone: 303/739-6660. Fax: 303/739-6657. E-mail: amain@ci.aurora.co.us.). Hours: vary with programs and events. Admission: varies by program or event.

Arts center

AURORA FOX ARTS CENTER

The Aurora Fox Arts Center, a community cultural center located in a renovated theater building, offers performances and occasional exhibits. The Fox Inter-Mountain Amusement Corporation built the 650-seat theater in 1946. It closed in 1983 due to declining attendance and a fire. The building was later restored by the city and reopened as an arts center. It consists of a Quonset hut fronted with an art moderne entrance, marquee, and neon sign.

Aurora Fox Arts Center, 9900 E. Colfax Ave., Aurora, CO 80010. Phone: 303/ 361-2908. Hours: vary with programs and events. Admission: varies by program or event.

AVON

Arts center

MAY GALLERY AT VILAR CENTER FOR THE ARTS

The Vilar Center for the Arts, one of the newest arts centers in Colorado, presents six exhibitions a year in its 2,200-square-foot May Gallery at the Beaver Creek Resort in Avon. In its inaugural exhibition in 1998, this showcase for the visual and performing arts featured diverse works—ranging from Renoir to Warhol—on loan from local private collections. Plans for future exhibitions include photographs, glass works, Native American art, invitational works by local and regional artists, and major traveling exhibitions.

May Gallery, Vilar Center for the Arts, 68 Avondale Lane, Beaver Creek Resort, Avon, CO 81620. (Contact: Vail Valley Arts Council, P.O. Box 1153, Vail, CO 81658. Phone: 970/748-1277. Fax: 970/949-5199. E-mail: vailarts@vail.net.) Hours: 10–6 daily. Admission: free.

BACHELOR

Historic ghost town

BACHELOR GHOST TOWN

The former mining town of Bachelor, Creede's largest and busiest neighbor during the 1890s, can be visited on the 17-mile Bachelor Historic Loop tour through Creede's silver-mining district (see separate listing under Creede). Only a few crumbling cabins, ruins of other structures and wooden sidewalks, and a cemetery remain.

Bachelor got its start in 1884, when John C. McKenzie located the Bachelor Mine south of the mining camp. But it was the Amethyst, Last Chance, and other nearby mines that brought prosperity to the community, increasing the population to an estimated 6,000.

The boom years lasted until 1908, when the town rapidly declined. Most of its residents eventually moved to Creede or settled elsewhere.

Bachelor Ghost Town, 4 miles north of Creede. Contact: Creede–Mineral County Chamber of Commerce, 1201 N. Main St., P.O. Box 580, Creede, CO 81130. Phones: 719/658-2374 and 800/327-2102. Fax: 719/658-2717.

BADITO

Historic ghost town

BADITO GHOST TOWN

Badito, founded in the 1850s, is one of Colorado's earliest settlements, and one of the most historic. It had the first courthouse and literary society in southern Colorado and was among the first in the state to have a flour mill, orchestra, and school.

Badito, which also was known as Boyce's, was a largely Spanish-American farming and ranching community that became a commercial center and the seat of Huerfano County in 1863.

The first settler was F. W. Poshoff, who opened a general store in the early 1850s. As others came to the area, Poshoff expanded his operations. He became a major supplier for the region, opening branch stores at Fort Garland and four other towns, as well as a commissary for cattle camps at La Loma.

By 1865, the population of Badito had increased to 3,000, but many of its residents relocated to nearby communities in the late 1870s due to poor farming and ranching conditions. The county seat also was changed to Walsenburg. Badito's decline continued into the twentieth century, and eventually only the adobe ruins of a church, a home that was once a hotel, and some farm buildings remained.

Badito Ghost Town, 20 miles northwest of Walsenburg. Contact: Huerfano County Chamber of Commerce, 400 Main St., Walsenburg, CO 81089-2002. Phone: 719/738-1065. Fax: 719/738-2506.

BAILEY

Historic museum park

McGraw Park

McGraw Park in Bailey covers five acres and features a number of historic structures, some of which have nineteenth-century furnishings. A trail leads to 10 additional acres.

The park opened in 1969, when Helen McGraw Tatum donated the land and its principal building, an 1864 log cabin, to the Park County Historical Society. It also has an 1898 one-room schoolhouse, an early-twentieth-century train stop station, a 1925 cabin, a 1929 wrought-iron bridge (which crosses the Platte River), and an ore wagon, caboose, and storage building.

The 1864 log cabin is furnished in rustic period style, and the schoolhouse contains nineteenth-century school items.

McGraw Park, Park County Historical Society, U.S. Hwy. 285, P.O. Box 43, Bailey, CO 80421. Phone: 303/838-9511. Hours: Memorial Day–Labor Day, 9–5 Sat., 10–4 Sun.; closed remainder of the year. Admission: free.

BALDWIN

Historic ghost town

Baldwin Ghost Town

The coal-mining town of Baldwin, 17 miles northwest of Gunnison, faced continual labor problems until the mines closed in the 1940s. The town site now is privately owned, but it is possible to see numerous early buildings from County Road 730.

When gold was discovered in 1881, the original community, Mount Carbon, was founded across the hill from what would one day be Baldwin. It became Baldwin, a company town, in 1887, when Citizens Coal and Coke Company opened a mine at the new site.

Baldwin suffered from labor violence as early as 1886, when a non-union miner was killed by a pro-union "Molly Maguire"—a member of a secret Irish-American organization that fought oppressive mining conditions and mine owners. By 1900, the mines had been crippled by a dozen strikes, leaving many miners destitute. A bridge was blown up by strikers at the turn of the twentieth century, and the violence later became so bad that the mining company shut down one of the mines for

20 years. In 1927, a mine superintendent was killed over a labor dispute. Labor problems continued until all the mines were closed in the late 1940s.

Baldwin Ghost Town, 17 miles northwest of Gunnison. Contact: Gunnison County Chamber of Commerce, 500 E. Tomichi Ave., P.O. Box 36, Gunnison, CO 81230. Phones: 970/641-1501 and 800/323-2453. Fax: 970/641-3467.

BALTIMORE

Historic ghost town

BALTIMORE GHOST TOWN

Little is known about the old mining town of Baltimore near South Boulder Creek about five miles west of Rollinsville, but the remaining structures and available information indicate it had an active life.

The town apparently had an opera house and a popular social club called the Baltimore Club. Its 1865 town hall and a building believed to have been a hotel survived until recently, when they collapsed. These and other ruins, plus log cabins, some of which have been converted into summer homes, still can be seen.

Baltimore Ghost Town, 5 miles west of Rollinsville. Contact: Boulder Convention and Visitors Bureau, 2440 Pearl St., Boulder, CO 80302. Phones: 303/442-2911 and 800/444-0447. Fax: 303/938-8837. Website: http://www.chamber.boulder.co.us.

BEECHER ISLAND

Historic site

BATTLE OF BEECHER ISLAND

The Battle of Beecher Island was fought in 1868 on a small island in the Arikaree River approximately 15 miles south of what is now Wray in Yuma County. It was one of the last battles between the U.S. Army and Native American tribes. Fifty army troops and Indian scouts, led by Colonel George Forsythe, were tracking a band of Indians who had attacked some freighters near Fort Wallace in Kansas when they were surprised by nearly 1,000 Sioux, Cheyenne, and Arapaho. The soldiers retreated to the island and managed to hold off the Indians for nine days before reinforcements arrived to drive off the raiding party. Sixteen troops were wounded and three died, including Lieutenant Fred H. Beecher, second in command, for whom the battle was named. The Indians suffered 75 dead, with many others wounded. Among the Indians killed was Chief Roman Nose.

An agricultural community later sprang up near the island and adopted the name of the historic battlefield. A number of abandoned buildings and ruins remain, as do a church and several homes, occupied by Beecher Island residents. A memorial for the Battle of Beecher Island was erected in 1905 but washed out, along with graves and markers, in 1935. It has been replaced by a monument and markers bearing the names of those killed in the battle. A museum was operated at the site from 1956 to 1966, when the contents were moved to the Wray Museum (see separate listing).

Battle of Beecher Island, 15 miles south of Wray. Contact: Wray Museum, 205 E. 3rd St., P.O. Box 161, Wray, CO 80758. Phone: 970/332-5063. E-mail: walborn@plains.net.

BELLVUE

Historic ranch

KOENIG-RAMSEY HOMESTEAD AND RANCH AT PINGREE PARK, COLORADO STATE UNIVERSITY

The Koenig-Ramsey Homestead and Ranch is part of Colorado State University's Pingree Park mountain campus in Bellvue, northwest of Fort Collins.

The ranch buildings were erected by Frank and Hazel Koenig in the mid-1920s. The couple farmed, raised cattle, and rented cabins to summer tourists and fishermen. In 1974, the property was sold to Colorado State University, though the family still maintains a cabin on the east side of the valley.

The university is developing a museum at the ranch and has begun collecting plants and mammals as part of an education and research program. The 1,600-acre mountain campus also is home to a conference and retreat facility centered around Hotchkiss Lodge. About half of the campus was destroyed by fire in the summer of 1994, but the buildings have since been replaced.

Koenig-Ramsey Homestead and Ranch, Pingree Park Campus, Colorado State University, 16301 Pingree Park Rd., Bellvue, CO 80512. (Postal address: Pingree Park Campus, Colorado State University, 211 Palmer Center, Fort Collins, CO 80523-8032.) Phone: 970/491-7377. Fax: 970/491-7427. Hours: open mid-May to late Oct. Admission: free.

BERTHOUD

History museum

LITTLE THOMPSON VALLEY PIONEER MUSEUM

The Little Thompson Valley Pioneer Museum in Berthoud features objects used by early settlers and later residents of the area from 1870 to 1955.

The Berthoud Historical Society opened the museum in 1977 in the 1893 Bimson Blacksmith Shop building, which was listed on the National Register of Historic Places in 1981. The museum later expanded into an adjoining building, a former machine shop from the 1930s.

Among the diverse displays are early drugstore, school, blacksmith's, and farming materials; a doctor's office; wedding dresses; a windmill; military uniforms; Native American artifacts; historic photographs; a fire-hose cart; a doctor's buggy; and an old surrey.

Little Thompson Valley Pioneer Museum, Berthoud Historical Society, 224 Mountain Ave., P.O. Box 225, Berthoud, CO 80513. Phone: 970/532-2147. Hours: 1–5 Thurs.–Sun.; closed Thanksgiving and Christmas. Admission: free.

Observatory

LITTLE THOMPSON OBSERVATORY

The Little Thompson Observatory, which opened in 1999 at Berthoud High School, features an 18-inch reflecting telescope that can be operated by students over the Internet. It is only the second such facility in the world, according to Chet Rideout, science teacher and one of the observatory's founders. The telescope was donated by Telescopes in Education, a California nonprofit group affiliated with NASA's Jet Propulsion Laboratory. Telescopes in Education operates the first remotely controlled Internet telescope used by students to view planets, constellations, galaxies, and other celestial bodies.

Remote users have access to the Berthoud telescope on weekdays for several hours after midnight. At other times the observatory is used by astronomy classes and visited by elementary school groups and the public. Special evening programs are presented for the public.

Though located on the Berthoud High School grounds, the observatory is operated independently. It is the brainchild of Chet Rideout; Tom Patterson, an English teacher at the school; and Tom Melsheimer, whose Berthoud company designs computer systems, including those that operate telescopes and other observatory equipment. Named for the nearby Little Thompson River, the observatory was built entirely with gifts and donations.

Little Thompson Observatory, Berthoud High School, 850 Spartan Ave., Berthoud, CO 80513. Phone: 970/532-2399. Hours: vary. Admission: free.

BLACK HAWK

Historic house

LACE HOUSE

One of the most decorative houses in Colorado is the 1863 Lace House in the former mining town of Black Hawk. It is an outstanding example of Carpenter Gothic, an architectural style popular in the nineteenth century.

The house was built by Lucien K. Smith. Smith's father, Nelson K. Smith, was a miner and tavern owner at nearby Smith Hill, from which the family built a toll road to Black Hawk. Then, with the help of W.A.H. Loveland, they constructed the Clear Creek Canyon–Black Hawk Toll Road in 1863.

In 1865, Lucien Smith sold the house and mining claims to C. W. Fiske for $4,000. The house had six subsequent owners before it was deeded to the City of Black Hawk. Restored as a bicentennial project in 1976, it was then leased to the Gilpin County Historical Society, which furnished and operated it as a historic house for a number of years.

The Lace House recently became a center of controversy when an adjacent gambling casino asked the city to relocate it to provide more parking space. After much debate, the city decided to move the house and other older homes to a historic village being developed in Mountain City, located between Black Hawk and Central City. Mountain City Historic Park will eventually feature 12 historically significant buildings.

The Lace House move will not take place for several years. Meanwhile, the house is open on a limited basis.

Lace House, 261 Main St., Black Hawk, CO 80422. (Contact: City of Black Hawk, 201 Selak St., Black Hawk, CO 80422. Phone: 303/582-5221.) Hours: irregular. Admission: free.

Historic district

CENTRAL CITY–BLACK HAWK HISTORIC DISTRICT

See description under Central City.

BOGGSVILLE

Historic ghost town

BOGGSVILLE GHOST TOWN

Boggsville in Bent County is one of the most historic sites in southeastern Colorado. Known as the cradle of southern Colorado's cattle industry, it was the first town in the region to have a school and a post office and was the final home of Kit Carson, who lived there briefly before his death in 1868.

Thomas O. Boggs, a great-grandson of Daniel Boone, was the first to settle in the area. A scout, guide, courier, and freighter, Boggs married the niece of Kit Carson's wife. She was given title to more than 2,000 acres in southern Colorado in 1865. Boggs built a 10-room Spanish-style home on the land the following year. In 1867, he was joined by John W. Prowers, who built a 6,000-square-foot mansion and soon became the area's largest landowner, with one of the biggest cattle herds in the region.

Boggs and Prowers grew wealthy as Boggsville became a major beef supplier to nearby Fort Lyons and other towns in the area. When Bent County was created in 1870, Boggsville was named the county seat. Prowers became the first county officer, and Boggs the first sheriff.

Boggs and Prowers planned to build a modern city at Boggsville but gave up when the Santa Fe Railroad decided to lay its tracks through Las Animas two miles to the north. Las Animas grew rapidly as a result and became the new county seat, while Boggsville remained a farming and cattle center with many large homes.

Not much is left of Boggsville. Most of the buildings are gone. Many of the structures were washed away or destroyed by the 1921 flood, including the ruins of Kit Carson's home. But the Pioneer Historical Society of Bent County has reconstructed the Boggs home and one wing of the Prowers home and is planning to erect a replica of the Carson home. The foundations of a number of buildings also can be seen on the 110-acre site, marked by a stone monument along Colorado Highway 101.

Boggsville Ghost Town, 2 miles south of Las Animas. Contact: Kit Carson Museum, Pioneer Historical Society of Bent County, 305 St. Vrain St., P.O. Box 68, Las Animas, CO 81054. Phone: 719/456-2005.

BOULDER

Art museum

BOULDER MUSEUM OF CONTEMPORARY ART

New art forms in the work of emerging and established contemporary artists are presented by the Boulder Museum of Contemporary Art in a historic two-story, loft-style former warehouse in downtown Boulder.

Founded in 1972, the 10,000-square-foot museum exhibits contemporary art by local, regional, national, and international artists. It also has an upstairs theater that presents cutting-edge music programs, dance performances, and traditional theater productions.

The museum facilitates exploration and understanding of contemporary art through lectures, panels, workshops, and special events. It hosts the annual Boulder Valley School Art Show, which features more than 1,000 artworks by children in kindergarten through twelfth grade, and presents a Young Curator's Program, which helps young people develop leadership and communication skills while learning contemporary art history.

The museum is located across the street from Boulder's Central Park and is adjacent to the Dushanbe Teahouse, a gift from Boulder's sister city in Tajikistan. Each Saturday from April through October, and on Wednesdays during the summer, the Boulder County Farmers' Market is held on 13th Street in front of the museum.

Boulder Museum of Contemporary Art, 1750 13th St., Boulder, CO 80302. Phone: 303/443-2122. Fax: 303/442-1633. Website: www.bmoca.org. Hours: 11–5 Tues.–Sun.; closed holidays. Admission: adults, $2; seniors, $1.50; children 12 and under, free.

Art Museum

LEANIN' TREE MUSEUM OF WESTERN ART

One of the nation's most extensive privately owned collections of western art can be seen at the Leanin' Tree Museum of Western Art in Boulder. The museum is housed in the corporate headquarters of Leanin' Tree Inc., the largest publisher of western, wildlife, and regional interest greeting cards in the nation.

More than 200 paintings and over 80 bronze sculptures are on display in the museum, which was opened in 1976 by the company's founder, Edward P. Trumble. The paintings depict Native Americans, cowboys, wildlife, pioneers, trappers, ranch life, railroads, and desert and mountain landscapes; the bronzes mainly represent bucking broncos and stagecoaches.

Approximately 40,000 visitors pass through each year to see works by such artists as Paul Hughes (monumental landscapes), Kenneth Riley (Plains Indians paintings), Jack Roberts (Colorado cowboy artist), Olaf Wieghorst (oils, watercolors, and pen-and-ink drawings), Gerard Curtis Delano (often considered Colorado's greatest painter of the Navajo and the American Southwest), John Hilton (paintings of the southwestern desert), Harry Jackson (bronze sculptures), and John Hampton (paintings and bronzes). These artists and others represented in the 12,000-square-foot museum are featured on many of Leanin' Tree's greeting cards.

Leanin' Tree Museum of Western Art, 6055 Longbow Dr., P.O. Box 9500, Boulder, CO 80301. Phones: 303/530-1442 and 800/777-8716. Fax: 303/530-7283. E-mail: artmuseum@leanintree.com. Website: www.leanintree.com. Hours: 8–4:30 Mon.–Fri., 10–4 Sat.–Sun.; closed major holidays. Admission: free.

History museum

BOULDER MUSEUM OF HISTORY

The Boulder Museum of History, founded by the Boulder Historical Society in 1944, has one of the largest collections of local-history artifacts, photographs, and documents in the region. The collection, totaling more than 600,000 items, is divided between the museum itself and the Boulder Public Library's Library of Local History.

The museum, located in the 1899 Harbeck-Bergheim House on University Hill, presents rotating exhibits from its collections, as well as traveling exhibitions of a historical nature. Artifacts on display include furniture, clothing, tools, machinery, household goods, memorabilia, accessories, and occupational and industrial objects from the Boulder area. The museum also hosts a lecture series; offers classes on such subjects as quilting, antiques collecting, and conservation and restoration; provides educational materials to schools; and sponsors such special events as period-costume fashion shows, turn-of-the-twentieth-century dancing, and an annual Victorian Fair.

Boulder Museum of History, 1206 Euclid Ave., Boulder, CO 80302. Phone: 303/449-3464. Fax: 303/938-8322. Hours: 10–4 Tues.–Sun. Admission: adults, $2; seniors and children, $1.

History Museum

CU HERITAGE MUSEUM AT THE UNIVERSITY OF COLORADO AT BOULDER

Achievements, artifacts, and anecdotes pertaining to the University of Colorado are celebrated at the CU Heritage Center, located on the third floor of Old Main on the Boulder campus.

Memorabilia, trophies, furniture, clothing, books, uniforms, photographs, and other materials connected to CU figures and events are displayed in seven galleries in Old Main, the university's first building. The galleries focus on university life; campus architecture; athletics; distinguished alumni, faculty, and presidents; space exploration; university yearbooks; and books by CU alumni and others.

Among those honored are Big Band leader Glenn Miller, archaeologist Earl Morris, Pulitzer prizewinner Jean Stafford, Supreme Court justices Wiley Rutledge and Byron "Whizzer" White, actor Robert Redford, composer Dave Grusin, golfer Hale Irwin, Nobel prizewinner Thomas Cech, astronauts Scott Carpenter and Elison Onizuka, Rhodes scholar Joe Romig, U.S. senators Eugene Millikin and Gordon Allott, artist and historian Muriel Sibell Wolle, Olympic medalists Bill Toomey and Billy Kidd, campus architect Charles Z. Kauder, and former Miss America Marilyn Van Derbur.

CU Heritage Center, University of Colorado at Boulder, Old Main, 3rd Floor, Campus Box 459, Boulder, CO 80309-0459. Phone: 303/492-6329. Fax: 303/492-6799. E-mail: oltmans_k@cufund.colorado.edu. Hours: 10–2 Tues.–Fri.; closed holidays. Admission: free.

Natural history museum

UNIVERSITY OF COLORADO MUSEUM AT THE UNIVERSITY OF COLORADO AT BOULDER

The University of Colorado Museum in Boulder is a comprehensive natural history museum featuring collections, exhibits, public programs, and educational services emphasizing the natural history and native cultures of the Rocky Mountains and adjacent Colorado Plateau, Great Plains, and Wyoming Basin.

The museum, founded in 1902 and housed in the Henderson Building on the university's Boulder campus, has more than 4 million objects, some of which are displayed in three permanent galleries on paleontology, anthropology, and zoology. The museum also has two temporary exhibition halls for special and traveling exhibitions, as well as a hands-on Discovery Center.

*The University of Colorado Museum on the Boulder
campus. Courtesy University of Colorado Museum.*

In addition, the museum offers a public program of lectures, family
events, and live demonstrations. Its extensive collections are used for teaching, research, and a master's degree program in museum and field studies.

The collections cover anthropology, botany, entomology, geology,
and zoology and include such objects as southwestern Native American
textiles and archaeological material; herbarium specimens of Rocky
Mountain plants; spiders and butterflies; Tertiary fossils from Colorado
and Wyoming; and significant holdings of small mammal, freshwater
snail, and snake specimens. Among the objects in the permanent exhibits are a complete *Triceratops* skull and other fossil dinosaur bones,
archaeological materials from sites near Mesa Verde, and birds of the
Rocky Mountain West.

University of Colorado Museum, University of Colorado at Boulder, Henderson Bldg., Campus Box 218, Boulder, CO 80309-0218. Phone: 303/492-6892. Fax: 303/492-4195. Website: www.colorado.edu/-ucm/home.html. E-mail: farnswor@stripe.colorado. Hours: 9–5 Mon.–Fri., 9–4 Sat., 10–4 Sun.; closed holidays. Suggested admission: adults, $3; seniors, $2; children 6 and older and students not enrolled at CU, $1; CU students, staff, faculty, and children under 6, free.

Children's museum

COLLAGE CHILDREN'S MUSEUM

The Collage Children's Museum in Boulder fosters children's curiosity about their world, largely through enjoyable hands-on experiences that enhance their knowledge of the arts and sciences, diverse cultures, and uses of technology.

The museum, which occupies 5,300 square feet in a storefront location, was founded in 1989 by a group of community-minded parents and professionals who envisioned a stimulating learning environment for children from preschool through third grade. The museum plans to move into a new downtown hotel complex within several years.

Among the varied exhibits are "Go Power," explaining the many forms of energy; "Good Vibrations," demonstrating how sound is created by vibrating objects; "Image-ination," enabling children to explore imagery and perception; "Playscape," dealing with tactile and motor skills; "Bubbles Galore," providing experiences with bubbles; and "Art Express," where children create original art using a variety of materials. The museum's Art Stream Gallery displays artworks by children from the Boulder and St. Vrain Valley School Districts and presents traveling exhibitions three times a year.

Educational programs include demonstrations of science experiments; hands-on activities; participatory workshops and performances led by professional artists; monthly Sunday entertainment introducing children to a variety of performances and workshops; opportunities to work with local artists; and annual celebrations exploring the diversity of arts and cultures in the area.

Collage Children's Museum, 2065 30th St., P.O. Box 2209, Boulder, CO 80306. Phone: 303/440-0053. Fax: 303/443-8040. Website: http://bcn.boulder.co.us/arts/collage. Hours: 10–5 Mon., Thurs., Sat.; 9–2 Wed.; 1–5 Sun.; closed Easter, Fourth of July, and Christmas. Admission: adults, $3.50; seniors, $2; children 2–7, $3.50; children under 2, free; families, $12; groups, $2 each.

Racing car museum

SHELBY AMERICAN COLLECTION

The Shelby American Collection in Boulder is a racing car museum specializing in Shelby Cobra, Shelby GT 350, and Ford GT 40 cars, historical records, and memorabilia. Founded in 1997, the museum is dedicated to the preservation of Shelby American cars—those designed by race-car driver Carroll Shelby—and to sharing the Shelby American team story with the public.

The 10,000-square-foot museum contains many of the original Shelby American team vehicles, including the legendary Cobra race cars. The collection of nearly 50 cars includes Sebring, LeMans, Ford Factory, FIA, and USRRC Cobra team cars driven by Ken Miles, Dan Gurney, Bob Bondurant, Phil Hill, and Dave McDonald. Also on display are the first Shelby GT 350 R model and the GT 40 Mk IV driven by Mario Andretti at LeMans in 1967.

The Shelby American Collection features prime examples of Cobra 427 S/C and competition models, 289 and 427 consumer cars, Cobra vintage racers, and an AC Bristol. In addition, the museum displays many rare prototypical and developmental parts, trophies, driving and crew uniforms, artwork, models, and other items related to Shelby American.

Carroll Shelby dreamed of developing a relatively inexpensive American sports car to compete with Europe's best. The result was the Cobra—a car that combined the assembly of a light European-style chassis with a powerful American V8 engine—which, through its design, speed, and endurance, set the tone for the 1960s muscle-car era. Shelby went on to design and develop the popular Shelby Mustang for the Ford Motor Company.

The collection was assembled and the museum opened by Steve Volk, a Shelby enthusiast.

Shelby American Collection, 5020 Chaparral Court, P.O. Box 19228, Boulder, CO 80308. Phone: 303/516-9565. Fax: 303/447-1380. Hours: 10–4 Sat. Admission: adults, $5; children under 12 accompanied by an adult, free.

Art galleries

UNIVERSITY OF COLORADO AT BOULDER

University of Colorado Art Galleries
UMC Art Gallery
Andrew J. Macky Gallery

The University of Colorado at Boulder has three art galleries, the largest and most comprehensive being the University of Colorado Art

Galleries. Smaller galleries are located in the University Memorial Center and Macky Auditorium.

University of Colorado Art Galleries

The University of Colorado Art Galleries on the Boulder campus enhance public understanding of the visual arts and advocate interdisciplinary approaches to the social, cultural, technological, and historical context of art.

The three adjoining galleries, opened in 1978 and located in the Sibell Wolle Building, present changing exhibitions and related educational events on twentieth-century art of regional, national, and international significance.

The galleries also sponsor in-state exhibitions of works from the Colorado Collection, a study and teaching resource under the facility's stewardship. The collection consists of approximately 4,000 objects, primarily works on paper, focusing on contemporary prints, photography, and nineteenth- and twentieth-century German etchings.

University of Colorado Art Galleries, University of Colorado at Boulder, Sibell Wolle Bldg., Campus Box 318, Boulder, CO 80309-0318. Phone: 303/492-8300. Fax: 303/492-8003. Website: http://stripe.colorado.edu/~gallery. Hours: 8–5 Mon. and Wed.–Fri., 8–8 Tues., 12–4 Sat.; closed holidays. Admission: $2 suggested donation for adults.

UMC Art Gallery

A wide variety of contemporary art is presented in the UMC Art Gallery on the entrance level of the University Memorial Center at the University of Colorado at Boulder. Exhibitions range from paintings and sculpture to multimedia shows.

UMC Art Gallery, University of Colorado at Boulder, University Memorial Center, Euclid Ave. and Broadway, Campus Box 204, Boulder, CO 80309-0204. Phone: 303/492-7465. Fax: 303/492-4327. Hours: 9–9 Mon.–Thurs., 9–5 Fri.; closed holidays. Admission: free.

Andrew J. Macky Gallery

The Andrew J. Macky Gallery features photography and art exhibits in the inner foyer of Macky Auditorium, a 2,047-seat concert hall on the University of Colorado campus in Boulder.

The exhibitions display the work of local, national, and international artists. Typically, three exhibitions are presented during the fall semester and three in the spring. The gallery is open on Wednesdays and during Macky Auditorium events.

The auditorium, which was built in 1914 and renovated in 1986, hosts performances including those of the university's band, choir, and orchestra; the Boulder Philharmonic Orchestra; and internationally known jazz, dance, classical, and pop artists. The auditorium also is used for lectures, a travel film series, commencement ceremonies, and conferences.

Andrew J. Macky Gallery, Macky Auditorium, University of Colorado at Boulder, 17th St. and University Ave., Campus Box 285, Boulder, CO 80309-0285. Phone: 303/492-8423. Fax: 303/492-1651. Hours: 10–5 Wed. and during auditorium events. Admission: free, except during events for ticketed patrons.

Arts center

DAIRY GALLERY AT THE DAIRY CENTER FOR THE ARTS

The Dairy Center for the Arts, located in a former dairy building in Boulder, presents exhibitions of diverse artworks in its Dairy Gallery.

The 40,000-square-foot building was abandoned by Watts-Hardy Dairy in 1987, when it merged with Sinton Dairy. Three years later, local artists obtained an option on the building and announced plans to convert the structure into an arts center. It opened in 1991.

Since then, the building has been renovated to include six music studios, three classrooms, an art gallery, a media center, a 99-seat theater, a conference room, and offices.

The arts center serves as landlord to a number of autonomous community arts groups, including the Boulder Philharmonic Orchestra and its affiliated Boulder Arts Academy; the Guild Theater; the Dairy Dance Partnership; the Naropa Institute School of Continuing Education; and the Arts and Humanities Assembly of Boulder County. It is also the site of various theater, dance, and music performances, as well as lectures, workshops, classes, and other arts programs.

Dairy Gallery, Dairy Center for the Arts, 2590 Walnut St., Boulder, CO 80302. Phone: 303/440-7826. Fax: 303/440-7104. Hours: 9–5 Mon.–Sat., 12–5 Sun.; closed major holidays. Admission: free.

Planetarium/science center/observatory

UNIVERSITY OF COLORADO AT BOULDER

Fiske Planetarium and Science Center
Sommers-Bausch Observatory

Planetarium shows and lectures, science exhibits, and observatory viewing are offered by the Fiske Planetarium and Science Center at the University of Colorado at Boulder.

The 8,000-square-foot facility, built with funds left to the university by Wallace Fiske, opened in 1975. Part of the Department of Astrophysical, Planetary, and Atmospheric Sciences, it offers programs for university classes, school groups, and the general public. The theater makes use of a Zeiss Mark IV projector, two panorama systems, more than 100 special-effects projectors, more than 70 slide projectors, and a digital automation projection system in its sky shows and other programs. A lobby exhibit features displays on telescopes, the solar system, and optics.

The Sommers-Bausch Observatory is open to public viewing on Friday evenings.

Fiske Planetarium and Science Center and Sommers-Bausch Observatory, University of Colorado at Boulder, Regent Dr., Campus Box 408, Boulder, CO 80309-0408. Phone: 303/492-5001. Fax: 303/492-1725. Hours: academic year, 8–5 Mon.–Fri. (also 7–9 Fri. evenings) and 1:30–3:30 Sat.; summer, 8–5 Mon.–Fri. (also 7:30–9:30 Fri. evenings); observatory, sunset to 11 P.M. Fri.; closed holidays. Admission: science center and observatory, free. Evening planetarium shows: adults, $3.50; seniors and children, $2. Matinee planetarium shows: adults, $2.50, children, $1.50.

Aquarium

EPOB AQUARIUM AT THE UNIVERSITY OF COLORADO AT BOULDER

The Department of Environmental, Population, and Organismic Biology at the University of Colorado at Boulder has a teaching aquarium that is open to the public when not in use for classes.

The 600-square-foot aquarium, housed in the Ramaley Biology Building, contains organisms representing the diversity of life. The aquarium features a coral-reef ecosystem tank with fan worms, banded coral shrimp, anemones, mollusks, fish, and at least 10 types of coral; an Amazon/ Nile tank with an African lungfish; a tide-pool tank with starfish, urchins, brittle stars, and other sea life; a boreal toad exhibit; and such other attractions as a horned shark, snapping turtle, snowflake eel, salamanders, and frogs.

EPOB Aquarium, University of Colorado at Boulder, Dept. of Environmental, Population, and Organismic Biology, Room C-154, Ramaley Biology Bldg., Campus Box 334, Boulder, CO 80309-0334. Phone: 303/492-8487. Hours: 10–5 Mon.–Fri.; closed holidays and when classes are not in session. Admission: free.

Visitor center

CELESTIAL SEASONINGS VISITOR CENTER

Celestial Seasonings Inc., the nation's largest specialty tea company, features a visitor center and tours at its corporate headquarters and manufacturing plant in Boulder.

Opened in 1991, the visitor center contains exhibits on the firm's history and products, a tea-tasting bar, a gift shop, and windows overlooking the tea production area. It also has an adjoining cafe and herb garden. Tours are offered hourly from 10 to 3 daily.

Celestial Seasonings Visitor Center, Celestial Seasonings Inc., 4600 Sleepytime Dr., Boulder, CO 80301-3292. Phone: 303/581-1202. Fax: 303/581-1331. Hours: 9–6 Mon.–Fri., 9–5 Sat., 11–4 Sun.; closed major holidays. Admission: free.

Exhibit spaces

BOULDER PUBLIC LIBRARY EXHIBIT SPACES

Changing exhibitions are presented in the Boulder Public Library, as well as the Carnegie Branch Library for Local History and the Meadows Branch Library.

Traveling exhibitions and exhibitions by contemporary Colorado artists are offered in The Exhibit Space at the main library. This gallery was created in a portion of the old library when the facility expanded in 1993. The library also houses an art collection.

The Carnegie Branch Library presents monthly exhibitions of historic Boulder photographs. The Meadows Branch Library schedules art exhibitions, some featuring individual artists, others showcasing the work of groups.

The Exhibit Space, Boulder Public Library, 1000 Canyon Blvd. (main entrance to library at 11th St. and Arapahoe Ave.), P.O. Drawer H, Boulder, CO 80306. Phone: 303/441-3100. Fax: 303/441-4119. Website: http://bcn.boulder.co.us/ library/btl/home.html. Hours: 9–9 Mon.–Thurs., 9–6 Fri.–Sat., 12–6 Sun.; closed major holidays. Admission: free.

Carnegie Branch Library for Local History, 1125 Pine St., P.O. Drawer H, Boulder, CO 80306. Phone and fax: 303/441-3110. Hours: 1–9 Mon., Tues., Thurs.; 9–5 Wed.; 11–5 Fri. and Sat.; closed major holidays. Admission: free.

Meadows Branch Library, 4800 Baseline Rd., Boulder, CO 80303. Phone: 303/ 441-4390. Fax: 303/441-4490. Hours: 9–5 Mon.–Thurs., 9–6 Fri.–Sat., 1–5 Sun. Admission: free.

Exhibit spaces

GEOLOGICAL SOCIETY OF AMERICA

The Geological Society of America displays geological maps, charts, photographs, and art, as well as samples of rocks and fossils, throughout its headquarters in Boulder. The first exhibits were installed when the society moved into the building in 1972.

Geological Society of America, 3300 Penrose Place, P.O. Box 9140, Boulder, CO 80301-9140. Phone: 303/447-2020. Fax: 303/447-1633. Hours: 8–4 Mon.–Fri.; closed major holidays. Admission: free.

Exhibit spaces

NATIONAL CENTER FOR ATMOSPHERIC RESEARCH

The National Center for Atmospheric Research, which studies the basic processes that drive weather and climate, presents science and art exhibitions at its Mesa Laboratory on Table Mesa in Boulder.

The center, managed by the nonprofit University Corporation for Atmospheric Research and housed in a prizewinning building designed by I. M. Pei, focuses on four major areas—storms and weather phenomena, climate, atmospheric chemistry, and the sun.

Exhibit spaces, located on the entrance level and balcony areas, are devoted primarily to the center's work, the processes behind weather and climate, and hands-on exhibits produced by The Exploratorium science center in San Francisco. Visitors can see such scientific instruments as an air sampler, portable weather station, and an eclipse camera/telescope. They may also enter a glassed-in observatory to watch scientists at work in the Computing Center. Two gallery areas feature changing art exhibitions by local artists.

Children and adults may also schedule a guided tour, make use of materials in the Educational Resource Center, and utilize hiking trails around the building and along the Flatirons.

National Center for Atmospheric Research, 1850 Table Mesa Dr., Boulder, CO 80303. Phone: 303/497-1174. Fax: 303/497-1172. Hours: 8–5 Mon.–Fri.; 9–3 Sat., Sun., and holidays. Admission: free.

Exhibit spaces

NORLIN LIBRARY EXHIBIT SPACES AT THE UNIVERSITY OF COLORADO AT BOULDER

Changing exhibitions of art, photography, books, manuscripts, and other materials are presented in five locations at Norlin Library, the largest of the University of Colorado at Boulder's libraries.

Norlin provides a gallery on the third floor, display cases in the first-floor east and west lobbies and the Special Collections Department on the second floor, and an exhibit area in the Archives Department on the lower level. Recent exhibitions include "Myths of the American West," "Racial and Ethnic Stereotypes," "The Book as Art," and "Land of Darkness: Remembering the Holocaust." Special Collections houses more than 60,000 rare books, manuscripts, and materials, making it one of the major collections of its kind in the West. Archives contains materials on such subjects as Western Americana, labor unions, politics and politicians, environment, human rights, and university history.

Other libraries on the Boulder campus also have exhibit spaces, among them the Engineering Library in the Mathematics Building, which features an exhibit on the history of the College of Engineering and Applied Sciences.

Norlin Library, University of Colorado at Boulder, Campus Box 184, Boulder, CO 80309-0184. Phone: 303/492-8302. Fax: 303/492-1881. Website: www-libraries.colorado.edu. Hours: 8 A.M.–12 midnight Mon.–Thurs., 8 A.M.–11 P.M. Fri., 10 A.M.–11 P.M. Sat., 12–12 Sun.; holidays, call for schedule (303/492-8705), but closed New Year's Day, Memorial Day, Thanksgiving, and Christmas. Admission: free.

Historic house

ARNETT-FULLEN HOUSE

The Arnett-Fullen House, a fanciful combination of Gothic Revival and Vernacular Masonry elements, is an 1877 architectural gem housing the offices of Historic Boulder Inc., a historical preservation organization.

Historic Boulder Inc. purchased the building in a public auction in 1993. Known as the "Gingerbread House" because of its steeply pitched gables with scrolled bargeboards, the structure is one of approximately 90 individually landmarked buildings in Boulder.

The Arnett-Fullen House was built by local businessman Williamette Arnett, who wanted the house to be a showplace. It was purchased in 1914 by Eliza Jane Fullen, widow of Hiram Fullen, one of Boulder County's first miners and discoverer of the Magnolia Mine at Magnolia and the American Mine at Sunshine, which turned out to be one of the county's richest. The house was completely renovated by the Fullen family in 1965, retaining many of its original features.

In addition to tours of the Arnett-Fullen House, Historic Boulder Inc. offers walking tours (for $6) of other historic houses, neighborhoods, and districts, including the University of Colorado campus;

University Hill, Whittier, and Mapleton neighborhoods; Columbia Cemetery; and the Downtown and Chautauqua Park historic districts (see separate listings for the districts).

Arnett-Fullen House, Historic Boulder Inc., 646 Pearl St., Boulder, CO 80302. Phone: 303/444-5192. Fax: 303/444-5309. Hours: 9–4 Mon.–Fri.; closed major holidays. Admission: free.

Historic ranch

WALKER RANCH

At 2,028 acres, Walker Ranch is the largest Colorado property listed on the National Register of Historic Places. It was homesteaded in the 1880s and retains many of its original buildings and other facilities, which are open to the public annually on two weekends in late September/early October. The ranch, located 7.5 miles west of Boulder on Flagstaff Road, was obtained by Boulder County in 1976 and is managed by the Parks and Open Space Department.

The annual "Walker Ranch: A Glimpse of the Past" festival, which began in 1985, features 65 costumed volunteers re-enacting life on a working ranch a century ago—churning butter, washing laundry, creating corn-husk and yarn dolls, caring for animals, and performing other chores.

Visitors can tour the ranch house, livestock/hay barn, wagon barn, scale house, log house, garage, turkey house, gas house, corn barn/pigpen, tack house/root cellar, springhouse, and blacksmith's shop, as well as a loading chute/dehorning gate, corrals, fenced pastures, and cultivated fields.

Founder James Walker came to the Boulder area from Missouri in 1869 with only $12. Suffering from yellow fever and longing to breathe the mountain air and see Indians before he died, Walker made his way to an Arapaho camp west of Boulder and built a lean-to nearby. A combination of fresh air, herbs, and Native American healing skill reportedly cured his illness. In 1882, he filed a homestead claim on a portion of the property now known as Walker Ranch. He and his family lived on the land until it eventually was sold. Boulder County purchased the 2,566 acres, of which 2,028 were designated open space and a historic district. The remainder was placed under the management of other agencies.

Walker Ranch is the trailhead for the 4.5-mile Eldorado Canyon Trail and several shorter trails, including a 1-mile trail leading to South Boulder Creek. A picnic area is located at the north end of the property.

Walker Ranch, 7.5 miles up Flagstaff Road from Boulder. (Postal address: Boulder County Parks and Open Space Dept., 2045 13th St., P.O. Box 471, Boulder, CO 80306.) Phone: 303/441-3950. Fax: 303/441-4594. Hours: 10–3 Sat.–Sun. on two weekends in late Sept./early Oct. Admission: free.

Historic hotel

HOTEL BOULDERADO

The Hotel Boulderado was built in 1909 through popular subscription by the citizens of Boulder, who envisioned a "first-class" hotel in a growing city that viewed itself as the "Athens of the West." The new building quickly became the center of business, social, and conference functions.

The five-story hotel, now listed on the National Register of Historic Places, retains much of its turn-of-the-twentieth-century charm, including a stained-glass lobby ceiling, cantilevered cherry staircase, Italianate and Mission-style brick architecture, and antique and reproduction furnishings.

The hotel has been largely restored to its original Victorian grandeur and expanded to provide additional guest rooms and meeting spaces. It now has 160 rooms, as well as banquet and conference facilities totaling 8,000 square feet.

Hotel Boulderado, 2115 13th St., Boulder, CO 80302. Phone: 303/442-4344. Fax: 303/442-4378. Website: www.boulderado.com. Hours: open 24 hours. Rates: vary with room and season.

Historic cemetery

COLUMBIA CEMETERY

The first interment at Boulder's historic Columbia Cemetery took place in 1870. Since then, approximately 3,500 people have been laid to rest here, including Tom Horn, the West's last hired gunfighter, and Mary Rippon, the University of Colorado's first female professor.

The cemetery was opened by the Columbia Masonic Lodge and the Odd Fellows, transferred to the City of Boulder in 1965, and designated a local historic landmark in 1977. It recently underwent a major restoration and improvement program funded by the Colorado Historical Society, Historic Boulder Inc., and the Boulder Parks and Recreation Department.

Columbia Cemetery, 9th and Pleasant Sts., Boulder. Contact: Historic Boulder Inc., 646 Pearl St., Boulder, CO 80302. Phone: 303/444-5192. Fax: 303/444-5309. Hours: sunrise to dusk.

Historic district

COLORADO CHAUTAUQUA HISTORIC DISTRICT

The Chautauqua movement promoting educational and cultural experiences and enjoyment of the outdoors began in 1874 at Lake Chautauqua in New York. The movement quickly spread, reaching its height in the 1920s, when 12,000 Chautauquas were scattered throughout the nation. Today, just 20 such facilities remain, and only 3 have been in continuous operation. One of these is the Colorado Chautauqua in Boulder, the lone continuously operating Chautauqua west of the Mississippi River.

The Colorado Chautauqua was established in 1898 by a group of educators and others, including some Texans, who were seeking a sylvan site in which to appreciate nature, learn, and enjoy the performing and visual arts. Initially, tents at the base of the Flatirons housed the Boulder Chautauqua's programming—as well as the facility's founders. Cabins, an auditorium, a dining hall, and other facilities were eventually built, and programming was expanded.

Today, many of the early-twentieth-century facilities still exist—as do more recent additions—on a 26-acre site that has become a historic district. It now has 40 cottages, two rental lodges, a performing arts center, a dining hall, a community house, a history/archives building, and other facilities near hiking trails and hundreds of acres of mountain parks.

Among the diverse educational, cultural, and performing arts offerings are lectures, films, concerts, plays, festivals, workshops, exhibits, and other activities. Chautauqua is the home of the Colorado Festival Orchestra, which presents approximately 60 concerts, ranging from classical to contemporary music, each summer. The Chautauqua grounds include a public park, where a Fourth of July concert is presented annually.

Colorado Chautauqua Historic District, 900 Baseline Rd., Boulder, CO 80302. Phone: 303/545-6924. Fax: 303/449-0790. Office hours: winter, open 8:30–5 Mon.–Fri.; summer, 8:30 A.M.–9 P.M. Mon.–Sat.; closed major holidays. Event hours vary. Admission: free to grounds and some events; varies with concerts and other events.

Historic district

DOWNTOWN BOULDER HISTORIC DISTRICT

The Downtown Boulder Historic District, listed on the National Register of Historic Places in 1980, is a showcase of late-nineteenth-

and early-twentieth-century commercial structures. Queen Anne, Italianate, Romanesque and Classical Revival, and art deco architectural styles predominate.

The historic district roughly includes the south side of Spruce Street from 10th to 16th Streets, Pearl Street from 9th to 16th Streets, and the north side of Walnut Street from Broadway to 9th Street, as well as the Post Office at 14th and Walnut Streets and the Hotel Boulderado at 13th and Spruce Streets. The district encompasses the city's oldest commercial section, which is located largely within the original 1859 Boulder town site.

The earliest Boulder settlement served as a service and supply center to adjacent booming mining areas. As the economy diversified in the late nineteenth and early twentieth centuries, the downtown filled with shops, offices, restaurants, and a courthouse. In 1976–1977, in an effort to revitalize the old commercial district, the city closed Pearl Street between 11th and 15th Streets to vehicular traffic and constructed a prizewinning open-air pedestrian mall that is one of the most successful of its type in the nation.

Among the nineteenth-century structures in the district are the 1876–1877 Soule-Coates House, 1878 Boettcher-Valentine Building, 1881 Brookfield-Holstein Building, 1882 Berlin-Boulder City Building, 1889 Fonda Drugstore Building, 1893 Boulder Hardware Building, 1895 Butsch-Paddock House, 1898 Armory, 1898 Buckingham Block, 1898 Willard Building, 1898 Odd Fellows Hall, and 1899 National State Bank Building.

Other notable structures in the historic district include the 1904 Elks Lodge Building, 1909 Hotel Boulderado, 1912 Mercantile Bank Building, 1906 Sternberg–Citizens National Bank Building, 1909 Boulder Post Office, 1911 Voegtle Building, 1912 Siena Square complex, 1933 Boulder County Courthouse, and the 1935–1936 Boulder Theatre.

Downtown Boulder Historic District. Contact: Historic Boulder Inc., 646 Pearl St., Boulder, CO 80302. Phone: 303/444-5192. Fax: 303/444-5309.

Historic District

MAPLETON HILL HISTORIC DISTRICT

Boulder's newest historic district is one of the city's oldest neighborhoods—Mapleton Hill, a tree-lined ridge with late-nineteenth- and early-twentieth-century mansions overlooking the Flatirons and much of the community.

Mapleton Hill was laid out by the Boulder Land and Improvement Company in 1882. More than 200 silver maples and cottonwoods were planted to attract prospective buyers. But development was slow until the Mapleton School opened in 1889 and the Boulder Sanitarium (now Mapleton Rehabilitation Center and Boulder Center for Sports Medicine, affiliated with Boulder Community Hospital) was built for tuberculosis patients in 1896 by the Seventh-Day Adventist Church.

Among the distinctive large homes built on Mapleton Avenue during this early period are the 1890 Giffin-Klinger House, 1891 Duncan House, 1895 Law House, and 1896 Daniel-Burnham House. Later additions include the 1900 Patton House, 1900 Culbertson-Ownbey House, 1905 McInnes House, and 1913 Eastman House.

Nineteenth-century homes such as the 1865 Squires-Tourtellot House (believed to be the oldest extant house in the city) on Spruce Street, 1890 Whitney-Holmes House on Highland Avenue, and 1879 Earhart-Degge House, 1882 Fonda House, 1890 Morrison-McKenzie House, and 1895 Dudge House on Pine Street can be found in the neighborhood.

Historic Boulder Inc. conducts walking tours of the Mapleton Hill Historic District, as well as four other historic districts—Colorado Chautauqua, Downtown Boulder, University Hill, and Whittier Neighborhood.

Mapleton Hill Historic District. Contact: Historic Boulder Inc. 646 Pearl St., Boulder, CO 80302. Phone: 303/444-5192. Fax: 303/444-5309.

BRECKENRIDGE

Historic houses and mines

SUMMIT HISTORICAL SOCIETY

Carter Museum and Barn
Gaymon Cabin
Briggle House
Milne House
Washington Mine
Lomax Placer Mine
Gold Dredge

The Summit Historical Society, founded in Breckenridge in 1966, oversees 13 historical properties in Summit County, 7 of which are located in Breckenridge and open to the public. The society also operates the Summit Historical Museum and the Montezuma Schoolhouse (see separate listings under Dillon and Montezuma). Four other properties are not open to the public.

The Carter Museum and Barn is said to be Colorado's oldest museum. It is located in the 1875 log cabin of Edwin Carter, who was known as the "log-cabin naturalist." It contains exhibits on Breckenridge history and Rocky Mountain fauna, features a slide show on the Breckenridge Historic District (see separate listing), and is on the walking tour of the town's historical sites.

Three other historic structures are the 1914 Gaymon Cabin, where the historical society and Breckenridge Resort Chamber of Commerce have their offices, the 1880 Briggle House, and the 1880 Milne House (Milne House is part of the Briggle House complex). Both homes are part of the historical walking tour.

Ninety-minute tours are offered at two mine sites dating from 1859 to 1863—the Washington Mine and the Lomax Placer Mine. Visitors can learn about the life of nineteenth-century hard-rock gold miners and see the tools they used and the structures they worked in. The Lomax Placer Mine, which includes three buildings, demonstrates how placer mining was conducted from the days of panning to those of hydraulic equipment and features actual gold panning and a slide show.

Another historical structure is the frame Gold Dredge, which can be seen along Tiger Road.

The Summit Historical Society also has four properties that are closed to the public—the Eberian House and Hoosier Pass Ski Cabin in Breckenridge, Slate Creek Hall in Silverthorne, and Rice Barn in Dillon.

Carter Museum and Barn, Summit Historical Society, 111 N. Ridge St., P.O. Box 745, Breckenridge, CO 80424-0745. Phone: 970/453-9022. Fax: 970/453-8135. Tour hours: mid-June through Sept., 1:30 and 3 Mon.—Fri; Oct.–May, 1 Thurs., plus slide show at 10 Wed. and Fri.; closed major holidays. Admission: museum tour, $3; slide show, $5.

Gaymon Cabin, Summit Historical Society, 309 N. Main St., P.O. Box 745, Breckenridge, CO 80424-0745. Phone: 970/453-9022. Fax: 970/453-8135. Hours: 9–5 Mon.–Fri.; closed major holidays. Admission: free.

Briggle House and Milne House, Summit Historical Society, 104 and 102 N. Harris St., P.O. Box 745, Breckenridge, CO 80424-0745. Phone: 970/453-9022. Fax: 970/453-8135. Hours: part of the walking tour and by appointment. Admission: donation requested.

Washington Mine, Summit Historical Society, Illinois Gulch Rd., P.O. Box 745, Breckenridge, CO 80424-0745. Phone: 970/453-9022. Fax: 970/453-8135.

Tour hours: mid-June through Sept., 1 Fri. and by appointment; closed remainder of the year. Admission: adults, $5; children 12 and under, $3.

Lomax Placer Mine, Summit Historical Society, 301 Ski Hill Rd., P.O. Box 745, Breckenridge, CO 80424-0745. Phone: 970/453-9022. Fax: 970/453-8135. Tour hours: mid-June through Sept., 3 Mon.–Fri. and by appointment; closed remainder of the year. Admission: adults, $5; children 12 and under, $3.

Historic mine

COUNTRY BOY MINE

The Country Boy Mine, a hard-rock mine that operated from 1887 to 1948 near Breckenridge, was reopened for tours in 1994.

The mine was initially a major gold and silver producer and later became an important source of lead and zinc. It was purchased by Doug and David Tomlinson, who wanted to create a tourist site demonstrating early underground mining techniques. The brothers worked for five months restoring the 1,200-foot-deep mine; then the blacksmith's shop, which has several troughs for gold panning in winter; and the compressor house, which contains a display of old mining equipment and other artifacts.

The mine tour begins with a brief history of the mine. Visitors then pass through the dry room (the miners' changing room) and the mine. Next comes a display and demonstration of mining equipment, with an opportunity to swing one of the sledgehammers and chisel-like tools used in mining. The tour ends with an opportunity to do some gold panning on the surface, which usually produces a few flakes of gold as souvenirs.

Country Boy Mine, 542 French Gulch Rd., P.O. Box 8569, Breckenridge, CO 80424. Phone: 970/453-4405. Website: http://summitnet.com/mine/. Hours: mid-May to mid-Oct., 10–4 (varies slightly in May and Oct.); mid-Dec. to mid-Apr., 11–4 (11–2 during most of Jan./Feb.); closed Mon. and mid-Apr. through mid-May and mid-Oct. through mid-Dec. Admission: adults, $11; children 4–12, $6; children under 4, free.

Historic district

BRECKENRIDGE HISTORIC DISTRICT

The 12-block Breckenridge Historic District is one of Colorado's largest, with 254 buildings in the old mining town (currently a year-round resort), now the oldest continuously occupied community on the Western Slope.

A gold strike in 1859 along the Upper Blue River and another discovery at Gold Run later that year resulted in a gold rush and the founding of the town of "Breckinridge," named for Vice President John

C. Breckinridge. When the Civil War broke out, local residents, who backed the Union, became so angered at Breckinridge's support of the Confederacy that they changed the spelling of the town's name to Breckenridge.

Later on, silver was discovered in the area. Virtually every method was used to extract it, and gold, from nearby streams and mountains. Large dredging machines, for example, dug up streams and rivers from 1898 to 1942, leaving piles of rock still visible near Breckenridge. The town's economy rose and fell as gold and silver deposits were mined and exhausted over the years.

Much of Breckenridge's architectural legacy is from the mining days of the late nineteenth and early twentieth centuries. The Summit Historical Society (see separate listing) now oversees 13 historical properties in Breckenridge and the surrounding area and operates guided walking tours of more than 40 historic structures. The buildings range from simple log cabins to restored Victorian false-front structures. The historic district was listed on the National Register of Historic Places in 1980.

Breckenridge Historic District. Contact: Summit Historical Society, 309 N. Main St., P.O. Box 745, Breckenridge, CO 80424-0745. Phone: 970/453-9022. Fax: 970/453-8135.

BRIGHTON

History museum

ADAMS COUNTY MUSEUM

The Adams County Museum, which houses historical collections and exhibits pertaining to the area, has five buildings at its cultural complex near Brighton.

The museum, founded in 1987 by the Adams County Historical Society, features a 1930s schoolhouse and a 1930s gas station with glass pumps, both originally built on the site; a working blacksmith's shop; an earth sciences center; and a cultural center containing most of the artifacts and exhibits.

The permanent exhibits cover such topics as the natural history and geology of the area; Native American cultures up to 1850; mountain men and explorers from 1820 to 1840; early western settlement from 1840 to 1902; the World War I period from an Adams County perspective; and the county's history and ethnic diversity.

The museum also displays works by local artists, presents special exhibitions, and holds various festivals, such as the Multi-Ethnic Cultural Arts Festival.

Adams County Museum, 9601 Henderson Rd., Brighton, CO 80601-9100. Phone: 303/659-7103. Hours: 10–4:30 Tues.–Sat.; closed New Year's Day, Fourth of July, Thanksgiving, and Christmas. Admission: free, but groups pay $.50 per person, with a minimum of $5.

Nature center

BARR LAKE NATURE CENTER

As recently as 1965, Barr Lake near Brighton was considered one of the most polluted bodies of water in the state (Denver sewage escaped into it via the South Platte River and a feeder canal).

Fortunately, things have changed, and the 2,500-acre Barr Lake State Park has been developed into a popular nature preserve featuring more than 300 species of birds, a variety of other wildlife, prairie grasslands and forests, a lake stocked with fish, a nine-mile lakeside trail, three picnic areas, and a nature center. It also offers guided nature walks and is home to the only pair of nesting bald eagles along the Front Range.

The Barr Lake Nature Center contains displays on the park's wildlife and habitat, including a replica of the bald-eagle nest. Nearby is a gazebo from which visitors can view the eagles and their nest with the aid of binoculars.

The park is one of 40 operated by the Colorado State Parks Department of Natural Resources.

Barr Lake Nature Center, 13401 Picadilly Rd., Brighton, CO 80601. Phone: 303/659-6005. Fax: 303/659-5489. Hours: 9–4 daily (park is open 5 A.M.–10 P.M. daily). Admission: $4 per vehicle.

BROOMFIELD

History museum

BROOMFIELD DEPOT MUSEUM

Broomfield's history and railroad heritage are featured at the Broomfield Depot Museum, located in a 1909 Colorado & Southern Railroad station moved from its original site at 120th Avenue and Wadsworth Parkway to Zang Spur Park.

The depot was purchased from the railroad in 1975 by the Broomfield Jaycees and opened by volunteers in 1983 after collections and exhibits were developed and the building extensively renovated.

The museum now has more than 3,000 artifacts and other materials, about one-third of which are on display. Visitors can see where the railroad agent sold tickets and controlled train traffic. They can also tour the waiting room, which now has an extensive railroad book collection, changing exhibits, and the original fixtures from the Broomfield Post Office; tour the upstairs master bedroom and children's room, where the depot agent and his family lived; and view a pictorial exhibit on the history of Broomfield.

Adjacent to the depot are the 1905 honey house, pump house, and outhouse, all from the Miles Crawford estate. The Crawford family was known for the honey it produced. The property was donated to the museum by Carolyn Lambert in memory of her parents.

Broomfield Depot Museum, 2201 W. 10th Ave., P.O. Box 531, Broomfield, CO 80020. Phone: 303/460-9014. Hours: 2–4 Sun.; closed holidays and Dec.–Feb. Admission: free.

BRUSH

History museum/cultural center

BRUSH AREA MUSEUM AND CULTURAL CENTER

After seven years of planning and fund-raising, the Brush Area Museum and Cultural Center opened to the public in January 1999.

The museum is located in the 5,000-square-foot Knearl School building, which operated from 1910 until 1971. Devoted to the history of the area, the museum contains artifacts, photographs, and other historical items. In addition to its permanent exhibits, the museum presents changing exhibitions. The old school building also serves as a center for community cultural events.

Brush Area Museum and Cultural Center, 314 S. Clayton St., P.O. Box 341, Brush, CO 80723. Phones: 970/842-4022 and 800/842-8659. Fax: 970/842-9113. Hours: 9–5 Mon.–Fri., 12–4 Sat.–Sun.; closed major holidays. Admission: free.

BUCKSKIN JOE

Historic ghost town

BUCKSKIN JOE GHOST TOWN

Nearly the only things left in Buckskin Joe, one of Colorado's earliest and wildest mining camps, are an arastra (used to crush ore) and a cemetery.

The town, originally called Laurette, was renamed for Joseph Higgenbottom, known as "Buckskin Joe" for his deerskin clothing. Higgenbottom was among the first to discover gold in the area in 1859. However, he traded his interest in the camp a year later for a horse, a gun, and settlement of a bar bill, then disappeared.

Although the gold boom was short-lived, more than 5,000 people, including H.A.W. Tabor, who later made a fortune in Leadville, came to this mining town two miles west of Alma before its decline. By 1866, it was nearly deserted.

One of the community's most famous figures was a dance-hall girl known as "Silver Heels" because of her fancy slippers. She cared for miners and their families during the 1861 smallpox epidemic, then caught the disease herself, which left her disfigured. After leaving town, she reportedly came back from time to time, heavily veiled, to place wildflowers on the victims' graves. Mount Silverheels later was named in her honor.

In recent years, the two remaining structures at the early mining camp were moved to the South Park City Museum, a re-created nineteenth-century mining village in Fairplay (see separate listing).

Buckskin Joe Ghost Town, 2 miles west of Alma. Contact: Alma Firehouse and Mining Museum, 1 W. Buckskin Rd., P.O. Box 336, Alma, CO 80420-0336. Phone: 719/836-3413.

BUENA VISTA

History museum

BUENA VISTA HERITAGE MUSEUM

The Buena Vista Heritage Museum is housed on the ground floor of the 1882 Chaffee County Courthouse in Buena Vista.

The museum, which opened in 1975, has four exhibit rooms. One focuses on mining and agriculture, another on clothing and textiles; the other two re-create an 1890s schoolroom, and an early living room and kitchen from the area. In addition, the Buena Vista Model Railroad

Society has built scale replicas of three 1880s narrow-gauge railroads from the Arkansas River valley. These model railroads are on view in a separate room.

The Chaffee County Council on the Arts runs an art gallery in the upstairs courtroom. The upper level also contains a research room on area history.

The Buena Vista Heritage Museum also operates the Turner Farm as a historic farm (see following listing).

Buena Vista Heritage Museum, 511 E. Main St., P.O. Box 1414, Buena Vista, CO 81211. Phone: 719/395-8458. Hours: May 25–Sept. 25, 9–5 daily; closed remainder of the year. Admission: adults, $2; children, $1.

Historic farm

TURNER FARM

The turn-of-the-twentieth-century Turner Farm, currently open for special events, is being converted to a living-history museum by the Buena Vista Heritage Museum.

The farm consists of a two-story frame farmhouse, a large log barn, the original homesteaders' cabin, farm equipment, and an orchard of 100-year-old apple trees. When the restoration is complete, the farm will be a living-history museum re-creating small homesteads typical of the area in 1900–1912.

Turner Farm, 829 W. Main St. (Contact: Buena Vista Heritage Museum, P.O. Box 1414, Buena Vista, CO 81211.) Phone: 719/395-8458. Hours: vary with event. Admission: free with appointment.

BURLINGTON

Living-history museum

OLD TOWN

More than 20 historic and re-created buildings, a collection of 40 vintage wagons, and numerous artifacts of the Old West are on display in a 6.5-acre living-history museum known as Old Town, opened by the City of Burlington in 1987. Most of the buildings have been moved from other Colorado communities and neighboring states, such as the 1889 train depot from Bethone, 1911 schoolhouse from Cope, early 1900s manor house from Vona, 1921 church from Armed, and early barn from Kanorado, Kansas.

Among the other historic and re-created structures are a general store, blacksmith's shop, law office, cream station, caretaker's house, bank/real estate office, drugstore, doctor's office, leather shop, saloon, newspaper office, woodworking shop, jail, dollhouse, soddies (sod houses), and heritage hall with farm machinery. An exhibit on Native Americans and a display of early western objects are also on view. Adjacent to the outdoor area is the Emporium, a shop featuring handcrafted and other gifts.

The museum is open throughout the year, but it is only during summer that visitors ride the Old Town Express, a wagon ride led by two Belgian draft horses; have an ice cream sundae in the cream shop; and see shows, mock gunfights, and other special events.

Old Town, 420 S. 14th St., Burlington, CO 80807. Phones: 719/346-7382 and 800/288-1334. Fax: 719/346-7169. E-mail: oldtownria.net. Website: www.burlingtoncolo.com. Hours: 9–6 Mon.–Sat., 12–5 Sun. (with extended hours in summer); closed New Year's Day, Easter, Thanksgiving, and Christmas. Admission: adults, $6; seniors, $5; children 12–17, $4; children 3–11, $2; children under 3, free; groups, $5 per person.

Carousel museum

KIT CARSON COUNTY CAROUSEL MUSEUM

A fully restored 1905 wooden merry-go-round and the building surrounding it are the focus of the Kit Carson County Carousel Museum on the county fairgrounds in Burlington.

The beautifully carved carousel, now a National Historic Landmark, was produced in 1905 by the Philadelphia Toboggan Company for the Elitch Gardens Amusement Park in Denver. It was operated at the park every summer until 1928, when it and the 1912 Wurlitzer Monster Military Band Organ inside it were sold to Kit Carson County for $1,250. The county commissioners were widely criticized for what was considered an extravagant expenditure in hard times—so much so that two of the three commissioners chose not to run for re-election.

The carousel was operated only during the county fair until 1984, when it became the functioning centerpiece of the museum, open between Memorial Day and Labor Day. Today, it is the only antique carousel in the United States to retain its original paint on both the animals and the scenery panels.

The merry-go-round has 46 hand-carved and -painted animals and four colorful chariots on a 45-foot-diameter platform housed in a 12-sided building. The military band organ, drive machinery, and center of the carousel are enclosed by 45 oil paintings depicting the Victorian era.

A visit to the carousel includes a 20-minute guided tour and a 4-minute ride. The history of the carousel and its intricately carved styles are explained by a tour guide.

Kit Carson County Carousel Museum, Kit Carson County Fairgrounds, Burlington, CO. (Postal address: P.O. Box 28, Stratton, CO 80836.) Phone: 719/348-5562. Fax: 719/348-5887. Hours: Memorial Day–Labor Day, 1–8 P.M. daily; closed remainder of the year (except to private group tours). Admission: $.25.

CALHAN

Wildlife refuge

BIG CATS OF SERENITY SPRINGS

More than 30 lions, tigers, cougars, bobcats, and lynxes make their home at Big Cats of Serenity Springs, a refuge for unwanted, abused, and retired wild felines on a 320-acre ranch near Calhan, northeast of Colorado Springs. Nick and Karen Sculac began caring for big cats in 1995, when they adopted a Bengal tiger kitten. Other homeless felines soon followed. Guided tours are offered on weekends by appointment.

Big Cats of Serenity Springs, P.O. Box 112, Calhan, CO 80808. Phone: 719/347-9200. Fax: 719/347-9100. E-mail: bigcatresq@aol.com. Hours: guided tours by appointment, 1–5 Sat., 11–5 Sun. Admission: adults and children, $5.

CAÑON CITY

History/natural history museum

CAÑON CITY MUNICIPAL MUSEUM

The Cañon City Municipal Museum is devoted to the history and natural history of the Fremont County region from about 1860 to 1950. The facility comprises three historical buildings, as well as two large galleries on the second floor of the Municipal Building.

Opened in 1928, the museum evolved from the vision of local businessman William Dallas DeWeese, who designed the two city-hall galleries to hold his collection of firearms, big-game trophies, and ethnographic artifacts. One of the galleries (the DeWeese Gallery) still features his collection and some of his furniture; the other (the Amick

Gallery) is dedicated to noted artist Robert Wesley Amick, who was born and educated in Cañon City.

The oldest of the three historic buildings is the 1860 log cabin built by Anson Rudd, blacksmith and first warden of the Colorado Territorial Prison. It is located on its original site. The other two structures are a small three-story stone house built in 1881 and occupied by the Rudd family until 1904, and a pioneer Catlin cabin moved to its present site in the 1980s. The cabin displays a collection of blacksmith's tools.

The museum and its collections are owned and funded by the City of Cañon City, which has contracted the management and operation of the museum to a private nonprofit organization, the DeWeese-Rudd Museum Group.

Cañon City Municipal Museum, 612 Royal Gorge Blvd., P.O. Box 1460, Cañon City, CO 81215-1460. Phone: 719/269-9018. Fax: 719/269-9017. Hours: 10–4 Tues.–Sat., also 10–4 Sun. in summer; closed New Year's Day and Christmas. Admission: adults, $1.50; children 6–12, $1; groups, half-price.

Prison museum

MUSEUM OF COLORADO PRISONS

A fascinating and grisly historical look at life in the state's prison system is offered at the Museum of Colorado Prisons—formerly the Colorado Territorial Prison Museum—in Cañon City.

The museum, opened by a nonprofit foundation in 1988, occupies Cellhouse 4, the former Women's Prison, built in 1935 and closed in 1980. It is located outside the east wall of the original 1868 federal territorial prison, which became a state facility in 1876. It is the only prison museum adjacent to an active prison.

The museum explains the history of Colorado's prison system from its founding in 1871 to the present. Of particular interest are historical prison equipment displayed in the museum's front yard and 30 prison cells featuring exhibits on various aspects of prison life and history.

Among the yard's exhibits are the gas chamber used in the final eight executions by gas in Colorado; two outdated cells from Cellhouse 7 at "Old Max," the former maximum-security prison; a large wagon once used to carry coal to the prison; a fire truck that was part of a cancelled pilot program to train inmates as firefighters; and early hand-pulled hose carts used to fight fires.

Each of the cell exhibits deals with a different topic, among them notorious inmates, the women's prison, wardens, early correctional officers, behavior control, the death penalty, prison industries, the 1929 riot, security towers, the prison cemetery, and modern cells. Material on view includes confiscated inmate weapons and contraband, disciplinary paraphernalia used from 1871 to the present, and historic photographs of prisoners and their life behind bars.

Museum of Colorado Prisons, 201 N. 1st St., P.O. Box 1229, Cañon City, CO 81215-1229. Phone: 719/269-3015. Fax: 719/269-9148. Hours: summer, 8:30–6 Mon.–Fri.; winter, 10–5 Mon.–Fri.; closed New Year's Day, Easter, Thanksgiving, and Christmas. Admission: adults, $4; seniors, $3.50; children 6–12, $2.50; children under 6, free; groups, $.50 discount per person.

Natural history museum

DINOSAUR DEPOT

Dinosaur Depot is an educational and interpretive facility in Cañon City that explains the history and significance of the Garden Park fossil area, a Jurassic dinosaur graveyard.

The area was one of three sites discovered in western North America in 1877 that provided paleontologists with their first look at the giant sauropod dinosaurs, some of the carnivorous dinosaurs, and *Stegosaurus*, whose existence was virtually unknown prior to the Garden Park discoveries.

The museum was opened in 1995 by the Garden Park Paleontology Society in partnership with the City of Cañon City, the Bureau of Land Management, and the Denver Museum of Natural History.

Visitors can see replica skulls and fossils of dinosaur finds made in the area, a life-size sculpture of an *Allosaurus*, and a laboratory where prep work is taking place on a *Stegosaurus* skeleton excavated in 1992. The facility also provides guided tours, educational programs for adults and children, and tours of the Garden Park fossil area.

Dinosaur Depot, 330 Royal Gorge Blvd., Cañon City, CO 81212. Phone: 719/269-7150. Fax: 719/269-7227. E-mail: depot@ris.net. Hours: summer, 9–5 daily; winter, 9–5 Wed.–Sun.; closed New Year's Day, Easter, and Christmas. Admission: adults, $2; children 4–12, $1; children 3 and under, free. Guided museum tours: adults, $3; children 4–12, $1.50; children 3 and under, free. Guided museum and fossil area tours: adults, $5; children 4–12, $2.50; children 3 and under, free.

Ethnic/religious history museum

MUSEUM AT HOLY CROSS ABBEY

Native American artifacts and religious historical materials are displayed in the Museum at Holy Cross Abbey, a Benedictine abbey near Cañon City.

The Royal Gorge Bridge near Cañon City. Courtesy Royal Gorge Bridge.

The museum, located in the basement of the Tudor/Gothic-style abbey founded in 1925, was developed in 1988 as an offshoot of a summer camp program. The Native American collection, which focuses on Plains Indians and includes arrowheads, axes, pots, blankets, and baskets, was assembled as a result of the youngsters' interest in Native American life. The religious materials—objects once used at the abbey—were added to the museum collection later and feature old vestments and the abbey's former throne.

Museum at Holy Cross Abbey, 2951 Colo. Hwy. 50, Cañon City, CO 81212. Phone: 719/275-8631. Fax: 719/275-7125. Hours: June–Aug., 9–4 daily; remainder of the year by appointment. Admission: free.

Arts Center

FREMONT CENTER FOR THE ARTS IN CAÑON CITY

The Fremont Center for the Arts in Cañon City opened in 1948 in the town's 1932 former post office building and continues to be managed by the nation's oldest community arts council.

Located in the downtown historic district, the arts center has a gallery, an eclectic collection of more than 150 artworks, and a program of changing exhibitions that includes a new show every month. It also hosts plays, music programs, poetry readings, and painting, language, and pottery classes.

The center's art collection ranges from lithographs to paintings by local artists. The changing exhibitions feature watercolors, oil paintings, lithographs, sculpture, photographs, quilts, and other works, created mainly by community and school groups.

Fremont Center for the Arts, 505 Macon Ave., Cañon City, CO 81212. Phone: 719/275-2790. Fax: 719/275-4242. E-mail: ftcarts@ris.net. Hours: 10–4 Tues.– Sat.; closed Sun.–Mon. and major holidays. Admission: free.

Historic site

ROYAL GORGE BRIDGE

The Royal Gorge Bridge near Cañon City is the world's highest suspension bridge, spanning the Arkansas River and Royal Gorge at a height of 1,053 feet. The bridge, which stretches for nearly a quarter mile, was built in 1929 and now attracts more than 500,000 visitors a year.

Although the Spanish explored the area in 1642, it was not until 1806 that American explorer Zebulon Pike became the first person to record seeing the canyon. In 1877, the Denver & Rio Grande Western Railroad laid track through the gorge to silver mines in the mountains near Leadville, and trains later became a popular way to view the Royal Gorge Bridge from below.

Today, visitors can walk or drive across the bridge; get a spectacular view of the canyon and bridge from a 35-passenger aerial tram; ride the world's steepest incline railway to the bottom of the canyon; and enjoy the Buckskin Joe Frontier Park and Railway, an Old West theme park near the bridge (see separate listing).

Royal Gorge Bridge, 4218 Fremont County Rd. 3-A, P.O. Box 549, Cañon City, CO 81215. Phones: 719/275-7507 and 888/333-5597. Fax: 719/269-3501. Hours: sunrise to sunset daily. Admission: adults, $12.50; seniors $9.50; children 4–11, $9.50; children 3 and under, free.

Historic railroad

CAÑON CITY & ROYAL GORGE RAILROAD

In 1999, a new railroad using a vintage diesel-powered locomotive and cars began offering 23-mile round-trip rides through the 1,053-foot-deep Royal Gorge from Cañon City to Parkdale three times daily from mid-May through mid-October. The fledgling rail line was founded in 1998 by Lindsey and Rosa Ashby, who operate the Georgetown Loop Railroad and once ran the half-mile-long Central City Railroad, now defunct.

The train travels over tracks used by the Denver & Rio Grande Western Railroad in the 1880s to carry settlers, prospectors, and cargo across the Rockies and, later, along a 173-mile route to Salida, Buena Vista, Leadville, Minturn, and Dotsero.

The gorge was the site of the legendary "Royal Gorge War" of 1878–1879, fought between the Rio Grande and Santa Fe railroads, which used gunmen, forts, and explosives to compete for sole right of access. Ultimately, the battle was settled in court in favor of the Rio Grande. The route most recently was owned by the Union Pacific Railroad.

The 11.6-mile route on the west side of the gorge and Arkansas River was purchased from the Union Pacific by Rock & Rail Inc. (which plans to develop a quarry at Parkdale and haul rocks to Pueblo and Colorado Springs) and the Royal Gorge Railroad. The Union Pacific intended to abandon the entire line but decided to reserve the right to carry freight in the future. The last regularly scheduled passenger service along the route ended in 1974.

Cañon City & Royal Gorge Railroad, Santa Fe Depot, 1st St. and Royal Gorge Blvd., Cañon City, CO 81215. (Additional contact: Georgetown Loop Railroad, 1106 Rose St., P.O. Box 217, Georgetown, CO 80444.) Phones: 303/569-2403, 800/691-4386, and 888/724-5748. Fax: 303/569-2894. Website: www.royalgorgeroute.com. Hours: departures mid-May to mid-October at 9, 12, and 3. Admission: adults, $24.50; children 3–12, $16.50; children under 3, free.

Historic town attraction

BUCKSKIN JOE FRONTIER PARK AND RAILWAY

Buckskin Joe Frontier Park and Railway is an Old West theme park consisting mainly of historic log buildings from around the state. It is located near the Royal Gorge, 9 miles west of Cañon City.

The 160-acre amusement park—the nation's largest with a western theme—opened in 1957. It has 27 relocated structures from the late nineteenth century, including a blacksmith's shop, general store, printing shop, livery stable, and barn. It also features a mine replica, a miniature railway, and an assortment of shops, saloons, food services, and entertainment. Staged gunfights are presented 11 times daily during the park season.

Buckskin Joe Frontier Park and Railway, 1193 and 1289 Fremont County Rd. 3-A, P.O. Box 1387, Cañon City, CO 81215. Phones: Buckskin Joe Frontier Park, 719/275-5149; Buckskin Joe Railway, 719/275-5485. Fax for both: 719/275-6270. E-mail: buckskinjoe@bemail.com. Website: buckskinjoes.com. Hours: Buckskin Joe Frontier Park, open May–Sept., 9–6 daily Memorial Day–Labor Day, with varying shorter hours before and after; Buckskin Joe Railway, open Mar.–Dec., 8–8 daily Memorial Day–Labor Day, with varying shorter hours before and after. Combination ticket admission: adults, $12; children 4–11, $10; children under 4, free.

CARBONDALE

History museum

MOUNT SOPRIS HISTORICAL MUSEUM

The Mount Sopris Historical Society in Carbondale traces its roots to the Carbondale Study Club in the early 1900s. But only in recent years has it presented historical displays in the town hall, library, and chamber of commerce. It plans to open the Mount Sopris Historical Museum in late 2000.

A century-old two-story log cabin built by homesteader Holland Thompson, a prominent prospector and rancher in the area, was donated to the historical society by his descendants in 1998. The structure was moved to a new location and will serve as the museum.

Mount Sopris Historical Museum, Mount Sopris Historical Society, 499 Weant Blvd. (off Colo. Hwy. 133), P.O. Box 373, Carbondale, CO 81623. Phone: 970/963-1890. Hours and admission to be determined.

CARIBOU

Historic ghost town

CARIBOU GHOST TOWN

Little is left of Caribou, once a thriving silver-mining town on a windswept hillside five miles northwest of Nederland near the Continental

Divide. Only portions of the stone foundations of an old hotel and an assay office remain.

A rock containing silver ore was found by prospector Sam Conger in 1860, but he failed to recognize the ore as silver. After seeing similar ore in Wyoming nine years later, Conger returned with five other prospectors and discovered the site of the Caribou Mine the very first day.

After the population rose to 3,000 and silver production peaked in 1875, the town suffered through two fires (1879 and 1899) that destroyed many of the buildings. The mines on Caribou Hill produced $20 million in silver ($8 million coming from the Caribou Mine alone) before the silver panic of 1893 sent prices plummeting and plunged the area into depression. Caribou was eventually abandoned.

Caribou Ghost Town, 5 miles northwest of Nederland. Contact: Nederland Visitors Center, Colo. Hwy. 19 and 1st St., P.O. Box 85, Nederland, CO 80466. Phone: 303/258-3936.

CARSON

Historic ghost town

CARSON GHOST TOWN

The mining town of Carson, 16 miles southwest of Lake City, sprang up in one of the most inaccessible mining areas in Colorado. It sat atop the Continental Divide in the San Juan Mountains, and runoff from heavy snows flowed to both the Gulf of Mexico and the Pacific Ocean.

Gold and silver were found at an elevation of 11,500–12,360 feet in an area blanketed with snow for much of the year. J. E. Carson first discovered ore on the mountaintop in 1881, staking claims on both sides of the Divide. Other prospectors quickly followed, and the camp became organized in 1882. Silver was mined during the 1880s; after the silver panic of 1893, the focus shifted to gold. Carson, also known as Carson City, reached its peak in the 1890s and early 1900s before sliding into decline and eventual abandonment.

A considerable number of crumbling structures and pieces of old mining equipment still survive; those on the Pacific slope have fared better against the elements than those on the Atlantic slope.

Carson Ghost Town, 16 miles southwest of Lake City. Contact: Lake City Chamber of Commerce, P.O. Box 430, Lake City, CO 81235. Phone: 970/944-2527.

CEDAREDGE

Living-history museum

PIONEER TOWN

Pioneer Town in Cedaredge is a five-acre re-created frontier community with historic and replica buildings outfitted with artifacts from the turn of the twentieth century.

The outdoor museum, opened in 1982 at the base of Grand Mesa (the world's largest flattop mountain) by the Surface Creek Valley Historical Society, contains more than 20 structures, including three wooden silos relocated from the Bar-I Ranch, the present site of Cedaredge.

Other buildings include working blacksmith's and printing shops, an award-winning chapel, and a depot, jail, cabin, bank, marshal's office, Wells Fargo office, barber shop/dental office, creamery, schoolhouse, livery stable, saloon, store/post office, packing shed, and two museums—the Charles States Museum, featuring mining equipment and geologic samples from the area, and the Sutherland Indian Museum, housing an extensive arrowhead and point collection.

Pioneer Town, Colo. Hwy. 65, P.O. Box 906, Cedaredge, CO 81413. Phone: 970/856-7554. Hours: Memorial Day weekend–Sept., 9–4 Mon.–Sat., 1–4 Sun.; closed remainder of the year. Admission: adults, $3; seniors, $2; children 8–17, $1.50; children under 8, free.

CENTRAL CITY

History museum

GILPIN COUNTY MUSEUM

The Gilpin County Museum, operated by the Gilpin County Historical Society, opened in 1974 in a former stone schoolhouse in Central City. The two-story building, which once housed all of Central City's classrooms and later became its high school, was built in 1870 by skilled Cornish stonemasons.

The six large rooms contain many possessions of the county's early pioneers. A re-creation of a Victorian home of a successful miner boasts a square grand piano, two Brussels carpets, a fainting couch, a pioneer kitchen, a child's bedroom with hand-carved furnishings, and other period items. The Vera Neal Memorial Room has a re-created barbershop, law office, and seamstress's shop, as well as a display of mining memorabilia.

Among the other exhibits are dioramas of a typical mining town and an early mill; personal belongings of Sheriff Dick Williams, who was fatally shot at the Mines Hotel in 1896; parts of the original Black Hawk and Central City post offices; an early dress shop; a general store; and a collection of old dolls.

Gilpin County Museum, Gilpin County Historical Society, 228 E. High St., P.O. Box 247, Central City, CO 80427-0247. Phone and fax: 303/582-5283. Hours: Memorial Day–Labor Day, 11–4 daily; other times by appointment. Admission: adults and children 12 and over, $3; children under 12, free. A combination ticket of $5 also enables purchasers to visit the Thomas House (see the following listing).

Historic house

THOMAS HOUSE

The Thomas House in Central City was built in 1874 and reflects period interest in European classical styling, with such features as Doric columns, entablature pedimented windows, applied plasters, and a secluded patio terraced with a Welsh mortarless rock wall.

The house was built by one of the Hendric brothers, who jointly owned a Central City foundry. In 1894, George Billings, owner of the Billings Millwork factory in Denver, gave the house to his daughter, Marcia, as a wedding gift, and it remained in the family until 1987, when it was taken over by the Gilpin County Historical Society.

The house is filled with advertising art and salesmen's samples, including dress lace and other items a mercantile store might sell (Billings's son-in-law, Ben Thomas, was vice president of the Sauer McShane Mercantile Co.). It also contains numerous paintings and drawings by Marcia Billings Thomas. Among the other items in the house are handmade quilts, dresses, large feather hats, a wood-burning cookstove, four pot-bellied stoves, 13 clocks, and an unusual ice chest used to store soda pop at the mercantile store.

Thomas House, Gilpin County Historical Society, 209 Eureka St., P.O. Box 247, Central City, CO 80427. Phone and fax: 303/582-5283. Hours: Memorial Day–Labor Day, 11–4 Fri.–Mon.; closed remainder of the year. Admission: adults and children over 12, $3; children under 12, free. A combination ticket of $5 also enables purchasers to visit the Gilpin County History Museum (see previous listing).

Historic hotel/museum

TELLER HOUSE HOTEL AND MUSEUM

The Teller House was built in 1872 as a grand Victorian hotel during Central City's boom days. It later became known for the mysterious "Face on the Barroom Floor" painted on the floor of its Face Bar.

The historic landmark was once known as the finest hotel (outside of Denver) west of the Mississippi River and hosted such notables as President Ulysses S. Grant. A path of silver brick was laid from Grant's carriage to the hotel's front door as a "welcome mat" during his 1873 visit.

The "Face on the Barroom Floor" was painted in 1934 by *Denver Post* artist Herndon Davis and continues to attract the attention of Central City visitors. The painting inspired Henry Mollicone to write a one-act play of the same name, which is performed each summer by the Central City Opera Apprentice Artists (one performance is staged in the bar itself). The walls of the Face Bar are decorated with restored murals of classic figures, including Leda and the swan, Venus with her apple, and Mars prepared for battle.

The Central City Opera House Association leased the property in 1932 and bought the hotel a few years later. In 1991, the Teller House was remodeled. The first floor was leased as a gambling casino (closed in early 2000) and restaurant, and the second floor became a historical

The Central City Opera House (right) *and Teller House* (left) *are among the historic attractions in the old mining town of Central City. Courtesy Central City Opera House and photographer Mark Kiryluk.*

museum (the Teller House Hotel Museum) featuring restored Victorian rooms with antique furniture and collectibles. Tours of the rooms—as well as the adjoining opera house—are given daily. Victorian artifacts and furniture (some of which belonged to such Colorado notables as Governor John Evans and Baby Doe Tabor) are found throughout the Teller House.

Teller House Hotel and Museum, 120 Eureka St., P.O. Box 8, Central City, CO 80427. Phone: 303/582-3200. Fax: 303/582-3678. E-mail: ccopera@mho.net. Hours: 10–1 daily, with tours (including Central City Opera House) 10–4 daily. Admission: museum, free; tours, $4.

Historic opera house

CENTRAL CITY OPERA HOUSE

Built in 1878, the Central City Opera House is the centerpiece of the Central City Historic District and the site of an annual summer opera festival in this former mining town.

The 552-seat opera house is a Victorian jewel, with an elaborately frescoed ceiling, excellent acoustics, and new theater-style seats, many of which are named after Colorado's pioneer families, illustrious figures in the performing arts, and opera benefactors.

The building's exterior is constructed of native granite and shows the stylistic influences of the great French Renaissance Château de Blois. The beautiful trompe l'oeil ceiling murals were painted by John C. Massman and refurbished in 1987. The building was designed by Denver architect Robert S. Roeschlaub and built by Welsh and Cornish miners.

The property was saved from decline in 1932 by the Central City Opera House Association, which renovated the building and has presented an annual summer opera festival there ever since. Tours of the opera house and the adjacent Teller House are offered year-round.

In addition to the excellent architecture of its opera house, the Central City Opera is known for its high-altitude performances (8,450 feet), the variety of the 30 properties the association maintains (including the Teller House Hotel, now also a casino and museum), and its highly regarded apprentice, youth, and artists-in-residence programs.

Central City Opera House, 200 Eureka St., Central City, CO 80427. (Postal address: 621 17th St., Suite 1601, Denver, CO 80293.) Phone: 303/292-6500. Fax: 303/292-4958. E-mail: ccopera@mho.net. Website: www.centralcityopera.org. Hours: tours, 10–4 daily; closed major holidays. Performances: late June through the *first week of August; matinees, 2:30; evenings, 8. Admission: tours, $4; performances, $30–$65.*

Historic district

CENTRAL CITY–BLACK HAWK HISTORIC DISTRICT

The nineteenth-century mining towns of Central City and Black Hawk form a historic district that is now a center of opera and gambling. (Central City and Black Hawk are two of three early Colorado mining communities—the other being Cripple Creek—where gambling has been legalized.)

The Central City–Black Hawk Historic District, which includes the commercial and residential areas of these adjoining communities off Colorado Highway 119, became a National Historic Landmark in 1961 and was listed on the National Register of Historic Places in 1966. Its boundaries were extended in 1991.

Two of Central City's principal historic properties are the 1872 Teller House, a Victorian hotel that is now a gambling casino and historical museum, and the 1878 Central City Opera House, which presents a summer opera festival (see separate listings). They are two of the thirty historic properties owned by the opera association.

Other historic structures in Central City include the 1864 Washington Hall, the original jail, now used for a summer-long arts-and-crafts show and sale; 1872 St. James Methodist Church; 1875 Wells Fargo Express Building; 1875 Belvidere Theatre; 1876 Williams Stables, now used for opera rehearsals and cabaret opera performances; 1897 City Hall; 1900 Gilpin County Courthouse; and the Register, First National Bank, Miller, Dostal, and Roworth blocks, most of which have been converted to gambling casinos behind historic facades.

The best-known historic structure in Black Hawk is the 1863 Lace House (see separate listing), an exceptional example of Carpenter Gothic, an architectural style popular in the nineteenth century.

Central City–Black Hawk Historic District. Contact: Gilpin County Museum, Gilpin County Historical Society, 228 E. High St., P.O. Box 247, Central City, CO 80427-0247. Phone and fax: 303/582-5283.

CHEYENNE WELLS

Jail museum

OLD CHEYENNE COUNTY JAIL MUSEUM

An 1894 jail designed by noted Denver architect Robert Roeschlaub is the home of the Old Cheyenne County Jail Museum in Cheyenne Wells. It is listed on the National Register of Historic Places.

After a new jail was constructed in 1961, the old jail was reopened as a museum by a group of women who also helped found the Eastern Colorado Historical Society, which now operates the facility.

The jail building has men's cells, a women's cell, tower office, work-room, staff room, and family living quarters for the sheriff—some of which were added in later years.

Old Cheyenne County Jail Museum, 85 W. 2nd St., P.O. Box 362, Cheyenne Wells, CO 80810. Phone: 719/767-8842. Fax: 719/767-5784. Hours: Memorial Day–Labor Day, 1–4 Mon.–Fri., 2–5 Sat.–Sun.; closed remainder of the year. Admission: adults, $1; students and children, $.50.

COKEDALE

Historic district

COKEDALE HISTORIC DISTRICT

The Cokedale Historic District is the best-preserved example of the many coal/coke camps that thrived in the early 1900s. Cokedale is also the site of the largest group of surviving coke ovens in the state.

Though most similar camps were dismantled when coal mines in the Las Animas–Huerfano district ceased operations after World War I, Cokedale functioned as a company town until 1946.

The community, constructed in 1906–1907 by the American Smelting and Refining Company, was heralded as a model camp, with housing, educational, and recreational facilities provided by the employer. Most of the homes, as well as the public and commercial buildings, have essentially survived intact.

Cokedale, near Trinidad, is located in Reilly Canyon in Cuchara Valley. Colorado Highway 12—known as the Highway of Legends—takes motorists through a series of former company towns (including Cokedale) and past large black slag piles left over from coal processing. Remnants of the double-sided coke ovens are visible on the south side of the highway.

The Cokedale Historic District was listed in the National Register of Historic Places in 1985.

Cokedale Historic District. Contact: Trinidad Chamber of Commerce, 309 N. Nevada Ave., Trinidad, CO 81082. Phone: 719/846-9285. Fax: 719/846-3545.

COLORADO SPRINGS

Art Museum

COLORADO SPRINGS FINE ARTS CENTER

The Colorado Springs Fine Arts Center is a major center for art and cultural activities in the Pikes Peak region. It comprises a fine arts museum, a performing arts theater, an art school, and an art library.

The arts center, which opened in 1936, was conceived by Alice Bemis Taylor, who envisioned a facility that would house her impressive collection of Hispanic, Native American, and Spanish colonial folk art and serve as a home for the fine and performing arts. It was one of the first institutions in the nation to combine the two genres.

The center is located in an attractive art deco building designed by renowned Santa Fe architect John Gaw Meem. The structure also reflects Mission and Pueblo architectural styles and incorporates Southwest Indian motifs. The center has nearly 11,600 square feet of gallery space for its permanent collections and more than 4,100 square feet for changing exhibitions, as well as a tactile gallery and a sculpture garden.

The fine arts permanent collection consists of nineteenth- and twentieth-century American paintings, graphics, and sculpture by such noted artists as Georgia O'Keeffe, John James Audubon, John Singer Sargent, Walter Kuhn, and Philip Pearlstein. The center also has an extensive collection of Charles M. Russell memorabilia on display, including sculptures, letters, and other personal effects.

The Native American and Hispanic art and artifacts are located in the Taylor Museum of Southwest Studies. These galleries contain Navajo textiles and sand paintings, Pueblo pottery and jewelry, and Guatemalan and Mexican tribal arts, including *santos* (Hispanic religious folk art images). Also on display is a reproduction of the Chapel of Our Lady of Talpa, a family chapel built in the 1830s in northern New Mexico, featuring *santos* and an altar screen from the original chapel.

The tactile gallery, which allows visitors to touch artworks, presents changing exhibitions drawn from the center's holdings and private collections. Braille and large-print labels provide information for the visually impaired.

The outdoor sculpture garden is a beautifully landscaped courtyard filled with contemporary, traditional, and Native American sculptures.

The fine arts center is also home to a 25,000-volume art research library, one of the largest in the region; the Bemis Art School, which offers classes in the visual arts and creative dramatics for children and adults; and a 450-seat performing arts theater that presents year-round professional drama, dance, music, and film programs.

Colorado Springs Fine Arts Center, 30 W. Dale St., Colorado Springs, CO 80903. Phone: 719/634-5581. Fax: 719/634-0570. E-mail: dturner@csfineartscenter.org. Hours: 9–5 Tues.–Fri., 10–5 Sat., 1–5 Sun.; closed national holidays. Admission: adults, $4; seniors, $2; students 13–21, $2; children 6–12, $1; children under 6, free.

History/general museum

COLORADO SPRINGS MUSEUM

The Colorado Springs Museum—formerly known as the Colorado Springs Pioneers Museum—is a general museum charged with preserving and interpreting the history of the Pikes Peak region.

Founded in 1937, the 70,000-square-foot museum occupies the former El Paso County Courthouse, an elegant 1903 building that has been restored and is now listed on the National Register of Historic Places.

The museum has collections and exhibits focusing on history and the fine and decorative arts. Among its more than 40,000 holdings are antique quilts; Native American artifacts; more than 700 pieces of Van Briggle art pottery; paintings of the Front Range from the late nineteenth and early twentieth centuries; papers of railroad builder William Jackson Palmer, founder of Colorado Springs; more than 30,000 historic photographs; and material relating to the city's founding and its mining, agricultural, health-resort, and military history. Many of these items are housed in the museum's Starsmore Center for Local History, a manuscript repository, reference library, and archive.

In addition to exhibits on the history and development of the city, the museum displays the reconstructed house of author Helen Hunt Jackson. Furnished with her possessions, it provides a view of a late-nineteenth-century home setting. The museum's restored Division 1 courtroom is frequently used as a motion picture location.

Colorado Springs Museum, 215 S. Tejon St., Colorado Springs, CO 80903. Phone: 719/578-6650. Fax: 719/578-6718. E-mail: cosmuseum@colospgs.co.us. Website: www.colorado-springs.com/cultredu/museums.htm. Hours: 10–5 Tues.–Sat., also 1–5 Sun. in May–Oct.; closed New Year's Day, Memorial Day, Fourth of July, Thanksgiving, and Christmas. Admission: free.

Children's museum

CHILDREN'S MUSEUM OF COLORADO SPRINGS

The Colorado Springs Museum. Courtesy Colorado Springs Museum.

Hands-on exhibits and activities are the focus of the Children's Museum of Colorado Springs, which is located in the Citadel Mall shopping center. Opened in 1989, the 2,000-square-foot museum serves young children up to the age of 10. The exhibits and activities pertain to health, animals, computers, the human body, video, and other fields. The museum also features a toddler room for children under five.

Children's Museum of Colorado Springs, Citadel Mall, 750 Citadel Dr. East, Colorado Springs, CO 80909. Phone: 719/574-0077. Hours: 10–5 Mon.–Sat., 12–5 Sun.; closed major holidays. Admission: adults, free; children 1 and over, $2; children under 1, free.

Aviation/space museum

PETERSON AIR AND SPACE MUSEUM

Air defense and the history of aviation, particularly in its connection to space, in Colorado and Colorado Springs are emphasized at the Peterson Air and Space Museum at Peterson Air Force Base in Colorado Springs.

Exhibits trace the history of the Army Air Corps, the Air Force, and aviation in the Pikes Peak region, and include such items as historic uniforms and flight suits, prisoners of war, historic military patches, aviation art, scale-model aircraft, full-size satellites, tracking stations, wall-size land-relief photos taken from space, and space-related films.

An outdoor display area features a CF-101B Voodoo, EC-121T Constellation, EV-57E Canberra, F-94C Starfire, F-89J Scorpion, T-33A Shooting Star, P-40N Warhawk, P-47 Thunderbolt, F-104A Starfighter, F-102A Delta Dart, F-86L Sabre, and CF-100 Canuck.

Five missiles also are on view—Nike Ajax, Nike Hercules, BOMARC, Hawk, and ATR-2N training missiles.

The museum and base are named for First Lieutenant Edward J. Peterson, a Colorado native and pilot who died when his photo reconnaissance plane crashed at the Colorado Springs Airport in 1942. The museum is housed in the original terminal building (1925–1940).

Peterson Air and Space Museum, Peterson Air Force Base, 150 E. Ent Ave., Colorado Springs, CO 80914. Phone: 719/556-4915. Fax: 719/556-4916. Hours: 8:30–4:30 Tues.–Sat.; closed national holidays. Admission: free.

Rodeo and cowboy museum/hall of fame

ProRodeo Hall of Fame and Museum of the American Cowboy

Professional cowboys and rodeos are the focus at the ProRodeo Hall of Fame and Museum of the American Cowboy in Colorado Springs. The hall of fame was founded in 1979 by the Professional Rodeo Cowboys Association; the Museum of the American Cowboy was developed in 1989 to preserve the legacy of rodeos and cowboys and to honor competitive champions.

Although cowboys usually are associated with the second half of the nineteenth century, many still are active on cattle ranches and compete in rodeos. Approximately 11 million people watch them perform at more than 700 rodeos annually.

The Professional Rodeo Cowboys Association—originally known as the Cowboys Turtle Association (cowboys allegedly were slow in getting things done)—was founded in 1936, when a number of cowboys walked out of a Boston rodeo to protest low prize money offered at these events (it often was less than the competitors' entry fees). Rodeo purses now often exceed several million dollars. The hall of fame/museum is adjacent to the association's national headquarters.

The hall of fame has more than 150 inductees, including rodeo contestants, stock contractors, clowns, announcers, contract personnel, other notables of the sport, and even rodeo animals. Among the honorees are world all-around rodeo champions Larry Mahan, Leo Camarillo, Casey

Tibbs, and Sharkey Irwin; saddle bronc riders Pete Knight and Yakima Cannute; bull riders Jim Shoulders, Kent Roberts, and Charles Sampson; steer wrestlers Homer Pettigrew and Bill Pickett; roper Ben Johnson; bucking horses Hell's Angel, Midnight, and Five Minutes 'til Midnight; and fighting bulls Oscar and Tornado.

The Hall of Fame Gallery has an exhibit case for each inductee, with a plaque, photographs, gear, memorabilia, and trophies. A new National Finals Gallery was added in 1996, when the facility was expanded from 25,000 to 45,000 square feet. It displays material pertaining to the rodeo "Super Bowl." The expansion also produced a large outdoor activity center with a full-size arena and barn.

Changing art exhibitions are presented throughout the museum. Rodeo animals, a sculpture garden, and an oversized bronze statue of nine-time world champion Casey Tibbs on his famed saddle bronc, Neckie, are on view outside the building.

ProRodeo Hall of Fame and Museum of the American Cowboy, 101 ProRodeo Dr., Colorado Springs, CO 80919. Phone: 719/528-4764. Fax: 719/548-4874. Hours: 9–5 daily; closed New Year's Day, Easter, Thanksgiving, and Christmas. Admission: adults, $6; seniors, $5; children 5–12, $3; children under 5, free.

The ProRodeo Hall of Fame and Museum of the American Cowboy in Colorado Springs. Courtesy ProRodeo Hall of Fame and Museum of the American Cowboy.

Figure skating museum/halls of fame

WORLD FIGURE SKATING MUSEUM AND HALL OF FAME
(including the U.S. Figure Skating Hall of Fame)

The World Figure Skating Museum and Hall of Fame in Colorado Springs traces the history of figure skating and operates two halls of fame—one national, the other international.

The United States Figure Skating Association ran a small museum at its headquarters in Boston from 1965 to 1979, when the organization moved to Colorado Springs. Shortly thereafter, it reopened the museum. The U.S. Figure Skating Hall of Fame and the World Figure Skating Hall of Fame were both established in 1976, the latter in collaboration with the International Skating Union. The museum and halls of fame are housed in a 10,000-square-foot building, which also contains an archive and a library.

Both halls of fame honor outstanding amateur and professional skaters, professional coaches, and others who have made significant contributions to the sport. Among the approximately 70 people enshrined in the world hall of fame are Sonja Henie of Norway, Barbara Ann Scott of Canada, Katarina Witt of Germany, James Koch of Switzerland, Dianne Towler and Bernard Ford of Great Britain, and Dick Button, Peggy Fleming, and Scott Hamilton of the United States. The more than 50 U.S. hall of fame inductees include Dorothy Hamill, Janet Lynn, Jojo Starbuck, and Kenneth Shelley. The halls of fame include plaques with a photograph and description of the skating accomplishments of each honoree.

On exhibit in the museum are historical ice skates, costumes, medals, trophies, posters, programs, photographs, films, and other materials pertaining to the history of figure skating and its outstanding performers. The museum houses the world's largest collections of skating art and memorabilia. One of the highlights is the Skating in Art collection of three-time Olympic champion Gillis Grafström of Sweden, featuring works from the seventeenth to twentieth centuries by artists such as Pieter Breughel the Elder, Hendrick Avercamp, and Winslow Homer, as well as unique silver, crystal, bronze, porcelain, and ivory pieces. Also on display are artworks by Toller Cranston, F. Buckley Moss, Andy Warhol, and other contemporary artists and sculptors.

Other exhibits include a collection of Sonja Henie dolls, more than 20 versions of the classic children's book *Hans Brinker and the Silver Skates*, artworks pertaining to figure skating, audio and video presentations on the world's great figure skaters, a display on U.S. Olympic gold medalists Brian Boitano and Scott Hamilton, and an exhibit on the U.S. figure skating team killed in a plane crash in Brussels in 1961.

World Figure Skating Museum and Hall of Fame, 20 1st St., Colorado Springs, CO 80906. Phone: 719/635-5200. Fax: 719/635-9548. Website: www.world skatingmuseum.org. Hours: 10–4 Mon.–Fri.; also June–Aug., 10–4 Sat., and Sept.–May, 10–4 first Sat. of the month; closed major holidays. Admission: adults, $3; seniors, $2; children 6–12, $2; children under 6, free.

Mining and industrial museum

WESTERN MUSEUM OF MINING AND INDUSTRY

The early history, equipment, and impact of mining in Colorado and the American West are the focus of the Western Museum of Mining and Industry, located across Interstate 25 from the U.S. Air Force Academy north of Colorado Springs.

Opened in 1975, the museum has an extensive collection of restored and working drills, pumps, generators, steam engines, and other mining/industrial equipment and provides more than 15,000 square feet of exhibits—many of a hands-on nature—in four buildings and outdoor displays on a 27-acre site.

Among the many pieces of working equipment exhibited and demonstrated are an 1895 Corliss steam engine that weighs 37 tons and has 500-horsepower capability; a steel hand drill with a four-pound hammer; a 100-pound rock-face blasting drill, and a huge turn-of-the-twentieth-century ore stamp mill.

Other attractions include a multimedia slide show, a simulated underground mine, a Colorado minerals exhibit, a restored 53-foot Elkton head frame from 1902, and demonstrations of a fire assay and gold panning.

The museum is located on the former Reynolds Ranch, a State Historic Landmark, and features a farmhouse and barn from the 1890s, as well as a reconstructed shop and hoist house and a 12,000-square-foot exhibit building and library.

Western Museum of Mining and Industry, 125 Gleneagle Dr., I-25 Exit 156A, Colorado Springs, CO. (Postal address: 1025 N. Gate Rd., Colorado Springs, CO 80921.) Phone: 719/488-0880. Fax: 719/488-9261. E-mail: admin@wmmi.org. Website: www.wmmi.org. Hours: 9–4 Mon.–Sat.; also June–Sept., 12–4 Sun.; closed major holidays. Admission: adults, $6; seniors, students 13–18, and college students, $5; children 5–12, $3; children under 5, free.

Money museum

MUSEUM OF THE AMERICAN NUMISMATIC ASSOCIATION

The Museum of the American Numismatic Association in Colorado Springs presents the nation's largest display of coins, medals, tokens, paper money, and related materials.

Opened in 1967, the museum, located in the association's headquarters building, has eight galleries for permanent exhibits and temporary exhibitions, including the Hall of Presidents, the Colorado Gallery, and the Tactile Gallery. The museum also contains photographs, artworks, tools, and machinery, as well as an archive and a 20,000-volume library related to numismatics.

Museum of the American Numismatic Association, 818 N. Cascade Ave., Colorado Springs, CO 80903-3279. Phone: 719/632-2646. Fax: 719/634-4085. E-mail: anamus@money.org. Website: www.money.org. Hours: 8:30–4 Mon.–Fri.; closed national holidays. Admission: free.

Natural history museum and space museum

MAY NATURAL HISTORY MUSEUM AND MUSEUM OF SPACE EXPLORATION

Two privately operated museums—the May Natural History Museum and the Museum of Space Exploration—are located at the John May Museum Center 10 miles southeast of Colorado Springs. It also is the site of Golden Eagle Ranch, a recreational-vehicle park and campgrounds with four lakes and five miles of mountain nature trails.

The natural history museum, consisting of a single large exhibit hall, features an extensive entomological collection gathered from tropical areas of the world over 53 years by James W.F. May, an Englishman who began collecting in 1903, and, later, by his son, John F. May. The collection started as a traveling exhibition in 1929 before being housed in the permanent museum in 1947.

Approximately 7,000 of the collection's more than 100,000 butterflies, beetles, scorpions, tarantulas, centipedes, weevils, and other invertebrates are displayed in the museum. Several cases of artifacts collected by James May on his travels—for example, a cowrie-shell necklace from New Guinea that could be used to help purchase a wife—are also on view.

Among the many unusual tropical specimens are a stick insect from New Guinea that measures 17 inches long and closely resembles a bundle of sticks; 10-inch-wide actius moths of India, whose markings imitate the appearance of a cobra's hood to scare off enemies; leaf insects of Borneo and leaf butterflies of Madagascar that look exactly like the leaves of the trees they rest on; Colombian beetles so large that they break street lights and can knock a person down if they hit him or her while flying; very large purple tarantula spiders from Peru that can catch and kill mice and small birds; and nine-inch-long poisonous scorpions from the Congo River region.

The space museum, which occupies three connecting trailers, was added in 1991. It features exhibits on topics ranging from early space flights to the latest space probes and space stations, making use of models, photographs, and films.

The admission fee covers both museums. The May family also plans to open several additional museums on other subjects.

May Natural History Museum and Museum of Space Exploration, John May Museum Center, 710 Rock Creek Canyon Rd., Colorado Springs, CO 80926-9779. Phones: 719/576-0450 and 800/666-3841. Fax: 719/576-3644. Hours: May–Sept., 8 A.M.–9 P.M. daily; remainder of the year by appointment. Admission: adults, $4.50; seniors, $3.50; children 6–12, $2.50; children under 6, free.

Transportation museum

CARRIAGE HOUSE MUSEUM

The Carriage House Museum, adjacent to The Broadmoor resort in Colorado Springs, is a transportation museum founded in 1941 and operated by the El Pomar Foundation. In addition to antique carriages, covered wagons, stagecoaches, and early automobiles, the 5,000-square-foot facility has a gun collection, Native American artifacts, horse tack, and other historical materials.

Carriage House Museum, The Broadmoor, 16 Lake Circle, Colorado Springs, CO 80906. Phone: 719/634-7711, ext. 5704. Hours: 10–12 and 1–5 Tues.–Sat., 1–5 Sun.; closed New Year's Day, Fourth of July, Veterans Day, Thanksgiving, and Christmas. Admission: free.

Street railway museum

PIKES PEAK HISTORICAL STREET RAILWAY FOUNDATION MUSEUM

The Pikes Peak Historical Street Railway Foundation was organized in Colorado Springs in 1982 to bring streetcars back to the city, where they operated from 1900 to 1932.

Plans call for the volunteer historical group to begin service, using vintage cars, from downtown Colorado Springs to Old Colorado City in 2000, and on to Manitou Springs later. Tracks now are being laid along the route.

Foundation workers are restoring 12 historic streetcars—a 1901 car once used in Colorado Springs, a 1919 car from Fort Collins, a 1942 car from Los Angeles, and nine 1947 cars from Philadelphia. Eight other cars will be added in the near future.

In 1996, the foundation opened a museum adjoining its offices and maintenance shop. Tours are given of the museum's collection of street-car models, artifacts, historic drawings and photographs, and operating plans, as well as the streetcars being restored in the shop.

Pikes Peak Historical Street Railway Foundation Museum, 2333 Steel Dr., P.O. Box 544, Colorado Springs, CO 80901. Phone: 719/475-9508. Fax: 719/475-2814. Hours: 10–4 Sat.; other times by appointment; closed New Year's Day, Thanksgiving weekend, Christmas Eve, and Christmas. Admission: adults, $2; children 5–12, $1; children under 5, free.

Zoological park

CHEYENNE MOUNTAIN ZOO

The Cheyenne Mountain Zoo, built on the eastern slope of Cheyenne Mountain at an elevation of 7,000 feet in Colorado Springs, is the only mountain zoo in the United States.

More than 500 animals representing 150 species can be found at the 75-acre zoological park, which opened in 1926 and is known for its diverse collection of exotic wildlife. Nearly 400,000 people visit each year to see such animals as reticulated giraffes, okapis, red pandas, bongos, Siberian tigers, rhinoceroses, amur leopards, Mexican gray wolves, gorillas, lions, orangutans, golden-lion tamarins, elephants, and zebras.

Cheyenne Mountain Zoo has four special-exhibition areas—Primate World, featuring gorillas and orangutans; Asian Highlands, containing Siberian tigers, red pandas, and amur leopards; Wolf Woods, where endangered Mexican gray wolves roam the mountainside; and Lion's Lair, housing African lions. Other attractions include the Elephant and Giraffe House, Bird and Reptile House, Monkey Pavilion, North American Cats, Rocky Cliffs, Birds of Prey, Bears, Aquatics, Hidden Prairie, Naked Mole Rats, and three gardens—the Butterfly Garden, Hummingbird Garden, and Life Zones Garden. The zoo also has a children's hands-on area, an antique carousel, and a 40-passenger tram that runs during the summer season.

Cheyenne Mountain Zoo, 4250 Cheyenne Mountain Zoo Rd., Colorado Springs, CO 80906. Phone: 719/633-9925. Fax: 719/633-2254. Website: www.cmzoo.org. Hours: Memorial Day–Labor Day, 9–6 daily; remainder of the year, 9–5 daily. Admission: adults, $7.50; seniors, $6.50; children 3–11, $4.50; children under 3, free.

Art gallery

COBURN ART GALLERY AT COLORADO COLLEGE

The Coburn Art Gallery in the Warner Campus Center at Colorado College in Colorado Springs presents a wide range of changing exhibitions.

Coburn Art Gallery, Colorado College, Warner Campus Center, 902 N. Cascade Ave., Colorado Springs, CO 80946. Phone: 719/389-6800. Hours: 12:30–7:30 Tues.–Sat.; closed Thanksgiving, Christmas, and when college is not in session. Admission: free.

Art gallery

GALLERY OF CONTEMPORARY ART AT THE UNIVERSITY OF COLORADO AT COLORADO SPRINGS

One of Colorado's most active contemporary art galleries is the Gallery of Contemporary Art at the University of Colorado at Colorado Springs.

Founded in 1981, the gallery presents changing exhibitions and offers guided tours, lectures, and educational programs for the university's students and visitors. Previous exhibitions have covered a wide range of contemporary art, from digital photography to leading artists of the twentieth century in Colorado collections.

Gallery of Contemporary Art, University of Colorado at Colorado Springs, 1420 Austin Bluffs Pkwy., P.O. Box 7150, Colorado Springs, CO 80933-7150. Phone: 719/262-3567. Fax: 719/262-3183. E-mail: griggs@uccs.edu. Website: http://harpy.uccs.edu/gallery/framesgallery.html. Hours: 10–4 Mon.–Fri., 1–4 Sat.; closed major holidays. Admission: adults, $1; seniors and students, $.50; children under 12 and UCCS students, faculty, and staff, free.

Visitor center

GARDEN OF THE GODS VISITOR CENTER

The Garden of the Gods is a 1,300-acre park of massive red sandstone formations in Colorado Springs. It was named in 1859 by Rufus Cable, an attorney and a charter resident of Colorado City, who was moved by the dramatic rock formations.

The Garden of the Gods Visitor Center, an excellent observation point for the rock formations and nearby Pikes Peak, presents a 12-minute multimedia show detailing the history and geology of the park and region and offers 30 exhibits focusing on the natural and cultural history of the park. The exhibits feature "talking rocks"—interactive

The Garden of the Gods in Colorado Springs. Shown here is the visitor center. Courtesy Garden of the Gods Visitor Center.

displays that resemble rocks and provide information about the park and the area.

The center also has in its collections—though not on display—a *Camptosaurus* skull found in the park, as well as other fossils, artifacts, and a herbarium.

Visitors can see five 14-foot-by-8-foot murals depicting the geological history of the area. Public programs such as walks, talks, and children's activities are offered throughout the year. In the summer, visitors also can take a guided bus tour of the park.

Garden of the Gods Visitor Center, 1805 N. 30th St., Colorado Springs, CO 80906. Phone: 719/634-6666. Fax: 719/634-0094. Hours: summer, 8:30 A.M.–9 P.M. daily; winter, 8:30–5:50 daily; closed New Year's Day, Thanksgiving, and Christmas. Admission: free. Multimedia show: adults, $2; children 5–12, $1; children under 4, free. Bus tour: adults, $3.75; children 5–12, $2.50; children 4 and under, free.

Visitor center

VAN BRIGGLE ART POTTERY VISITOR CENTER

Founded in 1899, Van Briggle Art Pottery in Colorado Springs has a visitor center and offers plant tours at its facilities, located in the old Midland Terminal Railroad roundhouse, a National Historic Landmark.

Van Briggle pottery, which can be found in the Metropolitan Museum of Art in New York and the Louvre in Paris, is produced from both old and new designs thrown on the potter's wheel or molded. The pottery comes in two glazes—a satin matte glaze, perfected by co-founder Artus Van Briggle at the beginning of the twentieth century, and a gloss glaze that is as smooth as polished glass.

More than 60,000 visitors take the factory tour each year and pass through the museumlike visitor center, which displays many of the firm's turn-of-the-twentieth-century pottery.

Van Briggle Art Pottery Visitor Center and Tour, 600 S. 21st St., P.O. Box 96, Colorado Springs, CO 80901. Phone: 719/633-7729. Fax: 719/633-7720. Hours: 8:30–5 daily; closed Easter, Thanksgiving, and Christmas. Admission: free.

Nature center

BEAR CREEK NATURE CENTER

Bear Creek Nature Center in Colorado Springs is one of two nature centers at regional parks operated by the El Paso County Parks Department (the other is Fountain Creek Nature Center near Fountain [see separate listing under Fountain]).

The Bear Creek center opened in 1977 at the 1,235-acre Bear Creek Regional Park and was remodeled extensively in 1995. It has a wildlife-viewing area and a 1,300-square-foot exhibit area featuring a large-scale topographic map of the Pikes Peak region, a foothills wildlife diorama dominated by a full-size black bear, a bear hibernation cave into which children can crawl, and displays on foothills history, geology, weather, plants, and animals. Most of the exhibits are interactive.

The center also presents a variety of environmental programs and offers two miles of nature trails; eight additional miles of trails for hiking, biking, and horseback riding; and archery, horseshoe, tennis, volleyball, basketball, playground, exercise, and picnic facilities.

Bear Creek Nature Center, 245 Bear Creek Rd., Colorado Springs, CO 80906. Phone: 719/520-6387. Fax: 719/520-6388. Hours: 9–4 Tues.–Sat.; also 9–4 Sun. in summer; closed major holidays. Admission: free.

Nature center

HELEN HUNT FALLS VISITOR CENTER

The Helen Hunt Falls Visitor Center is located in North Cheyenne Cañon Park, a 1,320-acre city park on the north side of Cheyenne Mountain in Colorado Springs.

Land for the park, operated by the Colorado Springs Parks and Recreation Department, was purchased in 1885. It was later expanded to its present size. The falls and visitor center are named for Helen Hunt Jackson, a noted author who wrote admiringly about the park's rocks, streams, and vegetation in the 1880s.

The visitor center is located in a late-nineteenth-century log building that contains exhibits on the park's animals, plants, trees, and other features and serves as the gathering point for nature talks and walks, one of which leads to the Starsmore Discovery Center at the south end of the park (see separate listing).

Helen Hunt Falls Visitor Center, 4075 N. Cheyenne Cañon Rd., Colorado Springs, CO 80906. Phone: 719/633-5701. Hours: Memorial Day–Labor Day, 9–5 daily; closed remainder of the year (although park is open year-round). Admission: free.

Nature center

STARSMORE DISCOVERY CENTER

The Starsmore Discovery Center is located at the southern end of the 1,320-acre North Cheyenne Cañon Park in Colorado Springs.

This nature center occupies the 1922 stone house of William and Mary Starsmore, which was moved to the park in 1990 and opened to the public in 1992 by the Colorado Springs Parks and Recreation Department.

Featured are nature exhibits, a mineral display, dioramas, and videos; a climbing wall; a bird-watching window; and information and photographs pertaining to the house and park. The center also offers a range of environmental programming, including school group programs, guest speakers, nature walks, and special events such as WaterQuest and the Hummingbird Festival.

One of the park's many trails leads to the Helen Hunt Falls and its visitor center (see previous listing).

Starsmore Discovery Center, 2120 S. Cheyenne Cañon Rd., Colorado Springs, CO 80906. Phone: 719/578-6146. Fax: 719/578-6149. Hours: Memorial Day through mid-Aug., 9 A.M.–9:30 P.M. daily; mid-Aug. through Labor Day, 9–5 daily; remainder of the year, 10–4 Thurs.–Sat., 12–4 Sun. Admission: free.

Environmental center

AIKEN CANYON PRESERVE FIELD STATION

The Nature Conservancy of Colorado operates a field station with exhibits at the 1,621-acre Aiken Canyon Preserve 16 miles south of

Colorado Springs. It has a similar center at the Carpenter Ranch adjacent to the organization's Yampa River Preserve near Hayden (see separate listing under Hayden).

The field station, a one-room straw-bale structure constructed in 1996, contains displays on the butterflies, birds, animals, plants, and history of the preserve. The preserve, which opened in 1993, has a diversity of geologic formations, plant communities, and wildlife, including 100 species of birds, and animals such as the black bear, mountain lion, gray fox, and tuft-ear and spruce squirrel.

Aiken Canyon Preserve Field Station, Nature Conservancy, 3350 Turkey Canyon Ranch Rd., Colorado Springs, CO 80926. Phone: 719/576-4336. Fax: 719/576-4453. Hours: summer, 9–5 Sat.–Mon.; remainder of the year, 10–3 Sat.–Mon. Admission: free.

Environmental center

BEIDLEMAN ENVIRONMENTAL CENTER

The Beidleman Environmental Center—adjacent to the 97-acre Sonderman Park, an urban wildlife sanctuary in Colorado Springs—emphasizes programs rather than exhibits.

Founded in 1986, the 1,200-square-foot facility operated by the Colorado Springs Parks and Recreation Department is named for Richard and Reba Beidleman, supporters of the community's open-space movement.

The center has a relief mural depicting the region's life zones and offers environmental programs for preschoolers through senior citizens, as well as school groups, focusing on wildlife and the protection of habitats and ecosystems.

Beidleman Environmental Center, 740 W. Caramillo St., Colorado Springs, CO 80907. Phone: 719/578-7088. Fax: 719/578-6717. Hours: vary with programs. Admission: usually free, but some programs charge fees.

Historic site

WILL ROGERS SHRINE OF THE SUN

The Will Rogers Shrine of the Sun is a 114-foot granite tower erected in memory of the cowboy humorist and political commentator. Located on a promontory on the eastern slope of Cheyenne Mountain, it sits 2,000 feet above Colorado Springs.

The shrine, a National Historic Site resembling a medieval castle, was dedicated to Rogers in 1937 by Spencer Penrose and other members of the End of the Trail Association, a civic organization. Rogers, a friend of Penrose's, was a frequent guest at Penrose's Broadmoor hotel.

Penrose wanted Rogers to be buried in the memorial tower, but the humorist's family had his remains transferred to his home state of Oklahoma. When Penrose and his wife, Julie, died, their ashes were entombed—along with the remains of two friends—in the chapel on the shrine's lower level.

The five-story Romanesque memorial has a winding staircase that leads to four rooms. Three are devoted to photographs and memorabilia pertaining to Rogers; the fourth contains regional historical materials and murals by noted artist Randall Davey depicting the Pikes Peak area.

A two-mile mountain drive takes visitors from the entrance to the Cheyenne Mountain Zoo to the Will Rogers Shrine of the Sun, now operated by the El Pomar Foundation.

Will Rogers Shrine of the Sun, 4250 Cheyenne Mountain Zoo Rd., Colorado Springs, CO 80906. Phone: 719/577-5737. Fax: 719/577-5702. Hours: 9–5 daily; closed New Year's Day, Thanksgiving, and Christmas. Admission: adults, $7.50; seniors, $6.50; children 3–11, $4.50; children under 3, free; families, $45 annual pass; groups of 15 or more, $6.50 per adult and $4 per child.

Historic ranch/living-history museum/arboretum

ROCK LEDGE RANCH HISTORIC SITE

The Rock Ledge Ranch Historic Site in Colorado Springs is a living-history farm and outdoor museum representing life in the Pikes Peak region from 1860 to 1910.

The 270-acre tract of land, formerly known as the White House Ranch, is located in Garden of the Gods Park. It was homesteaded in 1867 by Walter Galloway, who built a cabin in 1868 and worked the land. After struggling for a number of years, he sold the property to the Chambers family in 1874. The Chambers family built a home—called the Rock Ledge House—from rock quarried on the property. They also constructed two steam-heated greenhouses and raised fruit and produce. The ranch became one of the most productive in the area.

The Chambers era ended in 1900, when General William Jackson Palmer, founder of Colorado Springs, added Rock Ledge Ranch and its surrounding acreage to his Glen Eyrie estate. In 1907, William and Charlotte Schlater, relatives of Palmer, moved onto the property into the newly built Orchard House. Schlater, a prominent ornithologist, came from South Africa to become director of the Colorado College Museum.

This 1868 homestead cabin is part of the Rock Ledge Ranch Historic Site in Colorado Springs. Courtesy Rock Ledge Ranch Historic Site and photographer Don Stotts.

When development threatened to surround the historically significant land, the City of Colorado Springs purchased the property in 1968 with funds from the El Pomar Foundation and the Bemis-Taylor Foundation. The site was placed on the National Register of Historic Places in 1976 during the nation's bicentennial observance. It now is administered by the Colorado Springs Parks and Recreation Department.

Visits to the historic site focus on three separate periods—the 1868 homestead period, the 1895 working ranch period, and the 1907 estate period. In each case, historical interpreters dressed in costumes of the respective eras demonstrate the daily activities of the times. They till the soil, staff the general store (in the Rock Ledge House), and guide visitors through the reconstructed 1886 homestead cabin and restored 1907 Orchard House.

The site also offers a nature walk and the Rocky Mountain Arboretum, which features native plants of the region.

Rock Ledge Ranch Historic Site, 3203 Chambers Way (30th St. at the east entrance to Garden of the Gods Park), Colorado Springs, CO. (Postal address: Colorado Springs Parks and Recreation Dept., 1401 Recreation Way, Colorado Springs, CO 80905.) Phone: 719/578-6777. Fax: 719/578-6965. Hours: early June through Labor Day, 10–5 Wed.–Sun.; Labor Day through mid-Dec., 10–4 Wed.–Sun.;

closed remainder of the year. Admission: adults, $5; seniors, $3; children 6–12, $2; children under 6, free.

Historic house

GLEN EYRIE

Located in Colorado Springs, Glen Eyrie is a grandiose estate with a Tudor-style castle built by William Jackson Palmer, founder of the city, in 1904–1905. Listed on the National Register of Historic Places, it is now owned by the Navigators, a Christian evangelical group, and used primarily as a conference center.

The sandstone castle has 67 rooms and 24 fireplaces, some of which were imported from Europe. The original estate was virtually self-sufficient, possessing a schoolhouse, dairy, greenhouses, pool, stables, bowling alley, Turkish bath, and nine reservoirs. Many of these facilities still can be seen on the property.

Tours of Glen Eyrie are available. Visitors may also take afternoon tea, served at 2:30. Reservations are required for both.

Glen Eyrie, 3820 N. 30th St., P.O. Box 6000, Colorado Springs, CO 80934. Phone: 719/594-2287. Fax: 719/594-2517. Hours: tours offered at 1, 2, and 3 from June–Aug. and at 1 from Sept.–May; closed the week before Christmas. Tour cost: $5.

Historic house

McALLISTER HOUSE MUSEUM

In 1873, Civil War general William Jackson Palmer, who founded Colorado Springs, brought a young army major, Henry McAllister, to the fledgling city to serve as director of the Colorado Springs Company, a land-development firm that would contribute greatly to Palmer's envisioned "idyllic community" at the foot of Pikes Peak.

At the time, most houses in the emerging town were simple frame houses or mail-order homes. When fierce Chinook winds—strong enough to blow a narrow-gauge train from its rails—buffeted the area, these buildings often suffered damage. As a result, McAllister and his family built a brick and stone home that would withstand the worst of the elements: it had 20-inch-thick walls and a roof anchored into the masonry with thick iron rods.

In 1961, the Gothic-style cottage became the McAllister House Museum. Restored and furnished by the National Society of Colonial Dames of America, it retains much of its original charm and elegance.

McAllister House Museum, 423 N. Cascade Ave., Colorado Springs, CO 80903. Phone: 719/639-7925. Hours: May–Aug., 10–4 Wed.–Sat., 12–4 Sun.; Sept.–Apr., 10–4 Thurs.–Sat.; closed Jan. and major holidays. Admission: adults, $3; seniors, $2; children 6–16, $1; children under 6, free.

Historic house/bed-and-breakfast

HEARTHSTONE INN

The Hearthstone Inn in Colorado Springs, a bed-and-breakfast listed on the National Register of Historic Places, is actually two Victorian homes joined by a carriage house.

The inn has 25 rooms with furnishings from the late nineteenth century, including quilts, rocking chairs, cut-glass windows, ceramic fireplaces, and hand-carved-wood and brass beds. Each room is decorated around a different theme—the Solarium has plants and a skylight, and the Author's Den features a vintage typewriter.

Hearthstone Inn, 506 N. Cascade Ave., Colorado Springs, CO 80903. Phone: 719/473-4413. Fax: 719/473-1322. Hours: open 24 hours. Rates: vary with room and season.

Historic hotel

THE BROADMOOR

The Broadmoor, one of the world's premier resorts, began as a gambling casino in 1891 and was transformed into an elegant hotel complex in 1918 by Spencer Penrose, an entrepreneur who made a fortune in gold and copper mining.

The Colorado Springs resort now has 700 rooms and suites, 30 buildings, and 110,000 square feet of meeting space on 3,000 acres and boasts such amenities as a world-class spa and fitness center, 11 restaurants and lounges, a cigar bar and nightclub, three championship 18-hole golf courses, 12 tennis courts, three swimming pools, a skating rink, and riding stables. A small ski slope is nearby.

Penrose wanted to create the most beautiful resort in the world. He hired Warren and Wetmore, a noted New York architecture and design firm, and imported artisans from Italy and other European countries to fashion the ornate interior moldings and paintings and elaborate exterior detailing of the original Italian Renaissance–style hotel building and its four wings.

Penrose also built the Pikes Peak Road to the 14,100-foot summit, established the nearby Cheyenne Mountain Zoo, and purchased and

The Broadmoor in Colorado Springs is considered one of the world's premier resort hotels. Courtesy The Broadmoor.

modernized the Pikes Peak Cog Railway as a means of promoting the resort and the city's attractions.

The Broadmoor is now the nation's longest holder of the Mobil Five-Star and AAA Five-Diamond awards and has been the repeat recipient of numerous golf, tennis, meetings, food, wine, and hospitality honors.

Since its opening, The Broadmoor has hosted presidents, statesmen, foreign potentates, and celebrities, including U.S. presidents Hoover, Roosevelt, Eisenhower, Nixon, Reagan, and Bush; foreign dignitaries King Hussein of Jordan, Princess Anne of Great Britain, the King of Siam, and British prime minister Margaret Thatcher; entertainers John Wayne, Maurice Chevalier, Clark Gable, Jimmy Stewart, Jane Fonda, Jackie Gleason, and Reba McIntyre; and sports stars Joe DiMaggio, Stan Musial, Terry Bradshaw, and Sugar Ray Leonard.

After Penrose's death in 1939, a long-time colleague, Charles Tutt, Jr., took over as resort president. From 1961 to 1988, Tutt's sons, William and Russell, managed the property. In 1988, Tutt's controlling interest in The Broadmoor was obtained by the Oklahoma Publishing Company, chaired by Edward L. Gaylord.

The Broadmoor, 1 Lake Ave., P.O. Box 1439, Colorado Springs, CO 80906. Phone: 719/634-7711. Fax: 719/577-5700. E-mail: www.sales@broadmoor.com. Hours: open 24 hours. Rates: vary with room and season.

Historic cemetery

EVERGREEN CEMETERY

Many of Colorado Springs's notable citizens are buried at historic Evergreen Cemetery, the city's oldest continuously operating cemetery.

The cemetery site was deeded to the city in 1875 by General William Jackson Palmer, founder of Colorado Springs. He is buried in the cemetery, which is listed on the National Register of Historic Places.

Among the approximately 75,000 people laid to rest here are Helen Hunt Jackson, noted novelist; Winfield Scott Stratton, Cripple Creek's first millionaire and Colorado's greatest mining king; Rankin Scott Kelly, first sheriff of El Paso County; Artus Van Briggle, founder of Van Briggle Art Pottery; Maude McFerran Price, civic leader and lifetime curator of the Colorado Springs Pioneers Museum; Irving Howbert, bank president, mine owner, railroad pioneer, and state legislator; and Bob Womack, who discovered gold in Central City and sparked the last gold rush in Colorado in 1891.

The city-owned and -operated 220-acre cemetery is known for its 27 mausoleums, 1909 Romanesque stone chapel, 1922 World War I doughboy statue, 1992 granite monument to pioneers, and its rose trellises.

The City of Colorado Springs also operates another historic cemetery—Fairview Cemetery—located in Colorado City, a frontier town that was once the territorial capital and is now annexed to Colorado Springs. Many of the early settlers buried in other smaller cemeteries were moved to Fairview after Anthony Bott donated the site in 1895.

Evergreen Cemetery, 1005 S. Hancock Ave., Colorado Springs, CO 80903. Phone: 719/578-6077. Fax: 719/578-6077. Hours: summer, 6 A.M–8 P.M. daily; winter, 7–6 daily.

Historic town attraction

GHOST TOWN MUSEUM

The Ghost Town Museum in Colorado Springs is a privately operated collection of historic structures, artifacts, and memorabilia assembled to re-create an early Colorado town of the late nineteenth century.

The town, which looks as though its residents simply moved on and left all their possessions behind, is located in the former Colorado Midland Railroad complex, built in 1899. The buildings were transplanted from mining ghosts towns and other communities, and their turn-of-the-twentieth-century contents were gathered over the years from various sources.

The town has a general store, saloon, sheriff's office, jail, barbershop, blacksmith's shop, printing shop, Victorian home, and more. Visitors will find the general store fully stocked, the printing shop still in operation, the Victorian home presenting family life in the nineteenth century, and a short film showing how ghost towns evolved. Other attractions include old-time arcades and nickelodeons and gold panning.

The museum was opened in 1954 by Lois Akers and has been family-operated for three generations.

Ghost Town Museum, 400 S. 21st St., Colorado Springs, CO 80904. Phone: 719/634-0696. Fax: 719/634-2435. Hours: summer, 9–6 Mon.–Sat., 12–6 Sun.; remainder of the year, 10–5 Mon.–Sat., 12–5 Sun. Admission: adults, $4.50; seniors, $4; children 6–16, $2.50; children under 6, free.

Historic district

OLD COLORADO CITY HISTORIC COMMERCIAL DISTRICT

Once the territorial capital and an independent town, Colorado City now is a historic part of Colorado Springs. The Old Colorado City Historic Commercial District houses some of the city's oldest buildings and most popular art galleries.

Colorado City served as Colorado's first territorial capital; the legislature first caucused here in 1862. The building where the legislators met still stands in Bancroft Park near the center of the old town.

The historic district includes the north side of Colorado Avenue from 24th Street to 2611 Colorado Avenue, as well as 115 S. 26th Street and 2418 W. Pikes Peak Avenue. It was listed on the National Register of Historic Places in 1982.

Old Colorado City Historic Commercial District. Contact: Old Colorado City History Center, 1 S. 24th St., Colorado Springs, CO 80904. Phone: 719/636-1225.

COLUMBINE

Historic ghost town

COLUMBINE GHOST TOWN

Columbine was founded in 1897, when gold discoveries around Hahns Peak, five miles to the north, brought prospectors to the area. Several mines dug near Columbine were later incorporated into the Royal Flush Mine.

When mining faded, logging and sheep ranching became the primary enterprises in the area. Columbine was abandoned, but some of its surviving log cabins are used during the summer by fishermen. One even serves as a store.

Columbine Ghost Town, 5 miles north of Hahns Peak. Contact: Hahns Peak Area Historical Museum, 61110 Main St., Hahns Peak Village, General Delivery, Clark, CO 80428. Phones: 970/879-6781 and 970/824-5176.

COMMERCE CITY

Wildlife refuge/visitor center

ROCKY MOUNTAIN ARSENAL WILDLIFE REFUGE VISITOR'S CENTER AND NATIONAL EAGLE AND WILDLIFE PROPERTY REPOSITORY

The U.S. Army's Rocky Mountain Arsenal near Commerce City is the site of the Rocky Mountain Arsenal Wildlife Refuge and the National Eagle and Wildlife Property Repository, both opened in 1995 by the U.S. Fish and Wildlife Service.

The wildlife refuge has a visitor center with exhibits on many of the 300 species of wildlife—including deer, coyote, and bald eagles—found on the 17,000-acre arsenal grounds. The center also serves as the starting point for guided tours of the site.

The repository contains eagle feathers and contraband wildlife parts and products seized in illegal interstate and international trade. It can be visited only by appointment.

Rocky Mountain Arsenal Wildlife Refuge Visitor's Center, U.S. Fish and Wildlife Service, Commerce City, CO 80022-1741. Phone: 303/289-0930. Fax: 303/ 289-0579. Hours: 9–3 Sat.; tours by appointment. Admission: free.

National Eagle and Wildlife Property Repository, U.S. Fish and Wildlife Service, Rocky Mountain Arsenal Bldg. 619, Commerce City, CO 80022. Phone: 303/ 287-2110. Fax: 303/287-1550. Hours: by appointment only. Admission: free.

COMO

Natural history museum/art gallery

COMO MAMMOTH MUSEUM AND MOUNTAIN MAN GALLERY

The 20,000-year-old bones of a Columbian mammoth—a less hairy cousin of the Ice Age wooly mammoth—are the featured attraction at the Como Mammoth Museum and Mountain Man Gallery in the former steam-era railroad town of Como in South Park.

The fossils were found in a private dig outside of Como by Jack and Vicki Portice, who opened the museum/gallery in 1991. Among the findings on display are a tusk, ribs, fragments of leg bone, and a vertebra, all believed to have come from a prehistoric elephant that stood 10 feet tall at the shoulder. Five excavated prehistoric zebra or horse teeth found in the area also are on exhibit.

The fossils originally were kept in the Como Mercantile general store, which the Portices bought a dozen years ago. In 1990, they acquired a 1930s one-room log cabin in nearby Fairplay. In addition to the artifacts, the building contains a gallery of wood carvings Jack and Vicki have created from lightning-killed bristlecone pine.

Como Mammoth Museum and Mountain Man Gallery, 150 Broadway, P.O. Box 59, Como, CO 80432. Phone and fax: 719/836-2403. Hours: 9–5 daily; closed New Year's Day, Thanksgiving, and Christmas, and during February and two weeks in March. Admission: free.

CORTEZ

History museum/cultural center

CORTEZ CENTER

The Cortez Center in the southwest corner of Colorado was created in 1987 to promote intercultural understanding. It provides a community forum for educational, cultural, artistic, and scientific events and activities and operates a museum.

The center, founded with the help of the University of Colorado, is housed in a 1908 adobe building formerly used for retail business. Acquired in 1986, the building has been renovated and the adjoining lot landscaped, with the addition of a hogan and a stone plaza used for Navajo and Ute dances during the summer.

About half of the building's main level is devoted to the museum, which features an interior view of a kiva; dioramas of Basketmaker and Pueblo artifacts and ruins; findings from the Yellow Jacket dig; a collection of Anasazi pottery; overviews of Navajo, Pueblo, and Ute culture and crafts; a Ute beadwork display; and an exhibit of local pioneer artifacts. In the hands-on area, visitors can try their hand at weaving on a warped loom, grind corn, and touch scrapers, combs, pottery shards, animal bones, and arrowheads.

The Cortez Center's additional offerings include volunteer work experiences, food-stamp workfare, art and calligraphy classes, lectures, and summer dances and cultural programs. A farmers' market is held each summer on the dance plaza.

The center also manages and makes use of the 122-acre Hawkins Preserve in partnership with Jack Hawkins.

Cortez Center Inc., 25 N. Market St., Cortez, CO 81321. Phone: 970/565-1151. Fax: 970/565-4075. Hours: summer, 10–10 Mon.–Sat.; winter, 10–5 Mon.–Sat.; closed New Year's Day, Thanksgiving, and Christmas. Admission: donation requested.

National monument/visitor center

HOVENWEEP NATIONAL MONUMENT VISITOR CENTER

The Hovenweep National Monument Visitor Center, located in a 784-acre park 43 miles west of Cortez, tells the story of six groups of towers, pueblos, and cliff dwellings built by pre-Columbian Indians.

The national monument, which straddles the Colorado-Utah state line, was established in 1923. The visitor center, in Utah, is housed in a 1,500-square-foot former National Park Service ranger residence relocated from Mesa Verde in 1953. It is 15 miles north of the Ute Mountain Indian Reservation village of Aneth.

The exhibits consist of photographs, artifacts, and other materials dealing with the history and geology of the area.

Hovenweep, a Ute word meaning "deserted valley," aptly describes the remote mesas and canyons north of the San Juan River where prehistoric Pueblo Indians (similar to those inhabiting Mesa Verde National Park) once lived as farmers, hunters, and gatherers. Extended droughts in the tenth and eleventh centuries, followed by failing crops, diminishing water supplies, and perhaps warfare, caused the inhabitants to abandon the area and move south before 1300.

They left behind ruins of towers, many-roomed pueblos, and small cliff dwellings in six separate groups, all difficult to locate except the largest and best-preserved tower, Square Tower. The other five groups are the Holly, Hackberry Canyon, Cutthroat Castle, and Goodman Point ruins in Colorado and the Cajon ruins in Utah. The towers are the most prominent feature of each ruin and may be square, oval, circular, or D-shaped.

Hovenweep National Monument Visitor Center, National Park Service, McElmo Canyon Route, Cortez, CO 81321. Phone: 970/749-0510. Hours: 8–5 daily; closed New Year's Day, Thanksgiving, and Christmas. Admission: free, but monument admission is $6 per car.

Archaeological center

CROW CANYON ARCHAEOLOGICAL CENTER

The Crow Canyon Archaeological Center near Cortez is more training center than museum, but it does have a collection and display of archaeological artifacts from the area.

Week-long training programs offer classroom instruction and participation in on-site digs. During the summer, day programs include tours and working at an archaeological site. Weaving, jewelry making, and other classes are taught in the off-season.

Crow Canyon Archaeological Center, 23390 County Rd. K, Cortez, CO 81321. Phone: 970/565-8975. Fax: 970/565-4859. E-mail: ltbaca@crowcanyon.org. Website: www.crowcanyon.org. Hours: Mar.–Oct., 8–5 Mon.–Fri. (no public programs, but center staffed and open for inquiries); June–Sept., day programs (hours vary); closed New Year's Day, Thanksgiving, and Christmas. Admission: Mar.–Oct., public visits free; June–Sept. day programs, adults, $50; children, $25.

Historic site

FOUR CORNERS MONUMENT

Four Corners Monument, located off U.S. Highway 160 approximately 45 miles southwest of Cortez, is the only place in the nation where four states converge (Colorado, New Mexico, Arizona, and Utah).

The 25-foot-square concrete monument—with a plaque in the center precisely where the states meet—is administered by the Navajo Nation, although the land is shared by the Navajo and Mountain Ute tribes.

Four Corners Monument, off U.S. Hwy. 160 southwest of Cortez. Contacts: Navajo Parks and Recreation Dept., P.O. Box 9000, Window Rock, AZ 86515 (phone: 520/871-6647; fax: 520/871-6637) or Cortez Chamber of Commerce, 928 E. Main St., P.O. Box 968, Cortez, CO 81321 (phones: 970/565-3414 and 800/253-1616; fax: 970/565-4828). Hours: May–Aug., 7–7 daily; remainder of the year, 8–5 daily. Admission: $2.50 per person.

The Museum of Northwest Colorado. Courtesy Museum of Northwest Colorado and photographer Robert N. Nelsen.

CRAIG

History museum

MUSEUM OF NORTHWEST COLORADO

The Museum of Northwest Colorado in Craig is a 12,000-square-foot local history museum that features one of the nation's most comprehensive collections of cowboy and gunfighter gear.

Founded in 1964, this Moffat County museum moved to the restored and renovated 1921 Armory building in 1990.

The cowboy and gunfighter collection was assembled over four decades by Bill Macklin and consists of fine old cowboy gear such as guns, holsters, chaps, spurs, and saddles.

Other exhibits include displays on coal miners, farm implements, hardware, a re-created schoolroom, rocks and fossils, early wildlife photographer Allan G. Wallihan, former governor Ed Johnson, and the Moffat Road and Denver & Salt Lake Railroad. The largest stretched-canvas oil painting on the Western Slope—an 11-foot-by-16-foot painting depicting downtown Craig in 1895 by local artist F. Williams-Reust—is also on view inside the museum. A life-size bronze statue of James Robinson, a local cowboy from the early twentieth century, is located across the street from the museum in Estey Memorial Park.

Museum of Northwest Colorado, 590 Yampa Ave., Craig, CO 81625. Phone: 970/824-6360. Fax: 970/824-7175. E-mail: musnwco@cmn.net. Website: www.museumnwco.org. Hours: Memorial Day–Labor Day, 8:30–5 daily; remainder of the year, 10–5 daily; closed major holidays. Admission: free.

Historic ranch/museum

WYMAN ELK RANCH AND WESTERN MUSEUM

The Wyman Ranch and Western Museum near Craig is a working ranch and historical museum with collections focusing on aspects of life in Colorado since 1900.

The museum, on a ranch owned by Lou Wyman and his family since 1936, opened in 1990. Visitors can see diverse collections, including barbed wire, farm and ranch tools, soda bottles, lead soldiers, clocks, children's books, road signs, wagons, bicycles, grinding stones, pulleys, pumps, jacks, unusual mousetraps, and other materials, some dating to the turn of the twentieth century.

On the road leading to the ranch and museum, Wyman has assembled a wide range of antique tractors, farm equipment, automobiles, buses, and trucks, as well as two World War II tanks.

Among the collections under development are old and rare books, bottles and jars, kitchen tins and bottles, cowboy gear, advertisements, and materials related to the Moffat Tunnel and U.S. wars.

Wyman Elk Ranch and Western Museum, P.O. Box 278, Craig, CO 81626. Phone and fax: 970/824-6431. Hours: daylight hours daily (visitors should call ahead); closed Thanksgiving and Christmas. Admission: adults, $5; seniors, $3; children 12 and under, $3.

CREEDE

History museum

CREEDE MUSEUM

The Creede Museum, founded in the 1940s and operated by the Creede Historical Society, is located in the former Denver & Rio Grande Railroad depot next to Basham Park in downtown Creede, an old silver-mining town. The museum contains artifacts and memorabilia that provide insight into the lives of the homesteaders, prospectors, miners, entrepreneurs, and residents who helped shape Creede and Mineral County.

Among the objects on display are Creede's first hand-drawn fire wagon, early pioneer utensils, a horse-drawn hearse, gambling devices, historical photographs, early newspapers, and other items relating to the area's past.

Creede Museum, Creede Historical Society, Main St., P.O. Box 608, Creede, CO 81130. Phone: 719/658-2303. Hours: Memorial Day–Labor Day, 10–4 daily; remainder of the year by appointment. Admission: free.

Mining museum

CREEDE UNDERGROUND MINING MUSEUM

The Creede Underground Mining Museum is not actually located in a mine, though it certainly feels like it. Opened in 1992, the 25,000-square-foot museum takes visitors through a U-shaped tunnel designed to resemble an active hard-rock mine.

Creede, located in a side canyon of the Rio Grande Valley, was a thriving silver-mining town a century ago. Remnants of the original town, now called North Creede, are still visible in the sharply cut canyon beyond the present community's main street, where the museum is located adjacent to a rare underground firehouse.

The museum, a joint venture between the City of Creede and Mineral County, focuses on mining history and techniques from 1892 to 1960. Creede was a latecomer to Colorado's silver boom: the area's first silver lode was not discovered until 1889. Within a short time, however, mines like the Holy Moses, Ethel, Amethyst, and Last Chance were producing tons of high-grade ore, the population zoomed to nearly 10,000, and Creede became the leading producer of silver in the state. But prosperity was short-lived. With the repeal of the Silver Act in 1893, flash floods, and devastating fires, Creede nearly became a ghost town. It has since rebounded as an artists' colony and summer tourist community of 400.

Guides (usually former miners) take museum visitors on a one-hour tour through the underground simulated mine. The tour talks and displays paint a realistic picture of how silver ore was mined.

Creede Underground Mining Museum, 9 Forest Service Rd. 503, Creede, CO 81130. Phone: 719/658-0811. Hours: June–Sept., 10–4 Mon.–Fri.; closed remainder of the year. Admission: adults, $5; seniors, $4; children 5–16, $3; children under 5, free.

Historic site

BACHELOR HISTORIC LOOP

The Bachelor Historic Loop is a 17-mile tour route that takes visitors through Creede's silver-mining district and past two ghost towns (Weaver and Bachelor) and numerous abandoned mines.

The route begins at the south end of Creede (at the information/entrance station on Colorado Highway 149), travels north through town and up West Willow Creek to the Equity Mine, then turns south and follows the Bachelor Road back to Creede.

There are 16 numbered interpretive stops, marking such sights as the West Willow Creek–East Willow Creek Junction; the original Creede town site (now North Creede) and location of the Humphrey Mill and railroad junction; the Commodore Mine, site of the Amethyst vein and the first silver-mining claims in the area; the site of Weaver, base of the Amethyst and Last Chance Mines, the richest producing mines of the silver-boom era; the site of Bachelor near the Bachelor Mine; the Creede scenic overlook and the Bulldog Mine, which operated as late as 1985; and Creede Cemetery, including the grave of Bob Ford, who killed Jesse James in 1882. A number of surviving turn-of-the-twentieth-century structures can be seen along the way.

The tour route consists of very steep, narrow, winding, and unpaved mountain roads, but it is suitable for travel by cautious motorists, preferably with all-wheel-drive vehicles.

Located in a picturesque canyon of the Rio Grande Valley, Creede has become an artists' colony and vacation center.

Bachelor Historic Loop. Contact: Creede–Mineral County Chamber of Commerce, 1201 N. Main St., P.O. Box 580, Creede, CO 81130. Phones: 719/658-2374 and 800/327-2102. Fax: 719/658-2717. E-mail: creede@rmii.com.

Historic building

RIO GRANDE HOTEL

The 1892 Rio Grande Hotel in Creede was one of only a few wooden structures to survive a fire that devastated the town in 1892. It operated as a hotel for many years, then became a private residence, and now is being restored by the Creede Repertory Theatre to house visiting actors and host special events. The theatrical group purchased the old hotel, which originally had eight guest rooms, in 1992. It was listed on the National Register of Historical Places in 1995.

Rio Grande Hotel, 2 W. 2nd St., Creede, CO. (Contact: Creede Repertory Theatre,

125 W. Main St., Creede, CO 81130. Phone: 719/658-2541. Fax: 719/658-2343.) Hours: to be determined.

CRESTED BUTTE

History museum

CRESTED BUTTE MOUNTAIN HERITAGE MUSEUM

The history of this mountain mining community that has now become a vacation and skiing center is presented at the Crested Butte Mountain Heritage Museum.

Opened in 1995, the 2,500-square-foot storefront museum traces how the area evolved from Ute Indian summer hunting grounds to a coalmining hotbed in the late nineteenth century, then turned to tourism, and later skiing, when the mines closed in the early 1950s. Artifacts and photographs of the various historical periods describe the transformation.

The Mountain Bike Hall of Fame and Museum is located in the museum (see following listing).

Crested Butte Mountain Heritage Museum, 200 Sopris Ave., P.O. Box 2480, Crested Butte, CO 81224. Phone: 970/349-1880. Hours: summer, 1–6 daily; winter, 2–7 daily; closed Apr.–May and Oct.–Nov. Admission: adults, $2; children 12 and under, free; families, $5.

Biking hall of fame/museum

MOUNTAIN BIKE HALL OF FAME AND MUSEUM

The Mountain Bike Hall of Fame and Museum is located in the Crested Butte Mountain Heritage Museum (see previous listing). The museum was founded in 1988 to chronicle the history of mountain biking and honor the principal contributors to the sport, which has grown immensely in the last quarter century.

The museum features hundreds of memorabilia items and other objects tracing the development of mountain biking. Displays include vintage bikes, bike components, classic photographs, press clippings, and highlights from historic races and events.

The hall of fame has inducted approximately 60 individuals who have made major contributions to mountain biking. Bikers, manufacturers, organizers, promoters, and others are honored with photographs and biographies.

Each September, the Mountain Bike Hall of Fame and Museum hosts the longest-running mountain bike event in the world—the round-trip Pear Pass Tour to Aspen. The tour, which traverses the 12,705-foot pass, had its inaugural running in 1976.

Mountain Bike Hall of Fame and Museum, 200 Sopris Ave., P.O. Box 845, Crested Butte, CO 81224. Phone and fax: 970/349-6817. Hours: summer, 1–6 daily; winter, 2–7 daily; closed Apr.–May and Oct.–Nov. Admission: adults, $2; children 12 and under, free; families, $5.

Arts center

CENTER FOR THE ARTS

Art exhibitions, usually featuring the work of local artists, are offered at the Center for the Arts in Crested Butte. In addition to the small gallery, this community arts center, which opened in 1987, has a 215-seat auditorium where concerts, plays, and other performances are presented.

Center for the Arts, 606 6th St., P.O. Box 1819, Crested Butte, CO 81224. Phone: 970/349-7487. Fax: 970/349-5626. Hours: 10–5 Mon.–Fri. and for performances; closed New Year's Day and Christmas. Admission: varies with events.

Historic district

CRESTED BUTTE HISTORIC DISTRICT

Brightly painted false-front businesses and weathered miners' shacks constitute most of the Crested Butte Historic District. The historic district of this former coal-mining town (now a biking and skiing mecca) has been listed on the National Register of Historic Places since 1974.

The last coal mine in this alpine valley closed in the early 1950s. Popular shops, restaurants, and bars now occupy the century-old buildings along Elk Avenue, Crested Butte's main street. The town retains its old-time look and feel despite the major ski resort developed at the base of Mt. Crested Butte three miles away.

Crested Butte has become such a hotbed of biking that the Mountain Bike Hall of Fame and Museum has opened in the Crested Butte Mountain Heritage Museum, a storefront museum in the historic district (see separate listings).

Crested Butte Historic District. Contact: Crested Butte Mountain Heritage Museum, 200 Sopris Ave., P.O. Box 2480, Crested Butte, CO 81224. Phone: 970/349-1880.

CRIPPLE CREEK

History museum

CRIPPLE CREEK DISTRICT MUSEUM

The Cripple Creek District Museum, consisting of four buildings and a railroad passenger car, provides a glimpse into the past of this old mining camp, now a gambling center.

The museum's Main Building opened in 1953 and occupies the former Midland Terminal Railroad depot (in service from 1895 to 1949). Its 12 rooms are filled with displays of gold ore, mining equipment, railroad memorabilia, Victorian clothing and furniture, and other artifacts from the gold-mining boom days.

The Colorado Trading and Transfer Building, built in 1893, houses natural history exhibits, local wildlife displays, historic photographs of the district, a gallery of locally produced artwork, a restored Victorian-era flat, an entertainment and melodrama exhibit, and the museum gift shop.

The Assay Office features mining and geological exhibits and an extensive collection of assay equipment. The newly opened Archives Building features Cripple Creek and Victor newspapers from 1892 to the present, as well as cemetery records from Teller County and Alma.

The 1884 Midland Terminal Railroad passenger car contains railroad memorabilia and presents a slide show.

Cripple Creek District Museum, 500 E. Bennett Ave., P.O. Box 1210, Cripple Creek, CO 80813. Phone: 719/689-2634. Hours: summer, 10–5 daily; winter, 12–4 daily; closed Easter and Christmas. Admission: adults, $2.25; seniors, $1.50; children 7–12, $.50; groups, $1.75 per person; school groups, $.50 per person.

History museum

OLD HOMESTEAD MUSEUM

The Old Homestead Museum in Cripple Creek was a brothel in the gold-rush days at the turn of the twentieth century. It became a museum in 1958 and now is operated by the Jubilee Casino, one of Cripple Creek's gambling casinos. Cripple Creek, a former mining community, is one of three Colorado towns (Black Hawk and Central City are the others) where gambling is permitted.

The building retains much of its original furniture and decor. One room has wallpaper more than 100 years old.

Old Homestead Museum, 353 Myers Ave., P.O. Box 540, Cripple Creek, CO 80813. Phone: 719/689-3090. Hours: June, 11–4 daily; July–Sept., 10–5 daily;

May and Oct., 11–4 Sat.–Sun.; closed remainder of the year. Admission: adults, $3, children 11–12, $1.50; children under 11, free.

Historic mine

MOLLY KATHLEEN MINE

In 1891, Molly Kathleen Gortner discovered gold while hiking near Cripple Creek and became the first woman to register a mining claim in her own name. The Molly Kathleen Mine was opened near the site, one mile north of Cripple Creek on Colorado Highway 67.

Tours of the mine, which closed in 1961, are available (the first tours actually were given in the 1930s, while the mine was still being worked). Visitors descend 1,000 feet in the "skip" (a small elevator) during the 40-minute visit to this hard-rock mine.

A 90-minute bus tour also is offered of the nearby Cresson Mine, Colorado's largest open-pit mine still in operation; several ghost towns; and the old mining town of Victor.

Molly Kathleen Mine, Colo. Hwy. 67, P.O. Box 339, Cripple Creek, CO 80813. Phone: 719/689-2465. Hours: May–Oct., 9–5 daily; closed remainder of the year. Admission: adults, $10; children 3–11, $5; children 2 and under, free (same prices for bus tour).

Historic railroad

CRIPPLE CREEK & VICTOR NARROW GAUGE RAILROAD

The Cripple Creek & Victor Narrow Gauge Railroad, organized in 1968, takes visitors on a four-mile ride into history, passing many mines and ghost towns, among them the deserted community of Anaconda. Abandoned mines along the route include the Moon Anchor, Ducking, Mary McKinney, and E. Porter King. The tour is accompanied by a narration on the rich history of the once booming Cripple Creek/Victor mining area.

At the peak of the mining period, 55 narrow-gauge locomotives serviced Cripple Creek daily, hauling ore and carrying passengers.

During the tourist season these days, trains depart every 45 minutes from near the old Midland Terminal Railroad depot, now home of the Cripple Creek District Museum. They are pulled by a brightly painted, fully restored 15-ton locomotive typical of the early steam engines of the American West.

Cripple Creek & Victor Narrow Gauge Railroad, 520 E. Carr St., Cripple Creek, CO 80813. Phone: 719/689-2640. Fax: 719/689-3256. Hours: Memorial Day *weekend through the first week of Oct., 10–5 daily; closed remainder of the year. Admission: adults, $7.50; seniors, $6.75; children 3–17, $3.75; children under 3, free.*

Historic hotel

IMPERIAL HOTEL AND CASINO

The Imperial Hotel and Casino in Cripple Creek dates back to the town's mining boom at the turn of the twentieth century.

It has been in continuous operation (except for two years during World War II) since its opening in 1896. Now, however, it also operates a three-level gaming parlor in an adjacent building.

The hotel has 29 guest rooms whose furniture, antiques, and paintings date mainly from the Victorian era. Some rooms have bathrooms with claw-foot tubs; others share bathrooms down the hall.

One of the hotel's main attractions is the Imperial Melodrama Theatre, which first opened its doors in 1948.

Imperial Hotel and Casino, 123 N. 3rd St., P.O. Box 869, Cripple Creek, CO 80813. Phones: 719/689-7777 and 800/235-2922. Fax: 719/689-1008. Hours: open 24 hours. Rates: vary with room and season.

Historic district

CRIPPLE CREEK HISTORIC DISTRICT

The entire commercial and residential area of Cripple Creek—site of the nation's last major gold rush, at the turn of the twentieth century—constitutes the Cripple Creek Historic District.

More than $600 million in gold (more than $12 billion in today's dollars) was produced in the Cripple Creek area, said to have had the richest gold deposit on earth. Gold still is mined around Cripple Creek (mostly by open-pit mining), but gambling has replaced mining as the chief economic stimulant.

Cripple Creek is one of three old Colorado mining towns (Central City and Black Hawk are the others) that allow legalized limited-stakes gambling ($5 is the maximum bet). As a result, many historic structures have been converted into gaming casinos, attracting an influx of gamblers, and their money.

The first gold strike in Cripple Creek occurred in 1878 at Poverty Gulch. A ranch hand, Bob Womack, stumbled across some gold ore while riding his horse. He filed his first claim on the land in 1886 and his second in 1890, but shortly thereafter he sold his interests for only

$500 and later died penniless. Others were more fortunate. Winfield Scott Stratton, a friend of Womack's, struck gold with the Independence Mine in 1891 and became Cripple Creek's first millionaire.

By 1892, Cripple Creek had more than 2,500 residents, two banks, seven hotels, six mining and hardware supply companies, four butcher shops, two drugstores, an opera house, a stock and mining exchange, and at least 25 saloons. It called itself "the world's greatest gold camp."

In 1896, however, a dance-hall fire burned down most of the town; another blaze five days later nearly finished off what was left. But Cripple Creek was quickly rebuilt and by 1900 boasted 55,000 people, 150 saloons, 26 gambling halls, 49 grocery stores, 90 doctors, 34 churches, 15 newspapers, and a growing number of brothels.

The boom did not last long. Gold prices fell, and by 1912 most of the 475 mining companies in Cripple Creek had folded. Only 40 of the mines were still working eight years later. Today, numerous abandoned mines—and a few that still operate—can be seen in the Cripple Creek/ Victor area. Visitors also can tour a closed mine, the Molly Kathleen, outside Cripple Creek (see separate listing).

With the advent of legalized gambling, some buildings have been transformed into casinos (see previous listing for the Imperial Hotel and Casino). Others have been converted to different uses, including the 1901 Teller County Hospital, which is now the Hospitality House inn; a former house of prostitution, which has become the Old Homestead Museum; and the 1895 Midland Terminal Railroad depot, 1893 Colorado Trading and Transfer Building, and two other buildings, which now constitute the Cripple Creek District Museum (see separate listing).

Walking tours of the historic district are offered. The Cripple Creek & Victor Narrow Gauge Railroad (see separate listing), which follows some of the old rail lines, takes visitors on a four-mile round-trip journey that passes many of the old mines and ghost towns in the Cripple Creek/Victor area.

Cripple Creek Historic District. Contact: Cripple Creek Welcome Center, P.O. Box 430, Cripple Creek, CO 80813. Phones: 719/689-3315 and 877/858-4653. Fax: 719/689-2774.

CROOK

History museum

CROOK HISTORICAL MUSEUM

The town, historical society, and museum of Crook are named for General George Crook, the Civil War officer who led the fight against Indians as commander of the U.S. Army Department of the Platte in 1875.

The Crook Historical Museum, organized in 1975 by the Crook Historical Society, is housed in a former church built in 1910. It contains such diverse items as historical photographs, memorabilia, antique tools, early kitchen equipment, a tack room, wedding dresses, postal equipment, and a plaque commemorating Geronimo's surrender to General Crook in 1883.

Crook Historical Museum, Crook Historical Society, 401 N. 4th St., P.O. Box 194, Crook, CO 80726. Phone: 970/886-3612. Hours: Memorial Day–Labor Day, 2–4 Sun.; also by appointment. Admission: free.

CRYSTAL

Historic ghost town

CRYSTAL GHOST TOWN

The old silver-mining town of Crystal, originally known as Crystal City, was named after the crystalline quartz found along Rock Creek (later called the Crystal River) in 1880.

Five miles east of Marble, Crystal was difficult to reach because of the surrounding mountains and poor roads. For many years, Crystal was accessible only via Schofield Pass from the Gunnison area. It wasn't until a road was built to Carbondale that the town and mining flourished.

The first prospectors entered the Crystal area in the 1860s, but rich strikes were not made until the early 1880s. Mines such as the Lead King, Black Queen, and Sheep Mountain Tunnel boomed until the 1893 silver crash. Some mines made a comeback after the turn of the twentieth century by extracting lead and copper from ore piles, but even these mines declined after World War I.

Some of the early cabins remain, as do the old Crystal Club building and the picturesque ruins of the Crystal Mill, which once produced power on the Crystal River for the Sheep Mountain Tunnel Mine (still visible on the nearby mountainside). Some of the cabins have been converted to summer cottages, and a few new cabins have been built in recent years.

Crystal Ghost Town, 5 miles east of Marble. Contact: Marble Historical Society, 412 W. Main St., Marble, CO 81623. Phone: 970/963-0358.

DEARFIELD

Historic site/ghost town

DEARFIELD HISTORIC SITE AND GHOST TOWN

Dearfield was one of 14 rural towns established in the American West to provide African Americans the opportunity to own and work their own land.

The Dearfield town site, 11 miles west of Wiggins on Colorado Highway 34, is the only remaining example in the state of the national African-American colonization movement inspired by Booker T. Washington.

Dearfield was founded in 1910 by Colorado entrepreneur and African-American leader Oliver Toussaint Jackson, who filed a homestead claim for the initial 160 acres. Seven other black families filed land claims in 1914, and seven years later, the population had climbed to 700.

By 1917, 60 families lived in Dearfield. The town had numerous stores, a boardinghouse, a concrete-block factory, a blacksmith's shop, churches, and its own telephone service. But the Great Depression brought hard times, and the residents gradually moved and sold off most of the land. Only the remnants of a lunchroom, hotel, hunting shack, and corral are left. The town was listed on the National Register of Historic Places in 1995.

Dearfield Historic Site and Ghost Town, 25 miles southeast of Greeley. Contact: Greeley Municipal Museum Archives, City of Greeley Cultural Affairs Dept., Museums Div., 919 7th St., Greeley, CO 80631. Phone: 970/350-9220. Fax: 970/350-9475.

DEER TRAIL

History museum

DEER TRAIL PIONEER HISTORICAL SOCIETY MUSEUM

The Deer Trail Pioneer Historical Society Museum consists of four structures—a railroad depot, a log house, a one-room schoolhouse, and a museum building—in Deer Trail. The museum focuses on the history of the area and has displays of household items, tools, dolls, clothing, and other historical objects from various periods.

Deer Trail Pioneer Historical Society Museum, 2nd St., P.O. Box 176, Deer Trail, CO 80105. Phone: 303/769-4677. Hours: by appointment only. Admission: free.

DEL NORTE

History museum

RIO GRANDE COUNTY MUSEUM

The Rio Grande County Museum, which opened in 1967 in the county courthouse in Del Norte, now occupies a new building in the center of the community.

Among the historical objects on display are collections of arrowheads, rocks, and minerals, as well as examples of early carriages, clothing, furniture, room settings, regional rock art, and materials relating to John Charles Fremont's fourth and final expedition in the winter of 1848–1849, during which much of the party froze or starved to death just north of Del Norte in the La Garita Mountains.

During the summer, the museum offers lectures on the valley's history and wildlife and often features area artists-in-residence.

Rio Grande County Museum, 580 Oak St., Del Norte, CO 81132. Phone: 719/657-2847. Fax: 719/657-2627. Hours: Apr.–Sept., 10–5 Mon.–Fri., 1–4 Sat.; Oct.–Mar., 11–4 Mon.–Fri.; closed major holidays. Admission: adults, $1; children, $.50; families, $2.50.

DELTA

History museum

DELTA COUNTY MUSEUM

The Delta County Museum in Delta traces the history, development, and natural features of this Western Slope community and the surrounding area. The 10,000-square-foot museum, located in an old firehouse, was founded in 1964 by the Delta County Historical Society.

Among the museum's collections and exhibits are dinosaur fossils, butterflies, Native American artifacts, barbed wire, and agricultural, industrial, and transportation equipment, as well as collections of newspapers, photographs, and manuscripts.

Delta County Museum, 251 Meeker St., Delta, CO 81416. Phone: 970/874-8721. Hours: May–Sept., 10–4 Tues.–Sat.; Oct.–Apr., 10–4 Wed. and Sat.; closed major holidays. Admission: adults, $2; seniors, $1; children under 12 accompanied by an adult, free.

Living-history museum

FORT UNCOMPAHGRE LIVING HISTORY MUSEUM

Fort Uncompahgre, near present-day Delta, was a fur-trading post from 1828 to 1844. In 1989–1990, a replica of the fort was constructed and opened as a city-funded living-history museum at the entrance to Confluence Park, a 265-acre recreational facility near downtown Delta.

The original trading post, established by Antoine Robidoux, a member of one of the most influential families in the early American West, was erected at the confluence of the Uncompahgre and Gunnison (formerly Blue or Eagle Tail) rivers and consisted of a few log buildings enclosed in a quadrangle of pickets. Furs were brought and traded for goods from the East and Mexico for about 16 years, until most of the occupants were killed in an Indian attack.

The reconstructed fort covers three-and-a-half acres and features interpreters clothed in period attire. Visitors receive a guided tour of the Trade Room, where trappers and Indians exchanged furs for guns, knives, beads, and other prized goods; the Hide Room, where deer hides and beaver pelts were stored; and the living quarters, kitchen, adobe oven, and adobe forge, all part of the trading post. Churro sheep, the oldest and rarest breed in North America, are also on view at the fort.

Fort Uncompahgre Living History Museum, 205 Gunnison River Dr. (postal address: 530 Gunnison River Dr.), Delta, CO 81416. Phone: 970/874-8349. Fax: 970/874-1353. Hours: Mar. to mid-Dec., 10–4 Tues.–Sat.; closed Thanksgiving, and mid-Dec. to Mar. Admission: adults, $3.50; seniors, $2.50; children 6–12, $2.50; school groups, $1.50 per person; families of five or more and groups of eight or more, $2.50 per person.

DENVER

Art museum

DENVER ART MUSEUM

Exciting changes have been taking place at the Denver Art Museum, the largest and most comprehensive art museum between Kansas City and the West Coast. The museum's roots date back to 1893, when a group of men and women sought to further culture in Denver by forming the Artists' Club and beginning to collect artworks.

The museum occupied a number of different sites before opening in its present location, a castlelike building designed by Gio Ponti and James Sudler, in the Civic Center in 1971.

The Denver Art Museum features the largest and most comprehensive art collection between Kansas City and the West Coast. Courtesy Denver Art Museum.

The museum, which has more than 40,000 art treasures in its collections, recently completed a major renovation that features new galleries, centralized collections storage, a special-exhibitions space, a trendy restaurant, a colorful museum store, and a new museum entrance (facing the adjacent Central Library of the Denver Public Library). Changes include a spacious new home for art of the American West on the seventh floor; imaginative new European and American galleries on the sixth floor; a new gallery for architecture, design, and graphics on the second floor; reinstallation of modern and contemporary art on the first floor; creation of a new special-exhibition space where the museum restaurant and shop formerly were located on the first floor; and an underground connection to the Denver Public Library.

These improvements follow a 1993 renovation that provided new galleries for the pre-Columbian/Spanish colonial collection on the fourth floor and Asian works on the fifth floor. The Native American art galleries on the third floor had been previously redesigned. In 1999, voters approved a $62.5-million bond issue to double the museum's floor space.

The galleries devoted to art of the American West show how artists have depicted this region from about 1830 to the present. On display are landscapes by Albert Bierstadt, Thomas Moran, and Charles Partridge Adams; bronzes such as Frederic Remington's *The Cheyenne;* portraits including Winold Reiss's life-sized painting of a Native American chief, *Bob Riding Black Horse;* historic photographs by William Henry Jackson; and more contemporary views of the American West.

The European and American galleries are arranged by theme rather than period, focusing on such topics as Renaissance traditions; portraits and people; places; objects; textiles; and design arts. Works by Corot, Sisley, Renoir, Degas, Monet, Matisse, Rodin, and many others are on view. One of the highlights is a gallery featuring selections from the highly regarded Berger Collection of British paintings.

The Asian art galleries display exceptional works of Japanese painting and lacquer, Indian sculpture, Chinese ceramics and jade, and Korean, Tibetan, and Southwest Asian art.

More than 5,000 objects from the cultures of Central, South, and Mesoamerica are displayed in the pre-Columbian and Spanish colonial art galleries. The art and artifacts of Native Americans are featured on the third floor, with works of Northwest Coast Indians highlighted on the second floor. The museum has one of the nation's richest Native American collections, consisting of more than 16,000 items from more than 100 tribes across the United States and Canada.

The first floor now features two large exhibition spaces, one containing modern and contemporary works by artists like Warhol, Modigliani, Oldenburg, O'Keeffe, Rauschenberg, and Motherwell, and another for special and traveling exhibitions. Recent offerings have included ancient Egyptian art, architecture, and artifacts, and the works of Toulouse-Lautrec and the Impressionists.

Located on the lower level, the new education center, Adventures in Art, offers hands-on art classes and explorations and contains a lecture hall, classroom, studio, and concourse leading to the children's library, part of the Denver Public Library. The museum's main library, with more than 22,000 volumes, is located in the administrative annex several blocks away.

Denver Art Museum, 100 W. 14th Ave. Pkwy., Denver, CO 80204. Phones: 303/640-4433 and 303/640-2295. Fax: 303/640-5627. E-mail: webmail @denverartmuseum.org. Website: www.denverartmuseum.org. Hours: 10–5 Tues.–Sat., 10–9 Wed., 12–5 Sun.; closed major holidays. Admission: adults, $4.50; seniors and children 6–18, $2.50; children under 6, free.

History museum

COLORADO HISTORY MUSEUM

The Colorado History Museum in Denver is the flagship of the Colorado Historical Society's statewide network of 12 museum sites tracing the history of the state and region. The historical society, founded in 1879, maintains the collections and properties and is responsible for the exhibits and programs at the various sites. It is headquartered at the Denver museum.

The Colorado Historical Society, which began as a state agency and now operates partly as an independent nonprofit organization, has the state's most extensive collections of historical materials relating to Colorado and the American West.

The collections include more than 140,000 artifacts pertaining to the history and prehistory of Colorado and the region; more than 600,000 historical photographs, moving images, and negatives; and approximately 14 million documents, microfilms, books, serials, and ephemera collections in its library. The museum has one of the nation's largest collections of photographs by early photographers of the American West such as William Henry Jackson.

The Colorado History Museum (foreground) *is run by the Colorado Historical Society, which also operates 11 other historical museums and sites throughout the state. Courtesy Colorado Historical Society.*

The Colorado History Museum, located in Denver's Civic Center Historic District, has 28,000 square feet of exhibit space on two levels. The permanent and changing exhibits trace the lives, history, and diversity of Colorado's people—Native Americans, settlers, miners, cowboys, and others—making use of artifacts, photographs, dioramas, documents, and other items, including a sod house, a log cabin, mining equipment, period furniture, Tabor family memorabilia, and a 150-year Colorado timeline.

The museum also presents extensive education programming, including elementary- and secondary-school programs, guided tours, lectures, field trips, a speaker's bureau, videos, historic tours, sleepovers, traveling exhibitions, and school loan kits on such topics as cliff dwellers, mountain men, miners, and everyday life at the turn of the twentieth century.

The Colorado Historical Society also offers guidance on the rehabilitation of historic structures, administers the State Historical Fund preservation grant program, nominates properties to the National Register of Historic Places, and coordinates information about statewide historical and archaeological resources.

In addition to the Colorado History Museum, the society operates seven other museum sites on a year-round basis: the Grant-Humphreys Mansion, Pearce-McAllister Cottage, and Byers-Evans House and Denver History Museum in Denver; Fort Garland in Fort Garland; Ute Indian Museum in Montrose; Fort Vasquez Museum in Platteville; and El Pueblo Museum in Pueblo. Four other sites are open on a summer schedule: the Georgetown Loop Historic Mining and Railroad Park in Georgetown, the Healy House and Dexter Cabin in Leadville, Pike's Stockade in Sanford, and Trinidad History Museum in Trinidad. (See separate listings for all the regional sites).

Colorado History Museum/Colorado Historical Society, 1300 Broadway, Denver, CO 80203. Phone: 303/866-3682. Fax: 303/866-5739. E-mail: chssysop@usa.net. Hours: 10–4:30 Mon.–Sat., 12–4:30 Sun.; closed New Year's Day, Thanksgiving, and Christmas. Admission: adults, $3; seniors, $2.50; children, 6–16, $1.50; children under 6, free.

Natural history museum

DENVER MUSEUM OF NATURAL HISTORY

The Denver Museum of Natural History is the largest and most popular museum in the Rocky Mountain region, occupying 500,896 square feet and attracting nearly 2 million visitors annually.

This diorama of bighorn sheep is one of many at the Denver Museum of Natural History. Courtesy Denver Museum of Natural History and photographer Rick Wicker.

The museum was founded in 1900 after an organizing group purchased the extensive Colorado fauna collection of pioneer naturalist Edwin Carter, and two other naturalists—John T. Mason and John F. Campion—promised their collections of butterflies, moths, and crystalline gold.

The museum opened in 1908 in Denver's City Park upon completion of the building's central wing. The facility has since undergone numerous expansions. Its initial collection of 3,400 specimens of mammals, birds, rocks, and minerals has grown to more than 500,000 specimens and artifacts from the disciplines of anthropology, archaeology, geology, paleontology, and zoology as they pertain to the natural and cultural history of the region.

The Denver Museum of Natural History is one of the largest natural history museums in the nation. It is best known for its 95 world-renowned dioramas; extensive collections of gems, minerals, fossils, and other materials; exhibits on dinosaurs, Native American culture, and health; planetarium and IMAX theater; and education and research activities.

The dioramas of animals and habitats are considered among the best in the world. They include the Botswana Africa Hall, which offers a comprehensive survey of ecology in Botswana and features the largest diorama in the museum, with 22 mounted mammal specimens, including baboon, greater kudu, sable antelope, steinbok, warthog, and zebra in a savanna grassland setting; "Edge of the Wild" and "Explore Colorado: From Plains to Peaks" dioramas on Colorado wildlife and habitats. Other dioramas focus on Colorado wildlife and habitats; North American, South American, South Pacific, and Australian mammals; birds; bears; and sea mammals.

One of the newest and most popular attractions is "Prehistoric Journey," a permanent installation on dinosaurs. It contains numerous fossils in a parklike setting with a "time trail" and seven different "evidence areas," as well as dinosaur specimens and information pertaining to the 3.5-billion-year history of life on Earth.

Other exceptional exhibits include the Coors Gem and Mineral Hall, with approximately 2,500 specimens of gems, minerals, and Colorado gold, as well as a walk-through replica of a mine tunnel; the Crane North American Indian Hall, an ethnographic hall on the native peoples of North America, featuring a Cheyenne diorama, a reconstructed

One of the newest attractions at the Denver Museum of Natural History is "Prehistoric Journey." Courtesy Denver Museum of Natural History and photographer Annette Slade.

Navajo hogan, a Hopi pueblo, and a Northwest Coast gallery; and the Hall of Life, containing hands-on health science exhibits on anatomy, fitness, nutrition, genetics, how human life begins, stress, and substance abuse.

Sky shows are presented in the 232-seat Gates Planetarium (see separate listing), and spectacular 70-mm films are projected on a 4.5-story-tall, 6.5-story-wide screen in the 441-seat IMAX Theater.

The museum also hosts major special and traveling exhibitions (previous offerings have included "Aztec: The World of Moctezuma," "Imperial Tombs of China," and "Ramses II: The Great Pharaoh and His Time"); offers a wide range of educational classes, workshops, films, lectures, field trips, tours, and outreach programs; and conducts extensive excavations as part of its research programs.

The Denver Museum of Natural History is contemplating a name change to reflect the fact that many of its activities are science-oriented. One name under consideration is the Denver Museum of Nature and Science.

Denver Museum of Natural History, 2001 Colorado Blvd., City Park, Denver, CO 80205-5798. Phone: 303/370-6387. Fax: 303/331-6492. Website: www.dmnh.org. Hours: Memorial Day–Labor Day, 9–7 Mon.–Sat., 10–7 Sun.; remainder of the year, 9–5 daily; closed Christmas. Admission: adults, $6; seniors $4; children 3–12, $4; children under 3, free.

Children's museum

CHILDREN'S MUSEUM OF DENVER

In 1973, a group of parents and teachers sought a better way to educate children through play and family time. After considerable research, they created the Children's Museum of Denver, a place where kids can touch, explore, and learn from exhibits as they play.

A storefront museum was opened on Bannock Street and quickly became a popular attraction. In 1984, the museum moved into a new and larger building in the Platte Valley. It is now changing its focus to more strongly emphasize educational opportunities for newborns and children to the age of eight.

Approximately 3,700 square feet of the 24,000-square-foot building is being converted into the Center for the Young Child, which will include four exhibit areas targeting children from infancy to age four, as well as a resource center on early childhood development. The center will encourage sensory awareness; hands-on exploration activities; social, emotional, and large motor development; and cognitive learning and development, and will provide parents and caregivers with reference materials and Internet access.

The four early childhood exhibit areas will include The Pond (for children up to 9 months old), which provides exploration opportunities and requires the parent or caregiver to become involved in the play; The Meadow (for children 8–18 months old), which is similar to The Pond but also promotes language and cognitive development; The Grove (for children 16–36 months old), which encourages toddlers to use their imagination and parents to read to their children; and The Village (for children 3–4 years old), which provides a variety of participatory activities.

Among the museum's other exhibits are a weather station and a science center, exhibits on inventions and the workings of a grocery store, and two new exhibits on the creative arts and making the basketball team.

The museum also has educational programs; an interactive theater; an outdoor area where children can learn in-line skating, roller hockey, skiing, and snowboarding; special events; and publications for children and parents.

Children's Museum of Denver, 2121 Children's Museum Dr., Denver, CO 80211. Phone: 303/433-7444. Fax: 303/433-9520. Hours: 10–5 daily; special toddler program, 9 Tues.; closed Thanksgiving and Christmas. Admission: adults, $5; seniors, $3; children 3 and over, $5; children 1–2, $1; children under 1, free.

Cable television museum

NATIONAL CABLE TELEVISION CENTER AND MUSEUM

The National Cable Television Center and Museum is scheduled to open on the University of Denver campus in 2001. The center/museum, formerly based at Pennsylvania State University, relocated to Denver because of the city's leadership role in, and support of, the cable telecommunications field.

The new $60-million facility, housed in the Alan Gerry Cable Telecommunications Center Building, consists of a museum, theater, television studio, library, teaching center, atrium, and an outdoor amphitheater.

The educational center, the Magness Institute, will conduct research and provide education and training in the industry. The library will document the 50-year history of cable telecommunications. The atrium, or Great Hall, will feature a 40-foot-tall video tower capable of displaying 120 cable programs at once.

The museum will trace the history of the cable industry, using interactive touch screens, photographs, and information on the industry's important people and events. Three mini-theaters will present 10-minute videos on cable's past and the future influence it likely will have on entertainment, information dissemination, and finance. A nearby demonstration area will showcase state-of-the-art cable equipment and permit visitors to interact with the latest technology.

National Cable Television Center and Museum, 2000 Buchtel Blvd., Denver, CO 80208. Phone: 303/871-4885. Fax: 303/871-4515. E-mail: info@cablecenter.org. Website: www.cablecenter.org. Hours and admission: to be determined.

Aquarium

COLORADO'S OCEAN JOURNEY

The ocean came to Denver and the Rocky Mountains in 1999 with the opening of Colorado's Ocean Journey, a $93-million aquarium located in Denver's Central Platte Valley between Elitch Gardens and the Children's Museum of Denver.

The 106,514-square-foot aquarium, whose five major exhibits hold nearly 1 million gallons of water, seeks "to create experiences that inspire guests to discover, explore, enjoy, and protect our aquatic world."

The facility immerses visitors in the wonders of water on two journeys, from Colorado to Mexico's Sea of Cortez and from an Indonesian rain forest to the Pacific Ocean. In addition, the aquarium offers major exhibits on the Sea of Cortez and the Depths of the Pacific; the Sea Otter Cove; 16 dedicated focus areas; and three interactive stations.

The journey from the Continental Divide to the Sea of Cortez takes visitors down the Colorado River, through the Utah canyonlands and Lake Powell, and on to the Sea of Cortez and the Pacific Ocean. The other journey begins in a re-created Indonesian rain forest—complete with Sumatran tigers—and follows the Kiana River to the Pacific Ocean. A glass tunnel literally takes visitors through one of the aquarium's largest tanks, where fish swim over, under, and all around the public.

Approximately 15,000 specimens representing more than 300 species of fish, birds, and mammals are featured in the various exhibits.

The aquarium—the first major aquatic exhibit in the region—was conceived in 1991 by Bill Fleming and his wife, Judy Peterson-Fleming, who sought to create a world-class aquarium in a landlocked state.

Colorado's Ocean Journey, US West Park, 700 Water St., Denver, CO 80211. Phone: 303/561-4450. Fax: 303/561-4465. Website: www.oceanjourney.org.

Hours: summer, 9–6:30 Mon.–Fri., 9–8 Sat.–Sun.; remainder of year, 10–6 daily; closed Christmas. Admission: adults, $14.95; seniors, $12.95; young people 13–17, $12.95; children 4–12, $6.95; children under 4, free.

Botanic gardens

DENVER BOTANIC GARDENS

The Denver Botanic Gardens, located on 23 acres in the heart of Denver, seeks to encourage and increase the public's enjoyment and knowledge of plants and horticulture, with special emphasis on growing plants native to the Rocky Mountain region.

Opened in 1959, the facility has more than 14,000 species of plants and is internationally recognized for its water-lily, Japanese, xeriscape, plains, and rock alpine gardens, as well as its horticultural therapy pro-

The Denver Botanic Gardens focuses on plants of the Rocky Mountain region. Courtesy Denver Botanic Gardens.

gram, which promotes greater awareness of the therapeutic value of plants and plant-related activities.

The landscape is dominated by the award-winning and recently renovated Boettcher Memorial Conservatory, which houses the Tropical Botanica, a year-round haven for tropical and subtropical plants. Marnie's Pavilion at the gardens' west end houses collections of orchids and bromeliads and hosts seasonal floral displays. Changing exhibits also are presented in the Lobby Court.

The Water Garden, which contains the water-lily collection, received an award of excellence from the Royal Horticultural Society of England in 1991.

The Japanese Garden features pines, waterways, a teahouse, and more than 300 tons of stone. The Xeriscape Demonstration Garden displays plants gathered from arid lands of the American West and similar regions around the world. It was one of the first public gardens in the nation to focus on water-saving alternatives to traditional gardening.

The Plains Garden consists of grasses and other native prairie plants that re-create seven plant systems of Colorado's high plains. The Rock Alpine Garden is a one-acre western adaptation of a traditional English rock garden and is considered among the finest rock gardens in the nation.

Other gardens include the Gates Memorial Garden, which represents the transition zone between plains and mountains; the May Bonfils Stanton Rose Garden, containing more than 250 varieties of roses; the Endangered Plants Garden, created as part of a coordinated national effort to preserve rare and endangered plants; the Herb Garden, a garden filled with herbs that provide flavors and fragrances for vinegars, salts, and culinary spice mixes; and the Home Demonstration Garden, which shows how ground covers, perennials, shrubs, paving materials, and useful structures can help create a low-maintenance, inviting yard.

Among the Denver Botanic Gardens' other offerings are the Kathryn Kalmbach Herbarium, featuring changing displays of Colorado native plants, lichens, old herbariums, wood samples, and illustrations of plants; Helen Fowler Library, containing more than 21,000 books, periodicals, and catalogs on gardening, botany, and related subjects; education classes and lectures in horticulture, conservation, landscaping, botany, and floral arts; and a series of evening concerts featuring classical jazz, world music, and dance concerts, all performed at the gardens' outdoor amphitheater.

The Denver Botanic Gardens also operates the 700-acre Chatfield Arboretum near Chatfield Dam and Reservoir southwest of Denver (see separate listing under Littleton), the 20-acre Walter S. Reed Botanical

Garden research and education preserve near Evergreen, and the 160-acre Mount Goliath Alpine Unit west of Denver. The latter includes the two-mile M. Walter Pesman Nature Trail.

The Denver Botanic Gardens began in 1951 with the incorporation of the Botanic Gardens Foundation. Initial plantings were located in City Park near the Denver Museum of Natural History. The garden was moved to its present site in 1959 and today is operated in partnership with the Denver Department of Parks and Recreation.

Denver Botanic Gardens, 1005 York St. (office at 909 York St.), Denver, CO 80206-3799. Phones: 303/331-4000 and 303/370-8018. Fax: 303/331-4013. E-mail: dbg@dbg-usa.com. Website: botanicalgardens.org. Hours: May–Sept., 9–8 Sat.–Tues., 9–5 Wed.–Fri.; Oct.–Apr., 9–5 daily; closed New Year's Day and Christmas. Admission: May–Sept., adults, $5.50; seniors, $3.50; children 6–15, $3.50; children under 6, free. Oct.–Apr., adults, $4.50; children 6–15, $3; seniors, $2.50; children under 6, free.

Arboretum

CHESTER M. ALTER ARBORETUM AT THE UNIVERSITY OF DENVER

The approximately 400 species of trees on the University of Denver campus became the Chester M. Alter Arboretum, named for a former university chancellor, in 1999.

During his tenure, Alter sought to balance the construction of new buildings with beautifully planted open spaces.

Many of the trees on campus likely might not exist were it not for Rufus Clark, who sold 150 acres of prairie to the university in 1886, with the stipulation that 1,000 trees be planted on the new grounds. The trees were planted within a year, and many still survive.

The trees and shrubs are now being labeled, and additional plantings are being undertaken.

Chester M. Alter Arboretum, University of Denver, 2199 University Blvd., Denver, CO 80210. Phone: 303/871-2000. Hours: open 24 hours. Admission: free.

Zoological park

DENVER ZOOLOGICAL GARDENS

The Denver Zoological Gardens were founded in 1896 when an orphaned black bear was presented to the city's mayor and exhibited in a start-up zoo in Denver's City Park.

The zoo grew modestly under city stewardship until 1956, when a partnership was formed between the City and County of Denver and the

Denver Zoological Foundation, which was empowered to develop and improve the zoological gardens.

In ensuing years, the zoo added many new attractions, expanded its collections, and enhanced the quality of its exhibits throughout the 80-acre site. Today, it has nearly 3,500 animal specimens representing more than 660 species, making it one of the most diverse zoological collections in the country. Nearly 2 million visitors pass through annually. The animals include some of the most exotic and beautiful species on the planet, such as amur leopards, king cobras, black rhinos, coral-reef fish, elephants, zebras, gorillas, and many others. The zoo has 144 endangered species and 3 species that actually are extinct in the wild.

One of the zoo's newest and largest attractions is Primate Panorama, which features 29 species of primates, covers seven acres, and cost $14 million to construct. Its denizens range from a six-ounce pygmy marmoset to a 610-pound gorilla.

Another recent addition is Tropical Discovery, a rain forest housed in two glass pyramids, which takes visitors through a series of habitats: a mountain cave, tropical streams, waterfalls, temple ruins, a jungle river, and an offshore coral reef.

A third major exhibit is Northern Shores, which covers three-and-a-half acres and explores the wonders of Arctic life. It shows Arctic wolves roaming a pine forest, harbor seals frolicking in water, and polar bears and California sea lions playing along the rocks and shoreline of the Pacific coast.

Among the many other exhibits are Bird World, housing a variety of free-flying birds in walk-through habitats; the Humboldt Penguin Exhibit, offering simulated nest burrows for children to climb into; Jewels of the Emerald Forest, an exhibit of primates native to Madagascar and South America; Bear Mountain (the first zoo exhibit in the nation to be barless and re-create a natural habitat), which features grizzly and Asian black bears; and North American Wildlife, containing reindeer, musk ox, American bison, pronghorn antelope, and other animals.

A $62.5-million bond issue, passed in 1999, will pay for about half of a ten-year program to create even more natural settings for the zoo's animals.

The Gates Center is home base for the zoo's education programs and two interactive summer programs, Wild Encounter and Habitat Theater. The zoo also has a nursery for young animals that need medical care, and a conservation center for the propagation and reintroduction of rare and endangered animals.

Denver Zoological Gardens, 2300 Steele St., City Park, Denver, CO 80205-4911. Phone: 303/376-4800. Fax: 303/376-4801. E-mail: zooinfo@denverzoo.org.

Website: www.denverzoo.org. Hours: Apr.–Sept., 9–6 daily; Oct.–Mar., 10–5 daily. Admission: Apr.–Sept., adults, $8; seniors, $6; children 4–12, $4; children under 4, free. Oct.–Mar., adults, $6; seniors, $5; children 4–12, $3; children under 4, free.

Planetarium

CHARLES C. GATES PLANETARIUM AT THE DENVER MUSEUM OF NATURAL HISTORY

The Charles C. Gates Planetarium presents a wide variety of sky shows, which are included in the price of admission to the Denver Museum of Natural History in Denver's City Park (see separate listing).

The sky shows, offered on the hour, are produced by the planetarium's own research/production team and make use of a Minolta Series IV Star Projector to create images of more than 8,500 stars and star clusters. The planetarium projector is supplemented by 75 slide projectors, four video projectors, and special effect devices, which make it possible to simulate the surface of the moon, volcanic eruptions on a satellite of Jupiter, and even a space flight through the clouds of Venus.

The 232-seat planetarium, which opened in 1968 and is housed within the Museum of Natural History, also has lobby exhibits including a swinging Foucault pendulum, meteorites, Mars data collected by the Viking orbiter, and space art. Two astronomical murals created by Michael Carroll enhance the corridor leading to the planetarium. A major renovation of the planetarium is planned for 2000.

Charles C. Gates Planetarium, Denver Museum of Natural History, 2001 Colorado Blvd., City Park, Denver, CO 80205-5798. Phone: 303/370-6387. Fax: 303/331-6492. Website: www.dmnh.org. Planetarium hours: shows on the hour, but schedule varies. Museum hours: Memorial Day–Labor Day, 9–7 Mon.–Sat., 10–7 Sun.; remainder of the year, 9–5 daily; closed Christmas. Admission: free with museum admission of $6 for adults and $4 for seniors and children 3–12 (children under 3, free).

Observatory

CHAMBERLAIN OBSERVATORY AT THE UNIVERSITY OF DENVER

In 1890, the Chamberlain Observatory—funded by prominent landowner Humphrey Chamberlain—opened on the University of Denver campus. The observatory, a National Historic Landmark, is still in use today for instruction and research. It is also open to the public after sundown three evenings a week for telescope viewing and a slide show. The observatory is the home of the Denver Astronomical Society, which presents occasional special programs.

Chamberlain Observatory, University of Denver, 2930 E. Warren Ave., Denver, CO 80208. Phone: 303/871-5172. Hours: after sundown on Tues., Thurs., and Sat. (hours vary seasonally); closed major holidays. Admission: adults, $2; children 12 and under, $1.

Anthropology museum

MUSEUM OF ANTHROPOLOGY AT THE UNIVERSITY OF DENVER

The University of Denver houses the small Museum of Anthropology on the lower level of the Mary Reed Building on its Denver campus. Founded in 1931 and operated by the Anthropology Department, the museum has collections of textiles and artifacts and presents changing exhibitions.

Museum of Anthropology, University of Denver, Mary Reed Bldg., 2199 S. University Blvd. (postal address: Anthropology Dept., 2130 S. Race St.), Denver, CO 80208. Phone: 303/871-2406. Fax: 303/871-2437. E-mail: dsaitta@du.edu. Website: www.du.edu/dyna/duma.html. Hours: Sept.–June, 9–4:30 Mon.–Fri.; closed summer session and university holidays. Admission: free.

Art foundation/museum

VANCE KIRKLAND FOUNDATION AND MUSEUM

The diverse artworks of the late Vance Kirkland, who has been called the father of modern Colorado painting, are featured at the Vance Kirkland Foundation and Museum in Denver.

Kirkland, founding dean of the University of Denver School of Art, became a master watercolor painter of realistic and surrealistic works in the 1920s and 1930s; produced hard-edge abstractions and mixed water and oil to create abstract expressionist works in the 1940s and 1950s; then added specks of oil paint atop water-and-oil patterns to form dot paintings in the 1960s and 1970s.

Kirkland was the director of DU's art school from 1929 to 1932 and from 1946 to 1969. He also ran the Kirkland School of Art from 1932 to 1946 in the 1911 building where the foundation/museum now is located. The structure recently underwent an 8,000-square-foot expansion.

The foundation has more than 500 of Kirkland's artworks; nearly 100 are on exhibit in the museum at any given time. It also maintains a Kirkland archive, assists with traveling exhibitions of Kirkland's work, and maintains a collection of American dinnerware, furniture, metal works, textiles, sculpture, and paintings by such other artists as Harry Bertoia, Edgar Britton, Charles and Ray Eames, Frank Gehry, Isamu

Noguchi, Verner Panton, Warren Platner, George Rickey, Frank Lloyd Wright, Russel Wright, and Eva Zeisel.

Vance Kirkland Foundation and Museum, 1311 Pearl St., Denver, CO 80203. Phone: 303/832-8576. Fax: 303/832-8404. E-mail: vkfg@leith.cccall.com. Hours: 9–6 Mon.–Fri. by appointment; closed major holidays. Admission: free.

Art museum/gallery

TRIANON MUSEUM AND ART GALLERY

The Trianon Museum and Art Gallery in downtown Denver is a privately operated facility that houses a collection of eighteenth- and nineteenth-century European art and furnishings, including paintings, furniture, crystal, silver, porcelain, bronzes, and clocks, as well as oriental art objects and a rare gun collection.

The European collection features paintings by Watteau, Poussin, and Boucher; bronzes by de Bologne, Coysevox, Gregoire, Coustou, Barye, Mené, Dubucand, and Colinet; Carrara marble and gold Neptune bowls; a gold-on-bronze sculpture of Poseidon attributed to Cellini; a Napoleonic mahogany rolltop desk; an imperial clock created by Fabergé; and a Sèvres urn by Collot.

Among the other objects on display are a circa-1728 Stein-action 60-key piano, an eighteenth-century Savonnerie rug, Louis XVI service plates and a collection of rare china, a silver tray created by Ovchinnikov for Czar Peter the Great of Russia, and weapons from the sixteenth century to the present, including an 1877 Gatling gun.

Hourly tours are conducted through the museum and the adjoining art gallery, where some works are for sale.

Trianon Museum and Art Gallery, 335 14th St., Denver, CO 80202. Phone: 303/623-0739. Hours: 1–4 Mon.–Sat. Admission: $1; children under 12 accompanied by an adult, free.

Aviation/space museum

WINGS OVER THE ROCKIES AIR & SPACE MUSEUM

Twenty-four aircraft, including a huge B-52 Stratofortress bomber and a rare B-1A bomber, are on display at the Wings Over the Rockies Air & Space Museum, located in Hanger 1 at the former Lowry Air Force Base in Denver.

The museum, originally known as the Lowry Heritage Museum and dedicated to preserving artifacts of Lowry's colorful past, opened in 1982.

It was revamped, renamed, and moved to the cavernous Hanger 1 when the base was shut down in 1994.

The museum has added military and civilian aircraft and other exhibits as its mission has been expanded to preserve and interpret the history of aviation and space exploration.

Among the other aircraft at the museum are a 7D Corsair, F-86H, F-18A Bolo, B-57E Canberra, F4E Phantom, F-102A Delta Dagger, H-21C helicopter, RF-84K Thunderflash, T-33A T-bird, U3A Blue Canoe, D-V11 Fokker, and an Eaglerock biplane.

The museum also features the "Freedom" Space Module, a replica of a 1920s Primary Glider, and smaller exhibits on the Norden bombsight, Air Force Academy, World War I uniforms, President Dwight D. Eisenhower's "Denver White House," and other subjects.

Wings Over the Rockies Air & Space Museum, 7711 E. Academy Pkwy., Denver, CO 80220. Phone: 303/360-5360. Fax: 303/360-5328. Hours: 10–4 Mon.–Sat., 12–4 Sun.; closed New Year's Day, Easter, Thanksgiving, and Christmas. Admission: adults, $4; seniors, $2; children 6–17, $2; children under 6, free.

Button museum

JHB BUTTON MUSEUM

Antique, rare, and contemporary buttons and collectible thimbles are on view at the JHB Button Museum, a company museum opened in 1998 by JHB International Inc., a Denver button wholesaler.

The button company was started in 1969 by Jean Howard Barr, who still heads the firm. JHB International deals with more than 85 factories in 27 countries throughout Europe, Asia, and the Americas to obtain its wide range of classic and novelty buttons.

Visits to the museum are part of an hour-long tour of the company's assembly and distribution plant. The free guided tours are offered weekday afternoons by appointment.

JHB Button Museum, JHB International Inc., 1955 Quince St., Denver, CO 80231. Phone: 303/751-8100. Fax: 303/752-0608. Hours: 2:30–3:30 Mon.– Fri. by appointment; closed major holidays. Admission: free.

Doll museum

GOODWILL DOLL MUSEUM

A doll collection featuring 228 dolls—some more than 100 years old—is displayed at the Goodwill Doll Museum in Denver. The museum,

The Black American West Museum & Heritage Center in Denver is located in the historic house of Dr. Justina Ford, the first African-American woman doctor in Colorado. Courtesy Black American West Museum & Heritage Center.

located at and operated by Goodwill Industries, is open only on Thursday mornings, when tours are conducted by advance reservation.

Goodwill Doll Museum, Goodwill Industries, 6850 Federal Blvd., Denver, CO 80221. Phone: 303/650-7700. Fax: 303/650-7749. Hours: tours at 10 Thurs. by appointment. Admission: free.

Ethnic history/cultural museum

BLACK AMERICAN WEST MUSEUM & HERITAGE CENTER

The Black American West Museum & Heritage Center in Denver seeks to preserve the history and culture of the African-American men and women who helped settle and develop the American West.

Founded in 1971, the museum has been located in the historic home of Dr. Justina Ford, the first black female physician in Denver, since 1989. The Victorian house, which was moved to its present site in the Five Points area, was listed on the National Register of Historic Places in 1984.

The museum began as the hobby of Paul Stewart, a barber-turned-historian who became interested in cowboys and Indians as a child but found no reference to black cowboys. As an adult, he discovered that blacks played an important role in the development of the American West (one-third of the cowboys were African American) and began gathering artifacts, memorabilia, newspapers, documents, clothing, letters, photographs, and oral histories of black settlers, cowboys, soldiers, businesspeople, and others who helped settle and shape the West.

With his collection as the nucleus, Stewart opened a small museum at Clayton College, located at Martin Luther King and Colorado Boulevards, before moving to Five Points. The museum now exhibits an array of artifacts, photographs, and other historical materials relating to blacks involved in fur trading, homesteading, mining, cattle raising, military service, and other pursuits.

Black American West Museum & Heritage Center, 3091 California St., Denver, CO 80205. Phone: 303/292-2566. Fax: 303/892-1981. E-mail: bawhc@aol.com. Website: www.coax.net/people/lwf/bawmus.htm. Hours: May–Sept., 10–5 daily; remainder of the year, 10–2 Wed.–Fri., 10–5 Sat.–Sun.; closed major holidays. Admission: adults, $3; seniors and students, $2; children 13–17, $1; children 4–12, $.50; children under 4, free.

Ethnic history/cultural museum

MIZEL MUSEUM OF JUDAICA

Permanent, changing, and traveling exhibitions on Jewish history, culture, and art from around the world are presented at the Mizel Museum of Judaica in Denver. The museum, which is located in the BMH/BJ Synagogue, opened in 1982 and is the only museum of Judaica in the Rocky Mountain region.

The museum's principal permanent installation, "Bridges of Understanding," has two parts—Rites of Passage, and Ceremonies and Festivals. They highlight common themes, rituals, sights, flavors, and sounds that connect Jewish people from around the world, providing insight into their rich yet diverse Jewish heritages.

Among the recent changing and traveling exhibitions are "Ben-Zion: In Search of Oneself," "The Immigrant Adventure," and "Cuban Jewish Art Today."

Mizel Museum of Judaica, 560 S. Monaco Pkwy., Denver, CO 80224. Phone: 303/333-4156. Fax: 303/388-4210. E-mail: mizelmus@dnvr.uswest.net. Website: www.jewishmuseum.com/mizelmus.htm. Hours: 10–4 Mon.–Fri., 12–4 Sun.; closed major holidays. Admission: tour groups, $2 per person; all others, free.

Ethnic history/cultural museum

MUSEO DE LAS AMERICAS

Changing exhibitions of, and programs on, Latino art, culture, and history that celebrate the rich cultural diversity of Latin American countries and the southwestern United States are presented at the Museo de las Americas in Denver.

The museum, which opened in 1993, is located on Santa Fe Drive in the heart of one of Denver's most vibrant Hispanic neighborhoods.

The museum was founded by José Aguayo, whose life's dream was to open a Latino museum. However, he did not seriously pursue this goal until the early 1980s, when he earned degrees in anthropology and museum studies, worked as an intern at the Denver Art Museum, and became director of design at the Colorado Historical Society before launching the museum in 1991.

Past exhibitions presented at the museum include "Noche de Muertos—Chicano Journey into a Michoacán Night," "Visiones del Pueblo: The Folk Art of Latin America," "Peru: Traditions of Yesterday in Transition Today," and "José Guadalupe Posada: Mexican Printmaker."

Museo de las Americas, 861 Santa Fe Dr., Denver, CO 80204. Phone: 303/ 571-4401. Fax: 303/607-9761. E-mail: joseaguayo@mcione.com. Website: www.museo.org. Hours: 10–5 Tues.–Sat.; closed New Year's Day, Fourth of July, Thanksgiving, and Christmas. Admission: adults, $3; seniors and students, $2; children under 10, free.

Firefighting museum

DENVER FIREFIGHTERS MUSEUM

The Denver Firefighters Museum, housed in a 1909 fire station, is dedicated to preserving and presenting the history of firefighting in Denver. Opened in 1979, the 11,000-square-foot museum contains old fire engines, other firefighting equipment, historical photographs, and hands-on exhibits.

Among the historical items on display are three hand-drawn fire apparatuses dating from 1867, a horse-drawn steam pumper, and three motorized fire trucks dating from 1927 and 1952. The museum also has a collection of early leather fire helmets, trumpets, uniforms, and other firefighting objects.

Visitors can slide down one of the fire poles from the second floor, try on actual firefighting gear, and ring a fire alarm used from the turn of the twentieth century until 1977.

The fire station, known as Fire Station No. 1, was listed on the National Register of Historic Places in 1979.

Denver Firefighters Museum, 1326 Tremont Pl., Denver, CO 80204. Phone and fax: 303/892-1436. E-mail: info@firedenver. Website: www.firedenver.org. Hours: day after Memorial Day–Labor Day, 10–4 Mon.–Sat.; remainder of the year, 10–2 Mon.– Sat.; closed Memorial Day. Admission: adults, $3; seniors, $2; children 2–16, $2.

Living-history museum/historic site

FOUR MILE HISTORIC PARK

The oldest structure in metropolitan Denver—an 1859 building that served as a stage stop, wayside inn, and then farmhouse—is the centerpiece of Four Mile Historic Park, located four miles from downtown Denver.

The 11-acre park, operated in cooperation with the City and County of Denver, includes the original dwelling, outbuildings, and equipment of the Four Mile House, a former stage stop on the Cherokee Trail.

The frontier structure, listed on the National Register of Historic Places in 1969, was built by the Brantner brothers. In 1860, Mary Cawker, a 47-year-old widow with two children, turned the house into a stage stop and wayside inn. After a flood in 1864, she sold the 160-acre property to Levi and Millie Booth, who operated the stage stop and inn until the railroad reached Denver in 1870.

With the advent of rail, the Booths turned to farming. They put up an addition to the building in 1883, moved an 1860s frame house to the site (to produce the U-shaped house seen today), added 500 acres to the property, and became agricultural leaders in the valley and state.

Four Mile Historic Park, which functions as a living-history museum, has costumed interpreters who lead guided tours of the house and demonstrate old-time skills and crafts such as blacksmithing, plowing, harvesting, quilting, spinning, lace making, butter churning, and beekeeping. Visitors also have an opportunity to enjoy horse-drawn rides from 11 to 2 on Saturdays and Sundays. Children 6 to 11 years old can attend a Pioneer Summer Camp from June through August.

Four Mile Historic Park, 715 S. Forest St., Denver, CO 80222. Phone: 303/399-1859. Fax: 303/393-0788. Hours: Apr.–Sept., 12–4 Wed.–Fri., and 10–4 Sat.–Sun.; Oct.–Mar., 12–4 Sat.–Sun. Admission: adults, $3.50; seniors, $2; children 6–15, $2; children under 6, free; horse-drawn rides, $1.

Miniature/doll/toy museum

DENVER MUSEUM OF MINIATURES, DOLLS, AND TOYS

The Denver Museum of Miniatures, Dolls, and Toys is located in the historic Pearce-McAllister Cottage (see separate listing); its collections are exhibited throughout the building.

Founded in 1981, the museum features miniatures, dolls, teddy bears, and toys from around the world, including early dolls from 1740 and 1850 and a 1927 doll given to Colorado as a gesture of friendship by the City of Yokohama in Japan.

Among the other attractions are the 16-room Kingscote Doll House, the adobe Santa Fe Dollhouse, and a miniature Native American tepee scene with tiny basket weavings.

Denver Museum of Miniatures, Dolls, and Toys, Pearce-McAllister Cottage, 1880 Gaylord St., Denver, CO 80206. Phone: 303/322-1053. Fax: 303/322-3704. E-mail: Idsbc@aol.com. Website: www.westresearch.com/dmmdt/start. Hours: 10–4 Tues.–Sat., 1–4 Sun.; closed major holidays. Admission: adults, $3; seniors, $2; children 2–16, $2; children under 2, free.

Military museum

VFW POST 1 MUSEUM

The downtown Denver post of the Veterans of Foreign Wars—the nation's first VFW post—has a museum displaying artifacts and other historical materials from U.S. wars.

Among the objects on exhibit are weapons, knives, gas masks, swords, field phones, and part of a German airplane. Most of the materials are from the Spanish-American War, World War I, World War II, and the Korean War.

VFW Post 1 Museum, VFW Post 1, 955 Bannock St., Denver, CO 80204. Phone: 303/571-5659. Hours: 11–11 Mon.–Sat., 11–8 Sun.; closed Thanksgiving and Christmas. Admission: free.

Recycling museum

COMPLETE THE CYCLE MUSEUM

The Complete the Cycle Museum in Denver is more recycling showroom than museum. Better known as the Complete the Cycle Center, it encourages recycling by displaying the many products that can be made from recycled materials.

Guided tours, geared mainly toward school groups, are available. Visitors walk on a carpet made from plastic soft-drink bottles, sit at picnic tables constructed of plastic milk jugs, and see shingles made from car tires, floor tiles made from windshields, and a room with walls and ceiling made from recycled newspapers.

Complete the Cycle Museum, 3600 E. 48th Ave., P.O. Box 16664, Denver, CO 80216. Phone: 303/333-3434. Hours: by appointment. Admission: students, $3; teachers and parents, free.

Transportation museum

FORNEY TRANSPORTATION MUSEUM

The Forney Transportation Museum, once located in the old Denver Tramway Power Company building along the South Platte River near Speer Boulevard, has a new home—a renovated 146,000-square-foot former food distribution warehouse near the Denver Coliseum. The museum opened at this location in 1999.

The museum was started in Fort Collins in 1961 by J. C. Forney, whose soldering-iron and welding inventions led to the founding of Forney Industries. He began collecting vintage cars in the 1950s and soon needed a museum to house them. In 1967, the museum moved to the former power plant, which supplied electricity to the city's trolley cars. When the founder died, his son, Jack, took over and has spearheaded the museum's expansion.

More than half of the museum's collection is on display at the new site. Plans call for the remainder to be added in 2000. The museum's most notable exhibit is the 1941 "Big Boy" locomotive. At 135 feet long and 600 tons, it is the world's largest steam locomotive. Also on view are 171 automobiles, 60 buggies and carriages, 50 bicycles, 50 farm machines, 40 wagons, four airplanes, three other locomotives, two cabooses, and such other items as a trolley, cable car, crane, snowplow, and model railroad, as well as military uniforms, formal gowns, and wax figurines.

Among the prized automobiles at the museum are an 1899 four-passenger Locomobile, 1905 Ford, 1906 Pope Tribune Runabout, 1907 eight-passenger limousine with double running boards, 1912 Renault Opera Coupe, 1912 seven-passenger Vauxhall limousine, 1914 Detroit electric car, 1915 Cadillac, 1923 25-foot wheel-base Hispano Suiza, 1926 seven-passenger Lincoln, and such celebrity cars as President Teddy Roosevelt's parade car, Amelia Earhart's "Gold Bug" Kissel, and Prince Aly Khan's Rolls-Royce.

Forney Transportation Museum, 4303 Brighton Blvd., Denver, CO 80216. Phone: 303/297-1113. Fax: 970/498-9505. E-mail: forney@info2000.net. Website: www.forneymuseum.com. Hours: 9–5 Mon.–Sat.; closed New Year's Day, Easter, Fourth of July, Thanksgiving, and Christmas. Admission: adults, $5; seniors, $4; students 12–18, $3; children 5–11, $2; children under 5, free.

Art gallery

AMERICAN INSTITUTE OF ARCHITECTS GALLERY

The Colorado chapter of the American Institute of Architects in Denver has a gallery displaying award-winning architectural designs and examples of exceptional architectural projects.

American Institute of Architects Gallery, 1526 15th St., Denver, CO 80202. Phone: 303/446-2266. Fax: 303/446-0066. E-mail: aiadenco@aol.com. Website: www.aiacolorado.org. Hours: 9–5 Mon.–Fri.; closed major holidays. Admission: free.

Art gallery

CENTER FOR THE VISUAL ARTS, METROPOLITAN STATE COLLEGE OF DENVER

Exhibitions by culturally diverse artists, many of whom are nationally and internationally known, are presented at Metropolitan State College of Denver's Center for the Visual Arts, located off-campus in Denver's nearby LoDo (Lower Downtown) area.

Each year, the center mounts six or seven exhibitions emphasizing a diversity of mediums and themes. It also offers extensive programming, including tours, workshops, and lectures. Past exhibitions have featured paintings from Taiwan, textiles from Australia, art from West Africa, Japanese needlework, works by contemporary Latino artists, prints by Picasso, and works by the faculty, students, and other artists.

Center for the Visual Arts, Metropolitan State College of Denver, 1734 Wazee St., Denver, CO 80202. Phone: 303/294-5207. Fax: 303/294-5209. E-mail: morleyj@msc.edu. Website: www.mscd.edu/-metroarts. Hours: 11–5 Tues.–Thurs., 11–8 Fri., 12–4 Sat.; closed major holidays. Admission: free.

Art gallery

CHAC GALLERY, CHICANO HUMANITIES AND ARTS COUNCIL

Changing exhibitions of the works of Chicano and other artists are featured in the Chicano Humanities and Arts Council's CHAC Gallery, opened in 1978 in Denver. Shows usually last three weeks and are open to the public on Friday evenings and Saturday afternoons.

CHAC Gallery, Chicano Humanities and Arts Council, 772 Santa Fe Dr., Denver, CO 80204. Phone: 303/571-0440. Hours: 7–10 Fri. evenings, 1–4 Sat. Admission: free.

Art gallery

COLORADO INSTITUTE OF ART GALLERY

The artworks of students, faculty, and guest artists are displayed in changing exhibitions at the Colorado Institute of Art Gallery in Denver.

Colorado Institute of Art Gallery, 200 E. 9th Ave., Denver, CO 80203. Phone: 303/837-0825. Fax: 303/860-8520. Hours: 8 A.M.–9 P.M. Mon.–Thurs., 8–5 Fri., 9–12 Sat.; closed major holidays. Admission: free.

Art galleries

DENVER CENTER FOR THE PERFORMING ARTS
Boettcher Concert Hall Galleries
Temple Hoyne Buell Theatre Galleries
Helen Bonfils Theatre Main Lobby

The Denver Center for the Performing Arts is best known for its plays, concerts, and other performances, but it also displays artworks in three of its facilities—Boettcher Concert Hall, Temple Hoyne Buell Theatre, and Helen Bonfils Theatre.

Changing exhibitions are featured in Boettcher Concert Hall, which has two galleries, and the Temple Hoyne Buell Theatre, which has four. At the Helen Bonfils Theatre, occasional exhibitions related to performances are hung in the main lobby. A wide range of artworks are displayed, usually in month-long showings, at the Boettcher and Buell galleries, which are open only when performances and other special events are taking place. The Bonfils exhibitions are on view only for the duration of the related performances.

The curving lobby of the Bonfils Theatre also contains exhibits of the newly created Colorado Performing Arts Hall of Fame. The first inductees, honored in 1999, were bandleader Glenn Miller; actor Douglas Fairbanks, Sr.; playwright Mary Coyle Chase; benefactor Helen Bonfils; and actors Alfred Lunt and Lynne Fontanne.

Denver Center for the Performing Arts, 950 13th St., Denver, CO 80204. Phone: 303/640-2862. Fax: 303/640-2397. Website: www.artstozoo.org/. Hours: open only during performances and other special events. Admission: free, but there is a charge for events.

Art galleries

DENVER PUBLIC LIBRARY, CENTRAL LIBRARY
Vida Ellison Gallery
Western History Gallery

The new Central Library of the Denver Public Library contains two art galleries—the Vida Ellison Gallery, which presents changing exhibitions, and the Western History Gallery, which displays works from the library's western art collection.

The 540,000-square-foot downtown library, opened in 1995, has seven aboveground levels and three underground levels. It was designed by noted architect Michael Graves and the Klipp Colussy Jenks DeBois architectural firm of Denver.

The Vida Ellison Gallery features special and traveling exhibitions from the library's Douglas Collection of Fine Painting, as well as other works by professional artists. It is located on the seventh level. The Western History Gallery, part of the Western History and Genealogy Department on the fifth level, contains Albert Bierstadt's famous 1877 oil painting, *Estes Park*, and regional art, mainly nineteenth-century, from the library's 400-item western art collection, which includes works by Thomas Moran and Frederic Remington.

In addition to these two galleries, the Denver Public Library also has exhibition spaces in many of its 22 branches.

Vida Ellison Gallery and Western Art Gallery, Denver Public Library, Central Library, 10 W. 14th Ave. Pkwy., Denver, CO 80204-2731. Phones: 303/640-6377 and 303/640-6291. Fax: 303/640-6298. E-mail: kwisnia@denver.lib.com.us. Website: www.denver.lib.co.us. Hours: 10–9 Mon.–Wed., 10–5:30 Thurs.–Sat., 1–5 Sun.; closed major holidays. Admission: free.

Art gallery

EDGE GALLERY

Cutting-edge art is presented in changing exhibitions at the Edge Gallery, an artists' cooperative in Denver. Works range from fine art to video.

Edge Gallery, 3658 Navajo St., Denver, CO 80211. Phone: 303/477-7173. Hours: 7–10 Fri. evenings, 1–5 Sat.–Sun. Admission: free.

Art gallery

EMMANUEL GALLERY AT THE AURARIA HIGHER EDUCATION CENTER

Emmanuel Gallery at the Auraria Higer Education Center in Denver is shared by the three institutions located on the Auraria campus—Community College of Denver, Metropolitan State College of Denver, and University of Colorado at Denver.

The gallery is located in the Emmanuel Chapel Building, Denver's oldest church structure, which was listed on the National Register of Historic Places in 1969. Built as a non-denominational Sunday school in 1859, the building became an Episcopal chapel in 1874, a Jewish Orthodox synagogue in 1903, and an artist's studio in 1958 before the campus acquired in it 1973.

Eleven exhibitions are presented each year. They include three student and three faculty exhibitions and five shows featuring the work of regional and nationally known professional artists. The works are displayed in two exhibition spaces.

Emmanuel Gallery, Auraria Higher Education Center, 10th St. and Lawrence St. Mall, Campus Box Y, P.O. Box 173361, Denver, CO 80211. Phone: 303/556-8337. Fax: 303/556-8349. Hours: 11–5 Mon.–Fri.; closed major holidays. Admission: free.

Art gallery

HARRIET HOWE KELLY GALLERY AT THE ART STUDENTS LEAGUE OF DENVER

Monthly exhibitions of paintings, prints, sculpture, and artworks in various media by students, faculty, and others are presented in the Harriet Howe Kelly Gallery at the Art Students League of Denver, housed in the 1893 Sherman School landmark building.

The visual arts school offers a wide range of classes for adults and children of all abilities at minimal cost in a nonthreatening environment.

Harriet Howe Kelly Gallery, Art Students League of Denver, 200 Grant St., Denver, CO 80203. Phone: 303/778-6990. Fax: 303/778-6956. Hours: 8:30 A.M.–9:30 P.M. Mon.–Fri., 8:30–4:30 Sat.; closed major holidays. Admission: free.

Art gallery

LOWER-LEVEL GALLERY, COURTYARD BY MARRIOTT, UNIVERSITY OF COLORADO AT DENVER

The College of Arts and Media at the University of Colorado at Denver opened an off-campus gallery at the new Courtyard by Marriott hotel in downtown Denver in 1998.

The gallery, known as the Lower-Level Gallery, currently presents three exhibitions of student and faculty art each year, but it is planning to expand the offerings to include works by professional artists in the region.

Lower-Level Gallery, Courtyard by Marriott, 934 16th St., Denver, CO 80202. Phone: 303/571-1114. Fax: 303/571-1141. (Contact: Visual Arts Dept., College of Arts and Media, University of Colorado at Denver, Campus Box 177, P.O. Box 173364, Denver, CO 80217-3364. Phone: 303/556-4891. Fax: 303/556-2335.) Hours: open 24 hours. Admission: free.

Art gallery

PIRATE—A CONTEMPORARY ART OASIS

Pirate—A Contemporary Art Oasis is an artist-run cooperative featuring painting, sculpture, and installations in north Denver.

Pirate—A Contemporary Art Oasis, 3659 Navajo St., Denver, CO 80211. Phone: 303/458-6058. Hours: 7–10 Fri. evenings; 12–5 Sat.–Sun. Admission: free.

Art galleries

REGIS UNIVERSITY

O'Sullivan Arts Center Gallery
Main Hall Garden-Level Gallery

A wide range of professional artworks is presented in changing exhibitions in a 2,500-square-foot gallery at the O'Sullivan Arts Center at Regis University in Denver. The Arts Department also displays student art in the Garden-Level Gallery in Main Hall.

O'Sullivan Arts Center Gallery, Regis University, 3333 Regis Blvd., Denver, CO 80221. Phone: 303/458-3576. Hours: 11–2 Mon., Wed., and Fri.; 12–3 Tues.; 6–9 Thurs. evenings; closed major holidays. Admission: free.

Art galleries

ROCKY MOUNTAIN COLLEGE OF ART AND DESIGN

Philip J. Steele Gallery
Fine Arts Center Exhibition Space

The Rocky Mountain College of Art and Design in Denver has two art galleries—the Philip J. Steele Gallery and the Fine Arts Center Exhibition Space—in separate nearby locations. Changing exhibitions of artworks by students, faculty, and other artists are presented.

Philip J. Steele Gallery, Rocky Mountain College of Art and Design, 6875 E. Evans Ave. (the Fine Arts Center Exhibition Space is at 6850 E. Evans Ave.), Denver, CO 80224. Phone: 303/753-6046. Fax: 303/759-4970. Website: www.rmcad.edu. Hours: 8–6 Mon.–Fri., 9–4 Sat.; closed major holidays. Admission: free.

Art gallery

SCHWAYDER GALLERY AT THE UNIVERSITY OF DENVER

Changing art exhibitions are presented at the University of Denver School of Art and Art History's 2,300-square-foot Schwayder Gallery. Works from the school's collection of late-nineteenth- and early-twentieth-century European and regional art are sometimes displayed in the gallery.

Schwayder Gallery, University of Denver School of Art and Art History, 2121 E. Asbury Ave., Denver, CO 80210. Phone: 303/871-2846. Fax: 303/871-4112. Hours: Jan.–June and Sept.–Nov., 9–4 Mon.–Fri. and 12–4 Sat.–Sun. during exhibitions; closed major holidays. Admission: free.

Art gallery

Singer Gallery, Mizel Arts Center of the Jewish Community Center

Changing art exhibitions relating to Jewish culture are featured in the Singer Gallery, part of the Mizel Arts Center at the Jewish Community Center in Denver.

The gallery, which opened in 1995, schedules four to five exhibitions a year. Recent shows have highlighted Jewish humor, the impact of the McCarthy era on Jewish art, and an examination of the Holocaust through art. Each year, one of the exhibitions is interdisciplinary, accompanied by music, theater, and film programs.

Singer Gallery, Mizel Arts Center, Jewish Community Center, 350 S. Dahlia St., Denver, CO 80216. Phone: 303/399-2660. Fax: 303/320-0042. Website: www.mizelarts.org. Hours: 9–4 Mon.–Fri., 1–4 Sun.; closed major Jewish and national holidays. Admission: free.

Art gallery

Zip 37 Gallery

The Zip 37 Gallery in north Denver is an artists' cooperative that features changing exhibitions of works by regional contemporary painters and sculptors.

Zip 37 Gallery, 3644 Navajo St., Denver, CO 80211. Phone: 303/477-4525. Hours: 7–10 Fri. evenings, 12–5 Sat.–Sun. Admission: free.

Visitor center

United States Mint Visitor Center

Visitors can peruse monetary exhibits and see how 10 billion coins are produced each year at the United States Mint at Denver, one of the nation's four federal-government coinage-production facilities.

The exhibits on coins, early coinage equipment, and gold bullion are housed in the visitor center and along the route of the free 20-minute tours, which take members of the public through the production facilities, where coins are stamped, counted, and placed in shipping bags for transfer to Federal Reserve Banks.

Originally a U.S. Assay Office for gold and silver mined in the nearby mountains, the United States Mint at Denver, commonly known as the Denver Mint, began coining gold and silver in 1906. The Gothic Renaissance building, modeled after the Riccardi Palace in Florence, Italy, has been expanded five time to its current 80,000 square feet.

Operations at the Denver Mint include the blanking and striking of coins and the manufacturing of coining dies. The coinage metals are assayed, melted, and formed into slabs, which are then rolled to the proper thickness. For clad coinage (silver-color coins), two layers of copper-nickel alloy are bonded to a core of pure copper. The strip then is coiled and shipped to the mint (bonding is done elsewhere by private contractors) for blanking with punch presses.

Souvenir coin sets, commemorative coins, and other numismatic items are sold in the mint's salesroom.

United States Mint Visitor Center and Tour, 320 W. Colfax Ave., Denver, CO 80204-2693. Phone: 303/405-4763. Fax: 303/405-4604. Website: www.usmint.gov. Hours: 8–3 Mon.–Fri., but opens at 9 on Wed. from Sept.–Apr. and on the last Wed. of the month from May–Labor Day. Admission and tour: free.

Exhibit space

DAYTON MEMORIAL LIBRARY EXHIBIT WING AT REGIS UNIVERSITY

More than 200 *santos* and *retablos* are featured in the third-floor exhibit wing of the Dayton Memorial Library at Regis University in Denver. The bulk of the collection of wooden carvings of saints and religious paintings on wood was given to the university in 1993 by Rev. Thomas J. Steele, a Jesuit priest who teaches English at the university.

Dayton Memorial Library, Regis University, 3333 Regis Blvd., Denver, CO 80221. Phone: 303/458-4300. Fax: 303/964-5497. Hours: 8 A.M.–11 P.M. Mon.–Thurs., 8–7 Fri.–Sat., 12:30–11 Sun.; closed major holidays. Admission: free.

Exhibit space

DENVER INTERNATIONAL AIRPORT

Changing artistic and cultural exhibitions are presented on the passenger walkway connecting the terminal and Concourse A at Denver International Airport.

Since opening in mid-1997, the exhibition space has featured temporary shows on painting, pottery, tapestry, toys, costumes, folk art, architecture, and other subjects.

The DIA Art Program also administers the airport's permanent artworks and smaller displays.

DIA Art Program, Denver International Airport, 8500 Peña Blvd., Denver, CO 80249. Phone: 303/342-2200, ext. 2521. Fax: 303/342-2525. Website: flydenver.com. Hours: open 24 hours. Admission: free.

Exhibit space

REPUBLIC PLAZA EXHIBIT SPACES

Three or four changing art exhibitions are presented each year in the lobby and concourse exhibit spaces of the Republic Plaza building in downtown Denver. The exhibitions are part of Republic Plaza's Art in Public Spaces program, which began in 1995.

Republic Plaza Art in Public Spaces, 370 17th St., Denver, CO 80202. Phone: 303/733-1868. Hours: 8–6 Mon.–Fri., 8–2 Sat. Admission: free.

Historic house/museum

GOLDA MEIR MUSEUM, AURARIA HIGHER EDUCATION CENTER

The Denver house where Golda Meir, Israeli prime minister from 1969 to 1974, lived has become the Golda Meir Museum on the campus of the Auraria Higher Education Center.

The modest duplex, which she shared with her sister's family, originally was located at 1606–1608 Julian Street. When the house was threatened with demolition in the 1980s, a group of concerned citizens and the Auraria Foundation relocated it to the Auraria campus in 1988.

Meir left her parents' home in Milwaukee in 1913 to live with her sister, Shayna Korngold. She attended North High School for nearly two years before returning to Milwaukee. She also worked part-time as a presser for her brother-in-law at Korngold's Cleaning and Pressing Works near the Brown Palace hotel.

Meir's brief stay in Denver greatly influenced her life. The Korngold house was a social and intellectual haven for numerous Russian-Jewish immigrants. It was in this environment that she discussed politics, met her future husband, and developed her future political philosophy. She later became deeply involved in Zionism, deciding to emigrate to Israel in 1921.

The house, which was designated a Denver historic landmark in 1995, was moved to the campus, restored, and converted into a museum, conference center, and the Golda Meir Center for Political Leadership, a program of Metropolitan State College of Denver, which shares the campus with the Community College of Denver and the University of Colorado at Denver.

The living room and bedroom serve as exhibit spaces. The kitchen and bathroom have been restored to reflect their appearance when Meir lived there. In addition to photographs, the original objects on display include a mezuzah, a small container that holds a piece of parchment on which scripture is written; a *pushke*, a small box used to collect money for Jewish charities; a bank statement from Sam Korngold's business; a bathtub; and a Health Department notice imploring the duplex residents to "bury your dead chickens and stop throwing them out in the alley."

Golda Meir Museum, Auraria Higher Education Center, 1146 9th St. Park, Campus Box A, P.O. Box 173361, Denver, CO 80217-3361. Phone: 303/556-3291. Fax: 303/556-4403. Hours: by appointment. Admission: free.

Historical house/museum

BYERS-EVANS HOUSE AND DENVER HISTORY MUSEUM

Denver's colorful past is revealed at the 1883 Byers-Evans House and the adjoining Denver History Museum, located in the former service wing of the historic home.

This Denver landmark was built by William N. Byers, founder of the *Rocky Mountain News*. In 1889, the house was sold to William Gray Evans, president of the Denver Tramway Company and son of Colorado's second territorial governor, John Evans. The house stayed in the Evans family until donated—complete with furnishings—to the Colorado Historical Society. It opened for guided tours in 1989.

Docents and a short film explain the accomplishments of the Byers and Evans families, the architectural history of the house, and the background of the furniture and family belongings. Byers and Evans were instrumental in bringing the railroad to Denver and starting new business and civic organizations.

The Denver History Museum is a recent addition. It is housed in a renovated wing that once included the laundry room, servants' kitchen, and garage.

The museum combines interactive exhibits with traditional historical displays to tell the story of Denver's people, events, problems, and promises. It contains a wide range of photographs, moving images, artifacts, and other information relating to life in Denver from the mid-nineteenth-century gold rush to World War II.

By touching a video screen on one of the kiosks, visitors can obtain facts and figures about the history of Denver's weather, sports, politics, and transportation; a biographical profile of nearly 500 people who have been influential in Denver's development; and historical photographs of Denver and its residents as they went about their daily lives.

Artifacts and memorabilia, such as clothing, postcards, and political buttons, surround the kiosks in conventional display cases and pull-out drawers.

Byers-Evans House and Denver History Museum, 1310 Bannock St., Denver, CO 80204. Phone: 303/620-4933. Hours: 11–3 Tues.–Sun.; closed state holidays. Admission: adults, $3; seniors, $2.50; children 6–16, $1.50; children under 6, free.

Historical house/museum

GOVERNOR'S MANSION

The Governor's Mansion—formerly the Cheesman-Boettcher Mansion and now officially known as Colorado's Executive Residence—is the home of the governor and his family and the site of numerous social and special events.

The mansion, which underwent an $850,000 renovation in 1999, was built by Walter Cheesman, an early settler and Denver's first pharmacist, for his family in 1908. He died before the building was completed, but his wife and daughter lived in the house until 1926. The house then was sold to Claude Boettcher, whose father started the sugar-beet industry in northern Colorado. The mansion was donated to the state in 1960 by the Boettcher family and became a historic landmark in 1969.

Most of the house retains its original design, including the elegant 60-foot-by-70-foot Palm Room, which opens to a beautiful terraced garden designed by Cheesman; a large library and lounge off the main hall; an ornate dining room; and a grand stairway leading to the living quarters on the upper floors of the three-story red-brick building.

The mansion contains works of art from France, Italy, and China, a large 1740 Beauvais tapestry, a hand-carved Italian Baroque marble-top credenza from the sixteenth century, Italian walnut dining furniture, an eighteenth-century French chandelier with bronze and crystal drops, a Louis XIV desk with ormolu mounts, an 1800 Waterford crystal chandelier, a nymph with porpoises crafted in Italian marble, a collection of jade and quartz sculptures from the sixteenth and seventeenth centuries, and other priceless artifacts.

The mansion is open for free half-hour public tours on Tuesday afternoons from May through August and for a five-day period in early December.

Governor's Mansion, 400 E. 8th Ave., Denver, CO 80203. Phone: 303/866-3682. Fax: 303/866-5739. Hours: May–Aug., 12–2 Tues.; five days in Dec. from 10–1 Tues.–Fri. and 10–3 Sat. Admission: free.

Historical house/museum

GRANT-HUMPHREYS MANSION

The most elegant and historic Beaux Arts–style house in Denver is the 30-room Grant-Humphreys Mansion, erected in 1902 and associated with two prominent names in Colorado history—former governor and smelting-company owner James Benton Grant and wildcat oil industrialist Albert E. Humphreys.

The 15,000-square-foot mansion, opened to the public for guided tours in 1976 by the Colorado Historical Society, was known for its lavish entertaining and still can be rented for parties and meetings.

The turn-of-the-twentieth-century structure, listed on the National Register of Historic Places, actually is a mixture of styles, featuring grandiose proportions, detailed terra-cotta finishes, balustraded porches and balconies, an entablature, and a projecting facade supported by 20-foot columns.

Grant, who built the mansion, established the Grant Smelting Company in Leadville in 1877 and relocated the firm to Denver in 1882—the same year he was elected Colorado's third and youngest governor, serving from 1883 to 1885. Many of Denver's most wealthy and powerful families were among his friends and were guests at receptions, teas, dinners, and dances.

Upon Grant's death, his widow sold the mansion to Humphreys and his wife in 1917. Humphreys made—and lost—two fortunes in logging and mining before amassing a third through wildcat oil speculation. Humphreys remodeled the house, which continued to be a center of Denver social life. The mansion still has many of its period pieces.

Grant-Humphreys Mansion, 770 Pennsylvania St., Denver, CO 80203. Phone: 303/894-2506. Fax: 303/894-2508. Hours: 8:30–5 Mon.–Fri. by appointment; closed major holidays. Admission: donation requested.

Historical house/museum

JUSTINA FORD HOUSE

The Justina Ford House—the home of Colorado's first black female doctor—was built on Arapahoe Street in Denver, but it was relocated in the 1980s to 3091 California Street to house the Black American West Museum & Heritage Center (see separate listing).

The 1889 Victorian house was the home of Dr. Ford from 1912 to 1952. She maintained her office in it for 25 years. She is credited with delivering approximately 7,000 Colorado babies in the 50 years she practiced. She specialized in gynecology, obstetrics, and pediatrics. Many of her patients could not afford to pay, and when they did, she frequently used the money to buy groceries for their families.

Justina Ford House, Black American West Museum & Heritage Center, 3091 California St., Denver, CO 80205. Phone: 303/292-2566. Fax: 303/892-1981. Hours: summer, 10–5 Mon.–Fri., 12–5 Sat.–Sun.; winter, 10–5 Wed.–Fri., 12–5 Sat.–Sun.; closed major holidays. Admission: adults, $3; seniors and students, $2; children 13–17, $1; children 4–12, $.50; children under 4, free.

Historical house/museum

MOLLY BROWN HOUSE MUSEUM

The Colorado lavastone mansion known as the Molly Brown House Museum was home to one of the state's most colorful characters—the "Unsinkable" Molly Brown, who survived the 1912 *Titanic* disaster and assisted with the rescue and relief efforts.

The house, built in 1889, was designed by William Lang, one of Denver's great architects. It was purchased by gold-mine owner J. J. Brown and his wife, Molly, in 1894 and remained in the family until her death in 1932.

The Browns lived in the house only sporadically. From 1900 to 1910, they leased it to various prominent individuals, including Governor and Mrs. James Bradley Orman, while they traveled in Europe and the Orient.

By the 1920s, the building had been converted into a rooming house maintained by Molly's housekeeper. After Molly's death, the house was sold and the interior remodeled by various owners over the next 39 years. When the structure was threatened with demolition in 1970, Historic Denver Inc. was founded to save it. The house was bought the following year and gradually restored to its 1910 Victorian elegance. A carriage house also is located at the rear of the property.

Stone lions guard the entrance to the mansion, which is decorated in velvet, lace, and dark wood and contains period furniture—some of it original—and many art objects owned by the Brown family. Guided tours are conducted by costumed guides.

Molly Brown House Museum, 1340 Pennsylvania St., Denver, CO 80203. Phone: 303/832-4092. Fax: 303/832-2340. Website: www.mollybrown.org. Hours: 10–3:30 Tues.–Sat., 12–3:30 Sun.; also June–Aug., 10–3:30 Mon.; closed major holidays. Admission: adults, $5; seniors, $3.50; children 6–18, $1.50; children under 6, free.

Historical house/museum

PEARCE-McALLISTER COTTAGE

The 1899 Pearce-McAllister Cottage is one of Denver's earliest examples of Colonial Revival architecture, and the site of the Denver Museum of Miniatures, Dolls, and Toys.

The cottage was built by architect Frederick J. Sterner (best known for the design of the Daniels and Fisher Tower) for mining engineer Harold Pearce and his wife, who wanted a house similar to those in older areas of the East Coast.

The Pearce-McAllister Cottage in Denver includes the Museum of Miniatures, Dolls, and Toys. Courtesy Colorado Historical Society.

The cottage was bought by railroad lawyer Henry McAllister and his wife in 1907. They remodeled the interior in the 1920s. The house still contains all of the original McAllister furnishings. It became a historic landmark and a property of the Colorado Historical Society in 1972.

An independent nonprofit museum, the Denver Museum of Miniatures, Dolls, and Toys (see separate listing), is located in the cottage and exhibits its collections throughout the building.

Pearce-McAllister Cottage, 1880 Gaylord St., Denver, CO 80206. Phone: 303/322-1053. Fax: 303/322-3704. Hours: 10–4 Tues.–Sat., 1–4 Sun.; closed major holidays. Admission: adults, $3; seniors, $2; children 2–16, $2; children under 2, free.

Historic house/bed-and-breakfast

CASTLE MARNE

Castle Marne is a Victorian bed-and-breakfast in an 1889 castlelike stone structure with a four-story turret in Denver's Wyman Historic District in the Capitol Hill area.

The building was designed by eclectic architect William Lang as the home of real-estate developer Wilbur S. Raymond, who lived in it for only two years. Among the successive owners was John T. Mason, one of the founders and first curator of the Denver Museum of Natural History, who exhibited his collection of moths and butterflies in the mansion's third-floor ballroom.

In 1918, Mrs. Edwin Van Cise purchased the building, converted it into an apartment house, and lived there until her death in 1937. It was during that period that the house became known as "The Marne," reportedly because Mrs. Van Cise's son, Philip, fought in the Battle of the Marne in World War I and she wanted to commemorate the event.

The historic building had two more owners and then stood empty for six years before Jim and Diane Peiker bought the rundown structure, restored it, and converted it into a romantic 10-room bed-and-breakfast.

Castle Marne, which was listed on the National Register of Historic Places in 1974, has nineteenth-century charm, with large ornate stained-glass windows, chandeliers, a majestic staircase, and finely carved oak woodwork. Rooms are furnished with family heirlooms, antiques, and period reproductions. Breakfast is eaten in the original formal dining room, and afternoon tea is served in the parlor.

Castle Marne, 1572 Race St., Denver, CO 80206. Phones: 303/331-0621 and 800/926-2762. Fax: 303/331-0623. Hours: open 24 hours. Rates: vary with room and season.

Historic house/bed-and-breakfast

QUEEN ANNE INN

Two side-by-side Victorian buildings, designed in the Queen Anne style and erected in 1879 and 1886, constitute the Queen Anne Inn, a romantic bed-and-breakfast in the Clements Historic District near downtown Denver (see separate listing).

Opened in 1987, the inn consists of the 1879 Pierce House, which has 10 guest rooms, and the 1886 Roberts House, which features four new suites. The inn is beautifully decorated with fine antiques, original artwork, and freshly cut flowers.

Queen Anne Inn, 2147 Tremont Pl., Denver, CO 80205. Phones: 303/296-6666 and 800/432-4667. Fax: 303/296-2151. Hours: open 24 hours. Rates: vary with room and season.

Historic building

COLORADO STATE CAPITOL

The Colorado State Capitol, modeled after the historic United States Capitol in Washington, D.C., was completed in 1908, some 18 years after its cornerstone was laid. It is now a National Historic Landmark itself.

The imposing gray granite building overlooks Denver's Civic Center Historic District (see separate listing). Its gold-plated dome is visible for miles. High-rise buildings are forbidden by law from blocking the view.

The inside of the State Capitol is known for its native marble, brass banisters, vaulted ceilings, and rose onyx wainscoting. Stained-glass representations of early settlers and governors are visible above the legislative chambers.

Free 45-minute tours begin every 45 minutes. The building's observation deck affords panoramic views of Denver and is accessible via a 93-step staircase.

Colorado State Capitol, 200 E. Colfax Ave., Denver, CO 80203. Phone: 303/ 866-2604. Fax: 303/866-3855. Hours: tours, 9:30–2:30 Mon.–Fri.; observation deck, 9–3:30 Mon.–Fri. Admission: free.

Historic building

PARAMOUNT THEATER

The Paramount Theater in downtown Denver is the last remaining "movie palace" in the metropolitan area. It was designed in the art deco style in 1930 by prominent architect Temple H. Buell. It now is used primarily for live performances and special events.

The theater, located at 1621 Glenarm Place, was listed on the National Register of Historic Places in 1980. It contains the only existing Publix One Wurlitzer theater organ equipped with twin consoles.

Paramount Theater. Contact: Historic Denver Inc., 871 17th St., Suite 500, Denver, CO 80202. Phone: 303/296-9887. Fax: 303/296-2778.

Historic building

TIVOLI STUDENT UNION, AURARIA HIGHER EDUCATION CENTER

The Auraria Higher Education Center, which is home to three institutions (Community College of Denver, Metropolitan State College of Denver, and the University of Colorado at Denver), features one of the most historic and unusual student unions in the nation.

The student union is located in a former brewery constructed in 1866. The building underwent several expansions in the late nineteenth century and operated as a brewery until 1969. It was originally called Sigi's Brewery and then became successively the Colorado Brewery, Milwaukee Brewery, Tivoli Brewery, and Tivoli Union Brewery. In 1973, the building was listed on the National Register of Historic Places.

The structure, which adjoins the campus, was acquired by the Auraria Higher Education Center and leased to the Hahn Corporation, which turned it into the Tivoli Denver, an upscale shopping mall, in 1985. In 1994, the Tivoli was renovated and opened as a student union for Auraria's combined student body of more than 30,000.

The Tivoli Student Union now houses the student activities/student life office, student government, and some academic offices, as well as study lounges, a food court, a travel agency, a hair salon, an ice-cream and candy shop, a bookstore, a snowboard/skate shop, clothing stores, ticket services, movie theaters, and pool hall and arcade.

In a walking tour of the building, visitors can see historic photos of the Tivoli when it operated as a brewery, authentic copper kettles used in brewing beer, a grain roll mill, and an 1882 opera house built for the Turnvereins, a German gymnastic society.

Tivoli Student Union, Auraria Higher Education Center, 900 Auraria Pkwy., Suite 325, Denver, CO 80204. Phone: 303/556-6330. Fax: 303/556-6346. E-mail: romero@ahecas.ahec.edu. Hours: 6 A.M.–10:30 P.M. daily. Admission: free.

Historic hotel

THE BROWN PALACE

The Brown Palace, an elegant hotel built in 1892, is a National Historic Landmark located in Denver's central business and financial district.

The luxury hotel, constructed of Colorado red granite and Arizona sandstone, was one of the first hotels in the nation to have a central atrium. The Brown Palace's atrium features six stories of wrought-iron balconies rising to a stained-glass ceiling. The ground-floor Italian Renaissance–style lobby retains its intimate late-nineteenth-century feel, with leather sofas and overstuffed chairs arranged in small groupings. Afternoon tea, including sandwiches and pastries, is served in the lobby. The hotel also has four excellent restaurants—Ellyngton's, Palace Arms, Ship Tavern, and Brown Palace Club.

When the Brown Palace was built, during Colorado's mining heyday, it was at the edge of the city. Businessman Henry C. Brown, who donated the land for the State Capitol, hired architect Frank E. Edbrooke to design a building with a triangular footprint to fit the triangular lot he had purchased. As Denver grew, the hotel became part of the downtown.

Edbrooke used blocks of porous terra-cotta for the walls and floors and Mexican onyx for much of the interior. Each of the 230 rooms and suites faces onto a street and has a distinctive Victorian personality. Carvings of native Rocky Mountain animals, sculpted by James Whitehouse in the 1890s, are visible along the building's seventh-floor exterior.

Many prominent figures have stayed at the hotel. President Dwight D. Eisenhower, for example, used the hotel as his presidential campaign headquarters in 1952, and the Beatles were guests while performing at a Red Rocks concert in 1964.

The Brown Palace, 321 17th St., Denver, CO 80202. Phones: 303/297-3111 and 800/321-2599. Fax: 303/297-2954. Website: www.brownpalace.com. Hours: open 24 hours. Rates: vary with room and season.

Historic hotel

OXFORD HOTEL

The Oxford Hotel was built in 1891 during the height of the silver bonanza. Located near Union Station in the historic lower downtown district (now known simply as LoDo), it was conceived as a luxury hotel.

The five-story brick building, designed by architect Frank E. Edbrooke, had marble floors, frescoed walls, fine oriental rugs, private toilets, electric and gas lighting, and Denver's first elevator.

The hotel, listed on the National Register of Historic Places, prospered during Colorado's silver-mining days and the early twentieth century, undergoing expansions in 1902 and 1912. In the 1930s, the hotel was remodeled in an art deco motif. In the 1960s and 1970s, however, LoDo fell on hard times and the hotel deteriorated.

The Oxford Hotel closed and underwent a major overhaul, reopening in 1983, when the neighborhood began to bounce back as art galleries, restaurants, and office buildings sprang up. The lobby, mezzanine, and 81 rooms and suites were remodeled and furnished with English, French, and American antiques. The lobby, which contains Baby Doe Tabor's piano and a fireplace, opens to McCormick's Fish House and Bar, one of Denver's better seafood restaurants, and the Cruise Room, a restored art deco bar from the 1930s.

Oxford Hotel, 1600 17th St., Denver, CO 80202. Phones: 303/628-5400 and 800/228-5838. Hours: open 24 hours. Rates: vary with room and season.

Historic churches

AURARIA HIGHER EDUCATION CENTER
Emmanuel Chapel
St. Elizabeth's Church
St. Cajetan's Church

The Auraria Higher Education Center, home to three institutions of higher education in downtown Denver, is the site of three historic churches—the 1859 Emmanuel Chapel, 1898 St. Elizabeth's Church, and 1926 St. Cajetan's Church.

The churches became part of the campus grounds in 1969 when voters approved a $6-million bond issue for construction of the Auraria campus. The Denver Urban Renewal Authority acquired and cleared the initial 127 acres approved for the campus but left the churches and the Ninth Street historic houses intact (see separate listing for Ninth Street Historic District).

The Emmanuel Chapel, Denver's oldest church structure, was built as a nondenominational Sunday school in 1859 and became an Episcopal chapel in 1874. In 1903, the 20-foot-by-18-foot stone structure was purchased by a Jewish congregation and remodeled into a traditional Orthodox synagogue. However, when Auraria's Jewish population declined and services ceased in 1958, the chapel was sold to an artist, Wolfgang Pogzeba, for use as a studio.

In 1969, the building was listed on the National Register of Historic Places, and four years later it became part of the Auraria campus. It is now an art gallery shared by the three institutions on campus (see separate listing for Emmanuel Gallery).

St. Elizabeth's Church was the second church by that name in the Auraria area. The first was built by German Catholics in 1879, taken over by the Franciscan order in 1887, and later torn down and replaced by the present lavastone structure with a 162-foot spire in 1898.

The interior was remodeled in 1968. Stained-glass windows, new chandeliers, and a bank of organ pipes in the choir loft were added and other improvements made. In 1969, the church was listed on the National Register of Historic Places.

St. Elizabeth's faced one of its greatest challenges in the 1970s with the prospect of urban renewal and the development of the Auraria campus. The parish adjusted by creating the St. Francis InterFaith Center on the site, where students could gather and relax. In 1983, the Franciscans turned St. Elizabeth's over to the Capuchin order. After the property was acquired by the Auraria Foundation, the church building became a meeting and reception space for the campus and community.

St. Cajetan's Church was opened in 1926, as an increasing number of Spanish-speaking people began settling in the predominately German and Irish neighborhoods of Auraria. The brick-and-stucco Catholic church with two belfry towers provided religious services, medical aid, education, and even financial support to its parishioners until 1975, when they moved to a new church of the same name as the Auraria campus evolved. The old church building, which has become a Denver historic landmark and undergone renovation, is now used as a multipurpose auditorium for lectures, concerts, recitals, and other community functions.

Emmanuel Chapel, St. Elizabeth's Church, and St. Cajetan's Church. Contact: Auraria Higher Education Center, Campus Box A, P.O. Box 173361, Denver, CO 80217-3361. Phone: 303/556-3291. Fax: 303/556-4403.

Historic church

TRINITY UNITED METHODIST CHURCH

Trinity United Methodist Church, established in 1859, has occupied its imposing structure since 1888 and houses the longest continuously meeting congregation in Denver. When built, the historic church at 18th Street and Broadway was the tallest structure in Denver.

The church traces its origins to a sermon given by Methodist evangelist George Fisher to a congregation of trappers, miners, Native Americans, and others beneath a cottonwood tree at the confluence of the South Platte River and Cherry Creek in 1859. Several months later, the Denver and Auraria Mission, Trinity's predecessor, was founded by Reverend Jacob Adriance in a cabin.

The congregation soon outgrew the cabin and rented space in a carpenter's shop along Cherry Creek. When the 1864 flood swept the shop away, the church built a twin-towered structure at 14th and Lawrence Streets. Twenty years later, the present structure was erected as the congregation continued to expand. An adjoining education and office building was added in 1926. It was destroyed by fire and rebuilt in 1968, then replaced with a new structure in 1984.

The granite-and-sandstone church building, designed by Robert Roeschlaub, Colorado's first licensed architect, has a massive medieval look, with a soaring spire, steeply rising gables, and beautiful stained-glass windows. The church's imposing pipe organ, installed in 1888 and overhauled in the early 1970s, rises 32 feet and has more than 4,200 fully functional pipes. The church was listed on the National Register of Historic Places in 1970.

Trinity United Methodist Church, 1820 Broadway, Denver, CO 80202. Phone: 303/839-1493. Fax: 303/839-1901. Hours: 8–5 Mon.–Fri., varies Sat., 7–2 Sun.; closed major holidays.

Historic restaurant

BUCKHORN EXCHANGE

The Buckhorn Exchange, Denver's oldest continuously operated restaurant, is known as much for its mounted animals, Native American artifacts, and gun display as it is for its food (particularly game).

The restaurant was founded in 1893 by Henry H. "Shorty" Zietz, a cowboy, big-game hunter, and member of Buffalo Bill Cody's band of scouts, and still occupies its original off-downtown location.

The restaurant has more than 500 taxidermy items on display, including 235 large animal heads and whole animals (among them deer, elk, mountain lion, bighorn sheep, bear, moose, antelope, and bison); a variety of Native American artifacts; and some 125 guns, including a number of rare firearms.

The Buckhorn Exchange received Colorado's first liquor license, which is still displayed over the hand-carved 1857 bar in the upstairs Victorian parlor and saloon. The building's late-nineteenth-century

174 ✦ DENVER

western decor has been restored, and a covered roof garden has been added.

In addition to its steaks, prime rib, and baby-back ribs, the restaurant features elk, bear, deer, buffalo, and other game specialties.

Buckhorn Restaurant, 1000 Osage St., Denver, CO 80204. Phone: 303/534-9505. Fax: 303/534-2814. Hours: 11–10 Mon.–Fri., 5–11 Sat.–Sun.; closed New Year's Day, Mother's Day, Thanksgiving, and Christmas.

Historic cemetery

FAIRMOUNT CEMETERY

Many of Colorado's leading figures are interred in Fairmount Cemetery, founded in 1890 in southeast Denver, which is noted for its impressive architecture.

On the grounds are monuments by highly regarded Italian artists; a 90-foot-high 1891 French Gothic mortuary chapel; and the Gate Lodge, designed by prominent architect H.T.E. Wendell, which houses the cemetery offices and serves as the cemetery's entrance archway.

Among the notable people buried in Fairmount Cemetery are William Newton Byers, founder of the *Rocky Mountain News* and longtime civic leader; Methodist preacher John M. Chivington, who commanded the Colorado militia in the battle of La Glorieta Pass during the Civil War and in the controversial Sand Creek Massacre of 1864; Emily Griffith, founder of the Emily Griffith Opportunity School; Nathaniel P. Hill, a chemistry professor who discovered how to extract gold from embedded quartz and later was elected U.S. senator; John Wesley Iliff and his wife, Elizabeth Sarah, who assembled the greatest cattle herd in the West in the late nineteenth century; David H. Moffat, prominent banker, mine owner, and railroad builder for whom the Moffat Tunnel through the Continental Divide is named; Dr. Florence Sabin, noted doctor, scientist, and humanitarian whose statue is in the U.S. Capitol's Statuary Hall; Robert W. Speer, three-time Denver mayor known for his "City Beautiful" plan; and Henry M. Teller, who built the Teller House in Central City, worked for Colorado statehood, and was elected U.S. senator in Colorado's first election.

Fairmount Cemetery, 430 S. Quebec St., Denver, 80231. Phone: 303/399-0692. Fax: 303/399-1631. Hours: sunrise–sunset daily.

Historic cemetery

FORT LOGAN NATIONAL CEMETERY

Approximately 60,000 U.S. servicemen and -women are buried in Fort Logan National Cemetery on the southwestern edge of Denver. The national cemetery is one of two in Colorado, the other being Fort Lyon National Cemetery near Las Animas in the southeastern part of the state (see separate listing under Fort Lyon).

Fort Logan National Cemetery originated as the post cemetery at Fort Sheridan, whose name was changed to Fort Logan in 1889. The graveyard became a national cemetery in 1950.

The first recorded burial in the old post cemetery was Mabel Peterkin, daughter of an infantry private, in 1889; the first interment in the newly established national cemetery was Army Air Corps master sergeant Harry C. Miller of the 45th Bombing Squadron in 1950. Two Medal of Honor recipients killed in action in Vietnam—Army Major William Edward Adams of the 1st Aviation Brigade and Army First Sergeant Maximo Yabes of the 25th Infantry Division—are also buried here.

Fort Logan National Cemetery, 3698 S. Sheridan Blvd., Denver, CO 80236. Phone: 303/761-0117. Fax: 303/781-9378. Hours: sunrise–sunset daily.

Historic district

BAKER/SOUTH SIDE HISTORIC DISTRICT

The Baker/South Side Historic District is a well-preserved and cohesive middle-class Denver neighborhood built from the 1870s to the 1920s.

The Baker area, closely linked with the larger South Side section east of Broadway, contains approximately 847 structures, including 19 homes designed by William Lang, known for his imaginative residential architecture, and his partner, Marshall Pugh.

The district, listed on the National Register of Historic Places in 1985, underwent its greatest period of development in the late 1880s and early 1890s. Most of the houses were constructed in the Queen Anne style. The district is bounded roughly by Fifth Avenue, Broadway, Alameda Avenue, and Fox Street.

Baker/South Side Historic District. Contact: Historic Denver Inc., 821 17th St., Suite 500, Denver, CO 80202. Phone: 303/296-9887. Fax: 303/296-2778. Website: www.historicdenver.org.

Historic district

CIVIC CENTER HISTORIC DISTRICT

The Civic Center Historic District includes some of Denver's most notable government buildings and cultural facilities, such as the Colorado State Capitol, City and County Building, Denver Art Museum, Denver Public Library, and Colorado History Museum.

The district evolved rather slowly over a period of nearly 40 years from 1910 to 1949, even though the construction of the State Capitol began in 1890. Mayor Henry J. Arnold ordered the ground of the proposed center cleared in 1910, when the city's first public library was built.

The Greek Theatre, Colonnade of City Benefactors, and the Voorhies Memorial Gateway took shape in the 1920s after Arnold's successor, Mayor Robert W. Speer, employed E. H. Bennett, Chicago's city planner, to develop a plan for the Civic Center. The City and County Building was not constructed until 1932. The museum buildings and new library were erected even later.

The Colorado State Capitol, modeled after the U.S. Capitol, was completed in 1908 (see separate listing). This National Historic Landmark, with its gold-plated dome and gray-granite walls, sits on a hill overlooking the Civic Center. The interior features native marble, brass banisters, vaulted ceilings, rose onyx wainscoting, and stained-glass representations of early settlers and governors. Free tours are given throughout the year.

Civic Center Historic District. Contact: Historic Denver Inc., 821 17th St., Suite 500, Denver, CO 80202. Phone: 303/296-9887. Fax: 303/296-2778. Website: www.historicdenver.org.

Historic district

CLEMENTS HISTORIC DISTRICT

The Clements Historic District near downtown Denver was one of the city's first suburbs and home to many early prosperous businessmen. The area was platted in 1864 by Alfred Clements on a bluff southeast of Denver's original settlement.

The district features a number of Victorian buildings, including the Queen Anne Inn (see separate listing), a bed-and-breakfast consisting of two connected Queen Anne–style buildings erected in 1879 and 1886. Benedict Fountain Park, adjacent to the district, provides one of the best views of Denver's skyline.

The historic district, bordered roughly by 21st Street, Tremont Street, 22nd Street, and Glenarm Place, was listed on the National Register of Historic Places in 1979.

Clements Historic District. Contact: Historic Denver Inc., 871 17th St., Suite 500, Denver, CO 80202. Phone: 303/296-9887. Fax: 303/296-2778. Website: www.historicdenver.org.

Historic district

COLE NEIGHBORHOOD HISTORIC DISTRICT

The Cole Neighborhood Historic District in Denver features a considerable number of one- and one-and-a-half-story brick bungalows dating from the 1910s and early 1920s.

These bungalows were a popular type of single-family housing in the first three decades of the twentieth century. They were typically built in the Craftsmen style, although some followed the Mediterranean or Mission Revival styles.

The historic district, located in the 3200–3300 blocks of Vine and Race streets, was listed on the National Register of Historic Places in 1995.

Cole Neighborhood Historic District. Contact: Historic Denver Inc., 821 17th St., Suite 500, Denver, CO 80202. Phone: 303/296-9887. Fax: 303/296-2778. Website: www.historicdenver.org.

Historic district

COUNTRY CLUB HISTORIC DISTRICT

The Country Club Historic District, which contains many large homes designed by Denver's most important early architects, dates from 1902.

The district, which includes the 142 landscaped acres of the Denver Country Club, was listed on the National Register of Historic Places in 1979. Its boundaries were extended in 1985, and it now is bordered by Downing Street, University Boulevard, Fourth Avenue, and the north side of Alameda Avenue.

Among the architects who designed homes in the district are James Sudler and William, Alan, and Arthur Fisher, who also lived in the neighborhood.

Country Club Historic District. Contact: Historic Denver Inc., 821 17th St., Suite 500, Denver, CO 80202. Phone: 303/296-9887. Fax: 303/296-2778. Website: www.historicdenver.org.

Historic district

CURTIS-CHAMPA STREETS HISTORIC DISTRICT

The Curtis-Champa Streets Historic District—one of Denver's oldest residential areas still experiencing neighborhood growth—developed at the turn of the twentieth century as increasing commercial development forced middle-class residents to move from downtown.

The residents, most of whom worked downtown at the time, simply relocated farther down the same streets, which stretch into the downtown area. Many of the 1870–1890 homes still stand in this historic district bounded by 34th, Stout, Downing, and Arapahoe streets. The original district, expanded in 1983, was listed on the National Register of Historic Places in 1975.

Curtis-Champa Streets Historic District. Contact: Historic Denver Inc., 821 17th St., Suite 500, Denver, CO 80202. Phone: 303/296-9887. Fax: 303/296-2778. Website: www.historicdenver.org.

Historic district

GLENARM PLACE HISTORIC RESIDENTIAL DISTRICT

Large stately Victorian homes, mixed with smaller cottages and duplex-style double houses, give the one-block Glenarm Place Historic Residential District its diverse turn-of-the-twentieth-century architectural character.

The historic district, running from 2417 to 2462 Glenarm Place in Denver, features buildings of a quality and scale unlike those in the surrounding area. The houses were constructed during a period of economic growth in the late nineteenth century and reflect the opulence of the era.

The district was listed on the National Register of Historic Places in 1983.

Glenarm Place Historic Residential District. Contact: Historic Denver Inc., 821 17th St., Suite 500, Denver, CO 80202. Phone: 303/296-9887. Fax: 303/296-2778. Website: www.historicdenver.org.

Historic district

HIGHLAND PARK/SCOTTISH VILLAGE HISTORIC DISTRICT

Scottish Village is the last remaining section of Highland Park, a neighborhood planned and developed in 1874 by General William Jackson Palmer and Dr. William A. Bell, key figures in Colorado's early residential development.

Highland Park is one of only three known examples of nineteenth-century Romantic community planning along the Front Range (the other two are Corona Park in south Pueblo and the Fifth Addition in Colorado Springs)—all of them associated with Palmer and Bell.

What remains of Highland Park, which is characterized by curving streets with Scottish names, includes 136 brick and stone structures,

most of which are small and residential. The historic district, bounded
by Zuni Street, Dunkeld Place, Clay Street, and 32nd Avenue east of
Federal Boulevard, was listed on the National Register of Historic Places
in 1985.

*Highland Park/Scottish Village Historic District. Contact: Historic Denver Inc., 821
17th St., Suite 500, Denver, CO 80202. Phone: 303/296-9887. Fax: 303/296-
2778. Website: www.historicdenver.org.*

Historic district

HUMBOLDT STREET HISTORIC DISTRICT

The Humboldt Street Historic District contains some of Denver's
best residential architecture, built just before and just after 1900. In
1972, it was the city's first residential area to be designated a historic
district.

The district, which runs from 10th to 12th avenues on Humboldt
Street, features homes designed by some of Denver's most distinguished
architects. The development of Cheesman Park on the district's eastern
boundary stimulated much of the growth in the early twentieth century.

*Humboldt Street Historic District. Contact: Historic Denver Inc., 821 17th St.,
Suite 500, Denver, CO 80202. Phone: 303/296-9887. Fax: 303/296-2778.
Website: www.historicdenver.org.*

Historic district

LARIMER SQUARE HISTORIC DISTRICT

Larimer Square is a one-block historic downtown district consisting
of distinctive shops, restaurants, and nightclubs in 1880s Victorian buildings in one of Denver's oldest business areas.

Larimer Square (which is a street rather than a square) is located in
the 1400 block of Larimer Street, in the area where Denver started in
1858. The street was an important business center in the city's early days
but slid into severe decline before experiencing a resurgence, beginning
in the 1960s, as a shopping and entertainment area.

The historic district, listed on the National Register of Historic
Places in 1973, now has 28 specialty shops, seven restaurants, two night-
clubs, and other facilities. It is also the site of special events such as
Oktoberfest, Winterfest, and the Summer Night Concert Series.

*Larimer Square Historic District. Contact: Larimer Square Management, 1400
Larimer St., Suite 300, Denver, CO 80202. Phone: 303/534-2367. Fax: 303/
623-1041.*

Historic district

LOWER DOWNTOWN HISTORIC DISTRICT

Denver's Lower Downtown Historic District—affectionately known as LoDo—is a 25-block area of turn-of-the-twentieth-century warehouse, factory, and office buildings. It has recently undergone a renaissance as a popular mixed-use area filled with art galleries, restaurants, bars, shops, loft apartments, and business and professional offices.

The historic district, part of the original site of Denver, is bordered by Wynkoop, 20th, Market, and 13th streets and is adjacent to and northwest of the central business district. Unofficially, however, it is considered to extend as far as the Platte River, 23rd Street, Lawrence Street, and Speer Boulevard.

The district, which was listed on the National Register of Historic Places in 1988, includes more than 40 art galleries, nearly 60 restaurants and clubs, approximately 1,000 residential units, and dozens of retail businesses and professional services. Among the district's historic buildings are Union Station, the Oxford Hotel, and the 18th Street Atrium/Icehouse; Coors Field and Larimer Square are within the unofficial LoDo area.

Lower Downtown Historic District. Contact: Lower Downtown District Inc., 1616 17th St., Suite 368, Denver, CO 80202. Phone: 303/628-5428. Fax: 303/628-5495. E-mail: info@lodo.org. Website: www.lodo.org.

Historic district

NINTH STREET HISTORIC DISTRICT, AURARIA HIGHER EDUCATION CENTER

The Ninth Street Historic District, located in the heart of the downtown Auraria Higher Education Center, is the oldest restored residential block in Denver.

Three public institutions of higher learning—Community College of Denver, Metropolitan State College of Denver, and the University of Colorado at Denver—now share facilities and services on the Auraria campus.

The campus is located on the western bank of Cherry Creek, where the Russell brothers staked out the town of Auraria in 1858. It was the Russells' small gold strike that started the 1859 gold rush to the Rockies. Auraria became part of Denver in 1860.

The 14 structures in the three-acre Ninth Street Historic Park were saved and restored by Historic Denver Inc. when the land was acquired and cleared for construction of the Auraria campus. They represent middle-class housing of the late nineteenth century.

The two earliest houses were built in 1872; a number of other houses were constructed before 1876. The grocery store (now a restaurant) and two bungalows were built shortly after the turn of the twentieth century. The duplex where former Israeli prime minister Golda Meir once lived also has been moved to the area (see separate listing for the Golda Meir Museum).

The street retains its original granite curbing, and old flagstone from Auraria was used in replacing sidewalks. The street lamps came from Colorado Springs. The landscaping was designed to create an open village green area while retaining the linear quality of the streetscape. A small amphitheater was added south of the street.

Four other historic buildings are located on the Auraria campus—the 1866 Tivoli Student Union, 1859 Emmanuel Chapel, 1898 St. Elizabeth's Church, and 1926 St. Cajetan's Church (see separate listings).

Ninth Street Historic District. Contact: Auraria Higher Education Center, Campus Box A, P.O. Box 173361, Denver, CO 80217-3361. Phone: 303/556-3291. Fax: 303/556-4403.

Historic district

OLD HIGHLAND BUSINESS HISTORIC DISTRICT

The Old Highland Business Historic District, built between 1885 and 1890, contains a mixture of stores and office buildings reflecting a bygone era. The area came into being because developers of the nearby "utopian" town of Highlands (see following listing for Potter Highlands Historic District) would not permit commercial buildings.

The district, bordered by 15th, Boulder, 16th, and Central streets, is significant because of its architecture and its once important commercial role. It was listed on the National Register of Historic Places in 1979.

Old Highlands Business Historic District. Contact: Historic Denver Inc., 821 17th St., Suite 500, Denver, CO 80202. Phone: 303/296-9887. Fax: 303/296-2778. Website: www.historicdenver.org.

Historic district

POTTER HIGHLANDS HISTORIC DISTRICT

The Potter Highlands Historic District is a 36-block residential neighborhood in the northern portion of the Highlands, a community located on the hills west of the South Platte River. Originally planned as a utopian suburb in 1872, the Highlands was intended to have cleaner air and purer water than Denver's, and to attract residents of a higher moral character.

The residential neighborhood did not develop as anticipated, because public transportation into downtown Denver was inadequate. However, from the 1870s through the late 1930s, some of the area's prominent residents built exceptional homes in a wide range of architectural styles. Historic structures include a Prairie-style house and some of Denver's best examples of nineteenth-century-vernacular wood-frame houses.

The historic district, bounded by 38th Avenue, Zuni Street, 32nd Street, and Federal Boulevard, was listed on the National Register of Historic Places in 1986.

Potter Highlands Historic District. Contact: Historic Denver Inc., 821 17th St., Suite 500, Denver, CO 80202. Phone: 303/296-9887. Fax: 303/296-2778. Website: www.historicdenver.org.

Historic district

SAN RAFAEL HISTORIC DISTRICT

San Rafael Historic District is a well-preserved middle-class Denver neighborhood platted in 1877 by Henry A. DuBois, who named it for his hometown in California.

Development of the neighborhood, located eight blocks northeast of downtown, began in 1888 and continued until the silver crash of 1893. The historic district is bounded by Washington Street, 26th Avenue, Downing Street, and 20th Avenue. It was listed on the National Register of Historic Places in 1986.

San Rafael Historic District. Contact: Historic Denver Inc., 821 17th St., Suite 500, Denver, CO 80202. Phone: 303/296-9887. Fax: 303/296-2778. Website: www.historicdenver.org.

Historic district

STONEMEN'S ROW HISTORIC DISTRICT

The Stonemen's Row Historic District, located on the south side of 28th Avenue between Umatilla and Vallejo streets in Denver, consists of eight adjacent duplexes that form a small but unusually harmonious historic district.

The stone houses were built as rental units between 1891 and 1893 and are noteworthy for their unity of design, use of stone materials, and fine workmanship. Their facades, which make the buildings seem grander than they really are, have the heaviness and weight characteristic of Romanesque Revival architecture. The interiors are simple and undistinguished, but the exteriors are a monument to the talent of Denver's late-nineteenth-century stonemasons.

The duplexes were listed on the National Register of Historic Places in 1984.

Stonemen's Row Historic District. Contact: Historic Denver Inc., 821 17th St., Suite 500, Denver, CO 80202. Phone: 303/296-9887. Fax: 303/296-2778. Website: www.historicdenver.org.

Historic district

SWALLOW HILL HISTORIC DISTRICT

The Swallow Hill Historic District is associated with many of Denver's early business and political leaders and boasts one of the most significant groupings of turn-of-the-twentieth-century, architect-designed homes in the region.

The district, bounded by Clarkson Street, 17th Avenue, Downing Street, and Colfax Avenue, was developed between 1886 and 1910. It was listed on the National Register of Historic Places in 1988. Many of the homes in the neighborhood are individual historic landmarks. Today, Swallow Hill includes a mixture of residences, offices, and condominiums.

Swallow Hill Historic District. Contact: Historic Denver Inc., 821 17th St., Suite 500, Denver, CO 80202. Phone: 303/296-9887. Fax: 303/296-2778. Website: www.historicdenver.org.

Historic district

WESTSIDE NEIGHBORHOOD HISTORIC DISTRICT

The Westside Neighborhood Historic District, near Denver's Lincoln Park, looks much as it did in the late nineteenth century. The middle- and lower-income neighborhood, which came into being shortly after the 1858 settlement of Denver City, still retains many of its original small brick houses and red sandstone sidewalks, and much of its stone curbing, iron yard fencing, and curbside tree plantings. The historic district, bounded by Mariposa, Lipan, and Kalamath streets and 13th and 14th avenues, was listed on the National Register of Historic Places in 1975.

Westside Neighborhood Historic District. Contact: Historic Denver Inc., 821 17th St., Suite 500, Denver, CO 80202. Phone: 303/296-9887. Fax: 303/296-2778. Website: www.historicdenver.org.

DILLON

History museum

SUMMIT HISTORICAL MUSEUM

Three historic buildings form part of the Summit Historical Museum complex operated by the Summit Historical Society in Dillon. They include the 1883 Dillon schoolhouse, the 1885 Lula Meyers Ranch House, and a 1936 cabin.

Summit Historical Museum, Summit Historical Society, 403 LaBonte St., Dillon, CO 80435. (Contact: Summit Historical Society, P.O. Box 745, Breckenridge, CO 80424-0745. Phone: 970/453-9022. Fax: 970/453-8135.) Hours: Memorial Day–Labor Day, 1–5 Tues.–Sat.; closed remainder of the year. Admission: donation requested.

DINOSAUR

Visitor Centers

DINOSAUR NATIONAL MONUMENT

Headquarters Visitor Center
Quarry Visitor Center

The National Park Service's Dinosaur National Monument, where dinosaurs once roamed and their fossilized bones are now preserved in solid rock, straddles the border between northwestern Colorado and northeastern Utah and has two visitor centers, one in each state. The Headquarters Visitor Center is located two miles east of Dinosaur, Colorado, and the Quarry Visitor Center is seven miles north of Jensen, Utah.

Dinosaur National Monument, established in 1915, preserves internationally significant paleontological resources, cultural sites and artifacts, and the scenic canyon country of the Green and Yampa rivers. It has a collection of more than 35,000 specimens representing all categories of the monument's resources.

The Headquarters Visitor Center serves as the gateway to the monument area and provides an orientation. However, it does not include any dinosaur fossils in its informational exhibits.

It is at the Quarry Visitor Center that a 150-foot rock wall with more than 1,400 dinosaur bones can be seen. Some of the bones can even be touched. The wall contains 150-million-year-old fossils, such as those of the giant vegetarian *Stegosaurus* and meat-eating *Allosaurus*. Exhibits also explain various aspects of paleontology and dinosaur life.

Headquarters Visitor Center, Dinosaur National Monument, 4545 U.S. Hwy. 40, Dinosaur, CO 81610. Phone: 970/374-3000. Fax: 970/374-3003. Hours: winter, 8–4:30 Mon.–Fri., closed weekends and holidays; summer, hours may be extended (call 970/374-3000 for current information). Admission: free, but monument admission is $10 per vehicle.

Quarry Visitor Center, Dinosaur National Monument, P.O. Box 128, Jensen, UT 84035. Phone: 435/789-2115. Hours: winter, 8–4:30 daily (closed New Year's Day, Thanksgiving, and Christmas); summer, hours are extended (call 435/789-2115 for current information). Admission: free, but monument admission is $10 per vehicle.

DOLORES

Archaeology museum/interpretive center

ANASAZI HERITAGE CENTER

The Anasazi Heritage Center near Dolores is an archaeological museum and interpretive center explaining the history and culture of the Four Corners region. The center is operated by the U.S. Bureau of Land Management.

The 40,000-square-foot facility, which opened in 1988 as part of the McPhee Dam and Reservoir project, preserves and displays artifacts found on, and records concerning, public lands in the area, one of the richest archaeological regions in the nation.

The center has more than 2.5 million artifacts, archaeological samples, and manuscripts pertaining to excavations in the southwestern corner of Colorado, as well as films, exhibits, a pithouse replica, and a hands-on discovery area that explores the region's archaeology, history, and Pueblo, Ute, and Navajo lifeways.

Two twelfth-century Native American ruins are also on the museum grounds. The Dominguez and Escalante pueblos were named after Spanish friars who explored the area in 1776 and became the first to record prehistoric ruins in Colorado. The ruins were excavated and stabilized 200 years later. The Escalante Pueblo has a planned, formal architecture, whereas the Dominguez site is smaller and simpler. However, the latter has produced many artifacts, including nearly 7,000 turquoise, jet, and shell beads; ceramic vessels; bone tools; a shell-and-frog pendant; and other items, some typical of the Chaco Anasazi, a branch of the culture centered in New Mexico.

"Anasazi" is the Navajo name for an agricultural people who lived in the area between A.D. 1 and A.D. 1300. Their descendants belong to several modern tribes known as "Pueblo" Indians, referring to the apartment-house-style villages developed by the Anasazi. Many of these structures still survive.

Anasazi Heritage Center, Bureau of Land Management, 27501 Colo. Hwy. 184, Dolores, CO 81323. Phone: 970/882-4811. Fax: 970/882-7035. E-mail: meastin@co.blm.gov. Website: www.co.blm.gov/ahc/hmepge.htm. Hours: Mar.– Oct., 9–5 daily; Nov.–Feb., 9–4 daily; closed New Year's Day, Thanksgiving, and Christmas. Admission: adults, $3; children 17 and under and school groups, free.

DURANGO

History museum

ANIMAS MUSEUM

The Animas Museum in Durango is devoted to the history of the San Juan Basin, with emphasis on La Plata County. Founded in 1978, the museum, operated by the La Plata County Historical Society, is housed in the former 1908 Animas City School Building. An 1870s hand-hewn log cabin also is located on the grounds.

The museum has 2,500 square feet of exhibit space dealing with local and regional history, Southwest Indian arts and crafts, and a restored early schoolroom.

Animas Museum, 3065 W. 2nd Ave., P.O. Box 3384, Durango, CO 81302. Phone: 970/259-2402. Hours: May–Oct., 10–6 Mon.–Sat.; closed remainder of the year. Admission: adults, $1.75; children under 12, free.

Railroad museum

DURANGO & SILVERTON NARROW GAUGE RAILROAD MUSEUM

The history of railroading in southwestern Colorado is presented at the recently opened Durango & Silverton Narrow Gauge Railroad Museum, located in a nineteenth-century roundhouse near the Durango depot.

The roundhouse and an attached machine shop were built in 1881 but badly damaged in a devastating 1989 fire. Fortunately, workers were able to restore the structures in time for the 1990 summer tourist season.

Two brick walls that survived the fire are now part of the museum, which re-creates the atmosphere of the old roundhouse. The history of the Durango & Silverton Narrow Gauge Railroad is displayed on the walls. In addition, viewing windows allow visitors to observe engine inspections and repairs carried out by railroad mechanics in the working part of the roundhouse.

The museum, which opened in 1998, takes up almost half of the 36,000-square-foot roundhouse and occupies 8 of the 17 bays. Two bays contain glass cases filled with railroad historical items such as tools, signs, steam-engine gauges, oilcans, track equipment, furniture, and original communications equipment.

The remaining six bays feature early railroad equipment, including Engines #42 and #493, used by the Denver & Rio Grande and Rio Grande Southern railroads. Visitors can climb into the #493 locomotive, sit on the engineer's seat, and imagine what it felt like to operate an early coal-fired, steam-powered train.

Among the other displays are the General Palmer business car, immigrant sleeper cars, historic cabooses, and informational signs and videos. Visitors can look through viewing doors and watch the train-yard turntable, where working steam engines are turned around for their next trip out of the yard.

The Durango & Silverton Narrow Gauge Railroad also has a second museum in Silverton—the D&SNG Silverton Freight Yard Museum—devoted to the history of freight hauling in the region (see separate listing under Silverton). Admission to the museums is included in the price of round-trip train tickets.

Durango & Silverton Narrow Gauge Railroad Museum, 479 Main Ave., Durango, CO 81301. Phone: 970/247-2733. Fax: 970/247-9302. Website: www.durangotrain.com. Hours: May–Oct., 7 A.M.–8 P.M. daily; remainder of year, 8–5 daily; closed Christmas. Admission: adults, $5; children 5–11, $2.50; children under 5, free. Museum admission also included in round-trip train tickets. Summer round-trip ticket: adults, $53; children 5–11, $27. Winter round-trip ticket: adults, $41.55; children 5–11, $20.80.

Archive/library/museum

CENTER OF SOUTHWEST STUDIES, FORT LEWIS COLLEGE

The Center of Southwest Studies at Fort Lewis College in Durango was established in 1964 as a museum and research facility. It was also charged with developing an interdisciplinary Southwest curriculum drawing on anthropology, art, literature, history, and sociology.

The center now has an extensive collection of southwestern artifacts, historical records, photographs, books, and other printed materials. Holdings include 5,000 reels of microfilm, 600 oral histories, 35,000 photographs, 15,000 volumes, 7,000 linear shelf feet of manuscripts, and numerous periodicals, unbound printed materials, and artifacts.

Plans call for the Center of Southwest Studies to move to a new $7.5-million facility in 2000.

Center of Southwest Studies, Fort Lewis College, 1000 Rim Dr., Durango, CO 81301-3999. Phone: 970/247-7456. Fax: 970/247-7422. Hours: academic terms (late Aug. to mid-Dec., and Jan. through May), 9–5:30 Mon.–Thurs., 9–4:30 Fri., 2–5 Sun. (closed Sat. and holidays); summer, 10–2 Mon.–Fri. Admission: free.

Art gallery

FORT LEWIS COLLEGE ART GALLERY

Fort Lewis College Art Gallery in Durango is a showcase for artworks by students, faculty members, and local and regional artists. Traveling exhibitions are also presented in this 130-foot-long gallery opened in 1970 by the Art Department.

Fort Lewis College Art Gallery, 101 Art Bldg., 1000 Rim Dr., Durango, CO 81301-3999. Phone: 970/247-7167. Fax: 970/247-1774. Hours: Sept.–May, 10–4 Mon.–Fri.; closed major holidays and in summer. Admission: free.

Historic railroad

DURANGO & SILVERTON NARROW GAUGE RAILROAD

One of the nation's most popular historic railroads is the Durango & Silverton Narrow Gauge Railroad, which wends its way for 45 miles through the rugged San Juan Mountains from Durango to Silverton and back again.

Winding along the Las Animas River, this scenic route—whose construction is considered an engineering marvel—is one of the last vestiges of the old Denver & Rio Grande Railroad, which served many of Colorado's early mining towns. The Silverton Branch, as it was known, was completed in 1882 and operated by the Denver & Rio Grande until 1981, when it was sold to a private operator, renamed, and sold again in 1998. It became a National Historic Landmark in 1967.

Today, approximately 200,000 visitors a year ride the coal-fired steam train, which takes two-and-a-half to three hours to make the smoky trip from Durango to Silverton. The train makes a two-hour layover in Silverton before returning to Durango, so the expedition is typically an all-day affair. Four round-trips depart from Durango daily in the summer. During the winter season (Thanksgiving weekend and mid-December to early May), there is one departure a day, and, due to snow, the train goes only as far as Cascade Canyon.

The railroad operates two museums—the Durango & Silverton Narrow Gauge Railroad Museum in a roundhouse adjacent to the Durango depot, and the Silverton Freight Yard Museum near the Silverton Terminus (see separate listings). Round-trip train tickets include admission to the museums.

Durango & Silverton Narrow Gauge Railroad, 479 Main Ave., Durango, CO 81301. Phone: 970/347-2733. Fax: 970/259-9349. Website: www.durangotrain.com. Hours: summer—train to Silverton departs at 7:30, 8:15, 9, and 9:45 A.M. daily; winter—train to Cascade Canyon departs at 10 A.M. (closed first three weeks in Nov. and on Christmas). Summer round-trip ticket: adults, $53; children 5–11, $27; children under 5, free. Winter round-trip ticket: adults, $41.55; children 5–11, $20.80; children under 5, free.

Historic hotel

STRATER HOTEL

The Strater Hotel in Durango offers guests Victorian charm and a taste of the Old West. Built in 1887, the restored red-brick hotel has 93 individually designed period rooms with Victorian furnishings, a turn-of-the-twentieth-century honky-tonk saloon, and an old-fashioned summer melodrama theater.

This Durango landmark also features the nation's largest collection of American Victorian walnut antiques, priceless artifacts (including a Stradivarius violin and commemorative Winchester rifle), and ragtime piano music in the Diamond Belle Saloon.

In addition, the hotel has a restaurant (Henry's) with crystal chandeliers, oriental rugs, and southwestern cuisine. Six meeting and banquet rooms are also available.

The hotel has been owned and operated by the Barker family for three generations.

The 1887 Strater Hotel is a Durango landmark. Courtesy Strater Hotel.

Strater Hotel, 699 Main Ave., P.O. Drawer E, Durango, CO 81302. Phone: 970/ 247-4431. Fax: 970/259-2208. Website: www.strater.com. Hours: open 24 hours. Rates: vary with rooms and season.

Historic hotel

GENERAL PALMER HOTEL

Built in 1898, the General Palmer Hotel in Durango is named for General William Jackson Palmer, the calvary officer who brought railroad service to southern Colorado. The hotel, which has 39 Victorian rooms and suites, is located near the Denver & Silverton Narrow Gauge Railroad depot in Durango's Main Avenue Historic District.

General Palmer Hotel, 567 Main Ave., Durango, CO 81301. Phones: 970/247-4747 and 800/523-3358. Fax: 970/247-1332. Hours: open 24 hours. Rates: vary with room and season.

Historic districts

DURANGO MAIN AVENUE HISTORIC DISTRICT AND EAST THIRD AVENUE HISTORIC RESIDENTIAL DISTRICT

Durango has two historic districts—the Durango Main Avenue Historic District, which encompasses the historic downtown area, and the East Third Avenue Historic Residential District (known as The Boulevard), which features imposing Victorian homes from the turn of the twentieth century.

The Durango Main Avenue Historic District, listed in the National Register of Historic Places in 1980, consists of 86 buildings representing the architecture of the late nineteenth and early twentieth centuries.

The historic district is bounded roughly by Fifth Street, the Durango & Silverton Narrow Gauge Railroad right-of-way, 12th Street, and the alley between Main and Second Avenues. It includes such buildings as the 1882 railroad depot, 1887 Strater Hotel, and 1898 General Palmer Hotel (see separate listings), as well as the 1895 Palace Hotel, 1897 Newman Building, and other Victorian buildings now housing shops, galleries, and restaurants.

Durango was founded in 1879 when the small farming community of Animas City, two miles north of present-day Durango, refused to donate land to the Denver & Rio Grande Railroad for a depot. As a result, the railroad, which sought to extend its tracks from the eastern plains to the Animas River Valley, developed a new town site and rail hub—Durango—which soon became a mining-supply and smelter center for the region. Today, the town is a major tourist attraction and serves as a gateway to the Mesa Verde National Park and other sights in the area.

The East Third Avenue Historic Residential District, two blocks east of Main Avenue, contains many former homes of railroad, smelting, and business leaders. Architectural styles represented include Greek Revival, Gothic Revival, Queen Anne, Spanish colonial, and Mission designs. The district was listed in the National Register of Historic Places in 1984.

Durango Main Avenue Historic District and East Third Avenue Historic Residential District. Contact: Durango Chamber of Commerce, 111 S. Camino del Rio, P.O. Box 2587, Durango, CO 81302. Phones: 970/247-0312 and 800/525-8855. Fax: 970/385-7884.

DYERVILLE

Historic ghost town

DYERVILLE GHOST TOWN

The town of Dyerville, located just below Boreas Pass, 11 miles southeast of Breckenridge, sprang up around the cabin of preacher/prospector John L. Dyer, a fire-and-brimstone Methodist circuit rider, in the early 1880s.

In 1881, Dyer built the cabin a short distance from the Warriors Mark Mine, which he discovered. He set out to develop the mine, attracting other gold-seekers, a mill, and a spur of the Denver, South Park & Pacific Railroad. However, he sold his mining claim the following year and returned to spiritual pursuits, giving rousing sermons to miners in the area.

Dyerville prospered until 1885, then fell into decline. Mining ceased entirely in 1908, and the town was abandoned shortly thereafter. The ruins of cabins are still visible at the site.

Dyerville Ghost Town, 11 miles southeast of Breckenridge. Contact: Summit Historical Society, 309 N. Main St., P.O. Box 745, Breckenridge, CO 80424-0745. Phone: 970/453-9022. Fax: 970/453-8135.

EADS

History museum

KIOWA COUNTY MUSEUM

The Kiowa County Museum, operated by the Kiowa County Historical Society, opened in 1970 in a former bank building in Eads. The museum focuses on the homesteader period of the early twentieth century, featuring three period rooms—a living room, kitchen, and bedroom. But the museum also contains a diverse collection of other historical materials, including cowboy gear, clothing, farm equipment, photographs, and Native American arrowheads and relics.

Kiowa County Museum, Main St., P.O. Box 787, Eads, CO 81036. Phone: 719/438-2250. Hours: Memorial Day to mid-Sept., 1–4:30 Mon.–Sat. and by appointment; closed remainder of the year. Admission: free.

EAGLE

History museum

EAGLE COUNTY HISTORICAL SOCIETY MUSEUM

The Eagle County Historical Society Museum occupies a large barn in Chambers Park in Eagle. The park also contains a visitor center and rest area for travelers on Interstate 70.

Opened in 1992, the museum displays a range of items relating to the county history, including farming and mining equipment, carriages, Native American artifacts, and recreational materials. The museum grounds also feature a restored 1910 store building and a railroad caboose.

Eagle County Historical Society Museum, Chambers Park, Fairgrounds Rd., P.O. Box 192, Eagle, CO 81631. Phone: 970/328-6464. Hours: Memorial Day–Sept., 10–4 daily; closed remainder of the year. Admission: free.

EASTONVILLE

Historic ghost town

EASTONVILLE GHOST TOWN

The farming town of Eastonville, located in northern El Paso County about 12 miles south of Elbert, was one of the most prosperous agricultural communities in eastern Colorado, even touting itself as the "potato capital of the world."

The town got rail service in 1881 and a post office in 1883; boasted three churches, three hotels, and a two-story school by the 1890s; and reached its peak in the first decade of the twentieth century, when the population approached 500. But a potato blight, drought, and a major 1935 flood that washed away many of the town's buildings destroyed the community.

Many working farms and ranches still surround the old town site, but only scattered abandoned structures remain in Eastonville itself.

Eastonville Ghost Town, 12 miles south of Elbert. Contact: Colorado Springs Museum, 215 S. Tejon St., Colorado Springs, CO 80903. Phone: 719/578-6650. Fax: 719/578-6718. E-mail: cosmuseum@ci.colospgs.co.us. Website: www.colorado-springs.com/cultredu/museums.htm.

EMPIRE

Historic hotel

PECK HOUSE

Colorado's oldest operating hotel is the Peck House, an 1862 stage-coach stop in Empire on the former stage and wagon road (now U.S. Highway 40) up Berthoud Pass.

Peck House originally was a four-room home built by mining prospector James Peck for his wife. They opened their mountain home to travelers, prospectors, and investors who were exploring the West and Colorado's mining possibilities.

A second story and a verandah were later added, as was running water from a spring above the house. Today, the hotel has 11 guest rooms, all restored in 1986 with authentic period furniture. Guests can see the rolling Empire Valley from the front guest rooms, dining room, lounge, and barroom.

Among the many prominent figures who have stayed at the hotel are President Ulysses S. Grant, General William Tecumseh Sherman, and circus showman P. T. Barnum.

Peck House, 83 Dunny Ave., P.O. Box 428, Empire, CO 80438. Phone: 303/569-9870. Fax: 303/569-2743. Hours: open 24 hours. Rates: vary with room and season.

ENGLEWOOD

Art gallery

COYLE GALLERY AT ST. MARY'S ACADEMY

St. Mary's Academy in Englewood displays the artworks of students, and sometimes others, in its Coyle Gallery, housed in the institution's high-school building.

The academy, founded by the Sisters of Loretto in 1868, is the second-oldest private institution in the state and has been located on the 22-acre site of the historic Hickerson House in Cherry Hills Village since 1951.

Coyle Gallery, St. Mary's Academy, 4545 S. University Blvd., Englewood, CO 80110-6099. Phone: 303/762-8300. Fax: 303/783-6201. Hours: 8–4:30 Mon.–Fri. when classes are in session; closed major holidays. Admission: free.

Sculpture park

MUSEUM OF OUTDOOR ARTS

See description under Greenwood Village.

ESTES PARK

History museum

ESTES PARK AREA HISTORICAL MUSEUM

The Estes Park Area Historical Museum, founded in 1962 and operated by the Town of Estes Park, chronicles the community's history and that of the surrounding area.

The museum consists of a main exhibit building, a turn-of-the-twentieth-century homestead cabin, and the original administration building for Rocky Mountain National Park.

Among the collections and exhibits are pioneer artifacts; early clothing, implements, utensils, tools, and photographs; a Stanley Steamer automobile; and other historical materials relating to people and events of the area.

Estes Park Area Historical Museum, 200 4th St., P.O. Box 1601, Estes Park, CO 80517. Phone: 970/586-6256. Fax: 970/586-6909. E-mail: epmuseum @juno.com. Website: http://estes.on-line.com/epmuseum/. Hours: May–Oct., 10–5 Mon.–Sat., 1–5 Sun.; remainder of the year, 10–5 Sat., 1–5 Sun. Admission: adults, $2.50; seniors, $2; children 5–12, $1; children under 5, free; families, $10.

History museum

LULA W. DORSEY MUSEUM

The history of the YMCA of the Rockies and the surrounding area is the focus of the Lula W. Dorsey Museum, located on the campgrounds near Estes Park.

Opened in 1979, the museum consists of a two-story, 5,000-square-foot building and two historic cabins, one of which replicates the inside of a camp cabin in 1949. The museum building contains artifacts, memorabilia, photographs, and room settings representing various periods in the camp's history.

Lula W. Dorsey Museum, YMCA of the Rockies, Estes Park Center, 2515 Tunnel Rd., P.O. Box 20500, Estes Park, CO 80511-2800. Phone: 970/586-3341, ext. 1136. Fax: 970/586-6078. Hours: Memorial Day–Labor Day, 9–5 Mon.–Sat., 12–4 Sun.; remainder of the year, 9–11 and 12–4 Mon.–Fri., 9–3 Sat. Admission: $1 suggested donation.

History museum

STANLEY MUSEUM

The Stanley Museum opened in 1998 in two rooms on the lower level of the Stanley Hotel in Estes Park. It is operated by volunteers as a branch of the original and much larger Stanley Museum in Kingfield, Maine, where the Stanley family settled after emigrating from England in the early nineteenth century.

The satellite museum contains miniature replicas of Stanley Steamers, steam-powered automobiles invented by F. O. and F. E. Stanley at the turn of the twentieth century; information and photographs relating to the brothers, their inventions, and their contributions to Estes Park; and the history of the hotel, founded by F. O. Stanley in 1909. The museum also features photographs taken by the Stanleys' talented sister, Chansonetta Stanley Emmons.

Stanley Steamers once were used to transfer hotel guests from the railroad depot in Lyons to Estes Park. A 1903 model still is displayed in the hotel lobby.

Stanley Museum, Stanley Hotel and Conference Center, 333 Wonderview Ave., P.O. Box 1767, Estes Park, CO 80517. Phone: 970/577-1903. Fax: 970/586-4964. Hours: vary (call for information). Admission: free.

National park/natural history museum/visitor centers

ROCKY MOUNTAIN NATIONAL PARK

Moraine Park Museum
Beaver Meadows Visitor Center
Kawuneeche Visitor Center
Alpine Visitor Center
Lily Lake Visitor Center

Rocky Mountain National Park near Estes Park has a natural history museum and four visitor centers (a fifth will open shortly) that tell the story of the 265,727-acre park established in 1915. The park serves as a sanctuary for many animal species, including elk, deer, bears, bighorn sheep, mountain lions, beavers, otters, and such raptors as bald and golden eagles, hawks, and peregrine falcons. Approximately 3 million people visit annually.

Rocky Mountain National Park, which encompasses 76 peaks more than 12,000 feet high and straddles the Continental Divide for 40 miles, has one of the most dramatic alpine highways in the nation—Trail Ridge Road, which winds across the mountains for 50 miles, achieving an elevation of 12,183 feet. Trail Ridge Road is usually open from Memorial Day to mid-October.

The Front Range skyline is dominated by 14,255-foot Longs Peak, which can be seen from more than 100 miles away. It was near this peak in the early twentieth century that naturalist and writer Enos Mills spearheaded a conservation movement to create the park (see separate listing for Enos Mills Cabin).

Moraine Park Museum, located on Bear Lake Road and open only during summer, has exhibits pertaining to the park's geology, plants, wildlife, and history. It opened in 1931.

Two of the four visitor centers—Beaver Meadows and Kawuneeche—are open year-round. The other two—Alpine and Lily Lake—operate only from Memorial Day through September. A fifth visitor center east of the Fall River entrance is scheduled to open in late 2000.

Beaver Meadows Visitor Center, formerly known as Park Headquarters Visitor Center, is located at the park's east entrance. It features a three-dimensional map and other information on the park.

Kawuneeche Visitor Center, located at the west entrance near Grand Lake, contains natural history exhibits, a multimedia program, and other exhibits on the park.

Alpine Visitor Center, perched near the top of Trail Ridge Road, features exhibits on the tundra, weather, park, and adjacent Roosevelt National Forest.

Lily Lake Visitor Center, the newest of the four centers, overlooks Lily Lake eight miles south of Estes Park on Colorado Highway 7. It offers exhibits on natural history and the park.

Moraine Park Museum, Bear Lake Rd., Rocky Mountain National Park, Estes Park, CO 80517. Phone: 970/586-1206. Fax: 970/586-1256. Hours: mid-May through Sept., 9–5 daily. Admission: free.

Beaver Meadows Visitor Center, Rocky Mountain National Park, 1000 U.S. Hwy. 36, Estes Park, CO 80517. Phone: 970/586-1206. Fax: 970/586-1256. E-mail: bill_butler@nps.gov. Hours: Memorial Day–Labor Day, 8 A.M.–9 P.M. daily; remainder of the year, 8–5 daily; closed Easter and Christmas. Admission: free.

Kawuneeche Visitor Center, Rocky Mountain National Park, U.S. Hwy. 34, Grand Lake, CO 80047. Phone: 970/627-1260. Fax: 970/627-3270. Hours: Memorial Day–Labor Day, 8 A.M.–9 P.M. daily; remainder of the year, 8–5 daily; closed Easter and Christmas. Admission: free.

Alpine Visitor Center, Rocky Mountain National Park, U.S. Hwy 34, Estes Park, CO 80517. Phone: 970/586-1206. Fax: 970/586-1556. Hours: Memorial Day–Sept., 10–4:30 daily; closed remainder of the year. Admission: free.

Lily Lake Visitor Center, Rocky Mountain National Park, Colo. Hwy. 7, Estes Park, CO 80517. Phone: 970/586-1206. Fax: 970/586-1556. Hours: Memorial Day–Sept., 9–4:30 daily; closed remainder of the year. Admission: free.

Pewter museum/gallery

MICHAEL RICKER PEWTER MUSEUM AND GALLERY

The Michael Ricker Pewter Museum and Gallery in Estes Park features the pewter sculpture of its founder, Michael Ricker, who has operated a pewter sculpture studio for 35 years.

Approximately 1,000 pieces of pewter sculpture are displayed in the museum, which opened in 1993. The collection focuses on miniature sculptures portraying events in U.S. history. Other highlights include pewter sculptures of celebrities and sports figures; a miniature 1950s drive-in and cars of pewter; and a 35-foot-by-14-foot pewter sculpture depicting an American community scene.

Ricker also operates two pewter museum branches in Breckenridge and Denver.

Michael Ricker Pewter Museum and Gallery, 2050 Big Thompson Ave. (U.S. Hwy. 34 East), P.O. Box 2570, Estes Park, CO 80517. Phone: 970/586-2030. Fax: 970/586-4609. Hours: summer, 9–9 Mon.–Fri., 9–6 Sat.–Sun.; winter, 9–5 Mon.–Fri., 9–6 Sat.–Sun.; closed New Year's Day, Thanksgiving, and Christmas. Admission: free.

Art center

ART CENTER OF ESTES PARK

The works of northern Colorado artists are featured in changing exhibitions at the Art Center of Estes Park, located in the Stanley Village Shopping Center.

The nonprofit art center, opened in 1987, also presents other exhibitions and offers youth and adult art classes throughout the year. Past exhibitions have included paintings, prints, sculpture, photographs, weavings, jewelry, ceramics, and glassworks.

Art Center of Estes Park, 517 Big Thompson Ave., P.O. Box 3635, Estes Park, CO 80517. Phone: 970/586-5882. Hours: May–Sept., 11–5 daily; Oct.–Apr., 12–4 Fri.–Mon. Admission: free.

Historic house

ENOS MILLS CABIN

Enos Mills was a mountain adventurer, naturalist, and conservation pioneer instrumental in the establishment of the National Park Service and Rocky Mountain National Park near Estes Park.

His 1885 homestead cabin at the foot of Longs Peak was opened as a mini-museum in 1968 by his daughter, Edna, and now is operated by his granddaughter, Elizabeth.

The 150-square-foot cabin contains Mills memorabilia, correspondence, furniture, photographs, books, and other materials pertaining to his pioneering life. At the age of 14, Mills left his native Kansas to explore and settle in the (then) wilderness south of Estes Park. He worked as a mountain guide, miner, snow-measurement observer, innkeeper, park activist, and author of numerous books about his mountain experiences and wildlife encounters.

A gallery filled with many of Mills's photographs (which feature mountains and wildlife) and some of his books is located a short distance from the cabin.

Enos Mills Cabin, 6760 Colo. Hwy. 7, Longs Peak Rte., Estes Park, CO 80517-6404. Phone: 970/586-4706. Hours: Memorial Day–Labor Day, 11–4 Tues.–Sun.; remainder of the year by appointment. Admission: free, but groups are $2 per person.

Historic ranch

MacGregor Ranch

The MacGregor Ranch, a National Historic Landmark near Estes Park, is one of Colorado's oldest and largest homestead ranches to be converted into a pioneer living-history museum.

The cattle ranch was homesteaded in 1873, long before Rocky Mountain National Park, which it now adjoins, came into existence. When Muriel Lurilla MacGregor, the last member of the family, died in 1970, she thought she had left the 3,000-acre ranch in a charitable trust as a working ranch for educational purposes. Unfortunately, problems with the wording and execution of the will resulted in an enormous tax burden, as well as mounting legal fees, and it became necessary to sell off some of the land. The National Park Service bought a 400-acre parcel, which became part of Rocky Mountain National Park.

In 1976, trustees of the Muriel L. MacGregor Charitable Trust and a group of volunteers set about rectifying the financial and legal problems, and after years of hard work, they were successful. The ranch now is operated as a nonprofit organization by volunteers.

The National Park Service helped make the living-history museum possible by agreeing to a $4 million conservation easement in 1983 that permits ranching but bars commercial development.

The public now can visit the 1,221-acre ranch during summer. The 1896 ranch house is filled with the furniture and other possessions of

three generations of MacGregors. Much of the early ranching and farming equipment is still in use. The ranch also has cattle and horses, as
well as educational programs and two campgrounds.

*MacGregor Ranch, MacGregor Lane (Devil's Gulch Road), P.O. Box 4675, Estes
Park, CO 80517. Phone: 970/586-3717. Hours: Memorial Day–Labor Day, 11–
5 Tues.–Fri.; closed remainder of the year. Admission: free.*

Historic hotel

STANLEY HOTEL AND CONFERENCE CENTER

The majestic Stanley Hotel, overlooking Estes Park and the Rockies,
was opened in 1909 by F. O. Stanley, who, with his brother F. E. Stanley,
invented the Stanley Steamer automobile at the turn of the twentieth
century.

The white-pillared Georgian hotel, listed on the National Register
of Historic Places, is now a conference center as well. The Stanley has
hosted such guests as President Theodore Roosevelt, the "Unsinkable"
Molly Brown, folk singer Bob Dylan, astronaut Scott Carpenter, Crown
Prince Naruhito of Japan, and presidential candidate Alfred Landon,
who used the hotel as his campaign headquarters in the 1930s.

The hotel also serves as a performing arts center, hosting theater
productions and Colorado Music Festival concerts every summer.

Now operated by Grand Heritage Hotels International, the hotel
has 133 guest rooms and 16,450 square feet of meeting and banquet
space. One of the early Stanley Steamers, a 1903 Runabout, is on display
in the hotel lobby. Such cars once were used to transfer hotel guests
from the railroad depot in Lyons. The two-room Stanley Museum (see
separate listing) is located on the hotel's lower level.

*Stanley Hotel and Conference Center, 333 Wonderview Ave., P.O. Box 1767,
Estes Park, CO 80517. Phones: 970/586-3371 and 800/976-1377. Fax: 970/
586-4964. Hours: open 24 hours. Rates: vary with room and season.*

EUREKA

Historic ghost town

EUREKA GHOST TOWN

The ruins of the Sunnyside Mill, one of the largest in Colorado, are
all that remains of Eureka, site of the productive Sunnyside Mine eight
miles northeast of Silverton.

Charles Baker, founder of Baker City (later renamed Silverton), made the first gold strikes in Eureka and Animas Canyon in the 1860s, but it was not until 1873 that John Terry opened the Sunnyside Mine. Initial results were discouraging, so Terry sold the mine to a New York syndicate, which returned it to him after the mine failed to pay off. Soon, however, it became one of the richest mines in Colorado, operating for more than 50 years before closing in 1938.

The huge Sunnyside Mill was built to process ore from the Sunnyside Mine and other nearby mines, employing approximately 500 workers at the height of the mining boom. The mill's foundation is still visible in Eureka, which was plagued by snow and rock slides and eventually abandoned.

Eureka Ghost Town, 8 miles northeast of Silverton. Contact: Silverton Area Chamber of Commerce, 414 Greene St., P.O. Box 56, Silverton, CO 81433. Phones: 970/387-5654 and 800/752-4494. Fax: 970/387-0282.

EVANS

History museum

EVANS HISTORICAL MUSEUM

The Evans Historical Museum, founded and operated by the City of Evans, describes life, conditions, and historical events in the Evans area of the Colorado high plains. Its collections and exhibits feature, for the most part, everyday household objects of the past and present.

The museum is located in a historic 1887 house combining Queen Anne and Italianate styling. The building was home to several families before becoming a Victorian restaurant in 1975. The City of Evans acquired the house in 1985 and restored it as a museum. The building still contains its original woodwork, fireplace mantels, and staircase.

Evans Historical Museum, 3720 Golden St., Evans, CO 80620-2724. Phone: 970/506-2721. Hours: 1–5 Mon.–Fri. and Sun.; closed major holidays. Admission: free.

EVERGREEN

Historic house/museum

HIWAN HOMESTEAD MUSEUM

Hiwan Homestead Museum in Evergreen is housed in an 11,700-square-foot mountain retreat that began as a one-room log cabin in the 1880s, grew to a 17-room log mansion with outbuildings by the 1940s, and was converted into a historic house museum in 1974. It now is listed on the National Register of Historic Places.

Civil War widow Mary Neosho Williams and her daughter, Josepha, acquired the log cabin in the 1890s and hired John "Jock" Spence, a Scottish carpenter-builder, to transform it into a summer cottage. Thus began a series of architectural improvements that extended into the 1940s. In expanding the structure and erecting support buildings, Spence utilized individual design elements and distinctive touches reminiscent of the great Adirondack camps. The Williams compound was called "Neosho."

Josepha Williams Douglas, one of Colorado's first female doctors, died in 1938, and the house was sold to Tulsa oilman Darst Buchanan, who organized Hiwan Ranch, a 30,000-acre cattle ranch stretching from Evergreen to Central City. Much of the land was later sold off. The rustic mountain retreat was bought by Jefferson County Open Space in 1974. The museum opened the following year and is operated with the assistance of the Jefferson County Historical Society.

The main structure and its outbuildings, which now include a restroom facility, housekeepers' cabin, workshop, printing shop, and stone playhouse (used for temporary exhibitions), are furnished with period pieces, many of which belonged to the families that lived there.

The Douglas family was interested in Southwest Indian culture and made long collecting trips to New Mexico and Arizona. Many of the items they brought back are on display in the museum. Exhibits include a strong collection of Hopi basketry, pottery, and tiles. Other noteworthy offerings are the Julia Douglas doll collection, which features dolls collected through the 1930s from around the world, and quilts made by Hiwan's own Busy Bee crafters.

Hiwan Historical Museum, 4208 S. Timbervale Dr., Evergreen, CO 80439. Phone: 303/674-6262. Fax: 303/670-7746. Website: www.co.jefferson.co.us/dpt/ openspac/hiwan/hiwan.htm. Hours: June–Aug., 11–5 Tues.–Sun.; Sept.–May, 12–5 Tues.–Sun.; closed major holidays. Admission: free, but groups are $1 per person.

Bell museum

INTERNATIONAL BELL MUSEUM

Retired actor and makeup artist Winston Jones has been collecting bells for nearly seven decades, amassing more than 6,000 examples from around the world. In 1957, when his collection numbered only 2,000 bells, he converted his mountain log home into the International Bell Museum.

Exhibited outdoors are large bells made of iron, bronze, and brass. The rooms inside are filled with bells made of wood, leather, turtle shells, porcelain, glass, deer hooves, and other materials. The bells, which date from 1 B.C. to the present, range in size from one-quarter inch to one ton.

When taking visitors on a tour, Jones will often strike one of the outdoor bells, among them a giant bronze temple gong from Hong Kong, which reverberates throughout the canyon.

International Bell Museum, 30213 Upper Bear Creek Canyon Rd., P.O. Box 1601, Evergreen, CO 80439. Phone: 303/674-3422. Hours: mid-May through mid-Sept., Tues.–Sun. by appointment; closed remainder of the year. Admission: adults, $4; children under 12, $2.

Historic ranch/park/museum

HUMPHREY MEMORIAL PARK AND MUSEUM

The Humphrey Memorial Park and Museum in Evergreen consists of a 43-acre park, an 1880s ranch, Victorian gardens, and hiking trails. The property, formerly owned by Lucius and Hazel Humphrey and now listed on the National Register of Historic Places, was willed to five community organizations by the Humphreys' daughter in 1995, with the understanding that it was to be preserved for public benefit. Since then, a nonprofit organization has been created to administer the property as a park and museum.

The facilities, which opened to tours in 1997, include a 4,000-square-foot Victorian ranch house, barns, stables, and other support structures. The ranch house contains an eclectic collection of artifacts and other materials brought back by the Humphreys during their worldwide travels, primarily in the 1880s and 1890s. Among the artifacts are china, bells, necklaces, jewelry, swords, rugs, and other objects reflecting the cultures of China, Persia, Russia, Mexico, and other countries, as well as Native American tribes.

Humphrey Memorial Park and Museum, 620 S. Soda Creek Rd., Evergreen, CO 80439. Phone: 303/674-5429. Hours: June–Aug., 10–3 Thurs.–Sat. by appointment; closed remainder of the year. Admission: free.

FAIRPLAY

Living-history museum

SOUTH PARK CITY MUSEUM

South Park City Museum in Fairplay is a reconstructed mining village representative of mining towns in the Colorado Rockies between 1860 and 1900.

After gold was discovered in 1859, gold-seekers formed mining camps such as Tarryall, Leavick, Eureka, and Buckskin Joe in South Park, a 900-square-mile basin surrounded by mountains. In the decades that followed, the families of many early prospectors arrived, helping transform the rough camps into thriving communities. Now many of these mining villages are ghost towns or have vanished entirely.

South Park City Museum opened in 1959, 100 years after Colorado's first gold rush. The living-history museum collects, restores, and preserves representative architecture and period artifacts, which are used to re-create life in early Colorado mining towns (with emphasis on settlements in the South Park area).

The outdoor museum consists of 34 authentic early buildings. Seven are on their original sites in Fairplay; others have been moved from abandoned South Park mining camps.

The restored buildings, filled with 60,000 artifacts, feature period room settings and exhibits pertaining to the professions, trades, industries, and daily life of the mining towns. Among the buildings are a bank, church, courthouse, brewery, livery, inn, blacksmith's shop, schoolhouse, drugstore, newspaper office, water tower, head house (a locker room for miners), barn, log cabin, doctor's office, general store, saloon, railroad depot, and several pioneer houses.

South Park City Museum, 100 4th St., P.O. Box 634, Fairplay, CO 80440. Phone: 719/836-2387. Website: www.coloradodirectory.com/southparkmuseum/. Hours: mid-May to Memorial Day, and Labor Day to mid-Oct., 9–5 daily; Memorial Day–Labor Day, 9–7 daily; closed remainder of the year. Admission: adults, $5; seniors, $4; children 6–12, $2; children under 6, free.

FLAGLER

History museum/historic building

FLAGLER MUSEUM

The Flagler Museum is located on the second floor of Flagler's municipal building and library.

The building, which is on the National Register of Historic Places, was constructed in 1909 as a hotel and became a hospital in 1937. It was purchased by the town of Flagler in 1967. The building was renovated in 1993, and the museum opened that same year. It is devoted to the history of the hospital and hotel, as well as their role in the community.

In addition to artifacts, the museum offers a re-created 1909 hotel room, a typical early hospital room, a children's nursery, and photographs and information about the hotel and hospital.

Flagler Museum, 311 Main Ave., P.O. Box 126, Flagler, CO 80815. Phone: 719/765-4571. Fax: 719/765-4498. Hours: 8–12 and 1–5 Mon.–Fri.; closed national holidays. Admission: free.

Historic schoolhouse

SECOND CENTRAL SCHOOL BUILDING

The 1915 Second Central School Building, now undergoing renovation, will be the centerpiece of a developing historic park in Flagler. The building was moved from a remote location to Flagler's Maddle Park in 1993.

Eight grades were taught in two classrooms on the upper story of the 2,500-square-foot structure; high school classes were offered in the basement. The building contains historical materials pertaining to the school, such artifacts as a 1909 sewing machine and an early oil stove, and old photographs of the area. When the renovation undertaken by the Flagler Historical Society is completed in late 2000, the schoolhouse will become a museum.

Second Central School Building, Flagler Historical Society, 404 4th St., P.O. Box 263, Flagler, CO 80815. Phone: 719/765-4603. Hours: by appointment only. Admission: free.

FLEMING

Historic museum/park

FLEMING HERITAGE MUSEUM PARK

Fleming Heritage Museum Park, a 10-acre historically oriented facility, features a community museum, a restored railroad depot, a pioneer memorial, a craft shop, and a picnic area.

The Fleming Historical Society, founded in 1966, operates the museum, located in a restored 1905 Philarado one-room schoolhouse. The museum contains collections and exhibits pertaining to pioneer families and the history of the Fleming area.

The old Burlington depot features antique furniture in the upstairs living quarters once used by depot agents. The pioneer memorial, carved from white limestone, depicts modes of transportation used by early settlers, such as a covered wagon, a train, and a Model T Ford.

Fleming Heritage Museum Park, 400 W. Weston St., Fleming, CO. (Postal address: 313 W. Hall St., Fleming, CO 80728.) Phone: 970/265-2591. Park hours: open 24 hours. Museum hours: Memorial Day weekend–Aug., 1–4 Sun.; closed remainder of the year. Admission: free.

FLORENCE

History museum

PRICE MUSEUM

The Price Museum, formerly known as the Florence Price Pioneer Museum, depicts the history of Florence and the surrounding area. It is located in the city's first jail, built in 1894.

Founded in 1964, the museum displays artifacts, records, maps, photographs, and other materials relating to the area's farming, ranching, mining, oil fields, cement plant, and former processing plants for Cripple Creek gold.

The two-story museum contains, among other things, antique agricultural and mining equipment, early household appliances, a mineral exhibit, old newspapers, Native American artifacts, and a former post office.

Price Museum, Pikes Peak Ave. and Front St., Florence, CO 81226. Phone: 719/784-6424. Hours: May 15–Sept. 15, 1–4 daily; closed remainder of the year. Admission: free.

FLORISSANT

National monument/visitor center/historic homestead

FLORISSANT FOSSIL BEDS NATIONAL MONUMENT

Visitor Center
Horbek Homestead

The Florissant Fossil Beds National Monument was established in 1969 to protect the petrified redwood stumps and fossilized bones, teeth, shells, feathers, and other impressions of animals, fish, insects, and plants in an ancient forested valley near Florissant.

The fossil beds and petrified stumps were discovered in 1873. Paleontologists from leading universities and museums arrived soon after to explore, collect, and study the magnificent specimens. The work of one of the earliest paleontologists, Samuel Scudder, resulted in an extraordinary university museum collection—the 25,000 fossil insects at Harvard University's Museum of Comparative Zoology.

The fossil beds, created by volcanic eruptions 34 million years ago, are internationally known for the variety and number of their fossils, particularly of insects and plants. More than 60,000 specimens have been retrieved; many are in the collections of more than 20 museums and universities worldwide.

It is still possible to see petrified redwood stumps and fossil specimens at the 6,000-acre national monument, which is operated by the National Park Service. The best viewing is at the visitor center and along two interpretive trails. Some of the petrified stumps (of a species closely related to the Sequoia redwoods) are up to 15 feet tall and 45 feet in circumference. The visitor center also has exhibits on the creation and history of the fossil beds.

The national monument also features the 1878 Horbek Homestead, a National Historic Site that includes the original cabin and reconstructed barn, carriage shed, and root cellar. Herds of elk and other wildlife roam the monument's grounds.

Florissant Fossil Beds National Monument Visitor Center, National Park Service, 15807 Teller County Rd. 1, P.O. Box 185, Florissant, CO 80816. Phone: 719/748-3253. Fax: 719/748-3164. E-mail: jean_rodeck@nps.gov. Website: www.nps.gov/flfo. Hours: summer, 8–7 daily; winter, 8–4:30 daily; closed New Year's Day, Thanksgiving, and Christmas. Admission: free, but monument admission in summer is $2 for adults, free for children 16 and under, and $4 for families (there is no admission charge in winter).

FORT CARSON

Military museum

3RD CAVALRY MUSEUM

The history, equipment, weapons, vehicles, aircraft, documents, and photographs of the 3rd Armored Cavalry Regiment from 1846 to the present can be seen at the 3rd Cavalry Museum at Fort Carson near Colorado Springs.

The museum was founded at Fort Lewis, Washington, in 1959, when the regiment was based there; then moved to Fort Bliss, Texas, along with the regiment; and relocated to Colorado in 1996, when the 3rd Cavalry was transferred to Fort Carson.

In addition to the indoor collections and exhibits, the museum displays 13 armored vehicles and a helicopter on a pad outside the building.

3rd Cavalry Museum, Bldg. 2160, AFZC-DT-T-MM, Fort Carson, CO 80913-5000. Phone: 719/526-1368. Fax: 719/526-6573. E-mail: martinp@carson-cav3.army.mil. Hours: 9–4:30 Mon.–Sat.; closed federal holidays. Admission: free.

FORT COLLINS

History/general museum

FORT COLLINS MUSEUM

The Fort Collins Museum, founded in 1937, is a municipal general museum devoted primarily to the history and natural environment of the Fort Collins area.

Since 1977, the 16,000-square-foot museum has been housed in the 1904 Carnegie Library, which served as the public library until 1976.

The museum contains interpretive exhibits on the history of Fort Collins and northern Colorado, displays works of local artists, and features three historic buildings in its Pioneer Courtyard.

The first of these buildings is the Janis Cabin (fur-trapping era), former home of Antoine Janis, who homesteaded in the area in 1844; it is one of the oldest buildings in the state. The second is the Auntie Stone Cabin (army-fort era), built in 1864 as the fort officers' mess. Later on, it successively became the town's first school, an inn operated by Elizabeth Stone, a hotel kitchen, and, finally, a private residence. The third building is the Boxelder Schoolhouse (agricultural and settlement era), built in 1884 on the Maxwell Ranch in Upper Boxelder Canyon. It was in use continuously as a school until 1951.

The Pioneer Courtyard also has a collection of stone hitching posts, and architectural details such as stone lintels.

The museum hosts two annual celebrations—the Fur Trappers' Rendezvous in June and the Skookum Day celebration, which features live demonstrations and hands-on exhibits pertaining to pioneer life, tools, and techniques, in mid-July.

The museum houses one of the nation's largest collections of Folsom materials relating to prehistoric culture east of the Rockies. It also displays Native American artifacts, mineral specimens, and military artifacts from the area.

Fort Collins Museum, 200 Mathews St., Fort Collins, CO 80524. Phone: 970/221-6738. Fax: 970/416-2236. E-mail: jstilwell@ci.fort-collins.co.us. Website: www.ci.fort-collins.co.us/arts_culture/museum. Hours: 10–5 Tues.–Sat., 12–5 Sun.; closed major holidays. Admission: free.

Farm museum

FARM HERITAGE MUSEUM

The Farm Heritage Museum in Fort Collins reveals how farmers and ranchers worked the land, built barns and houses, and developed new ways to increase production and improve rural life in the twentieth century.

The museum was opened in 1985 on the farm in Lee Martinez Park by the City of Fort Collins Recreation Division in cooperation with the Rotary Club, which undertook the museum's creation as a community service project.

The farm is a 1920s former dairy farm, comprising the original barn, silo, chicken coops, and farmhouse, which was rebuilt in 1935. Several buildings—including the museum—and fenced pens for farm animals were added later.

Children's programs include the feeding and care of animals.

The museum has more than 30 displays, plus collections of barbed wire, model tractors, farm tools, and other items. In the farm's "North Forty" section, old farm machinery—corn shellers, stock scales, plow harrows, and a huge threshing machine—also can be seen.

Farm Heritage Museum, 600 N. Sherwood St., Fort Collins, CO. (Postal address: City of Fort Collins Recreation Div., 214 N. Howe St., Fort Collins, CO 80521.) Phone: 970/221-6665. Hours: Nov. to mid-Mar., 10–4:30 Wed.–Sat., 12–4:30 Sun.; mid-Mar. through Oct., 10–5:30 Wed.–Sat., 12–5:30 Sun.; also June–Aug., 10–5:30 Tues.; closed major holidays. Admission: free.

Science center/museum

DISCOVERY CENTER SCIENCE MUSEUM

The Discovery Center Science Museum in Fort Collins is a hands-on science center providing interactive explorations of scientific principles and technological applications for visitors of all ages.

The 15,000-square-foot museum, which opened in 1989, has more than 90 exhibits focusing on many areas of science and technology; a Starlab inflatable portable planetarium; and special science programs and classes.

Exhibit theme areas include Simple Machines; Energy in Motion; Biology; Communications and Home Science; Light and Optics; Electricity; and Predators. Popular individual exhibits highlight the Cartesian diver, Bernoulli blower, telescoping lever, vertical pulley, spinning top, shadow wall, laser, Whimshurst generator, black bear, and planetarium.

Discovery Center Science Museum, 703 E. Prospect Rd., Fort Collins, CO 80525. Phone: 970/493-2182. Fax: 970/493-4085. E-mail: dwhite@psd.k12.co.us. Website: www.csmate.colostate.edu/dcsm/. Hours: 10–5 Tues.–Sat., 12–5 Sun. Admission: adults and children 4 and over, $3.50; children under 4, free.

Art galleries

COLORADO STATE UNIVERSITY

Hatton Gallery
Curfman Gallery
Duhesa Lounge

Colorado State University in Fort Collins has three art galleries— the Hatton Gallery, Curfman Gallery, and Duhesa Lounge. The Gustafson Gallery, which exhibits historic costumes and textiles (see following listing), is located on campus as well.

Hatton Gallery

Historical and contemporary art exhibitions are presented at the art department's Hatton Gallery, housed in the Visual Arts Building.

The 1,850-square-foot gallery, founded in 1970, offers changing exhibitions of prints, posters, and other artworks from its collections and elsewhere. The gallery's collections consist of Japanese prints, Pop Art prints, and graduate-student work. Every two years, the gallery hosts an international poster exhibition, the only such display of contemporary poster design from around the world.

Hatton Gallery, Dept. of Art, Colorado State University, Visual Arts Bldg., Fort Collins, CO 80523-1770. Phone: 970/491-7634. Fax: 970/491-0505. E-mail: lfrickman@vines.colostate.edu. Hours: Sept.–May, 8–12 and 1–4:30 Mon.–Fri., 1–4 Sat.; closed New Year's Day, Fourth of July, Thanksgiving, Christmas, and semester breaks. Admission: free.

Curfman Gallery and Duhesa Lounge

Curfman Gallery and Duhesa Lounge are exhibition areas in CSU's Lory Student Center. Opened in 1968, the spaces present changing exhibitions, primarily of contemporary art.

Curfman Gallery and Duhesa Lounge, Lory Student Center, Colorado State University, Fort Collins, CO 80523. Phone: 970/491-0961. Fax: 970/491-6423. Hours: Sept.–May, 8:30 A.M.–9 P.M. Mon.–Thurs., 8:30 A.M.–9:30 P.M. Fri., 1–4 Sat.; remainder of the year, 8–4 Mon.–Fri.; closed Thanksgiving and semester breaks. Admission: free.

Costume and textile gallery

GUSTAFSON GALLERY AT COLORADO STATE UNIVERSITY

CSU's Gustafson Gallery is a historical costume and textile gallery that presents selections from the research collections of the Department of Design, Merchandising, and Consumer Services. It also hosts temporary exhibitions.

The 900-square-foot gallery recently was relocated to the Gifford Building, where the design department and its research collections are located.

The collections were started in 1950 and now consist of approximately 7,000 historical costumes and 500 textile pieces (primarily from the mid-nineteenth century on), as well as clothing accessories and sewing-related notions.

Gustafson Gallery, Dept. of Design, Merchandising, and Consumer Services, Colorado State University, 145 Gifford Bldg., 502 W. Lake St., Fort Collins, CO 80523. Phone: 970/491-1983. Fax: 970/491-7252. E-mail: carlson@cahs.colostate.edu. Website: www.colostate.edu/depts/dmcs. Hours: 9–5 Mon.–Thurs.; closed semester breaks and major holidays. Admission: free.

Arts center

LINCOLN CENTER

Monthly exhibitions featuring the work of local, regional, national, and international artists in all media are among the offerings of the Lincoln Center, a performing and visual arts complex operated by the City of Fort Collins.

Opened in 1978, Lincoln Center has three art galleries, two stages, an outdoor sculpture garden, and banquet and conference facilities. One of the annual highlights is ArtWear, a runway fashion show and sale of wearable art created by designers from across the country. It is presented in cooperation with Gary Hixon Interiors as a fund-raiser for the Visual Arts Department.

The Lincoln Center serves approximately 260,000 people each year.

Lincoln Center, 417 W. Magnolia St., Fort Collins, CO 80521-2646. Phone: 970/221-6735. Fax: 970/484-0424. Hours: 8–6 Mon.–Fri., 12–6 Sat. (except in summer), and during evening performances; closed national holidays. Admission: free.

Arts center

ONEWEST ART CENTER

Nearly a dozen contemporary art exhibitions are presented each year in the two gallery spaces at the OneWest Art Center, a 4,500-square-foot nonprofit facility in Fort Collins. The art center, which opened in 1991 in a renovated 1911 post office building, showcases the work of contemporary artists in the region.

OneWest Art Center, 201 S. College Ave., Fort Collins, CO 80524. Phone: 970/482-2787. Hours: 10–5 Tues.–Sat.; closed major holidays. Admission: free.

Sculpture park

SWETSVILLE ZOO

A collection of more than 150 outdoor sculptures made from old farm equipment and car parts can be seen at the Swetsville Zoo, located on a former dairy farm nine miles east of Fort Collins. Among other things, the sculptures represent domestic animals, birds, and flowers; nearly half are of dinosaurs.

Farmer Bill Swets began creating the sculptures in 1985. They are scattered on an island and along the shore of the Cache la Poudre River, which passes through his 100-acre farm.

Swets is still creating new works of sculpture.

Swetsville Zoo, 4801 E. Harmony Rd. (I-25 Exit 265), Fort Collins, CO 80528-9567. Phone: 970/484-9509. Hours: dawn to dusk daily. Admission: free.

Historic house

AVERY HOUSE

The 1879 Avery House in Fort Collins is a two-story Victorian sandstone structure with a distinctive Queen Anne tower. The building is the centerpiece of the Avery House Historic District, listed in the National Register of Historic Places.

The historic house, now owned and restored by the Poudre Landmarks Foundation, was built and expanded several times by Franklin and Sara Avery. The Queen Anne tower was among the additions. Other features of the property include a gazebo, foundation, and carriage house.

Franklin Avery surveyed Fort Collins in 1873 and is largely responsible for its wide streets. He later founded the First National Bank and was instrumental in developing water projects that enabled agriculture to flourish in northern Colorado.

The Poudre Landmarks Foundation, with assistance from Friends of the Water Works, is now working on restoration of the historic 1882 Fort Collins Water Works, located at North Overland Trail and Bingham Hill Road. The facility operated as a pump house for only 21 years, then was used for maintenance and storage from 1904 until recently. Plans call for the building to become an interpretive center detailing the history of the Fort Collins water system and the agricultural development made possible by early irrigation projects. The caretaker's residence and other outbuildings on the surrounding 25-acre site will be used by Colorado State University's Rocky Mountain Raptor Program, which will present displays and educational programs.

Avery House, Poudre Landmarks Foundation, 328 W. Mountain Ave., Fort Collins, CO. (Postal address: 108 N. Meldrum St., Fort Collins, CO 80521.) Phone: 970/221-0533. Hours: 1–3 Wed. and Sun.; closed major holidays. Admission: free.

Visitor center/tour

ANHEUSER-BUSCH BREWERY VISITOR CENTER

Anheuser-Busch Inc. offers brewery tours at 7 of its 12 plants, including the one in Fort Collins.

The Fort Collins brewery has given tours since it opened in 1989. The walking tours, which take 1 hour and 15 minutes, begin in an orientation room and conclude in the hospitality room with complimentary samples of Budweiser beers and soft drinks.

The tour takes visitors through eight production areas—mashing, straining, brew kettling, cooling, primary fermentation, beechwood aging, final finishing, and packaging—and then through the stables housing the famous Budweiser Clydesdales, the most recognizable symbol of Anheuser-Busch. On the first Saturday of each month, visitors can pose for pictures with one of the horses.

The Anheuser-Busch Brewery in Fort Collins offers free tours of its beer-making facilities. Courtesy Anheuser-Busch Brewery, Fort Collins.

Anheuser-Busch Brewery Tour, 2351 Busch Dr., Fort Collins, CO 80524. Phone: 970/490-4692. Fax: 970/490-4534. Hours: June–Aug., 9:30–5 daily; Sept.– Oct., 10–4 daily; Nov.–May, 10–4 Thurs.–Mon.; Budweiser Clydesdale Camera Day, 1–3 the first Sat. of every month. Admission: free.

Historic district

OLD TOWN HISTORIC DISTRICT

The Old Town Historic District in Fort Collins consists of upscale shops, galleries, cafes, and pubs, many of them in restored 1880s buildings along a pedestrian mall with dancing fountains.

The historic district, listed on the National Register of Historic Places in 1978, is roughly bounded by Mountain Avenue, College Avenue, Pine Street, the city's northeasternmost railroad tracks, and a line midway between Linden and Chestnut Streets. Sixteen historic buildings in the district—and five outside it—are featured on a walking tour.

The historic area, which was restored in the early 1980s as part of an urban renewal project, was the commercial center of Fort Collins in the late nineteenth and early twentieth centuries.

Fort Collins was established in the mid-nineteenth century as a military post to protect traders and settlers in the area and along the

Overland Trail. Prospectors were drawn to the nearby canyon of the Cache la Poudre River when gold was discovered in the Rockies in the late 1850s. Few were successful in their quest for gold, but a considerable number stayed on to farm or ranch.

Over the years, Fort Collins became an agricultural center, rich in alfalfa, sugar beets, and other crops, as well as an educational center with the founding of Colorado Agricultural and Mechanical College (later called Colorado State University) in 1879. In recent years, an increasing number of high-tech companies have located in the area.

Old Town Historic District. Contact: Fort Collins Convention and Visitors Bureau, 420 S. Howes St., Suite 101, P.O. Box 1998, Fort Collins, CO 80522. Phones: 970/482-5821 and 800/274-3678. Fax: 970/493-8061.

FORT GARLAND

Historic fort

FORT GARLAND MUSEUM

Fort Garland, 25 miles east of Alamosa, is a historic frontier military post established in 1858 in the San Luis Valley to protect settlers and travelers from Indian attack. It closed in 1883 following the large-scale removal of the Utes from much of Colorado in 1880.

The adobe buildings around the parade grounds have been restored by the Colorado Historical Society and feature a re-creation of the commandant's quarters in 1866, when frontiersman Kit Carson headed the garrison. Carson, who was commissioned colonel and brevet brigadier general during the Civil War, commanded a volunteer regiment assigned to the fort to keep peace and negotiate with the Utes. When regular troops returned in 1867, the volunteers were mustered out, and Carson settled in what is now Las Animas to become Colorado's Superintendent of Indian Affairs.

Fort Garland was built to replace nearby Fort Massachusetts, which was abandoned because of its vulnerability to Indian attack. Fort Garland was large enough to accommodate two companies of approximately 100 men and a handful of officers.

In addition to the commandant's quarters, the restored fort now contains exhibits illustrating military life at the time, as well as a display of folk art depicting Hispanic life in the San Luis Valley. Also on display is a Barlow and Sanderson stagecoach, a rare example of an Abbot-

Historic Fort Garland in the San Luis Valley has been re-opened as a museum. Courtesy Colorado Historical Society.

Downing mud wagon built around 1871, which provided basic transportation in the San Luis Valley in the late nineteenth century.

School tour programs, which focus on nineteenth-century military life, Hispanic culture, and Native Americans in the area at the time, are offered weekdays by appointment from September through May. The fort also presents six special activity days, including Live History Day, Pioneer Picnic, and Mountain Man Rendezvous, throughout the year.

Fort Garland Museum, U.S. Hwy. 160 and Colo. Hwy. 159, P.O. Box 368, Fort Garland, CO 81133. Phone: 719/379-3512. Hours: Apr.–Oct., 9–5 daily; Nov.– Mar., 8–4 Thurs.–Mon. Admission: adults, $2.50; seniors, $2; children 6–16, $1.50; children under 6, free.

FORT LUPTON

History museum

Fort Lupton Museum

Fort Lupton Museum is a one-room municipal museum featuring Weld County artifacts and other historical materials from 1860 to the present.

Opened in 1982, the museum is located in the 1929 Fort Lupton Library building. Among the museum's collections and exhibits are old clothing, arrowheads, toys, kitchen items, uniforms, medical equipment, Native American artifacts, books, and a model of early Fort Lupton.

Fort Lupton was established as a fur-trading outpost on the banks of the South Platte River in 1836 and served as a safe haven for settlers and others during Indian attacks in the 1860s. The town developed as a farming community whose growth was spurred when the Union Pacific Railroad laid track between Denver and Cheyenne in 1870.

Fort Lupton Museum, 453 1st St., Fort Lupton, CO 80621. Phone: 303/857-1634. Hours: 9–4 Mon.–Fri.; Sat. and Sun. by appointment; closed major holidays. Admission: free.

FORT LYON

Historic fort/cemetery

Fort Lyon National Cemetery

Fort Lyon National Cemetery is located at the second site of a historic frontier military post in Fort Lyon, Colorado, seven miles east of Las Animas in the southeastern corner of the state.

The original fort, built in 1860 and located near the trading post established by the Bent brothers and Ceran St. Vrain on the north side of the Arkansas River, was known as Fort Wise. In 1861, however, it was renamed Fort Lyon in honor of the first Union general to die in the Civil War.

Fort Lyon saw limited action until 1864, when Colonel John M. Chivington ordered most of the fort's troops to accompany his militiamen against a band of Cheyenne and other Indians 40 miles to the north. On the morning of November 29, the troops surrounded an Indian camp on Sand Creek and killed most of the occupants—mainly women, children, and old men. The controversial incident, known as the Sand Creek Massacre, resulted in Chivington's resignation.

After floodwaters overran the lowlands on which the fort was built, the post was relocated 20 miles to the west in 1867. Some of the fort's adobe and stone buildings remain, including the building in which Kit

Carson, former army scout, trapper, and commanding officer of Fort Garland, died in 1868. The building later was restored and converted into the Kit Carson Memorial Chapel.

When the U.S. Army abandoned Fort Lyon in 1897, the troops were transferred to other posts, and the bodies of soldiers interred there were moved to Fort McPherson National Cemetery in Nebraska.

Fort Lyon, however, did not stay closed for long. In 1906, the Navy established a tuberculosis sanitarium at the site, and it remained a U.S. Naval Hospital until 1922, when the Veterans Bureau (now the Veterans Administration) assumed operations. In 1933, the facility became a neuropsychiatric hospital. It remains an active VA hospital today, but is threatened with closure by federal cutbacks.

Approximately 2,000 servicemen and -women are buried in Fort Lyon National Cemetery, including two German prisoners of war who were treated for tuberculosis at Fort Lyon during World War I. The hospital graveyard became the Fort Lyon Hospital Cemetery under the Veterans Bureau in 1922. It was designated a national cemetery (one of two in Colorado, the other being Fort Logan National Cemetery in Denver [see separate listing]) after World War II.

Fort Lyon National Cemetery, Colo. Hwy. 183, Fort Lyon, Co 81038. Phone: 719/384-3143. Hours: sunrise–sunset daily.

FORT MORGAN

History museum

FORT MORGAN MUSEUM

The history of Fort Morgan, Morgan County, and northeastern Colorado is traced at the Fort Morgan Museum, which opened in 1975. The museum, operated by the Fort Morgan Heritage Foundation, has three galleries displaying artifacts and other historical materials on such topics as the old frontier fort, area history, the Cheyenne and Arapaho Indians, local bandleader Glenn Miller, German immigrants from Russia, a nearby buffalo kill site, early rail and auto transportation, and the once popular Hillrose soda fountain. The museum's other collections include agricultural implements, ranching equipment, quilts, china, textiles, clothing, materials relating to the sugar-beet industry, and historic photographs. These items, too, are sometimes exhibited.

A fund-raising campaign for a major museum expansion is currently under way.

*Fort Morgan Museum, 414 Main St., P.O. Box 184, Fort Morgan, CO 80701.
Phone: 970/867-6331. Fax: 970/542-3000. E-mail: ftmormus@ftmorganmus.org.
Website: www.ftmorganmus.org/. Hours: 10–5 Mon.–Fri. (also 6-8 Tues.–Thurs.),
11–5 Sat.; closed national holidays. Admission: free.*

History museum

OASIS ON THE PLAINS MUSEUM

The Oasis on the Plains Museum is located on a working ranch
approximately 15 miles southwest of Fort Morgan. Ranch owners Carl
and Lorraine Rigli started the museum in the early 1980s to house their
diverse collection of historical materials.

The Riglis store and display their growing collection in a block house,
a metal building, and two boxcars.

Among the items on exhibit are barbed wire, fencing tools, farm
machinery, furniture, dolls, appliances, arrowheads, and other household, farm, and personal objects from bygone eras.

*Oasis on the Plains Museum, 6877 Morgan County Rd. 14, Fort Morgan, CO
80701. Phone: 970/432-5200. Hours: summer, 1–5 Sun.; remainder of the year,
1–4 Sun.; other times by appointment. Admission: free.*

Military museum

U.S. MILITARY HISTORICAL MUSEUM

One of the newest Colorado museums is the U.S. Military Historical Museum, opened in late 1998 by Vietnam veteran Dan Lewis. The
museum, located in Fort Morgan, is dedicated to veterans of all wars.

The 2,000-square-foot museum occupies a renovated 1914 two-story
house and contains a display of 40 mannequins dressed in U.S. military
uniforms from the Revolutionary War to the Gulf War, a collection of
military uniforms worn by opposing armies from the same period, and 11
cases of military accoutrements and weapons from the American Revolution to the present.

The museum is only open by appointment.

*U.S. Military Historical Museum, 404 State St., Fort Morgan, CO 80701. Phone:
970/867-5520. Fax: 970/867-7343. Hours: individual and group tours must be
scheduled in advance. Admission: free.*

FOUNTAIN

Nature center

FOUNTAIN CREEK NATURE CENTER

The Fountain Creek Nature Center in Fountain Creek Regional Park focuses primarily on the ecosystems of the wetlands near Fountain. It is one of two nature centers operated in regional parks by the El Paso County Parks Department (the other is Bear Creek Nature Center in Colorado Springs [see separate listing]).

The Fountain Creek center, often referred to as "an oasis in the plains," opened in 1992. It provides approximately 1,000 square feet of exhibits (mostly interactive) and interpretive programs devoted to the five biological communities in the park—creek, woodlands, meadows, marsh, and ponds.

Nature trails and several observation pavilions permit wildlife viewing, including great blue herons and more than 230 other species of birds, in a wetlands environment. The park also has hiking, biking, and horseback-riding trails; fishing ponds at the north end; and an activity area that features picnic pavilions, a children's playground, playing fields, a volleyball court, and horseshoe pits.

Fountain Creek Nature Center, 320 Pepper Grass Lane, Fountain, CO 80817. Phone: 719/520-6725. Fax: 719/520-6746. Hours: 9–4 Tues.–Sat.; also 9–4 Sun. in summer; closed major holidays. Admission: free.

FRANKTOWN

Visitor center/historic homestead

CASTLEWOOD CANYON STATE PARK VISITOR CENTER

Castlewood Canyon State Park, five miles south of Franktown, stretches over more than 1,600 acres, most of it located in a canyon with steep sandstone walls. In it are the remains of the old Castlewood Canyon Dam, which was built for Denver-area water storage in 1890 and burst in 1933, flooding the Platte River's Cherry Creek drainage in Denver.

The park offers a network of canyon-bottom, canyon-rim, and woodland hiking trails; opportunities for climbers; picnic facilities; and the ruins of the turn-of-the-twentieth-century Lucas homestead.

In addition, the park has a visitor center, which opened in 1993, with exhibits on the history of the dam and the ecology of the park. A 14-minute multimedia presentation on the dam and park ecology is also available.

Castlewood Canyon State Park Visitor Center, S. Colo. Hwy. 83, P.O. Box 504, Franktown, CO 80116. Phone: 303/688-5242. Fax: 303/688-1190. Hours: 9–5 daily. Admission: $4 per vehicle.

FREELAND

Historic ghost town

FREELAND GHOST TOWN

The mining town of Freeland, five miles west of Idaho Springs via a ledge road notable for its frightening drop-offs, once attracted such prominent mining investors as Winfield Scott Stratton, Cripple Creek mine owner and millionaire, and John W. Mackay, the Comstock mining developer who headed a group of speculators from California.

The town was founded in 1880 during a period of rich gold and silver strikes. Successful mines of the area included the Freeland and Lone Tree. But prosperity did not last long, and Mackay's investors were disappointed.

However, durable structures were erected, and some of the log cabins, frame houses, and ruined stone structures are still visible, as are the remains of shaft houses and mine dumps along the route to Freeland.

Freeland Ghost Town, 5 miles west of Idaho Springs. Contact: Historical Society of Idaho Springs, 1416 Miner St., P.O. Box 1318, Idaho Springs, CO 80452. Phone: 303/569-4709. Fax: 303/567-4605.

FRUITA

National monument/visitor center

COLORADO NATIONAL MONUMENT VISITOR CENTER

Colorado National Monument near Fruita is a 20,000-acre park created in 1911 to preserve one of the grand landscapes of the American West.

The history and geology of the national monument are interpreted in the visitor center, which offers an introductory slide show, exhibits, and such programs as guided walks and campfire talks. The monument is administered by the National Park Service.

The brilliantly colored plateau-and-canyon country has towering masses of natural sculpted rock and embraces 32 square miles of rugged terrain. It is situated at the edge of the Uncompahgre Uplift and is part of the greater Colorado Plateau.

The high country of Colorado National Monument rises more than 2,000 feet above the Grand Valley of the Colorado River. Rim Rock Drive winds across the plateau, offering spectacular views of colorful sheer-walled canyons and fascinating rock sculptures. Among the sights in Monument and Wedding canyons are the 450-foot-high Independence Monument and Pipe Organ, as well as the Kissing Couple, Sentinel Spire, and Praying Hands formations, which rise from the canyon floor like stone skyscrapers.

The national monument was created through the tireless efforts of John Otto, who loved the wild and desolate canyon country, built miles of winding trails in it for others to enjoy, and spearheaded a campaign involving nearby Grand Junction residents and others to establish the park. His reward was being named a caretaker of the national monument—a job he gladly did for $1 a month.

Colorado National Monument Visitor Center, National Park Service, Rim Rock Dr., Fruita, CO 81521-9530. Phone: 970/858-3617. Fax: 970/858-0372. Website: www.nps.gov. Hours: Memorial Day–Labor Day, 8–7 daily; remainder of the year, 9–5 daily; closed Christmas. Admission: free, but monument admission is $4 per vehicle.

Dinosaur museum

DINAMATION'S DINOSAUR DISCOVERY MUSEUM

Robotic prehistoric creatures and realistic sculptures were the featured attractions of Dinamation's Dinosaur Discovery Museum in Fruita, just south of Interstate 70, until recently. The museum closed, but efforts are being made to reopen it with changes.

The museum, which opened in 1984 and was formerly known as the Devils Canyon Science and Learning Center, was operated by the Dinamation International Society, which produces robotic dinosaurs.

In addition to its animated dinosaur models, the museum featured 20 interactive displays, simulations of earthquakes, mounted dinosaur skeletons, and a working paleontology laboratory.

Dinamation's Dinosaur Discovery Museum, 550 Jurassic Court, Fruita, CO 81521. Phones: 970/858-7282 and 800/344-3466. Fax: 970/858-3522. Museum is now closed, but may reopen on a different basis.

FULFORD

Historic ghost town

FULFORD GHOST TOWN

The silver-mining town of Fulford, 22 miles southeast of Eagle, consisted of adjacent upper and lower mining camps. They were settled in 1889 and named in 1896 for Arthur H. Fulford, a mine owner killed in a snowslide.

The site originally was called Nolan's Creek Camp, after an early prospector who discovered gold in 1887. More than 500 mining claims were filed shortly thereafter, but few hit pay dirt. Some of the mines were dug in natural cliffs, and it often was necessary for miners to be lowered into the caves from above. The town flourished twice—in the 1890s and early 1900s, and again from 1912 to 1918—before faltering.

Only the ruins of several cabins remain in deserted upper Fulford, though a summer community of cabins has developed in lower Fulford. One of the Fulford caves also has become a tourist attraction.

Fulford Ghost Town, 22 miles southeast of Eagle. Contact: Eagle Visitors Center, 100 Fairgrounds Rd., Eagle, CO 81631. Phone: 970/328-5220.

GENOA

General museum/viewing tower

WONDER VIEW TOWER AND MUSEUM

The Wonder View Tower and Museum in Genoa on Colorado's eastern plains is a 65-foot view tower and a 22-room museum whose collections and exhibits focus on historical artifacts and natural history.

The facility is best known for its odd assortment of specimens, artifacts, and curiosities, and the fact that on a clear day, six states are visible from the observation tower.

Among the museum's diverse holdings are a 75,000-year-old mammoth tusk and bones found by the owner, Jerry Chubbuck; more than 20,000 arrowheads, some of which are rare; nearly 1,000 pictograph paintings; 500 glass insulators from electric utility poles; 100 horse collars; three preserved two-headed calves; and a wide array of other items, including antique bottles, locks and keys, branding irons, cash registers, china cherry pitters, bows and arrows, oil lamps, jewelry, coils, fish fossils, and firearms.

The tower was built as a tourist attraction around the turn of the twentieth century by C. W. Gregory and Myrtle le Bow. In addition to its observation area, the tower originally featured a cafe, a dance hall, a room walled with rocks from every state, and a fireplace of petrified wood. The rock-walled room and petrified-wood fireplace still remain. Jerry Chubbuck bought the tower when it came up for sale and added to its existing collections.

Wonder View Tower and Museum, 30121 Frontage Rd. (I-70 Exit 371), Genoa, CO 80818-8805. Phone: 719/763-2309. Hours: Mar.–Sept., 8–8. Admission: adults, $1; children 12–17, $.50; children under 12, free.

GEORGETOWN

Energy museum

GEORGETOWN ENERGY MUSEUM

The Georgetown Energy Museum, which opened in 1993, is housed in a working hydroelectric plant constructed in 1900 to provide electricity for Georgetown and its nearby mines, which needed power for hoists and air compressors.

The plant's principal feature is the century-old generating equipment, still in operation. The plant uses two Pelton waterwheels powered by high-pressure flow from a reservoir one mile away and 700 feet higher than the generating station.

In addition, the plant has two alternating-current generators, two direct-current exciters, and governors for the waterwheels, all displayed in the museum as examples of generating technology in the early twentieth century.

The museum also contains a collection of historical equipment related to the electrical industry, such as direct-current generators, alternating-current generators, electric motors, voltmeters, ammeters, and such consumer appliances as electric stoves, washing machines, and power tools. In addition, it has more than 300 photographs related to the Georgetown hydro plant and area, as well as books on the electric power industry dating back to the turn of the twentieth century.

Georgetown Energy Museum, 600 Griffith St., P.O. Box 398, Georgetown, CO 80444. Phone and fax: 303/569-3557. Hours: June–Sept., 10–4 daily; reduced hours the remainder of the year. Admission: adults, $2; children 10 and older, $1; children under 10, free.

Historic hotel/museum

HOTEL DE PARIS MUSEUM

The Hotel de Paris in Georgetown opened in 1875 and quickly became one of the most elegant places to stay and dine in the Old West. Today, it is a historic hotel/museum operated by the Colorado branch of the National Society of Colonial Dames of America.

The two-story stone-and-stucco hotel, known for its unique design, original furnishings, and colorful history, was built by Louis Dupuy, a Frenchman who came to Georgetown as a miner and eventually became an innovative innkeeper, master chef, scholar, and philosopher. It was his dream to create a luxurious hostelry and restaurant similar to the inns of Normandy, his homeland.

The Hotel de Paris was the site of the famous "millionaires' dinner" in 1879. Nine tycoons, including mine owners, railroad operators, and financial leaders representing combined assets of more than $200 million, joined Dupuy for dinner. They included Jay Gould and his son, George; General Grenville M. Dodge; Sidney Dillon; Russell Sage; Captain G. H. Baker; Oliver Ames; W.A.H. Loveland; and E. K. Berthoud.

The hotel featured steam heat and hot and cold running water (unusual for the time), decorative arts objects, a well-stocked library, hand-carved furniture, a courtyard, and excellent food. Celebrities from around the country came to enjoy the accommodations, food, ambiance, and conversation with Dupuy.

Dupuy died in 1900, and the hotel slid into decline before closing in the 1940s. Fortunately, the Colonial Dames purchased the once famous hotel and began restoring it to its 1875–1900 splendor in 1954. Extensive renovations also were conducted in the 1970s.

Among the original pieces are Haviland china, diamond-dust mirrors, a large pendulum clock, carved walnut furniture, lace curtains, tapestry drapes, paintings and etchings, and many of the books in the library.

The large kitchen still contains an antique stove and accessories, as well as washing and ironing equipment. The wine cellar has some of the old barrels, bottles, and early food containers.

Tours of the historic hotel are guided by volunteers from the Colonial Dames.

Hotel de Paris Museum, 409 6th St., P.O. Box 746, Georgetown, CO 80444. Phone: 303/569-2311. Hours: June 1–Sept. 30, 9–5 daily; remainder of the year, 12–4 Sat.–Sun. Admission: adults, $4; seniors, $3; children 6–16, $2; children under 6, free; groups, $2 per person.

Historic house/museum

HAMILL HOUSE MUSEUM

The Hamill House Museum in Georgetown is located in a country-style Gothic Revival house built in 1867 and later expanded by a silver-mining family. It now is owned and operated by Historic Georgetown Inc., which is restoring four other historic structures—the Bowman-White House, Tucker-Rutherford House, Kneisel House, and Johnson Cabin—as well.

The Hamill House was built by Joseph Watson, brother-in-law of William Arthur Hamill, a silver-mining speculator who acquired the house in 1874. He and his wife, Priscilla, expanded the house to its present dimensions in 1879, adding a dining room, conservatory, and rear wing, as well as central heating, gas lighting, bay windows, walnut woodwork, and interior decor.

At the same time, Hamill built the two chateauesque buildings at the rear of the property, using granite from his quarry west of Silver Plume. The larger building served as offices for Hamill's silver-mining and other business interests; the smaller structure was used as the carriage house, stable, and stable-hand's quarters.

After the family's fortunes declined following the 1893 silver crash, Hamill moved to Denver. The family's tenure in Georgetown ended in 1914. Between 1914 and 1970, the house was successively a rooming house, a historic house museum, and a restaurant/mountain lodge. Historic Georgetown Inc. purchased the property and reopened it as a museum in 1971.

When the house was acquired, it still possessed its walnut woodwork, downstairs wall and ceiling papers, light fixtures, and four fireplace mantels, but there was little else inside. It now is decorated with period pieces, including some of the original furniture (donated by Hamill descendants). Restoration was temporarily set back by fire in 1974, but the work is now virtually complete.

Hamill House, Historic Georgetown Inc., 305 Argentine St., P.O. Box 667, Georgetown, CO 80444. Phone: 303/569-2840. Fax: 303/674-2625. E-mail: preservation@historicgeorgetown.org. Website: www.historicgeorgetown.org. Hours: Memorial Day–Sept., 10–4 daily; Oct.–Dec., 10–4 Sat.–Sun.; closed remainder of the year. Admission: adults, $5; seniors and students, $4; children under 6, free; groups, $1 discount per person.

Historic railroad and mine

GEORGETOWN LOOP HISTORIC MINING AND RAILROAD PARK

The Georgetown Loop Railroad carries tourists between the mining towns of Georgetown and Silver Plume during summer. Courtesy Georgetown Loop Railroad and photographer Ron Ruhoff.

The Georgetown Loop Railroad, an engineering marvel originally built in 1884 as part of the Colorado Central Railroad, connects two historic mining towns, Georgetown and Silver Plume. Though the towns are only 2 miles apart, it takes 4.5 miles to travel between them by rail, because of the difficult terrain.

On its journey, the restored narrow-gauge train, owned by the Colorado Historical Society and operated by Georgetown Loop Railroad Inc., climbs 640 feet up steep mountain valley walls, twisting around 14 sharp curves and crossing four bridges, including the spectacular Devil's Gate trestle, which spans 300 feet and towers 95 feet above Clear Creek. It takes the old steam engine 1 hour and 10 minutes to make the round-trip.

The railroad, which connected with Denver in 1877 but never made it across the Continental Divide to Leadville as its owners once hoped, originally hauled silver ore and was a popular tourist attraction until 1939, when the line was closed and later dismantled. The Colorado Historical Society purchased the rail route in the 1950s and reopened the restored Georgetown–Silver Plume line in 1975.

Today, the Georgetown Loop Railroad is a National Historic Landmark and part of the Georgetown Loop Historic Mining and Railroad

Park, which also includes the 1877 Old Georgetown Station, a ticket office with historical displays; the Morrison Valley Center, an interpretive center in Georgetown offering exhibits and an audiovisual presentation; the original 1884 Silver Plume Depot, whose indoor displays are complemented by vintage engines and cars on exhibit in its yards; and the Lebanon Mine, a silver mine that operated in Silver Plume in the 1870s and 1880s. The historical society conducts guided tours of the mine and remaining support facilities (mine manager's office, change room, blacksmith's shop, and toolshed). The quarter-mile walking tour takes 1 hour and 20 minutes.

Visitors can take the train ride from Memorial Day through the first weekend in October. The mine tour is open only in summer. Tickets for the two attractions are purchased separately, and advance reservations are recommended. There are 11 departures daily, some boarding at Georgetown, others at Silver Plume.

Also available at the Old Georgetown Station are Trails and Rails Downhill Mountain Bike Tours, which combine biking down old mountain railroad beds and roads and riding the train. The half- and full-day tours depart daily at 8 A.M. and 1 P.M. and include a mountain bike rental, uphill transportation, protective gear, guided downhill tour, lunch, and the train ride. Four tour routes are offered—Guanella Pass and Argentine Central for a half-day, and Mount Evans and Mount McClellan for a full day.

Georgetown Loop Historic Mining and Railroad Park, 1106 Rose St., P.O. Box 217, Georgetown, CO 80444. Phones: 303/569-2403 and 800/691-4386. Fax: 303/569-2894. Website: www.georgetowncolorado.com. Train departures: Memorial Day weekend through the first weekend in Oct., trains leave Georgetown at 10, 11:20, 12:40, 2, and 3:20 daily and Silver Plume at 9:20, 10:40, 12, 1:20, 2:40, and 4 daily. Mine tours: Memorial Day weekend–Labor Day, times vary with train arrivals. Train tickets: adults, $12.95; children 3–15, $8.50; children under 3, free. Mine tour: adults, $5; children 3–15, $3; children under 3, free. Bike tour/ train ride: $65 to $95.

Historic building

OLD GEORGETOWN STATION

The Old Georgetown Station is the original 1877 terminal of the Colorado Central Railroad for trains between Denver and Georgetown. In 1884, it also served the rail line leading to Silver Plume. But the station closed when railroad service was discontinued in 1939.

The depot was reactivated in 1975, when the Colorado Historical Society purchased the rail route and restored summer tourist service between Georgetown and Silver Plume. It now functions primarily as a ticket office for the Georgetown Loop Railroad and Lebanon Mine tours. It also houses a cafe, gift shop, information center, historical displays, and affiliated booking office for downhill mountain bike tours.

Old Georgetown Station, 1106 Rose St., P.O. Box 217, Georgetown, CO 80444. Phones: 303/607-1686 and 800/691-4386. Fax: 303/569-2894. Website: www.georgetowncolorado.com. Hours: Memorial Day weekend through the first weekend in Oct., 7:30–5 daily. Admission: free.

Historic district

GEORGETOWN–SILVER PLUME HISTORIC DISTRICT

The entire commercial and residential areas of two early mining communities—Georgetown and Silver Plume—and the railroad grade connecting them are part of the Georgetown–Silver Plume Historic District.

The historic district, designated in 1966, contains many structures from the silver-mining boom in the latter part of the nineteenth century.

Among Georgetown's early buildings are the 1867 Hamill House, 1875 Hotel de Paris, 1877 Georgetown Station, 1900 hydroelectric plant, and such other structures as the Alpine Hose Company No. 2 station, Grace Episcopal Church, and McClellan House.

The Colorado Central Railroad grade between Georgetown and Silver Plume was built in 1884. The 4.5-mile track was considered an engineering marvel because of its steep grades, sharp curves, and many trestles and bridges. The rail line hauled silver ore and passengers until 1939, when the route was abandoned and dismantled. In the 1950s, the Colorado Historical Society purchased the route, restored the line over the next two decades, and resumed passenger service on a seasonal basis in 1975 as the Georgetown Loop Railroad. It now is one of Colorado's most popular tourist attractions.

The 1884 train depot is one of the surviving early structures in Silver Plume. Others include the Lebanon Mine and some of its support buildings from the 1870s–1880s and the 1894 schoolhouse, which held classes until 1959.

Georgetown–Silver Plume Historic District. Contact: Historic Georgetown Inc., 305 Argentine St., P.O. Box 667, Georgetown, CO 80444. Phone 303/569-2840. Fax: 303/674-2625. E-mail: preservation@historicgeorgetown.org. Website: www.historicgeorgetown.org.

GILLETT

Historic ghost town

GILLETT GHOST TOWN

Gillett, located in the Cripple Creek Mining District, was better known for its horse racing than its mining. Some of the leading horses of the day raced at the Gillett track, which was also the site of an 1895 bullfight attended by thousands of people.

The bullfight—the only one ever to be staged in the United States—featured bulls and bullfighters from Mexico, but it turned out to be a failure, ending in a riot on the first day of the three-day event. Several tired and frightened bulls were slaughtered, the promoters arrested, and the remainder of the event cancelled.

A number of gold mines, including the Lincoln, were located near Gillett, which had a reduction plant, an electric power plant, a railroad terminal and freight yard, and some of the finest houses and churches in the district. Only the ruins of an old church, the jail, and a few houses remain.

Gillett Ghost Town, 6 miles northeast of Cripple Creek on Colo. Hwy. 67. Contact: Cripple Creek Welcome Center, P.O. Box 430, Cripple Creek, CO 80813. Phones: 719/689-3315 and 877/858-4653. Fax: 719/689-2774.

GILMAN

Historic ghost town

GILMAN GHOST TOWN

Gilman, founded in 1886 and perched on Battle Mountain 1,200 feet above the Eagle River, became a ghost town after mining operations ended in 1984 and the Environmental Protection Agency declared the town a major cleanup site.

For years, Gilman competed with nearby Redcliff, where many of the area's miners lived. The towns were only three miles apart, but travel between the communities in winter was treacherous.

The miners worked in the Iron Mask, Star of the West, and Belden Mines in Gilman. In 1915, the mines were purchased and consolidated by the New Jersey Zinc Company, which ran the massive underground mining operation until 1977. Then the mine and town were sold to two other companies before closing in 1984. The last residents left the following year. However, many of Gilman's buildings still stand.

Gilman Ghost Town. Contact: Eagle County Historical Society Museum, Chambers Park, Fairgrounds Rd., Eagle, CO 81631. Phone: 970/328-6464. Alternate contact: Redcliff Community Center, 400 Pine St., P.O. Box 40, Redcliff, CO 81649. Phone: 970/827-5303. Fax: 970/827-5300.

GLENWOOD SPRINGS

History museum

FRONTIER HISTORICAL SOCIETY MUSEUM

Exhibits on local history, the Ute Indians, and John "Doc" Holliday, a hard-drinking gambler (and friend of gunfighter Wyatt Earp) who died in Glenwood Springs, are featured at the Frontier Historical Society Museum in Glenwood Springs.

The 2,500-square-foot museum is located in a beautifully preserved 1905 house that still retains its original wood facings and decor. Founded in 1964, the museum occupied the house in 1971.

Frontier Historical Society Museum, 1001 Colorado Ave., Glenwood Springs, CO 81601. Phone: 970/945-4448. Hours: May–Oct., 11–4 Mon.–Sat.; remainder of the year, 1–4 Mon., Thurs., Sat.; closed major holidays. Admission: adults, $3; seniors, $2; children under 12, free; groups, $1 per person.

Historic site

GLENWOOD HOT SPRINGS POOL

Opened in 1890, this historic pool in Glenwood Springs is 615 feet long and 75 feet wide, making it the world's largest outdoor hot springs pool.

The pool is fed by the Yampah Spring, which flows at 3.5 million gallons a day and is believed to be one of the hottest in the world. The spring was discovered in 1860 by a geological expedition led by Captain Richard Sopris, for whom a nearby mountain is named.

In 1886, the Devereux brothers and a group of British investors bought the spring and 10 acres of land, intending to build the world's largest hot springs pool. The two-block-long pool and a red sandstone bathhouse and lodge opened in 1890. Hoping to make Glenwood Springs a major resort, the Devereux brothers also built the adjacent Hotel Colorado in 1893 (see following listing). The hotel is still in operation but is now separately owned.

The outdoor hot springs pool in Glenwood Springs is the world's largest.
Courtesy Hot Springs Lodge and Pool.

In 1956, a group of local businessmen purchased the pool, bathhouse, and lodge and began long-term major renovations. Improvements
included an updated pool with a filtration system in the 1960s; a new
bathhouse complex with a sport shop, athletic club, and restaurant-
lounge in the 1970s; a new 107-room lodge and additional parking in
the 1980s; and changes to the original stone bathhouse, which now also
contains an athletic club and offices, in the 1990s. The facility, known
today as the Hot Springs Lodge and Pool, has a main pool kept at 90
degrees and a smaller therapy pool kept at 104 degrees.

Hot Springs Lodge and Pool, 401 N. River Rd., Glenwood Springs, CO 81601.
Phone: 970/945-2846. Fax: 970/945-6683. Hours: summer, 7:30 A.M.–10 P.M.
daily; winter, 9 A.M.–10 P.M. daily. Pool admission: adults $7.25; children 3–12,
$4.75; children under 3, free; groups of 20 or more, $6.25 for adults and $4.25 for
children.

Historic hotel

HOTEL COLORADO

The Hotel Colorado in Glenwood Springs opened in 1893 as part of an effort to make the hot springs community a world resort.

The Victorian hotel was built by the Devereux brothers—Walter, Horace, and James—adjacent to their newly opened Glenwood Hot Springs Pool, still the world's largest outdoor hot springs pool (see previous listing).

Modeled after the Villa de Medici in Italy, the hotel has hosted European royalty, U.S. presidents and senators, movie stars, and others who came to enjoy the pool and the Glenwood Springs area.

The hot springs resort maintained its appeal almost until World War I, then fell into decline in the 1920s and 1930s. During World War II, the hotel served as a U.S. Navy convalescent hospital; the pool was used therapeutically to help rehabilitate disabled sailors and marines from 1943 to 1945.

Following the war, the 128-room hotel was sold and began operating independently from the pool. The hotel, which changed its name to Village Inn for a number of years, became a National Historic Landmark in 1979. The hotel has undergone a number of renovations and currently is completing a $2.5-million improvement program.

Hotel Colorado, 526 Pine St., Glenwood Springs, CO 81601. Phone: 970/945-6511. Fax: 970/945-7841. Hours: open 24 hours. Rates: vary with room and season.

GOLDEN

History museum

GOLDEN PIONEER MUSEUM

The Golden Pioneer Museum was created as a Works Progress Administration (WPA) project in 1938 but closed during World War II. It did not reopen until 1953, when the Daughters of the American Revolution (DAR) took over the facility. It now is operated by the City of Golden and managed by the local DAR chapter.

During its history, the museum has moved several times—from an old schoolhouse to the old county courthouse, from there to a wing of city hall, and finally to the old library building in 1996.

The museum tells the story of Golden and the surrounding area from the Indian and pioneer days of the nineteenth century through

World War II, featuring artifacts from Golden and other parts of Jefferson County. Among the displays are period clothing and furniture, household items, mining equipment, military accessories, Native American tools, and Golden's first galvanized bathtub.

The museum is also home to the Mary Wallenhorst Johnson Research Center, which contains genealogical resource materials, an extensive photograph collection, and more than 250 genealogical volumes.

Golden Pioneer Museum, 923 10th St., Golden, CO 80401. Phone: 303/278-7151. Fax: 303/278-2755. Website: www.henge.com/-goldenpm. Hours: 10–4:30 Mon.–Sat.; closed major holidays. Admission: free.

History museum

BUFFALO BILL MEMORIAL MUSEUM AND GRAVE

William F. "Buffalo Bill" Cody died at his sister's house in Denver in 1917 and was buried (at his request) on Lookout Mountain near Golden. Four years later, Cody's foster son, Johnny Baker, founded what is today's Buffalo Bill Memorial Museum and Grave at the burial site.

Baker, a marksman with Cody's Wild West shows, created the museum to house mementoes from Buffalo Bill's life and his popular western shows. Because of his close relationship to Cody, Baker was able to collect many of Buffalo Bill's personal effects and compile one of the nation's largest collections of Wild West show posters.

The original museum building now is a National Historic Site and contains a gift shop. The collections and exhibits are now housed in an adjacent modern building. The museum, operated by the City of Denver, is located in Lookout Mountain Park, a 65-acre Denver mountain park.

The museum features women of the Wild West shows, a Native American gallery, a changing-exhibition area, and a historical timeline of Buffalo Bill's life. The collections consist of items associated with Cody and his times, including objects and documents, historic photographs, and the extensive show posters. Among the unique items are one of the few remaining scripts from a Buffalo Bill stage appearance, Sitting Bull's bow and arrows, firearms used by Cody, and a painting of Cody by Frederic Remington.

Buffalo Bill Memorial Museum and Grave, 987½ Lookout Mountain Rd., Golden CO 80401. Phone: 303/526-0747. Fax: 303/526-0197. Hours: May–Oct., 9–5 daily; Nov.–Apr., 9–4 Tues.–Sun.; closed Christmas. Admission: adults, $3; seniors, $2; children 6–15, $1; children under 6, free; groups, $2 per person for adults and $.75 for children.

Geology/mineralogy museum

COLORADO SCHOOL OF MINES GEOLOGY MUSEUM

Established in 1874, the Colorado School of Mines Geology Museum in Golden is one of the first museums in Colorado.

The museum houses extensive collections on mineralogy, paleontology, geology, and Colorado mining, and contains two floors of exhibits on minerals, gems, scientific instruments, and mining equipment and artifacts.

The Colorado School of Mines also offers, through its mining engineering department, public tours of the Edgar Experimental Mine, an underground classroom and laboratory it operates in Idaho Springs (see separate listing under Idaho Springs).

Colorado School of Mines Geology Museum, 16th and Maple Sts., Golden, CO. (Postal address: Geology Museum, 1500 Illinois St., Golden, CO 80401-1887.) Phones: 303/273-3815 and 303/273-3823. Fax: 303/273-3859. E-mail: vamast@mines.edu. Hours: 9–4 Mon.–Sat.; also 1–4 Sun. in Sept.–June; closed major holidays. Admission: free.

Living-history museum

CLEAR CREEK HISTORY PARK

Life in Golden in the late nineteenth and early twentieth centuries is re-created at the Clear Creek History Park, which features costumed interpreters giving demonstrations and tours amid historic structures relocated from elsewhere in the area.

Among these structures is the 1876 Guy Hill School, a one-room schoolhouse originally erected in Golden Gate Canyon. It was placed on the Mitchell Elementary School grounds during the nation's 1976 bicentennial observance and then relocated to Clear Creek History Park in 1996.

Other structures at the 3.5-acre park include two old log cabins (an 1873 cabin and an 1878 cabin with an 1897 addition); an early barn, privy, and chicken coop; and replicas of a turn-of-the-twentieth-century blacksmith's shop, smokehouse, and root cellar. The park also contains gardens typical of the period.

The historical park, which opened in 1997, is operated by the Friends of Astor House and Clear Creek History Park.

Clear Creek History Park, 11th and Arapahoe Sts., Golden, CO 80401. (Contact: Astor House, 822 12th St., Golden, CO 80401. Phones: 303/278-3557 and 303/216-1243. Fax: 303/278-8916. E-mail: cchpark@aol.com.) Hours: May 15–Oct. 15, 11–5 Wed.–Sun; remainder of the year, 9–4 Tues.–Sat.; closed major holidays, except Fourth of July. Admission: adults, $3; children 5–12, $2; children under 5, free.

Mountaineering museum

AMERICAN MOUNTAINEERING MUSEUM

The American Alpine Club, founded in 1902 by alumni of Ivy League universities, moved its headquarters, library, and museum from New York City to Golden in 1993; it now shares Golden's 35,000-square-foot former junior high school building with the Colorado Mountain Club and the Colorado Outward Bound School.

Originally limited to individuals with significant climbing experience, the Alpine Club has opened its membership to anyone interested in mountaineering.

The museum—scheduled to reopen by mid-2000—houses such items as a diary kept by William Howard during the first American ascent of Mont Blanc, the U.S. flag carried up Mount Whitney in 1865, and a scale model of Mount Everest. Other resources include an 18,000-volume library of mountaineering books, which range from fifteenth-century rare volumes to contemporary books of practical advice for climbers.

American Mountaineering Museum, 710 10th St., Suite 50, Golden, CO 80401. Phone: 303/384-0110. Website: www.mountaincenter.org. Hours: to be determined. Admission: to be determined.

Quilt museum

ROCKY MOUNTAIN QUILT MUSEUM

The Rocky Mountain Quilt Museum in Golden is dedicated to the preservation and promotion of the art and history of American quilts and quilt making.

It was founded in 1982 by Eugenia Mitchell, a Golden resident who donated 100 quilts, some of which she made herself, to the facility. The museum is one of only six museums in the nation devoted exclusively to quilting. It now has more than 200 quilts in its collection.

The museum moved into its present site in 1990. It has two galleries, which display quilts from its collections and those on loan from other sources.

Rocky Mountain Quilt Museum, 1111 Washington Ave., Golden, CO 80401. Phone: 303/277-0377. Fax: 303/215-1636. E-mail: rmqm@worldnet.att.net. Website: www.rmqm.org. Hours: 10–4 Mon.–Sat.; closed New Year's Day, Thanksgiving, and Christmas. Admission: adults, $3; children 6–12, $1; children under 6, free.

Railroad museum

COLORADO RAILROAD MUSEUM

More than 60 narrow- and standard-gauge locomotives, passenger and freight cars, cabooses, and other historical rolling stock can be seen outdoors on early tracks at the Colorado Railroad Museum in Golden.

More than 50,000 railroad artifacts, photographs, and documents, plus a 45-foot-by-20-foot HO-scale model railroad layout are located in the museum building, a replica of an 1880s-style masonry depot.

The museum, founded in 1959, occupies 4 acres at the foot of North Table Mountain and is the largest railroad museum in the Rocky Mountain region.

The locomotives and cars on display are surviving examples of the thousands that once operated in the mountains and plains of Colorado and surrounding states. Several are open to inspection; others are being restored or used to store artifacts and archives. One narrow-gauge locomotive—the 1881 Denver & Rio Grande Western No. 346—and a 1930s "Galloping Goose" rail car are run on the museum's one-third-mile track a number of times each year.

Among the historic locomotives and cars are an 1880 Denver Leadville & Gunnison locomotive; a 317-ton Chicago Burlington & Quincy locomotive that could haul 100-car freight trains; three "Galloping Geese" rail cars, which replaced steam trains in the mountains of southwestern Colorado from 1931 to 1951; an 1872 Denver & Rio Grande business car that was rebuilt in 1884 as an office and home for rail officials out on the line; an 1887 Colorado Midland observation car built by Pullman; an 1899 Colorado & Southern steam-powered rotary snowplow; an 1881 Denver & Rio Grande caboose; and the oldest existing freight car from a Colorado railroad—the 1887 Rio Grande Southern bunk car used to house maintenance workers out on the line.

The Colorado Railroad Museum started a hall of fame to honor outstanding Colorado railroad figures, inducting the first four honorees in 1998.

Colorado Railroad Museum, 17155 W. 44th Ave., Golden, CO 80402-1121. Phones: 303/279-4591 and 800/365-6263. Fax: 303/270-4229. E-mail: mail@crrm.org. Website: www.crrm.org. Hours: 9–5 daily; closed Thanksgiving and Christmas. Admission: adults, $4; seniors, $3.50; children under 16, $2; families $9.50.

Art center/art galleries

FOOTHILLS ART CENTER

The Foothills Art Center, located in two historic buildings in Golden, seeks to further the fine arts through a variety of changing exhibitions and educational programs.

Founded in 1968, the art center has six galleries in which an annual theme show, several self-curated exhibitions, two annual juried exhibitions (Colorado Clay Exhibition and Rocky Mountain National Watermedia Exhibition), and two biennial juried exhibitions (Colorado Art Open Exhibition and North American Sculpture Exhibition) are presented.

The Foothills Art Center, which also has an extensive education program and an art library, is housed in an 1872 former Presbyterian church and an adjacent Victorian mansion, both listed on the National Register of Historic Places.

Foothills Art Center, 809 15th St., Golden, CO 80401. Phone: 303/279-3922. Fax: 303/279-9470. Hours: 9–4 Mon.–Sat., 1–4 Sun.; closed national holidays. Admission: free.

Visitor center

COORS VISITOR CENTER

Informal tours of the Coors Brewing Company's plant in Golden began a year after the brewery was founded in 1873 and were formalized in the late 1940s. Today, up to 300,000 visitors tour the plant annually.

Visitors park their cars in the lot at 13th and Ford Streets, take the shuttle bus through downtown historic Golden, and enter the Coors Visitor Center, where the 30-minute walking tour of the brewery begins.

Among the exhibits in the entrance area are five themed dioramas (The Dream, Prohibition, Innovations, Mystique, and The Future) and a changing display of memorabilia covering more than 125 years of brewing.

The guided tour of the brewery takes visitors through malting, packaging, and related processes. The brewhouse is filled with 50 beautiful hand-hammered copper kettles, each containing 15,500 gallons of liquid. In the packaging area, up to 1,800 aluminum cans per minute roll off each assembly line. The tour concludes in a hospitality lounge, where visitors can sample Coors beers and non-alcoholic beverages.

Coors Visitor Center and Tour, Coors Brewing Co., 12th and Ford Sts., P.O. Box 4030, Golden, CO 80401-1295. Phone: 303/277-2337. Fax: 303/277-5337. Hours: 10–4 Mon.–Sat.; closed major holidays. Admission: free.

Visitor center

DAN SCHAEFER VISITORS CENTER AT THE NATIONAL RENEWABLE ENERGY LABORATORY

The National Renewable Energy Laboratory in Golden is the nation's premier center for the research and development of solar, wind, geothermal, biofuel, and other renewable and alternative energy sources.

Originally called the Solar Energy Research Institute, the facility began operations in 1977 and gained national-laboratory status in 1991. It is operated by Midwest Research Institute for the U.S. Department of Energy on a contract basis.

The laboratory's mission is to lead the nation toward a sustainable energy future by developing renewable energy technologies, improving energy efficiency, advancing related science and engineering, and facilitating commercialization.

The laboratory's visitor center—named for former congressman Dan Schaefer—features exhibits on renewable energy and energy efficiency, including interactive exhibits and videos that explain how people can use such technologies in their homes, vehicles, and communities. The building itself incorporates passive solar energy technologies, including a Trombe wall that provides light and heat.

Dan Schaefer Visitors Center, National Renewable Energy Laboratory, 15013 Denver West Pkwy., Golden, CO 80401. Phone: 303/384-6565. Fax: 303/384-6568. Hours: 8–5 Mon.–Fri.; closed national holidays. Admission: free.

Visitor center

GOLDEN GATE CANYON STATE PARK VISITORS CENTER

Golden Gate Canyon State Park near Golden covers more than 14,000 acres and has 35 miles of hiking trails, 15 miles of mountain biking trails, and a visitor center with exhibits on the park.

The Golden Gate Canyon State Park Visitors Center, located inside the southeast entrance, opened in the late 1960s and was extensively remodeled in 1995. Its exhibits pertain to the history, wildlife, geology, ecology, recreational opportunities, and weather of the park, which is operated by the Colorado State Parks Division of the Natural Resources Department.

Golden Gate Canyon State Park Visitors Center, 3873 Colo. Hwy. 46 (Golden Gate Canyon Rd.), Golden, CO 80403. Phone: 303/582-3707. Fax: 303/582-3212. Hours: 8–4:30 daily; closed Thanksgiving and Christmas. Admission: $4 per vehicle.

Nature center/visitor center

LOOKOUT MOUNTAIN NATURE CENTER

The Lookout Mountain Nature Center near Golden is both a nature center and a travelers' visitor center in the 110-acre Lookout Mountain Nature Preserve.

The center, part of the Jefferson County Open Space Park System, was opened in 1985 and recently moved into a new 7,900-square-foot building, which hosts nature exhibits, programs, and lectures and serves as the starting point for hikes and field trips. The nature preserve has 8.5 miles of hiking trails.

The first of the center's new exhibits deals with migratory birds and the plants and animals of the ponderosa pine country. Other exhibits interpret the region's ecosystem. In addition to general programs, the center offers tailored programs for children under 5, children 5–10, and others. Programs are free but require advance registration.

The center is located several miles from Interstate 70 via Exit 256.

Lookout Mountain Nature Preserve, 910 Colorow Rd., Golden, CO 80401. Phone: 303/526-0694. Fax: 303/321-5368. Hours: 10–4 Tues.–Sun. Admission: free.

Historic site

MOTHER CABRINI SHRINE

The Mother Cabrini Shrine on Lookout Mountain in Golden honors Frances Xavier Cabrini, one of the founders of the Institute of the Missionary Sisters of the Sacred Heart of Jesus and the first U.S. saint.

Born in Italy, she came to New York to help Italian immigrants, then moved to Colorado in 1902 to open a school in north Denver's Mount Carmel parish. In 1905, the Queen of Heaven Orphanage, where young girls were cared for and educated by the Missionary Sisters, was built on Federal Boulevard. Mother Cabrini later purchased the Golden property for a summer camp for the orphans. With her beatification in 1938, the site became a place of prayer and devotion.

Today, the shrine continues to attract pilgrims. An imposing 22-foot statue of the Sacred Heart on an 11-foot base is visible to motorists traveling on Interstate 70. Also located on the site are a 1915 stone house and barn, a building for prayer and meetings, and a 1970 main building with a chapel, convent, and gift shop.

The shrine is open daily to visitors. Mass is celebrated at 7:30 A.M. daily, as well as 11 A.M. on Sunday. Retreat facilities are available.

*Mother Cabrini Shrine, 20189 Cabrini Blvd., Golden, CO 80401. Phone: 303/
526-0758. Fax: 303/526-9795. Hours: summer, 7–7 daily; winter, 7–5 daily.
Admission: free.*

Historic site

ROCKY FLATS NUCLEAR WEAPONS PRODUCTION PLANT

The former Rocky Flats nuclear weapons production plant—now
called the Rocky Flats Environmental Technology Site—is listed on the
National Register of Historic Places for "making a significant contribu-
tion to the broad patterns of U.S. history."

The U.S. Department of Energy facility, which used radioactive and
hazardous materials to make components for nuclear weapons for nearly
40 years, is now a Superfund cleanup site destined to be closed down.

Rocky Flats comprises more than 750 structures on a 385-acre industrial area surrounded by nearly 6,000 acres of controlled open space
north of Golden. Its legacy of contaminated facilities, soils, and ground
water must be cleaned up before the site can be closed and converted to
another use.

The cleanup work is being conducted by the Kaiser-Hill Company
and the Department of Energy under a 10-year agreement that runs
through 2006. The former manufacturing buildings are being decon-
taminated and decommissioned, and steps are being taken to correct the
soil and water problems and remove hazardous materials. Meanwhile, an
informational exhibit has been installed in the Kaiser-Hill office building,
and a visitor center is under development at the site. The site will be
open at least through 2006.

*Rocky Flats Environmental Technology Site, Colo. Hwy. 93, P.O. Box 464, Golden,
CO 80402-0464. Phone: 303/966-8164. Hours: 6–4:30 Mon.–Fri.; closed
major holidays. Admission: free.*

Historic house/museum

ASTOR HOUSE MUSEUM

The Astor House Museum in Golden is located in a former hotel
that is listed on the National Register of Historic Places. The hotel,
erected in 1867, was among Colorado's finest of the era. It was built by
Seth Lake, a Baptist deacon, to house legislators (at the time, Golden
City was the territorial capital of Colorado).

After the capital moved to Denver, the hotel served other guests
until it was purchased by Ida Goetze and converted into a boarding-

house. Mrs. Goetze's family operated the boardinghouse until the 1950s. In 1971, when the old Astor House Hotel was slated to become a parking lot, concerned citizens formed the Golden Landmarks Association. They fought the impending demolition by petitioning for a ballot initiative, which passed in 1972.

The building, now a museum, has been restored as a turn-of-the-twentieth-century western Victorian hotel. Rooms now offer different glimpses into the life and times of Golden City when it was the capital of the Colorado Territory.

Astor House Museum, Golden Landmarks Assn., 822 12th St., Golden, CO 80401. Phone and fax: 303/278-3557. E-mail: goldenlm@aol.com. Website: www.webspan.com/fastpart/astorhouse.html. Hours: 11–4 Tues.–Sat.; closed Dec. 25–Jan. 2. Admission: adults, $3; children 12 and under, $1.

Historic house/museum

BOETTCHER MANSION

The 1917 Boettcher Mansion on Lookout Mountain in Golden was the summer home and hunting lodge of Charles Boettcher, one of Colorado's early entrepreneurs. It is now a historic house operated by Jefferson County on 110 acres of open space.

The two-story Craftsman-style mansion, listed on the National Register of Historic Places, was opened to the public in the mid-1970s. It contains a collection of arts-and-crafts-style furnishings and information and photographs on the Boettcher family, Lookout Mountain, and Golden. The mansion may be rented for special events.

Boettcher Mansion, 900 Colorow Rd., Lookout Mountain, Golden, CO 80401. Phone: 303/526-0855. Fax: 303/526-5519. Hours: 8–5 Mon.–Fri., Sat.–Sun. by appointment; closed major holidays. Admission: free.

Historic district

12TH STREET HISTORIC RESIDENTIAL DISTRICT

The 12th Street Historic Residential District in Golden features a row of exceptional 1860s brick buildings, including the Astor House Museum, an 1867 former hotel with period furnishings (see separate listing).

The historic district, which was listed on the National Register of Historic Places in 1983, also contains Colorado's first National Guard Armory. Built in 1913, it is the largest cobblestone building in the United States.

12th Street Historic Residential District. Contact: Golden Landmarks Assn., 822 12th St., Golden, CO 80401. Phone and fax: 303/278-3557.

GOLDFIELD

Historic ghost town

GOLDFIELD GHOST TOWN

Near the turn of the twentieth century, during the height of the gold-mining craze, Goldfield was the third-largest town in the Cripple Creek Mining District. Today, it is a ghost town with boarded-up buildings and abandoned mines.

Located one mile northeast of Victor, Goldfield was founded in 1895 by the owners of the Portland Gold Mining Company and grew rapidly as a heavily unionized miners' town. By 1899, it was competing with Cripple Creek to become the county seat of the newly formed Teller County. Goldfield, however, lost out. It suffered further in a 1904 labor dispute in which strike leaders—including several town officials—were forced to leave the mining district.

The combined town hall/fire station is the principal surviving building in Goldfield and was listed on the National Register of Historic Places in 1984. Most of the other historic structures are weathered homes and storefronts.

Goldfield Ghost Town, 1 mile northeast of Victor. Contact: Victor Chamber of Commerce, P.O. Box 83, Victor, CO 80860. Phone: 719/689-3553.

GOLD HILL

Historic district

GOLD HILL HISTORIC DISTRICT

Gold Hill, a mountain community 11 miles northwest of Boulder, is one of Colorado's oldest mining camps. When gold was discovered in 1859 near present-day Gold Hill, thousands of prospectors rushed to the area, but few hit pay dirt. A few years later, gold-bearing quartz was found at the Horsfal Mine, setting off another surge of prospecting, mostly unsuccessful.

The original Gold Hill mining camp burned down in a fire in 1860 but was quickly rebuilt. In 1872, when tellurium ore was discovered in the area, a new town of Gold Hill was established close to the original site.

This later Gold Hill is now part of the Gold Hill Historic District, listed in 1989 on the National Register of Historic Places. It includes early log cabins, frame structures, and more recent buildings, bounded by Main, Pine, College, and Horsfal Streets. Among the district's historic structures are the Bluebird Lodge (originally the Westworth House), Gold Hill Inn, Gold Hill General Store, and 1873 Gold Hill School, the oldest continuously operating school in Colorado.

No longer a mining center, rustic Gold Hill has become a tourist attraction and a mountain bedroom community for people who work in Boulder.

Gold Hill Historic District. Contact: Boulder Convention and Visitors Bureau, 2440 Pearl St., Boulder, CO 80302. Phones: 303/442-2911 and 800/444-0447. Fax: 303/938-8837. Website: www.chamber.boulder.co.us.

GOTHIC

Historic ghost town

GOTHIC GHOST TOWN

The mining town of Gothic, eight miles north of Crested Butte, was short-lived. Gold and silver ores were discovered at the foot of Gothic Mountain in 1879, but by 1884 the gold and silver deposits were depleted; most of Gothic's 8,000 residents left shortly thereafter.

Garwood Hall Judd, however, stayed on until his death in 1930. Once the town's mayor, Judd was Gothic's only resident for many years. Found dead in his cabin, he was cremated, and his ashes were scattered around town.

The highlight of Gothic's boom years was an 1880 visit by General Ulysses S. Grant, who toured many of Colorado's early mining towns. The citizens gave him a noisy parade in which the general drove his own stagecoach at the head of the procession.

Several old buildings located at the town site now are used by the Rocky Mountain Biological Laboratory in its summertime studies of the area's plant and animal life.

Gothic Ghost Town, 8 miles north of Crested Butte. Contact: Crested Butte–Mt. Crested Butte Chamber of Commerce, 601 Elk Ave., Crested Butte, CO 81224. Phones: 970/349-6438 and 800/545-4505. Fax: 970/349-1023.

The Regional History Museum, part of the Museum of Western Colorado in Grand Junction, traces area history from the 1880s to the present. Courtesy Museum of Western Colorado Research Center and Special Library and photographer Jerry Van Wyngarden.

GRAND JUNCTION

History/natural history museum

MUSEUM OF WESTERN COLORADO

> Regional History Museum
> Dinosaur Valley Museum
> Cross Orchards Historic Farm Site

The Museum of Western Colorado, the largest museum between Denver and Salt Lake City, operates three museums and manages three natural resource areas in the Grand Junction region.

Founded in 1966, the former main museum is now the Regional History Museum. The two other museums are the Dinosaur Valley Museum, which features dinosaur fossils, and Cross Orchards Historic Farm Site, a living-history museum re-creating the early 1900s.

The three natural resource areas where dinosaur fossils have been found are Riggs Hill, site of the 1900 discovery of the world's first known

Brachiosaurus; Dinosaur Hill, where the *Apatosaurus* displayed at the Field Museum in Chicago was quarried in 1901; and Rabbit Valley, where ongoing excavations continue to uncover new fossil specimens. All three outdoor sites, located west and northwest of Grand Junction, have self-guided trails that teach about each area's geology and paleontology.

Regional History Museum

The Regional History Museum in downtown Grand Junction features Native American artifacts, natural history exhibits, and a timeline tracing the history of western Colorado from 1880 to the present.

The museum contains collections of costumes, small arms, minerals, fossils, and historical, archaeological, ethnological, botanical, zoological, and other materials relating to western Colorado, as well as an extensive research library and collections of historical documents and photographs.

Regional History Museum, Museum of Western Colorado, 233 S. 5th St., P.O. Box 2000-5020, Grand Junction, CO 81502. Phone: 970/242-0971. Fax: 970/242-3960. Website: www.mwc.mus.co.us. Hours: winter, 10–4 Tues.–Sat.; summer, 10–4 Mon.–Sat.; closed major holidays. Admission: adults, $3; seniors, $2.50; children 2–12, $2; children under 2, free; families, $8.

Dinosaur Valley Museum

The Dinosaur Valley Museum, located two blocks from the Regional History Museum, explores the science of paleontology and features fossil specimens from the area and realistic robotic dinosaurs that stomp, roar, startle, and amuse visitors. Other displays include examples of early paleontology work and ancient dinosaur trackways. An active paleontology laboratory is also on view to visitors.

Dinosaur Valley Museum, Museum of Western History, 362 Main St., P.O. Box 2000-5020, Grand Junction, CO 81502. Phone: 970/243-3466. Fax: 970/242-3960. Website: www.mwc.mus.co.us. Hours: winter, 10–4 Tues.–Sat.; summer, 9–4 daily; closed major holidays. Admission: adults, $4; seniors, $4.50; children 3–12, $2; children under 3, free; families, $10.

Cross Orchards Historic Site

Cross Orchards Historic Site is a 25-acre living-history museum that re-creates the lifeways and agricultural traditions of the early 1900s in western Colorado.

Authentically costumed guides provide tours and perform demon-strations of such old-time crafts as candle making, woodworking, blacksmithing, woodstove cooking, weaving, and spinning as practiced during the farm's heyday in the 1910s.

The Cross family from Massachusetts owned and operated the original 243-acre orchard/farm, which was planted with 22,000 apple trees, from 1896 to 1923. It was the largest of many fruit-producing orchards in Mesa County. The property was sold in 1924, acquired by a community preservationist group in the 1970s, and opened as a museum in the 1980s.

The barn/packing shed and the workers' bunkhouse are listed on the National Register of Historic Places. Other buildings and early agricul-tural equipment are also on the site.

In addition, the museum property has three auxiliary exhibits—a section of the narrow-gauge Uintah Railway, with a historic engine, several cars, caboose, and trestle; vintage road-building equipment; and turn-of-the-twentieth-century farming equipment and household items.

A number of seasonal events and workshops reflecting the area's agricultural heritage and traditions are presented.

Cross Orchards Historic Farm Site is part of the Museum of Western Colorado in Grand Junction. Courtesy Museum of Western Colorado Research Center and Special Library and photographer Jerry van Wyngarden

Cross Orchards Historic Farm Site, Museum of Western Colorado, 3073 Patterson Rd./F Rd., Grand Junction, CO 81504. Phone: 970/434-9814. Fax: 970/523-7914. Website: www.mwc.mus.co.us. Hours: Apr.–Oct., 9–3 Tues.–Sat.; closed Sun.–Mon. and remainder of the year. Admission: adults, $3; seniors, $2.50; children 2–12, $2; children under 2, free; families, $8.

Children's museum

DOO ZOO CHILDREN'S MUSEUM

The Doo Zoo Children's Museum in Grand Junction was established in 1984 as a hands-on museum promoting learning and parent/child interaction.

Among the museum's most popular exhibits are the grocery store, playhouse, post office, bank, manipulative toys, fish and animals, and miniature fire truck.

Doo Zoo Children's Museum, 248 Colorado Ave., Suite B, Grand Junction, CO 81501. Phone: 970/241-5225. Hours: 10–5 Mon.–Sat.; closed Fourth of July, Thanksgiving, and Christmas. Admission: adults, $1; children 2–14, $4; children 1 year old, $2; children under 1, free.

Art gallery

JOHNSON ART GALLERY AT MESA STATE COLLEGE

The Johnson Art Gallery in the W. W. Campbell College Center at Mesa State College in Grand Junction presents art exhibitions by students, faculty, and professional regional artists during the academic year.

Johnson Art Gallery, Mesa State College, W. W. Campbell College Center, 12th and Elm Sts. (postal address: Art. Dept., Mesa State College, 1175 Texas Ave.) Grand Junction, CO 81501. Phone: 970/248-1233. Fax: 970/248-1199. Hours: late Aug.–early May, 9–4 Mon.–Thurs., 9–12 Fri., call for hours on Sat.; closed major holidays and when classes are not in session. Admission: free.

Arts center

WESTERN COLORADO CENTER FOR THE ARTS

Changing exhibitions of arts and crafts are presented in three galleries of the Western Colorado Center for the Arts in Grand Junction. The arts center, founded in 1953, also offers theater, music, dance, film, and other programs, as well as classes in arts and crafts.

Western Colorado Center for the Arts, 1803 N. 7th St., Grand Junction, CO 81501. Phone: 970/243-7337. Fax: 970/243-2482. Website: newcomersnet/ artcenter.com. Hours: 9–4 Tues.–Sat.; closed national holidays. Admission: adults and children, $2; Tuesdays are free.

Botanic gardens/butterfly house

WESTERN COLORADO BOTANICAL GARDENS

The Western Colorado Botanical Gardens in Grand Junction feature a 4,000-square-foot greenhouse with 600 varieties of tropical plants and a butterfly house containing North American native species.

Opened in 1997, the gardens cover more than 12 acres. A rose garden and 32 varieties of dahlias were recently supplemented with a color and harmony garden (plantings showing color throughout the year), a sensory garden used in cultural therapy classes, and an amphitheater for outdoor programs.

The facility is operated by the Western Colorado Botanical Society.

Western Colorado Botanical Gardens, 641 Struthers Ave., Grand Junction, CO 81501. Phones: 970/245-3090 and 970/245-3288. Fax: 970/245-9001. E-mail: webotanical@gvii.net. Website: www.wcbotanic.org. Hours: 10–5 Wed.–Mon.; closed New Year's Day, Thanksgiving, and Christmas. Admission: adults, $3; seniors and students, $2; children 5–12, $1.50; children under 5, free.

Historic district

NORTH SEVENTH STREET HISTORIC RESIDENTIAL DISTRICT

A variety of architectural styles—including Queen Anne, Colonial Revival, and Mission—are represented in the North Seventh Street Historic Residential District, the most intact historic residential area in Grand Junction.

The five-block historic district, located on Seventh Street from Hill to White Avenues, was developed between the 1890s and 1930s and reflects a progression from modest cottages to elaborate bungalows. It has a wide tree-lined boulevard with a grassy median.

The district was listed on the National Register of Historic Places in 1984.

North Seventh Street Historic Residential District. Contact: Grand Junction Visitors and Convention Bureau, 740 Horizon Dr., Grand Junction, CO 81506. Phones: 970/244-1480 and 800/962-2547. Fax: 970/243-7393.

GRAND LAKE

Historic house/museum

KAUFFMAN HOUSE MUSEUM

The Kauffman House Museum, operated by the Grand Lake Area Historical Society, is located in Ezra Kauffman's 1892 tourist hotel and residence in Grand Lake.

The two-story hotel, run by Kauffman until his death in 1920, is listed on the National Register of Historic Places because of its all-log construction and its role in Grand Lake's early development. It operated as a hotel until 1946. The building was bought and managed by various owners until purchased by the historical society in 1973.

The building has been restored and contains much of its original furniture, as well as representative items from the turn of the twentieth century. It also features a collection of historical materials from the area, including early photographs, clothing, china, bowling balls, and locally made skis.

Kauffman House Museum, Grand Lake Area Historical Society, Lake Ave. at Pitkin St., P.O. Box 656, Grand Lake, CO 80447. Phone: 970/627-9277. Hours: Memorial Day–Labor Day, 11–5 daily; remainder of the year by appointment. Admission: free.

GRAND MESA

Visitor centers

GRAND MESA NATIONAL FOREST

Grand Mesa Visitor Center
Lands End Observatory

Two visitor centers—Grand Mesa Visitor Center and Lands End Observatory—are located in Grand Mesa National Forest about 25 miles east of Grand Junction.

Grand Mesa, one of the world's largest flat-topped mountains, covers 380,000 acres, has more than 300 lakes and a wide range of plants and animals, and rises to an average elevation of more than 10,000 feet. It was formed by lava flows, glaciers, and erosional forces over millions of years.

The Grand Mesa Visitor Center, operated year-round by the U.S. Forest Service, opened in 1992 at Cobbett Lake (formerly Carp Lake) in the center of the mesa at the intersection of Colorado Highway 65 and

Forest Road 121. It has exhibits covering the history and utilization of the mesa's water resources, which supply 11 nearby communities.

The Lands End Observatory, listed on the National Register of Historic Places, is located on Forest Road 100 at the edge of a cliff at the western end of the mesa. The observatory marks the terminus of the Grand Mesa Scenic and Historic Byway.

Built by the Civilian Conservation Corps in the 1930s, the observatory is open only during summer. It has an exhibit on the construction of the facility and the byway, as well as photographs related to the scenic highway. Two newly installed scopes allow visitors to better enjoy the vast landscape visible from the cliff.

The 55-mile Grand Mesa Scenic and Historic Byway snakes its way from the orchards of the 5,000-foot-elevation valley floor to the alpine meadows of Grand Mesa at its nearly 11,000-foot-high summit before terminating at the Lands End Observatory.

Grand Mesa Visitor Center, Colo. Hwy. 65 and Forest Road 121, Grand Mesa National Forest. (Contact: Grand Junction Ranger District Office, U.S. Forest Service, 2777 Crossroads Blvd., Grand Junction, CO 81506. Phone and fax: 970/242-8211.) Hours: mid-June through Oct., 9–5 daily; remainder of the year, 9–5 Sat.–Sun. Admission: free.

Lands End Observatory, Forest Rd. 100, Grand Mesa National Forest. (Contact: Grand Junction Ranger District Office, U.S. Forest Service, 2777 Crossroads Blvd., Grand Junction, CO 81506. Phone and fax: 970/242-8211.) Hours: July to late Sept., 9–4 daily; closed remainder of the year. Admission: free.

GREELEY

History museums

CITY OF GREELEY MUSEUMS

The Greeley Department of Cultural Affairs, located in the civic center complex, operates four city-owned museums in Greeley. They are the Greeley Municipal Museum, Meeker Home Museum, Centennial Village Museum, and Plum Farm Museum.

Greeley Municipal Museum

The Greeley Municipal Museum, established in 1969, houses the administrative offices for the museum system and contains an extensive collection of historical documents and other materials relating to the early history of Greeley and Weld County.

Interpretive historical exhibits and traveling exhibitions are presented in the museum's gallery. The facility also has an archives/research room with the original Union Colony records and documentary and photographic resources on people, places, and events in the region.

Greeley Municipal Museum, City of Greeley Cultural Affairs Dept., Museums Div., 919 7th St., Greeley, CO 80631. Phone: 970/350-9220. Fax: 970/350-9475. Hours: 10–4 Tues.–Sat.; closed major holidays. Admission: free.

Meeker Home Museum

The Meeker Home Museum in Greeley is located in a two-story adobe brick structure built in 1870 as the residence for Nathan Cook Meeker, the city's founder.

Meeker, who was agricultural editor of the *New York Tribune*, organized a joint-stock company called the Union Colony in 1869 whose purpose was to establish a farming community in the American West. Each participant paid a $155 membership fee used to purchase land for the colony.

The town of Greeley was established at the colony site in 1870 and quickly became one of the most successful colonies in the West, emphasizing temperance, religion, education, agriculture, irrigation, and cooperation.

The 1870–1885 pioneer era of Greeley's history is interpreted through guided tours of the historic house, which is listed on the National Register of Historic Places. The six-room home is furnished with Meeker family belongings and other nineteenth-century artifacts and materials.

Entry fee includes same-day admission to Centennial Village.

Meeker Home Museum, 1324 9th Ave., Greeley, CO 80631. (Contact: City of Greeley Cultural Affairs Dept., Museums Div., 919 7th St., Greeley, CO 80631.) Phone: 970/350-9220. Fax: 970/350-9475. Hours: mid-Apr. through Memorial Day, 10–3 Tues.–Sat.; Memorial Day–Labor Day, 10–5 Tues.–Sat.; Labor Day through mid-Oct., 10–3 Tues.–Sat. Admission: adults, $3.50; seniors, $3; children 6–12, $2; children under 6, free.

Centennial Village Museum

The settlement history of Greeley and Weld County from 1860 to 1920 is interpreted at the Centennial Village Museum, established in 1976.

Twenty-eight historic structures are featured at the 5.5-acre park-like museum complex containing artifacts and other historical materials pertaining to homesteaders, Union Colonists, farmers, ranchers, civic leaders, early businesses, and activities of the period.

Among the buildings are an 1863 log-cabin courthouse, 1872

cottage, 1885 pavilion, 1900 Queen Anne–style house, and 1908 homestead house, 1917 wagon house, and 1917 rural church, as well as a one-room schoolhouse, ice house, stable and carriage house, Union Pacific depot, Swedish-American home, Colonial Revival–style house, German-Russian beet shanty, adobe brick farm shed, and wooden granary.

Visitors can take guided or self-guided tours. Centennial Village tickets also include same-day admission to the Meeker Home Museum.

Centennial Village Museum, 1475 A St., Greeley, CO 80631. (Contact: City of Greeley Cultural Affairs Dept., Museums Div., 919 7th St., Greeley, CO 80631.) Phone: 970/350-9220. Fax: 970/350-9475. E-mail: dillc@ci.greeley.co.us. Hours: mid-Apr. through Memorial Day, 10–3 Tues.–Sat.; Memorial Day–Labor Day, 10–5 Tues.–Sat.; Labor Day through mid-Oct., 10–3 Tues.–Sat.; also, 1–5 first Sun. of every month. Admission: adults, $3.50; seniors, $3; children 6–12, $2; children under 6, free.

Plum Farm Museum

The newest addition to the City of Greeley's museum system is Plum Farm Museum, located on land that has been farmed since the 1880s. The farm, donated by Charles Plumb, opened as a museum in 1998.

The original 160-acre farm was owned by Colonel Charles White, a Civil War veteran who settled in Greeley as part of Nathan Meeker's Union Colony. White farmed the land but did not live on the property until his farmhouse was built in 1904. Plumb became the owner in 1922 after White's death.

Interpretive programs on the 1900–1940 history of the farm and agriculture of the period are presented. In addition to the farmhouse, a barn and a number of outbuildings and farm equipment are located on the 5.2-acre site.

Plum Farm Museum, 4001 W. 10th St., Greeley, CO 80634. (Contact: City of Greeley Cultural Affairs Dept., Museums Div., 919 7th St., Greeley, CO 80631.) Phone: 970/350-9220. Fax: 970/350-9475. E-mail: dillc@ci.greeley.co.us. Hours: mid-Apr. through mid-Oct., 10–5 Sat. and 1–5 Sun.; closed major holidays and remainder of the year. Admission: free.

Art gallery

MARIANI GALLERY AT THE UNIVERSITY OF NORTHERN COLORADO

Regional and student art exhibitions are presented at the Mariani Gallery, run by the Department of Visual Arts at the University of

Northern Colorado in Greeley. The gallery, established in 1972, mounts exhibitions in the Oak Room Gallery in Crabbe Hall.

Mariani Gallery, Dept. of Visual Arts, University of Northern Colorado, 8th Ave. and 18th St., Greeley, CO 80639. Phone: 970/351-2184. Fax: 970/351-2299. Hours: 9–4 Mon.–Fri. (also 7–9 Mon. and Wed.); closed during summer. Admission: free.

GREENWOOD VILLAGE

Sculpture park

MUSEUM OF OUTDOOR ARTS

The Museum of Outdoor Arts is a "museum without walls" whose works are displayed throughout the 400-acre Greenwood Plaza business park in Greenwood Village. But arrangements are being made to move all or part of the collection to the new Englewood City Center, site of the former Cinderella City mall, in late 2000.

The outdoor museum, which features more than 50 sculptures and other artworks, was founded in 1982 to bring together the many works distributed throughout the Greenwood Plaza properties owned and managed by the John Madden Company. The Madden family wanted to enhance the aesthetics of their business environments and provide the community with direct access to quality art.

The nonprofit museum presents a broad spectrum of offerings, ranging from decorative works to exquisite pieces of fine art, blended into the surrounding architecture and landscape. Sculptures include Jon Leitner's *Sampson*, a bronze tribute to a Yorkshire terrier, and Lynn Tillery's *Child of Peace*, an abstract work whose mirrored concave surface is couched within bronze folds.

In addition to guided tours of the artworks, the museum presents concerts, lectures, classes, school programs, special exhibitions, and other educational and cultural activities.

Museum of Outdoor Arts, 7600 E. Orchard Rd., Suite 160N, Greenwood Village, Englewood, CO 80111. Phone: 303/741-3609. Fax: 303/741-1029. Hours: 8:30–5:30 Mon.–Fri. and selected Sats.; closed national holidays. Admission: free. Guided tours: adults, $3; seniors, $1; children 17 and under, $1.

Art galleries

DUNCAN GALLERIES AT THE KOELBEL LIBRARY

Changing exhibitions of works by local artists are presented in the west and south wings of the Duncan Galleries at the Koelbel Library, part of the Arapahoe Library District in Greenwood Village.

Duncan Galleries, Koelbel Library, 5955 S. Holly St., Littleton, CO 80121. Phone 303/220-7704. Fax: 303/220-1651. Hours: 9–9 Mon.–Thurs., 9–5 Fri.–Sat., 1–5 Sun.; closed holidays. Admission: free.

Arts/humanities center

Curtis Arts and Humanities Center

Changing art and historical exhibitions, concerts, lectures, poetry readings, and workshops are among the offerings of the Curtis Arts and Humanities Center in Greenwood Village.

The center, operated by Greenwood Village, opened in 1991 in a 1914 brick schoolhouse that was expanded in 1930. The schoolhouse, which served children in the area until 1967, is listed on the National Register of Historic Places.

Curtis Arts and Humanities Center, 2349 E. Orchard Rd., Greenwood Village, CO 80121. Phone: 303/797-1779. Hours: 10–5 Tues.–Fri.; 10–2 Sat. only for special programs; closed major holidays. Admission: free.

Historic schoolhouse

Cherry Creek Schoolhouse

One of the oldest surviving school buildings in Colorado is the 1874 Cherry Creek Schoolhouse, now located on the Cherry Creek High School campus in Greenwood Village. It is one of two historic schoolhouses that are owned by Cherry Creek School District 5. The other is the Melvin Schoolhouse Museum-Library at Smoky Hill High School in Aurora (see separate listing).

The historic schoolhouse was originally a one-room elementary school located near the present-day intersection of Arapahoe and Parker Roads. The schoolhouse was closed in 1951 shortly after its district was consolidated with six other small districts to form the present Cherry Creek School District.

The school building was sold at auction and served for many years as a farmer's shed. In 1963, Cherry Creek teacher Ed Berger interested his social studies class and members of the Key Club in local history. The students learned about the old school and raised funds to purchase the structure. With help from the school district, the old schoolhouse was moved to the Cherry Creek High School campus in 1969, then restored and opened in 1971. Programs on turn-of-the-twentieth-century schooling now are presented to school groups and members of the public during the academic year.

Cherry Creek Schoolhouse, Cherry Creek High School, 9300 E. Union Ave., Englewood, CO 80110. Phone: 303/486-2285. Fax: 303/486-2239. Hours: during the school year by appointment; closed during summer. Admission: free.

GROVER

History museum

GROVER DEPOT MUSEUM

The Grover Depot Museum, located in one of two historic two-story railroad stations in Colorado, traces the history of railroading, farming, and ranching near the Pawnee National Grassland and Pawnee Buttes, not far from where the Colorado, Wyoming, and Nebraska state lines meet.

The railroad depot operated from 1888 to 1975, when it was acquired by the Pawnee Historical Society and converted into a museum in 1976 as part of the nation's bicentennial observance.

The depot housed a ticket window, a waiting area, and a freight and baggage storage section on the main floor, with living quarters for the stationmaster and his family upstairs. The main floor now contains collections of railroad, post office, and other materials. The upstairs living quarters have been restored as a kitchen, living room, and bedroom furnished with articles donated by farming and ranching families in the area.

Grover Depot Museum, Pawnee Historical Society, Logan St. and Stony Ave., Grover, CO 80729. Phone and fax: 970/895-2482. Hours: May–Labor Day, 1–4 Sun.; other times by appointment. Admission: free.

GUNNISON

History museum

GUNNISON PIONEER MUSEUM

The Gunnison Pioneer Museum, which traces the cultural history and heritage of Gunnison County, was opened in 1964 by the Gunnison County Pioneer and Historical Society.

The museum now has eight historic buildings, including an 1876 post office, an 1880 dairy barn, and a 1905 rural schoolhouse, as well as collections of arrowheads, minerals, costumes, tools, dolls, toys, antique cars and wagons, ranch machinery, saddles, silverware and pewter, turn-of-the-twentieth-century furnishings, and a narrow-gauge train.

The Denver & Rio Grande train consists of Engine #268 and a flanger, gondola, boxcar, livestock car, and caboose. Along the track are a D&RG water tank (moved in 1971 from Marshall Pass) and a D&RG depot (moved from Sargents in 1975).

The museum also owns the Aberdeen Quarry on Beaver Creek near Gunnison. Granite from the quarry was used in building the Colorado State Capitol in Denver. Jeep tours of the historic site are offered as part of the museum's summer program.

Gunnison Pioneer Museum, Gunnison County Pioneer and Historical Society, S. Adams St./U.S. Hwy. 50, Gunnison, CO. (Postal address: 696 County Rd. 16, Gunnison, CO 81230.) Phone: 970/641-4530. Hours: Memorial Day–Labor Day, 9–5 Mon.–Sat.; closed remainder of the year. Admission: adults, $5; children 6–12, $1; children under 6, free.

National recreation area/visitor centers

CURECANTI NATIONAL RECREATION AREA

Elk Creek Visitor Center
Lake Fork Visitor Center
Cimarron Visitor Center
East Portal Information Center

Four National Park Service visitor centers are located at the Curecanti National Recreation Area, which consists of three reservoirs that parallel U.S. Highway 50 between Gunnison and Montrose. Visitors to the area can enjoy picnicking, camping, fishing, boating, and hiking.

The construction of three dams on the Gunnison River to provide irrigation and hydroelectric power as part of the Bureau of Land Reclamation's Upper Colorado River Storage Project has transformed a semi-arid area into a water-based recreational mecca, which opened in 1965.

The largest of the reservoirs is 10-mile-long Blue Mesa Lake. Most of the power is generated at the Morrow Point Lake dam. The Crystal Lake dam maintains an even flow of water through the adjacent Black Canyon of the Gunnison National Park, which also is administered through the National Park Service's Curecanti headquarters (see separate listing under Montrose).

Elk Creek Visitor Center, located at the east end of Blue Mesa Lake and closest to Gunnison, opened in 1968. The first of the visitor centers, it features natural history specimens from the area and has exhibits on ancient inhabitants, early surveyors, water development in the Gunnison Basin, and the Denver & Rio Grande Railroad's history in the area.

Lake Fork Visitor Center, at the Blue Mesa Lake dam near Sapinero, contains exhibits on flora and fauna associated with the lake.

Cimarron Visitor Center, in Cimarron near the Morrow Point Lake dam, has displays on the reservoir basin's construction and the operation of the Denver & Rio Grande Railroad, which mainly transported livestock. Adjacent to the center are four railroad cars from the 1930s and 1940s, and a mile away in the canyon is a railroad trestle with a locomotive, tender, and two cars.

At the far western end of the recreation area is the East Portal Information Center, which is open only intermittently in the summer. Located at the Crystal Lake dam and east portal of the Gunnison Diversion Tunnel, it has displays on irrigation and the tunnel.

Curecanti National Recreation Area Visitor Centers, 102 Elk Creek, Gunnison, CO 81230. Phone: 970/641-2337. Fax: 970/641-3127. Hours: Elk Creek Visitor Center, 8–6 daily Memorial Day–Labor Day and intermittently at other times; Lake Fork Visitor Center, 9–4 daily Memorial Day–Labor Day; Cimarron Visitor Center, 8:30–4 daily Memorial Day–Labor Day; East Portal Information Center, intermittently Memorial Day–Labor Day. Admission: free.

HAHNS PEAK VILLAGE

History museum

HAHNS PEAK AREA HISTORICAL MUSEUM

The Hahns Peak Area Historical Museum in Hahns Peak Village near Clark is located at the site of the first permanent settlement in Routt County and northwest Colorado.

The museum, founded by the Hahns Peak Area Historical Society in 1972 and moved to a 1912 former jail building in 1976, now also features a restored 1911 schoolhouse. Its collections and exhibits include such local historical items as mining equipment, household objects, sleds, furniture, and school materials.

Hahns Peak Area Historical Museum, 61110 Main St., Hahns Peak Village, General Delivery, Clark, CO 80428. Phones: 970/879-6781 and 970/824-5176. Hours: June–Sept., 10–5 daily. Admission: donation requested.

HANCOCK

Historic ghost town

HANCOCK GHOST TOWN

The mining and railroad town of Hancock, 25 miles southwest of Buena Vista, is best known for its role in building and maintaining the historic Alpine Tunnel, the first railroad tunnel to pierce the Continental Divide (see separate listing under Alpine Station).

The 1,771-foot-long tunnel was built in 1881 by the Denver, South Park & Pacific Railroad in its race to reach the Gunnison area. But the Denver & Rio Grande Railroad got there nearly a year earlier, going over Marshall Pass south of Poncha Springs.

The railroad and tunnel played an important role in the development of the St. Elmo, Romley, and Hancock mining area, hauling out ore and bringing in equipment and other supplies. Previously, these communities had only been accessible via mountain passes plagued by unpredictable weather conditions.

Much of the railroad equipment and many of the workers who built the tunnel were based in Hancock, located about three miles from the east tunnel entrance. Once the tunnel was completed, Hancock became a rail shipping and maintenance center. After the last train passed through the tunnel in 1910, Hancock fell into decline but did not disappear completely until mining ceased.

Mining began in the Hancock area in the late 1870s. The town was named for the Hancock Placer claim, the first in the area. It was followed in 1879 by the opening of the Stonewall Mine, the largest producer, which operated until 1915.

The old railroad grade to Alpine Tunnel still remains, but the tracks have been removed. A few deteriorating cabins are all that is left of the town. The ruins of one mine are nearby.

Hancock Ghost Town, 25 miles southwest of Buena Vista. Contact: Greater Buena Vista Area Chamber of Commerce Visitors Center, 343 S. U.S. Hwy. 24, Buena Vista, CO 81214. Phone and fax: 719/395-6612.

HASTINGS

Historic site

HASTINGS MINE DISASTER SITE

Colorado's greatest coal mine disaster occurred on April 27, 1917, when a mine explosion killed 121 men in Hastings, only three miles from the scene of the Ludlow Massacre (see separate listing under Ludlow).

The explosion occurred at the No. 2 Mine, owned and operated by the Victor-American Fuel Company, in Hastings, 17 miles northwest of Trinidad in Las Animas County.

The blast apparently was caused by an open flame coming in contact with a deadly mine gas known as "fire damp" on a day when two critical machines were not working—the electric mining machine and an adobe duster used to spray the coal facings to lessen the dust.

After the mine reopened, production declined. The mine finally was abandoned and the portal sealed in 1923. The mine tipples, trestles, other structures, and rail tracks later were removed; only the cement foundations with their anchor bolts, the ruins of coke ovens, and a monument commemorating the dead miners remain at the site.

Hastings, 17 miles northwest of Trinidad. Contact: Trinidad History Museum, 300 E. Main St., Trinidad, CO 81082. Phone: 719/846-7217. Fax: 719/846-6872. Alternate contact: Walsenburg Mining Museum, 110 5th St., Walsenburg, CO 81089. Phone: 719/738-1065. Fax: 719/738-2506.

HAYDEN

History museum

HAYDEN HERITAGE CENTER

The Hayden Heritage Center, which opened in 1969 in the 1914 former Denver & Rio Grande Railroad depot in Hayden, houses exhibits and collections ranging from an exceptional rock collection to an array of artifacts from the early 1900s.

The museum contains clothing, farm machinery, and even a threshing machine burned by the Ute Indians at the turn of the twentieth century. In addition, it has extensive information on, and photographs of, early settlers in the area.

Hayden Heritage Center, 300 Pearl St., P.O. Box 543, Hayden, CO 81639. Phone: 970/276-4380. Hours: Memorial Day–Labor Day, 11–5 Fri.–Mon.; closed remainder of the year. Admission: free.

Historic ranch/environmental center

CARPENTER RANCH INTERPRETIVE CENTER

The 850-acre Carpenter Ranch, operated by the Nature Conservancy of Colorado near Hayden, has an interpretive center in the property's ranch house.

The ranch, homesteaded in the late nineteenth century and opened to the public in 1997, is one of the oldest in the area with the original buildings still intact. It is adjacent to the Nature Conservancy's 251-acre Yampa Valley Preserve. A similar center is located at the organization's Aiken Canyon Preserve near Colorado Springs (see separate listing under Colorado Springs).

The Carpenter Ranch Interpretive Center contains exhibits on the natural, cultural, and agricultural history of the working ranch and the Yampa Valley. It also offers self-guided walks along a one-mile trail. More than 80 bird species have been documented on the ranch, including nesting bald eagles and greater sandhill cranes.

Carpenter Ranch Interpretive Center, 13250 W. Hwy. 40, P.O. Box NN, Hayden, CO 81639. Phone: 970/276-4626. Fax: 970/276-4625. Hours: June–Sept., 9–12 Thurs.–Fri., 9–3 Sat.; closed major holidays and remainder of the year. Admission: free.

HEARTSTRONG

Historic ghost town

HEARTSTRONG GHOST TOWN

The crossroads town of Heartstrong, 19 miles southeast of Yuma, was an offshoot of another farming community, Happyville, several miles to the east.

Richard John Gilmore, who came to Colorado for his health, was instrumental in the development of Happyville near his homestead in 1908. The town grew rapidly and by 1911 had a post office, school, store, dairy, garage, and machine shop.

One of the leading merchants of Happyville was Cleve Mason, who built a large store in 1915 and owned several other buildings in town. When differences developed with other residents, Mason decided to start another town. He moved his store and three other buildings to the new site, Heartstrong, and many of his friends followed.

Heartstrong, which also became known as Headstrong, grew rapidly in the early 1920s and became a commercial and social center. Happyville, on the other hand, fell into decline as a remaining store burned and other buildings were torn down or moved to Heartstrong.

Heartstrong, however, suffered from the farm depression of the late 1920s and the Dust Bowl drought of the 1930s. By the 1940s, it was virtually deserted. Only the ruins of several buildings and some foundations remain today.

Heartstrong Ghost Town, 19 miles southeast of Yuma. Contact: Yuma Museum, 306 S. Detroit St., P.O. Box 454, Yuma, CO 80759. Phone: 970/848-5430.

HOLYOKE

History museum

PHILLIPS COUNTY MUSEUM

The Phillips County Museum in Holyoke tells the story of this northwestern Colorado county first settled by homesteaders in sod houses.

Opened in 1975 by the Phillips County Historical Society, the 4,600-square-foot museum features four rooms filled with pioneer furnishings; objects from an early general store, dentist's office, and hospitals; a doll collection; and exhibits of early automobiles, cattle ranching items, Native American artifacts, quilts, military objects, school photographs, and other historical materials. An outdoor display of early agricultural equipment is adjacent to the museum building.

Phillips County Museum, 109 S. Campbell St., Holyoke, CO. (Contact: Phillips County Historical Society, 220 S. Baxter Ave., Holyoke, CO 80734. Phone: 970/ 854-3311.) Hours: Memorial Day–Labor Day, 1–4 Sun.–Fri.; closed remainder of the year. Admission: free.

HOTCHKISS

History museum

HOTCHKISS-CRAWFORD HISTORICAL SOCIETY MUSEUM

The Hotchkiss-Crawford Historical Society operates a museum that collects and displays artifacts of settlers in the section of the North Fork Valley of the Gunnison River encompassing the towns of Hotchkiss and Crawford (another museum in Paonia covers the rest of the valley).

The society was founded in 1974 and the 4,000-square-foot museum opened in 1990. The museum is located in a World War II–era building that was moved to Hotchkiss from Grand Junction.

Among the collections and exhibits are saddles, guns, clothes, pots and pans, a chuck wagon, Native American artifacts, and other items relating to the history of the valley.

Hotchkiss-Crawford Historical Society Museum, 180 S. 2nd St., P.O. Box 370, Hotchkiss, CO 81419. Phone: 970/872-3780. Hours: May 30–Labor Day, 1–4 Wed. and Fri.; closed remainder of the year. Admission: adults and children, $1; infants, free.

HOT SULPHUR SPRINGS

History museum

GRAND COUNTY MUSEUM

The Grand County Museum in Hot Sulphur Springs occupies a 1924 schoolhouse, maintains five other historic buildings on-site, and operates an 1874 ranch house, stage stop, and post office near Winter Park.

The museum, which opened in 1974, contains 102 maps, 173 oral histories, more than 6,500 photographs and 400 manuscripts, and 3,000 artifacts relating to the history of Grand County.

Among the exhibits in the schoolhouse are displays on the development of the ski industry, the German prisoners-of-war camp located in Fraser during World War II, archaeological findings in Windy Gap, pioneer women, and early schools, post offices, and towns. The artifacts range from butter churns to bear traps.

The five buildings that have been restored on-site are an 1897 county jail, 1900 courthouse, 1920 Forest Service cabin, 1920 one-room schoolhouse, and 1920 blacksmith's shop. The jail walls are still covered in the original graffiti.

The museum is run by the Grand County Historical Association, which also operates the Cozens Ranch Museum on U.S. Highway 40 between Winter Park and Fraser (see separate listing under Winter Park).

Grand County Museum, 110 Byers Ave., P.O. Box 165, Hot Sulphur Springs, CO 80451. Phone: 970/725-3939. Fax: 970/725-0129. E-mail: gcha@rkymtnhi.com. Website: www.grandcountymuseum.com. Hours: summer, 10–5 Mon.–Sat., 12–5 Sun.; winter, 11–4 Wed.–Sat.; closed New Year's Day, Thanksgiving, and Christmas. Admission: adults, $4; seniors, $3; children 6–18, $2; children under 6, free; families, $10.

HUGO

History museum

LINCOLN COUNTY MUSEUM

The Lincoln County Museum in Hugo is located on the 1880 home-stead site of the town's founder. The municipal museum was created in 1972 and contains collections of, and exhibits on, period furniture, fur-nishings, and clothing; glassware; utensils; firearms; and historic photo-graphs and postcards.

Lincoln County Museum, 7th St. and 3rd Ave., P.O. Box 367, Hugo, CO 80821. Phone: 719/743-2485. Fax: 719/747-2447. Hours: by appointment. Admis-sion: free.

IDAHO SPRINGS

History museum

HERITAGE MUSEUM

The Heritage Museum, located in the old mining community of Idaho Springs, shares a building with the Idaho Springs Chamber of Commerce, which operates a visitor center there.

The 7,500-square-foot museum, which opened in 1994, is run by the Historical Society of Idaho Springs, which also operates the long-established Underhill Museum, where it maintains its offices.

The Heritage Museum covers the social, mining, and transportation history of the Idaho Springs area at the turn of the twentieth century. It contains historical photographs, mining equipment, Native American and Spanish colonial artifacts, and other historical materials, as well as a period schoolroom, hotel room, and newspaper office from the Victorian era.

Heritage Museum, Historical Society of Idaho Springs, 2400 Colorado Blvd., P.O. Box 1318, Idaho Springs, CO 80452. Phone: 303/567-4100. Fax: 303/567-4605. Hours: 9–5 daily. Admission: free.

Mining/milling museum

CLEAR CREEK HISTORIC MINING AND MILLING MUSEUM

The six-story Argo Gold Mill in Idaho Springs processed rich ore from area mines—much of it delivered via a 22,000-foot tunnel—from 1913 until its closure in 1943. The mill and tunnel are now the centerpieces of the Clear Creek Historic Mining and Milling Museum, which opened in 1977.

The mill and tunnel, listed on the National Register of Historic Places in 1978, still contain much of their original machinery and are open to self-guided tours. The museum also contains historic photographs, journals, ledgers, and other materials relating to the history of the mill, mining, and Clear Creek County. Ore cars and parts of a stamp mill are also visible on the grounds.

Clear Creek Historic Mining and Milling Museum, 2350 Riverside Dr., P.O. Box 1990, Idaho Springs, CO 80452. Phone: 303/567-2421. Fax: 303/567-9304. Hours: Memorial Day–Labor Day, 10–7 daily; remainder of the year, 10–5 daily. Admission: adults, $10; children 7 and older, $8; children 3–6, $5; children 2 and under, free.

Historic house/mining museum

UNDERHILL MUSEUM

The 1912 assay office and home of James Underhill, mineral surveyor and Colorado School of Mines professor, is the site of the Underhill Museum in Idaho Springs.

The museum, founded by the Historical Society of Idaho Springs in 1964, is devoted to the area's mining history and features an equipped assay office, historical photographs, mining equipment, and a historic house with period furniture.

The historical society, which has its offices in the Underhill Museum, also operates the Heritage Museum, which shares a building with the local chamber of commerce (see separate listing).

Underhill Museum, Historical Society of Idaho Springs, 1416 Miner St., P.O. Box 1318, Idaho Springs, CO 80452. Phone: 303/567-4709. Fax: 303/567-4605. Hours: Memorial Day–Labor Day, 11–5 daily; remainder of the year by appointment. Admission: free.

Historic mine

EDGAR EXPERIMENTAL MINE

From the 1870s through the 1890s, the Edgar Mine in Idaho Springs yielded high-grade silver, gold, lead, and copper. But production tapered off to a trickle, and the mine was given to Colorado School of Mines in Golden in 1921. Today, the mine is used for teaching, research, and public tours.

Now called the Edgar Experimental Mine, it is primarily an underground classroom and laboratory for the university's Mining Engineering Department and various state and federal agencies.

Students and staff members conduct guided tours of the mine throughout the year. Tours cover more than a half-mile of underground workings. Lighted displays show past and present drilling, blasting, and mucking equipment. The mine also features an exhibit of mining artifacts.

Edgar Experimental Mine, 365 8th Ave., Idaho Springs, CO 80452. (Contact: Mining Engineering Dept., Colorado School of Mines, Golden, CO 80401. Phone: 303/273-3700.) Phone: 303/567-2911. Fax: 303/567-9133. Tour hours: June 1–Aug. 15 at 9, 11, 1, and 3 Tues.–Sat.; Aug. 16–May 31, 9–3 for institutional groups by appointment (but closed Fri. from Sept.–Dec.). Admission: adults, $6; seniors, $4.50; children 6–16, $3; children under 6, free; families, $15.

Historic mine

PHOENIX GOLD MINE

Visitors can enter a working gold mine, which first opened in 1871, to see how hard-rock mining is done at the Phoenix Gold Mine in Idaho Springs.

Half-hour tours of the mine, which opened to the public in 1986, are available. Visitors are taken 400 feet into the mine by owner Al Mosch, a former miner, and other tour guides who relate the history of the Phoenix Gold Mine and mining in the area, as well as describing gold-mining techniques.

An old stamp mill, an ore crusher, and other mining equipment are also visible on the property.

Phoenix Gold Mine, Trail Creek Rd., P.O. Box 3236, Idaho Springs, CO 80452. Phone: 303/567-0422. Hours: 11–4 daily. Admission: adults, $9; seniors, $8; children 12 and older, $9; children 5–11, $5; children under 5, free.

Historic district

IDAHO SPRINGS DOWNTOWN COMMERCIAL DISTRICT

The first major discovery of placer gold in Colorado took place in 1859 in Idaho Springs, which became an important mining, milling, and supply center for the Clear Creek mining region.

Prospector George A. Jackson found bits of gold in rocks near the confluence of Clear Creek and Chicago Creek during a winter hunting trip in 1859. The following spring, he returned with a party of men and extracted more than $1,500 of gold in one week. News of this success spread quickly, and soon thousands of miners and merchants had arrived at the site initially known as Jackson's Diggins. The name was changed to Sacramento and then Idaho Bar before becoming Idaho Springs, largely because of the hot springs in the area. These hot springs boosted the local economy, supporting the construction of spas and the bottling of mineral water.

The Idaho Springs Downtown Commercial District, which was listed on the National Register of Historic Places in 1984, has been the business center of the Idaho Springs area since its development in the late nineteenth century. A historic collection of late-Victorian-era structures, such as the Hanchett Building, Mining Exchange, and Queen Hotel, forms the core of this old mining community.

Near the downtown are two early gold mines—the Edgar Mine and the Phoenix Mine—that can be toured and an old gold mill—the Argo Mill—that processed ore from are mines. The Argo Gold Mill is part of the Clear Creek Historic Mining and Milling Museum. (See separate listings for the mines and the museum.)

Idaho Springs Downtown Commercial District. Contact: Historical Society of Idaho Springs, 1416 Miner St., P.O. Box 1318, Idaho Springs, CO 80452. Phone: 303/ 569-4709. Fax: 303/567-4605.

IGNACIO

Ethnic history/cultural museum

SOUTHERN UTE INDIAN CULTURAL CENTER MUSEUM

The history, arts, and culture of the Southern Ute Indians are featured at the Southern Ute Indian Cultural Center Museum on the Southern Ute Indian Reservation in Ignacio.

Visitors to the 7,000-square-foot center, which opened in 1972, are greeted by a large painting of a buffalo hunt and a mural depicting a Southern Ute campground. The mural serves as the background for a tepee, a willow backrest, a drying rack, and a replica of a sweat lodge.

Also on view are many turn-of-the-twentieth-century photographs depicting the traditional dress and adornments of the Utes, beautiful beadwork and leather materials dating from the early 1800s to the present, and artifacts of Anasazi origin from excavations in the area.

A permanent exhibit on the life of the Southern Utes displays clothing, tools, and other objects. In addition, there is a 17-minute multimedia slide show that traces the Ute legacy, as well as a 10-minute video on the Bear Dance. The museum also presents changing exhibitions, art festivals, dance programs, workshops, lectures, and an annual Southern Ute Fair and Powwow.

*Southern Ute Indian Cultural Center Museum, Colo. Hwy. 172 North, P.O. Box
737, Ignacio, CO 81137. Phone: 970/563-9583. Fax: 970/563-4641. E-mail:
sumuseum@southern-ute.nsn.us. Hours: mid-May through mid-Oct., 10–6 Mon.–
Fri., 10–3 Sat.–Sun.; remainder of the year, 10–5:30 Tues.–Fri. Admission:
adults, $1; children 10 or under, $.50.*

INDEPENDENCE (Pitkin County)

Historic ghost town

INDEPENDENCE GHOST TOWN

East of Aspen, the mining ghost town of Independence, a National
Register Historic Site, is located at an elevation of 10,800 feet, approximately two miles from the summit of Independence Pass on the Continental Divide.

Prospectors discovered gold in the area in 1879; by 1880, a community of 300 people were living there in tents. The population grew to
1,500 by 1882, and the number of businesses reached 40. However,
prosperity was short-lived. Gold production decreased, and the miners
were lured away by more abundant work, better pay, and the milder
climate in Aspen. By 1888, only 100 residents remained in the high
mountain town. When the worst storm in Colorado's history cut off
supply routes in 1899, miners dismantled their homes to make skis and
escaped en masse to Aspen.

A number of Independence's abandoned structures have survived
but are in poor condition. They now are maintained by the Aspen Historical Society and include the collapsed Ted Ackerman boardinghouse,
a building believed to have been the general store, traces of the stables,
a building said to be the J. B. Conners boardinghouse, and the Farwell
Stamp Mill, built in 1880 to process gold from the mines. A cabin used
by a summer intern from the Aspen Historical Society who watches the
property and answers visitors' questions also is on-site.

*Independence Ghost Town, 13.5 miles east of Aspen off Colo. Hwy. 82.
Contact: Aspen Historical Society, 620 W. Bleeker St., Aspen CO 81611.
Phone: 970/925-3721. Fax: 970/925-5347. E-mail: ahistory@rof.net. Hours:
summer tours at 11, 1, and 3 daily. Admission: free, but suggested donation of
$2 for adults and $1 for children.*

INDEPENDENCE (Teller County)

Historic ghost town

INDEPENDENCE GHOST TOWN

Teller County's ghost town of Independence, located between Altman and Goldfield, is two miles north of Victor in the Cripple Creek Mining District. It is best known for the violence that took place there during the 1904 gold miners' strike.

The town, named for the Independence Mine founded by Winfield Scott Stratton, was the site of two explosions set by Harry Orchard, a terrorist with ties to the Western Federation of Miners. One explosion aimed at scabs at the Independence Depot killed 13 people and injured others. The second, a trial blast at the Vindicator Mine, killed two mine officials. Orchard later was convicted of killing the former governor of Idaho in the labor wars.

Independence, which once boasted a population of 1,500, later was consolidated with expanding Goldfield. Much of the town still exists, but the structures are weathered and decaying.

Independence Ghost Town, 2 miles north of Victor. Contact: Victor Chamber of Commerce, P.O. Box 83, Independence Ghost Town, Victor, CO 80860. Phone 719/689-3553.

IRONTON

Historic ghost town

IRONTON GHOST TOWN

Unlike most early towns in the San Juan Mountains, Ironton was more of a transportation and supply center than a mining hot spot. Located on the north side of Red Mountain Pass, eight miles south of Ouray, it served as the major freighting junction between Red Mountain mines and Ouray.

Founded in 1883, Ironton played an important role in the development of the mining area, especially before good roads were built in the area. Ironton ore wagons and then its Silverton Railroad connection carried ore from the Yankee Girl, Saratoga, Silver Belle, and other Guston and Red Mountain Town mines even after a toll road was extended to those mining communities.

Ironton had a population of more than 1,000 during the boom years but began a steady decline in the 1890s. The community was abandoned in 1926, when the railroad tracks were removed. But a number of crumbling structures remain.

Irontown Ghost Town, 8 miles south of Ouray. Contact: Ouray Historical Society, 420 6th Ave., P.O. Box 151, Ouray, CO 81427. Phone: 970/325-4576.

JULESBURG

History museums

FORT SEDGWICK DEPOT MUSEUM AND FORT SEDGWICK MUSEUM

The Fort Sedgwick Historical Society operates two museums in Julesburg, an important Overland Trail crossroads where a historic military fort and Colorado's only Pony Express station were located. The frontier town was once burned to the ground by Indians.

The complementary museums are the Fort Sedgwick Depot Museum, which opened in 1975 in a 1930s Union Pacific Railroad depot, and the Fort Sedgwick Museum, which opened in 1998 in a newly constructed building several blocks away.

The historical society's original museum was located in the basement of Julesburg's public library from 1940 to 1975. When the railroad depot became available, all the collections and exhibits were moved to the 6,000-square-foot restored station.

The depot museum now contains a wide range of artifacts and other historical materials, including Native American artifacts, prehistoric fossils, Pony Express memorabilia, pioneer utensils, period clothing, railroad equipment, barbed wire, western paintings, firearms, champion cowboy Thad Sowder memorabilia, and items relating to the four stages of Julesburg's development.

The new Fort Sedgwick Museum functions as a year-round interpretive center dealing primarily with the old military fort, which protected settlers, travelers, and the mail route along the South Platte River in northeast Colorado. Although the original sod, adobe, and wood structures no longer exist, the museum had collected many artifacts from the period.

Julesburg was named for Jules Beni, who ran a trading post in the area during the 1850s and became an agent for the Overland Stage Company when it was established in 1859. Julesburg also served as a Pony Express horse-relay mail stop in 1860–1861 and became the site of Camp Rankin, later renamed Fort Sedgwick, in 1864. The following year, Indians destroyed Julesburg by fire. The frontier town was relocated three times before settling at its present location in 1881, when a Union Pacific branch line was built to Denver.

Fort Sedgwick Depot Museum, 201 W. 1st St., P.O. Box 69, Julesburg, CO 80737. Phone: 970/474-2264. Hours: Memorial Day–Labor Day, 9–5 Mon.–Sat., 11–5 Sun.; closed remainder of the year. Admission: adults, $1; children, $.50.

Fort Sedgwick Museum, 114 E. 1st St., P.O. Box 69, Julesburg, CO 80737. Phone: 970/474-2061. Hours: by appointment. Admission: adults, $1; children, $.50.

KERSEY

Visitor Center

CONAGRA KUNER FEEDLOT VISITOR CENTER

ConAgra, one of the nation's leading beef, pork, and lamb processors, has a visitor center at its Kuner cattle feedlot in Kersey near Greeley.

The 500-acre feedlot, which normally contains approximately 100,000 head of cattle, opened in 1974 and is operated by Monfort Inc., a ConAgra division. The visitor center features displays on cattle byproducts.

Visitor Center, ConAgra Cattle Feeding—Kuner, 28625 U.S. Hwy. 34, Kersey, CO 80644. Phone: 970/356-2323. Fax: 970/356-6070. Hours: 8–4 Mon.–Fri.; also 8–4 Sat. in summer; closed major holidays. Admission free.

KIOWA

History museum

ELBERT COUNTY MUSEUM

Period rooms, dioramas, interpretive panels, photographs, and artifacts pertaining to Elbert County are on display at the Elbert County Museum in Kiowa.

The museum was opened in 1993 by the Elbert County Historical Society in the old 1921 Kiowa High School building. Among the exhibits are an early doctor's office, general store, courtroom, and turn-of-the-twentieth-century parlor; hand-carved dioramas of trails through the county to the goldfields; interpretive panels and photographs on the county's history; and such objects as early clothing, furniture, household items, and farm equipment from the area.

Elbert County Museum, 515 Comanche St., P.O. Box 43, Kiowa, CO 80117. Phones: 303/621-2448 and 303/621-2229. Hours: Memorial Day–Labor Day,

11–2 Thurs., 12–4 Sat., 2–4 Sun.; *remainder of the year by appointment. Admission: free.*

KIT CARSON

History museum

KIT CARSON HISTORICAL SOCIETY

The Kit Carson Historical Society, founded in 1968, displays Native American artifacts, natural history objects, and other historical materials from the area in a 1907 former Union Pacific Railroad depot in Kit Carson.

Kit Carson Historical Society, Park St., P.O. Box 107, Kit Carson, CO 80825. Phone: 719/962-3306. Hours: Memorial Day–Labor Day, 9–5 daily; closed remainder of the year. Admission: free.

KREMMLING

History museum

KREMMLING MUSEUM

The Kremmling Museum, which opened in 1977, is located in the 1904 former jail building in the town square but is planning to move. The new expanded facilities will include a homestead house and a 1903 livery barn. When the move takes place, the museum will change its name to the Heritage Museum.

At present, exhibits consist mainly of historical photographs and the former jail, but the expansion will enable the museum to add other historical materials to its collection.

Kremmling Museum, Town Square, P.O. Box 204, Kremmling, CO 80459. Phone: 970/724-3396. Hours: by appointment only. Admission: free.

LAFAYETTE

History/mining museum

LAFAYETTE MINERS MUSEUM

Coal mining from 1861 to 1979—with emphasis on tools and equipment of the hand-loading era—is the focus of the Lafayette Miners

Museum in this former coal-mining center, now a suburban bedroom community.

The 900-square-foot museum, located in the 1890s Lewis Home since its founding in 1976, traces the history of Lafayette from the early mining days to the present.

Coal was first discovered on the property of city founder Mary Miller. By the peak of the coal-mining boom at the turn of the twentieth century, Lafayette's Old Town area boasted six mines.

The six-room Lewis residence originally housed miners from the Gladstone Mine northwest of Lafayette. When the mine closed, the house was moved into town and then purchased by coal miner William E. Lewis and his family in 1913. The house served as a meeting place for coal miners during a strike that lasted into 1915. Lewis died in 1914, but his wife lived in the house until her death in 1975. The Lafayette Historical Society acquired the building the following year.

Among the museum's attractions are a kitchen full of unusual household items used by Lafayette's early families; an extensive collection of mining tools and equipment; a re-created schoolroom containing pictures, trophies, and memorabilia from the past; and a bedroom featuring vintage clothing and accessories from the turn of the twentieth century.

Lafayette Miners Museum, Lafayette Historical Society, 108 E. Simpson St., Lafayette, CO 80026-2322. Phone: 303/665-7030. Hours: 2–4 Thurs. and Sat.; tours by appointment; closed Thanksgiving and Christmas. Admission: free.

Art gallery

LAFAYETTE ART CENTER/LAFAYETTE PUBLIC LIBRARY

The lobby of the Lafayette Public Library serves as a gallery for bi-monthly art exhibitions presented by the Lafayette Art Center as part of the Lafayette Cultural Arts Commission's community arts program.

The art center opened an office and began presenting exhibitions in the library in 1998 after having mounted exhibitions in other locations for nearly a decade. A library hallway also is used for shows by local artists and students and, occasionally, regional artists.

Lafayette Art Center, Lafayette Public Library, 775 W. Baseline Rd., Lafayette, CO 85026. Phones: 303/665-5200 and 303/665-5222. Fax: 303/665-8936. Hours: 10–9 Mon.–Thurs., 10–5 Fri.–Sat., 1–5 Sun.; closed major holidays. Admission: free.

LA JUNTA

History museum

OTERO MUSEUM

The Otero Museum in La Junta (the town formerly was known as Otero) contains a wide range of exhibits and collections highlighting local life from the 1870s to recent years. The facility comprises seven buildings, some of which date to the late nineteenth century.

The museum opened its doors in 1984. It was founded by the Otero Museum Association in an 1890 home and grocery store listed on the National Register of Historic Places. Over the years, other buildings were added, including the 1873 Nancy Wickham boardinghouse, the first frame house in La Junta; a coach house to store and display the museum's collection of vehicles; and a replica (built with some of the structure's original logs) of the community's 1876 schoolhouse.

Among the objects on display are farming and ranching equipment, early grocery-store items, guns, saddles, histories of local sugar-beet factories, arrowheads, a room pertaining to the local history of the Santa Fe Railroad (which came to La Junta in 1875), and such historic vehicles as an 1865 Concord stagecoach, 1900 surrey, 1905 Reo "sidewinder" car, and 1916 chuck wagon.

Otero Museum, Otero Museum Assn., 3rd and Anderson Sts., P.O. Box 223, La Junta, CO 81050. Phone: 719/384-7500. Hours: May–Sept., 1–5 Mon.–Sat.; remainder of the year by appointment. Admission: free.

Ethnic history/cultural museum

KOSHARE INDIAN MUSEUM

The Koshare Indian Museum in La Junta seeks to preserve, interpret, and perpetuate Native American culture, focusing primarily on the art and artifacts of the Southwest and Plains Indians.

The museum, which opened in 1949 and was expanded in 1959 and 1980, is home to the Koshare Indian Dancers, a Boy Scout (Troop 232) dance group known for its interpretation of Plains and Pueblo Indian dances. The Koshares were organized in 1933 to honor and perpetuate the cultural legacy of the nation's first people.

The centerpiece of the 20,600-square-foot building is the Kiva, a 60-foot-diameter ceremonial round room where the Koshares perform their dances. The structure, which resembles the great kivas of the

Pueblos, contains more than 620 logs and has one of the largest self-supported roofs in the world.

The Koshare Indian Dancers have used the proceeds of their performances to expand the museum's collections of Native American art and artifacts. The Koshares present school shows in the spring and perform during the summer and in late December at the museum. They also have performed in 44 states.

The museum collections and exhibits feature pottery, beadwork, quillwork, instruments, and jewelry from many Native American tribes, including the work of such renowned potters as the Nampayo family of the Hopi First Mesa and Maria Martinez of the San Ildefonso Pueblo; artworks by 9 of the 10 founding artists of the Taos school; and a large collection of work by other well-known artists.

Koshare Indian Museum, 115 W. 18th St., P.O. Box 580, La Junta, CO 81050. Phone: 719/384-4411. Fax: 719/384-8836. E-mail: koshare@iguana.ruralnet.net. Website: www.koshare.org. Hours: 10–5 daily; open until 9 P.M. Mon., Wed., and show nights; closed major holidays. Admission: adults, $2; seniors and children, $1. Koshare performances: adults, $5; children, $3.

Historic fort

BENT'S OLD FORT NATIONAL HISTORIC SITE

In 1833, William and Charles Bent and Ceran St. Vrain built an adobe trading post on the banks of the Arkansas River eight miles east of La Junta on what became known as the Santa Fe Trail. Today, a reconstructed version of the post—Bent's Old Fort National Historic Site—has been constructed on the site by the National Park Service.

The original trading post, called Fort William, was a commercial enterprise exchanging goods with Native Americans (Arapaho, Cheyenne, Kiowa, and Comanche) and served as a way station for traders, hunters, and travelers, many on their way to Santa Fe and Colorado. The fort flourished for nearly two decades, but its importance later waned with declining trade, cholera epidemics, and Indian hostilities.

Because the Bents had developed a close relationship with the Native American tribes, the fort, now known as Bent's Fort, was designated headquarters for the Upper Platte and Arkansas Indian Agency in 1846. Shortly thereafter, the fort became involved in the Mexican War, serving as a staging point for the invasion of Mexico's northern provinces.

After the death of Charles Bent in 1847, Ceran St. Vrain tried unsuccessfully to sell the fort to the U.S. Army. It is believed that William

Bent set fire to the fort in 1849, destroying it before moving his trading activities approximately 40 miles down the Arkansas River to Big Timbers, where he constructed Bent's New Fort in 1853.

Over time, the old fort's ruins virtually disappeared, and title to the land passed to the federal government. After considerable research, Bent's Old Fort was reconstructed in 1976 as part of the nation's bicentennial observance. Based on archaeological findings and historical drawings of the fort, the reconstruction closely resembles the original trading post. It is now a National Historic Site.

The fort, which occupies two levels, is built around a courtyard. A huge fur press dominates the central plaza. The fort has approximately 20 rooms furnished largely with replicas of furniture and implements used during the mid-1840s. Among the rooms are a trade room, where Indians, trappers, and Mexicans exchanged their furs and hides for goods; a council room, where the terms of trade frequently were agreed upon; a smithy and a carpenter's shop, where tradesmen worked and lived; a dining room (the largest room in the fort) for the owners and their guests; a billiard room, used for entertainment, drinking, and gambling; warehouses where furs, barrels, boxes, and sacks of trade goods were stored; trappers' and hunters' quarters; laborers' quarters, which housed the Mexican laborers who built and maintained the fort; and the cooks' room.

Bent's Old Fort National Historic Site along the old Santa Fe Trail near La Junta. Courtesy Bent's Old Fort National Historic Site.

Bent's Old Fort National Historic Site, National Park Service, 35110 Colo. Hwy. 194, La Junta, CO 81050. Phone: 719/383-5010. Fax: 719/384-5031. E-mail: BEOL-interpretation@nps.gov. Website: www.nps.gov/BEOL. Hours: summer, 8–5:30 daily; winter, 9–4 daily; closed New Year's Day, Thanksgiving, and Christmas. Admission: summer, adults and children 17 or older, $2; children under 17, free. Free remainder of the year.

LAKE CITY

History museum

HINSDALE COUNTY MUSEUM

An 1877 stone mercantile structure is the home of the Hinsdale County Museum in Lake City. Opened in 1975, the museum presents changing exhibits on different aspects of the area's history.

Past exhibits have featured Alferd Packer, convicted of killing and eating his companions during an ill-fated winter prospecting expedition; the 120th anniversary of suffragette Susan B. Anthony's visit to Lake City; mining in the region; and local business and family histories.

Hinsdale County Museum, Hinsdale Historical Society, 130 Silver St., P.O. Box 353, Lake City, CO 81235. Phone: 970/944-9515. Hours: June–Sept., 10–4 Mon.–Fri., 1–4 Sat.–Sun.; closed Oct.–May. Admission: adults, $2; children under 12, $.50.

Historic district

LAKE CITY HISTORIC DISTRICT

The San Juan Mountains surround Lake City and its historic district, located in a canyon at the confluence of Henson Creek and the Lake Fork of the Gunnison River in Hinsdale County.

Gold was discovered in the area in 1874 by Enos Hotchkiss, bringing a flood of prospectors to Lake City. Within two years, the town boasted 1,000 residents, seven saloons, five blacksmiths' shops, four laundries, two banks, and two breweries.

Like many mining communities, Lake City has had its ups and downs; its economy stabilized somewhat after the Denver & Rio Grande Railroad came to town in 1889. It now is noted for its excellent hiking and fishing in the Uncompahgre National Forest and especially Lake San Cristobal.

Lake City, however, is best known for the gruesome Alferd Packer case. Packer was tried and convicted in Lake City for killing and eating five prospecting companions during a winter trip through the nearby mountains in 1874. While awaiting trial, he escaped from jail and was not recaptured for nine years. Packer was sentenced to death, but the trial was declared unconstitutional on a technicality. He was tried again and sentenced to 45 years of hard labor in prison, though he later was pardoned by the governor.

The Lake City Historic District, listed on the National Register of Historic Places in 1978, is one of the largest in the state. It has a collection of false-front Victorian buildings, gingerbread-trim houses, and the 1876 Community Presbyterian Church, the first church on the Western Slope. The Hinsdale County Museum is housed in an 1877 former mercantile building (see previous listing).

Lake City Historic District. Contact: Lake City–Hinsdale County Chamber of Commerce, P.O. Box 430, Lake City, CO 81235. Phones: 970/944-2527 and 800/ 569-1874.

LAKEWOOD

History museum

LAKEWOOD'S HERITAGE CENTER

The City of Lakewood is in the process of transforming Historical Belmar Village Museum and Park into Lakewood's Heritage Center, a more comprehensive museum and a major cultural and artistic center.

Belmar Village opened in 1976 on the 126-acre estate of the late May Bonfils Stanton, a prominent Denver philanthropist. The museum originally was housed in the Stanton farmhouse and barn and featured changing exhibits and early agricultural equipment.

Several years ago, Lakewood decided to broaden the museum's scope and provide a wider range of cultural, artistic, and interactive learning experiences. As a result, the current emphasis is on exhibits highlighting Lakewood's history and twentieth-century historical themes; educational classes; arts programs; and special events. A 500-seat outdoor amphitheater for music, dance, and theatrical productions has also been added.

The evolving heritage center now covers 15 acres and features a number of historical structures, either original to the site or moved there, including an 1870s farmhouse and country school (being updated to reflect the 1920s), 1922 working windmill, 1935 interurban trolley stop, and 1948 International-style commercial building with art deco touches. A collection of farm tractors and equipment from 1910 through the 1940s is also on display.

Lakewood's Heritage Center, 797 S. Wadsworth Blvd., Lakewood, CO 80226. Phone: 303/987-7850. Fax: 303/987-7851. Hours: 10–4 Tues.–Fri., 12–4 Sat.– Sun.; closed major holidays. Admission: adults, $2; children 3–12, $1; children under 3, free.

Art gallery

RED ROCKS COMMUNITY COLLEGE ART GALLERY

The Red Rocks Community College Art Gallery in Lakewood presents changing exhibitions of works by Jefferson County elementary and secondary students and community artists, as well as shows by the college's students and faculty. The gallery opened in 1994.

Red Rocks Community College Art Gallery, 13300 W. 6th Ave., Lakewood, CO 80228. Phone: 303/914-6382. Fax: 303/914-6666. Hours: 8 A.M.–10 P.M. Mon.– Fri., 8–6 Sat.–Sun.; closed major holidays. Admission: free.

Planetarium

ROBERT H. JOHNSON PLANETARIUM, JEFFERSON COUNTY SCHOOL DISTRICT

The Jefferson County School District operates the Robert H. Johnson Planetarium in Lakewood as an educational service for county schoolchildren in grades 3–6 and other interested groups.

The planetarium, which opened in 1964, has a 33-foot dome, a 1995 Zeiss ZKP3 star projector, and 125 seats. The astronomical programs are educational in nature and can be tailored to meet the needs of individual groups.

The school district also operates two observatories that are not open to the public: one is on Mount Evans near Evergreen and the other is on Windy Peak near Bailey.

Robert H. Johnson Planetarium, Jefferson County School District, 200 Kipling St., Lakewood, CO 80226. Phone: 303/237-4386. Hours: 9:30–5 Mon.–Fri. and by appointment; Sat.–Sun. by appointment. Admission: $2 per person.

Historic cemetery

CROWN HILL CEMETERY TOWER OF MEMORIES

The Tower of Memories, a seven-story mausoleum at the Crown Hill Cemetery in Lakewood, was listed on the National Register of Historic

Places in 1987. The cemetery was founded in 1907 by George W. Olinger, who inherited his father's chain of mortuaries.

Construction of the Tower of Memories began in 1926 and continued for nearly 60 years, reflecting the influence of different architects and the popularity of various architectural styles.

The original design was Gothic, with a vaulted, churchlike interior. In the late 1920s, new architects replaced the Gothic detailing with a modernistic treatment and articulation of the tower. Construction continued until labor and material shortages halted work during World War II. In 1948, construction resumed under a new architect, who increased the height of the tower by eight feet and added a front stairway.

The result is a striking modernistic building featuring an entrance hall with a pictorial history of the cemetery, a chapel, a drawing room for smaller services, and a multi-tiered mausoleum, the first in the Denver area.

Among those buried at Crown Hill Cemetery are brewery founder Adolph Coors, author Mary Coyle Chase, and boxer George V. Manley.

Crown Hill Cemetery Tower of Memories, 8500 W. 29th Ave., Lakewood, CO. Cemetery address: 7777 W. 29th Ave., Denver, CO 80215. Phones: 303/233-4611 and 888/276-9645. Hours: summer, 8 A.M.–dusk daily; winter, 6:30 A.M–8 P.M. daily.

Historic cemetery

GOLDEN HILL CEMETERY, HILL SECTION

Lakewood's Golden Hill Cemetery, established in 1908 by the West Side Benevolent Society, includes the Hill Section, reserved for indigent Jews buried at community expense, Jews who committed suicide (they were denied burial in the main portion of the cemetery by Jewish custom), and tuberculosis patients from the Jewish Consumptive Relief Society sanitarium and hospital. Most of those interred in the Hill Section, which is listed on the National Register of Historic Places, were tuberculosis victims.

Golden Hill Cemetery, Hill Section, 12000 W. Colfax Ave., Lakewood, CO 81215. Phone: 303/237-0573. Hours: 8:30 A.M.–sunset Sun.–Fri., closed Sat.

LAMAR

History museum

BIG TIMBERS MUSEUM

The 1928 bank robbery in which four people were killed by the Fleagle gang is recalled at the Big Timbers Museum in Lamar. On display are the getaway car and guns, as well as photographs and newspaper clippings relating to the event.

The museum was opened in 1966 by the Prowers County Historical Society in the 1929 AT&T repeater station building.

Among the facility's varied collections and displays are turn-of-the-twentieth-century gowns, carriages, saddles, furnishings, Native American artifacts, photographs, and other historical materials pertaining to the area.

Big Timbers Museum, Prowers County Historical Society, 7515 U.S. Hwy. 50, P.O. Box 362, Lamar, CO 81052. Phone: 719/336-2472. Hours: June through mid-Sept., 10–6 daily; remainder of the year, 1–5 daily; closed New Year's Day, Good Friday, Thanksgiving, and Christmas. Admission: free.

LAS ANIMAS

History museum

KIT CARSON MUSEUM

The Kit Carson Museum is a complex of eight historic buildings operated by the Pioneer Historical Society of Bent County in Las Animas near the old Santa Fe Trail in southeastern Colorado.

Opened in 1961, the museum's main building has 15 rooms filled with collections and exhibits. The structure was built in 1940 to house German prisoners during World War II. It later provided housing for migrant workers, then widows and the indigent.

The other buildings, most of which have been moved from elsewhere, include an 1860 stage station, 1876 county jail, 1882 city jail, the 1891 Kreybill schoolhouse, a blacksmith's shop, and a carriage house.

The buildings contain historical exhibits on such topics as Kit Carson, the cattle industry, Native Americans, carriages, Fort Lyon, railroads, agriculture, and prominent citizens from the area.

The historical society is in the process of restoring the historic ghost town of Boggsville, two miles south of Las Animas. Several of the large houses have been reconstructed, and a replica of Kit Carson's home is planned (see separate listing for Boggsville).

Kit Carson Museum, Pioneer Historical Society of Bent County, 305 St. Vrain St., P.O. Box 68, Las Animas, CO 81054. Phone: 719/456-2005. Hours: Memorial Day–Labor Day, 1–5 daily; closed remainder of the year. Admission: donation requested.

LA VETA

Historic fort

FORT FRANCISCO MUSEUM

The Fort Francisco Museum, located on the site of an 1863 adobe fort in La Veta, consists of nine buildings, including three from the original trading post erected by John Francisco.

The fort has 10 rooms—three in the east wing and seven in the west wing—and contains a re-created general store. Among the other buildings are a one-room schoolhouse and a blacksmith's shop, both moved to the site; a former store that was converted to a saloon and a post office; and a building with exhibits on mining and an early doctor's office.

The museum was founded in 1956 by the Huerfano County Historical Society, which also operates the Walsenburg Mining Museum (see separate listing under Walsenburg). Among its collections are settlers' furniture, manuscripts, photographs, taxidermy examples, Native American artifacts, and early clothing, tools, farm and ranch implements, guns, musical instruments, currency, and coal-mining materials.

Fort Francisco Museum, Huerfano County Historical Society, Main St., P.O. Box 428, La Veta, CO 81055. Phone: 719/742-3506. Hours: Memorial Day–Labor Day, 9–5 daily; other times by appointment. Admission: adults, $4; children 10–17, $2; children 9 and under, free.

LEADVILLE

History museum/gallery

HERITAGE MUSEUM AND GALLERY

The history of Leadville, once a mining boomtown, is the focus of the Heritage Museum and Gallery, founded in 1971 and housed in a 1902 former Carnegie Library building in the Leadville Historic District.

The museum, operated by the Lake County Civic Center Association, contains exhibits and collections of mining artifacts, ore samples, clothing, household items, topographic maps, fine art, and materials relating to the 10th Mountain Division, which trained at nearby Camp Hale in World War II.

Perhaps the most popular exhibit is a quarter-inch-scale replica of Leadville's 1896 Ice Palace. Designed to resemble a Norman castle, the

Ice Palace covered five acres and had 90-foot towers at its entrance. More than 10 million pounds of ice were used to create the ice castle, which Leadville hoped would boost its economy after the 1893 silver panic. The 9-foot-by-6-foot model, built by Frank Goris, is a cutaway with skating and dancing figures.

A park is being developed adjacent to the museum. It already features an 1870 prospector's cabin, wagons, and other materials.

The Lake County Civic Center Association also oversees Leadville's historic Old Church, built in the 1880s.

Heritage Museum and Gallery, 102 E. 9th St., P.O. Box 962, Leadville, CO 80461. Phone: 719/486-1878. Hours: May–Oct, 10–6 daily; closed remainder of the year. Admission: adults, $2.50; children 6–16, $1.50; children under 6, free.

Mining museum/hall of fame

NATIONAL MINING HALL OF FAME AND MUSEUM

The mining industry's colorful history and the contributions of pioneers in the discovery, development, and processing of the nation's natural resources are chronicled in the National Mining Hall of Fame and Museum in Leadville.

Opened in 1988 in a 70,000-square-foot renovated Victorian schoolhouse (the 1899 former high school), the institution is one of only several federally chartered museums created through an act of Congress.

Individuals who have played a significant role in the mining industry are honored in the National Mining Hall of Fame, which has approximately 150 members. Six people are inducted each year. Plaques describing the life and contributions of each honoree can be seen in the Hall of Fame Gallery.

The museum features gold and artifacts from each of the 17 states that experienced significant gold rushes; hundreds of mineral specimens, including exceptional specimens on loan from the Smithsonian Institution and the Harvard Mineralogical Museum; 22 miniature dioramas by woodcarver Hank Gentsch depicting the history of gold mining; murals of historical moments in mining and metallurgy by noted artist Irving Hoffman; a model railroad with trains passing through an early mining camp; a coal exhibit dramatizing both underground and surface mining; an exhibit of industrial minerals; bronze and metal sculptures throughout the museum; and a walk-through replica of an underground hard-rock mine.

National Mining Hall of Fame and Museum, 120 W. 9th St., P.O. Box 98, Leadville, CO 80461. Phone: 719/486-1229. Fax: 719/486-3927. E-mail:

The National Mining Hall of Fame and Museum in Leadville. Courtesy National Mining Hall of Fame and Museum.

nationalminingmuseum@bemail.com. Website: www.leadville.com/mining museum. Hours: May–Oct., 9–5 daily; Nov.–Apr., 10–2 Mon.–Fri.; closed New Year's Day, Thanksgiving, and Christmas. Admission: adults, $4; seniors, $3.50; children 6–12, $2; children under 6, free.

Fish hatchery/visitor center

LEADVILLE NATIONAL FISH HATCHERY VISITOR CENTER

The Leadville National Fish Hatchery, established in 1889 near Leadville, is the oldest federal fish hatchery west of the Mississippi River and the second oldest in the nation.

In 1980, it opened a visitor center in the original hatchery building. The center consists of two display rooms—one devoted to the history and early equipment of the hatchery and the other to current operations and fish propagation methods.

The hatchery, operated by the U.S. Fish and Wildlife Service, also features a picnic area, a nature trail leading to the Evergreen Lakes, and hiking and cross-country skiing trails.

Leadville National Fish Hatchery Visitor Center, 2844 Colo. Hwy. 300, Leadville, CO 80461. Phone: 719/486-0189. Fax: 719/486-3343. Hours: Memorial Day– Labor Day, 7:30–5 daily; remainder of the year, 7:30–4 daily. Admission: free.

Historic houses

HEALY HOUSE AND DEXTER CABIN

Two of Leadville's earliest dwellings, the 1878 Healy House and the adjacent 1879 Dexter Cabin, are operated by the Colorado Historical Society as historic house museums.

Healy House is a restored Victorian mansion featuring furniture, clothing, photographs, maps, and other materials representative of the late-nineteenth-century mining era. Dexter Cabin is a two-room rough log cabin with fine woodwork and wood floors. They were acquired by the Leadville Historic Association in 1942 and became the property of the Colorado Historical Society in 1948.

Healy House was built by August Meyer, a prominent mining engineer, sold during the mining boom of 1881, and converted into a boardinghouse in 1897 by Daniel Healy, who added a third floor to the original two-story structure. Healy House contains a family suite, lavishly furnished parlor, hand-embroidered silk fireplace screen, unusual wall and ceiling coverings, and several pieces of furniture that once belonged to silver magnate H.A.W. Tabor and his first wife, Augusta.

The log cabin, built by banker and investor James Dexter, has a surprising interior featuring inlaid oak and walnut floors, wall coverings imported from England, built-in cabinets, and window lambrequins. It also houses a collection of walking sticks, historical photographs, and Dexter family possessions.

Healy House and Dexter Cabin, 912 Harrison Ave., Leadville, CO 80461. Phone: 719/486-0487. Hours: Memorial Day–Labor Day, 10–4:30 daily; Labor Day through the end of Sept., 10–4:30 Sat.–Sun.; remainder of the year by appointment. Admission: adults, $3.50; seniors, $3; children 6–16, $2; children under 6, free.

Historic house

TABOR HOME

Guided tours of the 1877 Leadville home of silver king Horace A.W. Tabor and his first wife, Augusta, are conducted for groups of 10 or more by the City of Leadville during the summer.

The house, occupied by the Tabors until 1880, when they moved to Denver, was relocated from Harrison Avenue to its present site on Fifth Street in 1879, when the street became more commercial and residential property too expensive.

The Tabors still occupied the frame dwelling when they entertained former president Ulysses S. Grant and his wife in 1880. After the Tabors left for Denver, the house was sold to Augusta Tabor's sister, who lived in it for many years.

The Tabors' marriage broke up over the "Baby" Doe affair, which became a national scandal. The Tabors later divorced and Horace married Elizabeth Doe.

Tabor Home, 116 E. 5th St., Leadville, CO 80461. (Contact: Dept. of Administrative Services, City of Leadville, 800 Harrison Ave., Leadville, CO 80461. Phone: 719/486-0349. Fax: 719/486-1040.) Hours: Memorial Day–Labor Day, groups of 10 or more by appointment only; closed remainder of the year. Admission: free.

Historic house/bed-and-breakfast

ICE PALACE INN

The Ice Palace Inn, a Leadville bed-and-breakfast, occupies two adjacent Victorian houses built in 1898–1899 on the site of the Ice Palace castle, which opened and melted away in 1896.

The original Ice Palace, made from 5,000 tons of ice, was constructed in 36 days by 300 out-of-work miners in hopes of boosting Leadville's sagging economy. The spectacular 450-foot-by-320-foot structure had an indoor ice rink, ballroom, theater, dining hall, snack bar, kitchen, and two 90-foot towers. But an unusually warm spring doomed the icy complex earlier than expected.

The Ice Palace Inn bed-and-breakfast has eight guest rooms, each individually decorated. All feature private baths. Five bedrooms have fireplaces. Breakfast is served on small tables in a formal dining room decorated with photographs of the original Ice Palace.

Ice Palace Inn, 813 Spruce St., Leadville, CO 80461. Phones: 719/486-8272 and 800/754-2840. E-mail: ipalace@sni.net. Website: www.icepalaceinn.com. Hours: open 24 hours. Rates: vary with room and season.

Historic opera house

TABOR OPERA HOUSE

The lavish Tabor Opera House was opened in Leadville in 1879 by Horace A.W. Tabor, who made and lost a fortune in silver mining. Many leading entertainers of the Victorian era came to the boomtown to perform, including Shakespearean actor Laurence Barrett, magician Harry Houdini, Al Field's Minstrels, and Sousa's Marine Band.

Tabor lost the opera house in the 1893 silver panic, but it continued to operate under a succession of owners until 1955, when Florence Hollister, a 74-year-old retired schoolteacher, purchased the historic three-story building and saved it from demolition.

Mrs. Hollister undertook a restoration program and opened the building to tourists. When she died in 1965, her heir, Evelyn E. Furman, completed the restoration.

The opera house still has its original hand-painted scenery, some of its plush Victorian seats, dressing rooms with antique furniture, and large autographed photos of many of the stage stars who performed there. Visitors also can tour the five-room Tabor Suite, with its Victorian furnishings, on the second floor.

Tabor Opera House, 308 Harrison Ave., Leadville, CO 80461. Phone: 719/486-1147. Fax: 303/471-5224. Hours: 9–5 Sat.–Sun. Admission: adults, $4; children 5–12, $2; children under 5, free.

Historic mine

MATCHLESS MINE

The Matchless Mine in Leadville generated millions of dollars for Horace A.W. Tabor in the 1880s and early 1890s. But the silver panic of 1893 dealt a knockout blow to silver mining—and the Matchless Mine. As a result, Tabor and his second wife, Elizabeth Doe, lived in poverty in Denver after the mine closed.

But Tabor never lost faith in the mine, and on his deathbed he told his wife, "Hang on to the Matchless. It will make millions again." Baby Doe (as she was known) moved to a cabin near the mine and struggled and starved for nearly 36 years to follow his injunction. She sometimes was seen on the streets of Leadville with her feet wrapped in burlap sacks to keep out the cold. She refused food and clothing from sympathetic friends. Her frozen body was found in the cabin in 1935.

After her death, the mine machinery was removed and the property was vandalized. In 1953, a community nonprofit group, Leadville Assembly Inc., initiated a successful movement to restore the cabin and open the property to the public. Guided tours now are offered of the cabin, hoist room, and head frame.

Matchless Mine, 414 E. 7th St., Leadville, CO 80461. Contact: Leadville Assembly Inc., 3940 Colo. Hwy. 91, Leadville, CO 80461. Phone: 719/486-0371. Hours: early June through Labor Day, 8–5 daily; closed remainder of the year. Admission: adults, $3.50; children under 6, $1.

Historic railroad

Leadville, Colorado & Southern Railroad

Summer visitors to Leadville can take a 23-mile round-trip ride to the Climax mining area on the Leadville, Colorado & Southern Railroad.

The railroad, which began operations in 1987, makes use of the 1894 Colorado & Southern depot and travels over the old railroad's high line. The Colorado & Southern once served the mining camps and carried passengers between Leadville and Denver.

The scenic railroad now makes the 2.5-hour narrated round-trip journey to and from the Climax Molybdenum Mine area near Fremont Pass. The trip is offered twice daily from mid-June through Labor Day and once daily in early June and the rest of September.

Leadville, Colorado & Southern Railroad, 321 E. 7th St., P.O. Box 916, Leadville, CO 80461. Phone: 719/486-3936. Fax: 719/486-0671. Hours: mid-June through Labor Day, two trips daily at 11 and 2; Memorial Day weekend through mid-June, and day after Labor Day through the last week in Sept., one trip daily at 1. Prices: adults, $22.50; children 4–12, $12.50; children under 4, free.

Historic hotel

Delaware Hotel

The Delaware Hotel, which opened in Leadville in 1886, once served mining prospectors, businessmen, and such notorious figures as Billy the Kid, Doc Holliday, and Butch Cassidy. But nearly 100 years later, the Victorian-era hotel was closed and auctioned off in a delinquent-tax sale.

In 1992, however, the hotel, named by its founders for their home state, came back to life under new owners Scott and Susan Brackett, who restored many of its original Victorian features and made a number of improvements.

Perhaps the most noticeable change was the conversion of the first floor, which had been the Crew Beggs Dry Goods Company since the hotel first opened, into the hotel's lobby and restaurant (Calloway's), which formerly had been located on the second floor.

All 36 rooms now have baths (previously, the entire hotel had only four). The rooms contain Victorian furniture, brass beds, exposed brick walls, and other touches from the turn of the twentieth century. Some of the original uneven floors have been retained.

The hotel is listed on the National Register of Historic Places and is a principal attraction of the Leadville Historic District, which includes most of the city's historic downtown buildings.

Delaware Hotel, 700 Harrison Ave., Leadville, CO 80461. Phones: 719/486-1418 and 800/748-2004. Fax: 719/486-2214. Hours: open 24 hours. Rates: vary with room and season.

Historic district

LEADVILLE HISTORIC DISTRICT

The downtown and surrounding areas of Leadville—at 10,152 feet, the nation's highest incorporated town—are part of the old mining community's historic district.

The Leadville Historic District, which became a National Historic Landmark in 1961, includes more than 70 square blocks of Victorian architecture and is roughly bounded by Hazel, Second, James, and 10th Streets.

In 1880, during the silver-mining boom, Leadville was Colorado's second-largest city, with a population of more than 24,000. Today, it has approximately 3,000 residents. It was during the late nineteenth and early twentieth centuries that nearly all of the buildings in the historic district were constructed. Fortunately, most were preserved and can be seen during a walking tour of the historic area.

These self-guided tours usually begin at the Ice Palace Park, site of a winter ice-sculpture festival in the 100 block of W. 10th Street. Participants then head south on Harrison Avenue, Leadville's main street.

On the east side of Harrison are such historic structures as the 1878 Healy House and adjacent 1879 Dexter Cabin, both operated as historic house museums by the Colorado Historical Society; 1902 Carnegie Library building, which now houses the Heritage Museum and Gallery; 1900 former high school, now the site of the National Mining Hall of Fame and Museum; 1905 Leadville City Hall building, which served as the town's post office until 1973; 1886 Delaware Hotel, restored and reopened in 1992; 1880 Annunciation Church (the one with the tall steeple), where "the Unsinkable" Molly Brown was married and funeral services were held for Baby Doe Tabor; 1893 Iron Building, apparently so called because iron was used in its construction; 1892 American National Bank building, with its bell-shaped, copper-plated dome; 1887 Breene Block building, which formerly housed a liquor store and now features a bar/lounge on its first floor; Hyman Block, built between 1885 and 1890, where Doc Holliday shot his last man; and 1879 Tabor Opera House, said to be the finest theater between St. Louis and San Francisco of its time.

Crossing the street and heading north on Harrison Avenue, visitors can see the 1883 Clipper Building, which originally was the Board of

Trade Saloon and has housed the Silver Dollar Saloon since 1935; 1880 St. George's Episcopal Church, a smaller replica of St. George's Church in New York City; 1881 Western Hardware Building, where Manville and McCarthy Hardware operated for more than 100 years; 1955 Lake County Courthouse, which replaced an 1880 courthouse (elsewhere on the block) that was partially burned in 1942; 1897 clapboard commercial building, once a drugstore and saloon; 1885 Tabor Grand Hotel designed by noted architect George King; and 1889 Presbyterian Church, notable for its open Gothic-style bell tower.

Leadville Historic District. Contact: Greater Leadville Area Chamber of Commerce, 809 Harrison Ave., P.O. Box 861, Leadville, CO 80461. Phones: 719/486-3900 and 800/933-3901. Fax: 719/486-8478.

LIMON

History museum

LIMON HERITAGE MUSEUM

The Limon Heritage Museum is a complex of historical buildings, objects, and exhibits along a six-block railroad right-of-way in Limon on the eastern plains.

The museum was opened by the Limon Heritage Society in 1992 in a turn-of-the-twentieth-century Rock Island Railroad depot, which has been restored and now contains exhibits on early settlers, Native American artifacts, posters, weather station equipment, railroad memorabilia, farm machinery, and a working model railroad set in 1940s Limon.

Adjacent to the depot are four rail cars—a 1914 lunch-counter/dining car, a Union Pacific caboose, a Milwaukee Road passenger/baggage car, and a Union Pacific/Rock Island snowplow.

Located near the depot are an 1892 boxcar with a collection of saddles, tack, and western memorabilia; a 1900s one-room schoolhouse; a sheepherder's wagon; an 1892 scale; and a Prairie Monument honoring pioneer families of the eastern plains.

Railroad Park is being developed by the museum, with the assistance of the Town of Limon, about six blocks from the depot. So far, it contains antique farm machinery, picnic tables, playground equipment, a grandstand, and two of six windmills planned for the park.

The museum also intends to construct a new 41-foot-by-100-foot building east of the depot to display large objects and present additional exhibits.

Limon Heritage Museum, Limon Heritage Society, 899 1st St., P.O. Box 341, Limon, CO 80828. Phone: 719/775-2373. Hours: June–Aug., 1–8 Mon.–Sat.; closed remainder of the year. Admission: free.

LINCOLN

Historic ghost town

LINCOLN GHOST TOWN

The early mining town of Lincoln (formerly Paige City), four miles northeast of Breckenridge, was the site of the "Ten Years War," during which three men lost their lives in a shootout. It is also near the site where a 9.5-ounce solid gold nugget—said to be Colorado's largest—was found in 1869.

The shooting war followed the discovery of an unusual form of gold—high-quality crystallized gold deposited in twisted, wire-thin strands—in French Gulch by Harry Farncomb in the early 1860s. Farncomb quietly bought up the "wire patch," though not in accordance with accepted mining practices. When he turned the gold in to a Denver bank, a group of investors and jealous prospectors sought to wrest control of the land in a lengthy legal battle that ended in a shootout involving 40 men. Farncomb was able to keep his land claims but later sold his interests to a third party.

The giant gold nugget was found by Tom Groves and Harry Lytton in a placer claim in French Gulch. The gulch and the hillside north of the gulch—called Farncomb Hill—proved to be especially rich in gold; small nuggets were found there as late as the 1970s. But Lincoln, which was home to the Farncomb Hill miners and those who worked the Wellington Mine and the French Gulch dredges, eventually was deserted. Only a few collapsing cabins remain at the foot of Farncomb Hill. Huge piles of rock from dredging operations are still visible at French Gulch, as are the ruins of old mining and milling sites. The last huge dredge boat also can be seen in the area.

Lincoln Ghost Town, 4 miles northeast of Breckenridge. Contact: Summit Historical Society, 309 N. Main St., P.O. Box 745, Breckenridge, CO 80424-0745. Phone: 970/453-9022. Fax: 970/453-8135.

LITTLETON

Living-history museum

LITTLETON HISTORICAL MUSEUM

Pioneer life in Littleton and the South Platte Valley during the latter half of the nineteenth century and the early twentieth century is re-created at the Littleton Historical Museum, located on 14 acres adjacent to Gallop Gardens and Ketring Park and Lake.

Founded in 1969, the museum features two living-history farms—an 1860s homestead farm and an 1890s farm—with costumed interpreters demonstrating chores, crafts, and occupations of the time.

The museum also has an 1864 schoolhouse, an early 1900s blacksmith's shop, and a 1910 icehouse, as well as a museum building with three galleries and a library/collections center containing more than 30,000 historical artifacts used in exhibits, educational programs, and research.

The 1860s homestead farm comprises the 1861 log home (decorated with original and reproduced furnishings of the period) built by Isaac McBroom to house his wife and three children; an 1860s sheep and goat shelter; a 1910 icehouse; and a reconstructed barn, oxen shelter, poultry coop and storage shed, pigsty, and corncrib. The farm also has an orchard, vegetable garden, and four fields planted on a rotating basis. The 1890s farm includes the 1889 farmhouse built by Fred Bemis, an early windmill, a reconstructed barn and blacksmith's shop, and a tool shed, corncrib, privy, poultry coop, smokehouse, pigsty, and garden. The 1864 schoolhouse was relocated to the property.

Littleton Historical Museum, 6028 S. Gallup St., Littleton, CO 80120. Phone: 303/795-3950. Fax: 303/730-9818. Website: www.littleton.org/lcn. Hours: 8–5 Tues.–Fri., 10–5 Sat., 1–5 Sun.; closed major holidays. Admission: free, but $1 per person for non-city groups.

Art gallery

COLORADO GALLERY OF THE ARTS AT ARAPAHOE COMMUNITY COLLEGE

Traveling art exhibitions are featured at the Colorado Gallery of the Arts at Arapahoe Community College in Littleton. The 2,128-square-foot gallery, founded in 1979, also presents lectures, films, concerts, and education programs for students, adults, and children.

Colorado Gallery of the Arts, Arapahoe Community College, 2500 W. College Dr., P.O. Box 9002, Littleton, CO 80160. Phone: 303/797-5649. Fax: 303/797-

5935. *Hours: 10–5 Mon.–Fri., 10–1 Sat.; closed major holidays and when college is not in session. Admission: free.*

Arts center

STANTON GALLERY, TOWN HALL ARTS CENTER

Town Hall Arts Center is a multicultural facility in downtown Littleton that presents theater, music, dance, comedy, and visual-arts programming. Opened in 1983 in a historic landmark building, the arts center mounts a different art exhibition each month in the Stanton Gallery. Some shows highlight the work of a single artist; others feature the work of guilds.

Stanton Gallery, Town Hall Arts Center, 2450 W. Main St., Littleton, CO 80120. Phone and fax: 303/794-6580. Hours: 9–5 Mon.–Fri., 10–2 Sat. Gallery admission: free. Theater admission: adults, $12; seniors and children, $10.

Botanic gardens

HUDSON GARDENS

Hudson Gardens, a 30-acre display garden along the South Platte River in Littleton, features 16 distinctive gardens reflecting the trees, plants, and flowers of Colorado.

The garden was created by the late Evelyn Hudson. She and her husband, Colonel King C. Hudson, purchased part of the site for a log restaurant in 1941. Over the next two decades, the couple operated their popular restaurant, added to the property, and cared for the riverbank running through it. Hudson Gardens exists today because Evelyn created the Hudson Foundation prior to her death in 1988 to help fund the gardens.

Hudson Gardens opened in 1993. The log restaurant is now known as the Inn at Hudson Gardens and hosts weddings, receptions, meetings, parties, and other special events at the garden.

Within the 16 gardens are displays devoted to roses, wildflowers, prairie grasses, deciduous trees, aquatic plants, and 40 types of conifers. Other gardens include a rock garden, a demonstration garden, a wetlands area with native plants and wildlife, and other specialty displays. Featured are fragrant plants, a three-season display of colorful flowers, and plantings designed to attract butterflies.

Hudson Gardens, 6115 S. Santa Fe Dr. (postal address: 2888 W. Maplewood Ave.) Littleton, CO 80120. Phone: 303/797-8505. Fax: 303/797-3650. Hours: 10–dusk daily. Admission: adults, $4; seniors, $3; children 6–10, $2; children under 6, free.

Arboretum/historic farms/nature center

CHATFIELD ARBORETUM

> Hildebrand Homestead
> Green Farm
> Polly Steele Nature Center

Chatfield Arboretum, operated by the Denver Botanic Gardens, is located on 700 acres leased from the U.S. Army Corps of Engineers southwest of Littleton. Opened in 1989, the arboretum features native flora and fauna, flower gardens, several distinct ecosystems, two nineteenth-century farms, an 1870s one-room schoolhouse, and a nature center.

The grasslands have been reseeded with more than a dozen native grass species, and many trees and shrubs have been planted to form windbreaks for research purposes. Wetland ponds also have been developed to demonstrate habitat restoration and add beauty to the area.

The Dryland Perennial Gardens and Kim Sterne Survival Garden display plants from throughout the West, many of them used by Native Americans and early settlers.

One of the farms—that homesteaded by Frank Hildebrand in 1866—is on the National Register of Historic Places; the other—the former Green farm—has been renovated to house the arboretum's administrative offices, a small classroom, and a maintenance shop. An old bunkhouse has been converted into the Polly Steele Nature Center, from which a beehive can be viewed. The Deer Creek School, which once was downstream from the farms, has been moved to higher ground, restored, and is now a visitor center. Guided tours of the site are offered only by reservation.

Chatfield Arboretum, 8500 Deer Creek Canyon Rd., Littleton, CO 80128. Phone: 303/973-3705. Fax: 303/973-1979. Hours: 9–5 daily; closed New Year's Day and Christmas. Admission: adults, $1; children under 16, free.

Visitor center/historic house

GEORGE T. O'MALLEY VISITORS CENTER AND PERSSE HOUSE, ROXBOROUGH STATE PARK

The 3,265-acre Roxborough State Park near Littleton is known for its spectacular razor-backed rock formations, lush meadows, wooded foothills, and variety of wildlife. But it also contains the George T. O'Malley Visitors Center (named for the first director of the Colorado State Parks Division), as well as more than 13 miles of hiking trails, interpretive nature walks, cart tours, and a historic house.

The visitor center, which opened in 1986, offers a 15-minute slide show on the park, and changing exhibits on its plants, animals, birds, and geology. The park's wildlife includes deer, bobcats, elk, coyotes, mountain lions, and eagles.

The historic 1903 stone Persse House, located about a mile north of the visitor center, formerly was the vacation home of businessman Henry Persse.

George T. O'Malley Visitors Center, Roxborough State Park, 4751 N. Roxborough Dr., Littleton, CO 80125. Phone: 303/973-3959. Fax: 303/973-4044. Hours: May–Aug., 8 A.M.–9 P.M. daily; Sept.–Oct., 8–7 daily; Nov.–Feb., 8–5 daily; Mar.–Apr., 8–6 daily. Admission: $4 per vehicle.

Visitor Center

SOUTH PLATTE VISITOR CENTER

The South Platte Visitor Center is an extension of the Chatfield Dam flood control project administered by the U.S. Army Corps of Engineers near Littleton. Opened in 1982, the visitor center has exhibits on the Corps of Engineers' mission in the South Platte basin, historical and cultural resources in the area, and environmental resources and concerns.

South Platte Visitor Center, U.S. Army Corps of Engineers, 9307 Colo. Hwy. 121, Littleton, CO 80128-6901. Phone: 303/979-4120. Fax: 303/979-0602. Hours: May–Sept., 8–4:30 daily; Oct.–Apr., 9–5 daily. Admission: free.

LONGMONT

History museum

LONGMONT MUSEUM

The Longmont Museum traces the history of the residents of Longmont and the St. Vrain Valley from the days of the early Plains Indians to the present.

The museum, a division of the city's Department of Human and Cultural Services, was founded in 1936, opened in 1940, became a municipal museum in 1970, and moved into its 11,100-square-foot current home in the mid-1970s. An even larger museum is now planned.

The museum's exhibits and programs focus on local people but usually cover a much wider geographic, historical, or social landscape.

The principal exhibit, detailing the history of the area, is "Western Visions: A History of the People of Longmont and the St. Vrain Valley," including Native Americans, explorers, mountain men, prospectors, settlers, farmers, ranchers, businesspeople, educators, and immigrants, from 10,000 B.C. to the present.

Among the other exhibits are "Kidspace," an interactive gallery for children and parents, and "Exploring the Future," dealing with local astronaut Vance Brand and space exploration. The museum also has two galleries for changing exhibitions on history, art, and science.

Museum collections include more than 30,000 artifacts from the mid-nineteenth century to the present, 6,000 historical photographs of Longmont and the area, and more than 250 linear feet of documentary archives related to the social, economic, political, and cultural history of Longmont and the St. Vrain Valley.

Longmont Museum, 375 Kimbark St., Longmont, CO 80501. Phone: 303/651-8374. Fax: 303/651-8590. Hours: 9–5 Mon.–Fri., 10–4 Sat.; closed major holidays. Admission: free.

History museum

DOUGHERTY ANTIQUE MUSEUM

Ray and Dorothy Dougherty have collected and restored a wide variety of cars, farm equipment, musical instruments, and other objects, many relating to the history of Boulder County. In 1977, they opened their collection to the public as the Dougherty Antique Museum on their farm one mile south of Longmont on U.S. Highway 287.

The museum faltered later when Ray died and Dorothy and their children could no longer maintain the collection or operate the museum. Fortunately, Boulder County officials stepped in to provide funds and volunteers to run the museum in 1998.

The 29,000-square-foot museum has 38 restored classic cars, including a 1902 Mobile Steamer and a 12-passenger 1915 Stanley Steamer mountain wagon, which took people from railroad depots in Longmont and Loveland to the Stanley Hotel in Estes Park.

Among the other collections are more than a dozen player pianos and organs, a 1928 American La France pumper fire truck used by Longmont until 1955, and an 80-year-old Aultman and Taylor steam tractor that stands more than 10 feet high.

Dougherty Antique Museum, 8306 N. 107th St. (U.S. Hwy. 287), Longmont, CO 80501. Phone: 303/441-3500. Hours: Memorial Day–Labor Day, 10–4

Fri.–Sun.; closed remainder of the year. Admission: adults, $4; children 6–12, $3; children under 6, free.

Historic house

HOVERHOME

Hoverhome is an elegant 1913–1914 Tudor country mansion in Longmont. It is now operated as a historic house and event center by the St. Vrain Historical Society, which also owns the adjacent 1893 farmstead. Both buildings are local historic landmarks.

The gracious 8,000-square-foot house and the farmstead were the property of Charles and Katherine Hover. He was involved in agribusiness ventures; she was active in church affairs and dreamed of creating a comfortable retirement community where the elderly could live in dignity. Retirement housing was later developed on a portion of the Hover Farm.

Hoverhome has remained virtually unaltered, retaining its original furniture and woodwork, leaded glass, and built-in features typical of the Arts-and-Crafts style of the period. The historical society sponsors historical programs and tours and rents the house and its spacious grounds for weddings, retreats, parties, and other special events.

Only two acres remain of the 160 farmstead acres once owned by the Hovers. But the original farmhouse, barn, mill, and other buildings are still in place, all under restoration. The house and the farmstead are virtually surrounded by residential development.

The St. Vrain Historical Society also owns the 1881 Old St. Stephen's Church, which is leased to the Polar Bear Gallery, and operates the Old Mill Park, which features a number of historic structures (see following listing).

Hoverhome, St. Vrain Historical Society, 1309 Hover Rd., Longmont, CO 80503. Phone: 303/774-7810. Fax: 303/774-7811. Hours: by appointment, and during programming and special events. Admission: varies with events.

Historic park/houses

OLD MILL PARK

Old Mill Park, established in Longmont in 1970 by the St. Vrain Historical Society, features a collection of historic structures dating mainly from the early settlement days of the late nineteenth century.

The park's creation began with the purchase of the 1871 Townley House and the donation of the Secor Centennial Garden. In the years that followed, the 1860 Affolter Cabin, 1860 Hauck Milk House, 1873 Hubbard House, 1890 Billings Cabin, and 1904 Gildner Gazebo were added, as were the mill pond, Denio-Taylor Mill Ditch, and mill wheel.

The result is an impressive array of historic structures in a community park with a garden, water features, and even antique streetlights once located on Longmont's Main Street.

The 1871 Townley House was built by John and Sarah Townley, who came to Longmont from Massachusetts. Their New England–style cottage was expanded in 1881 by the second owners, who added a dining room with a bay window and a larger kitchen. The house was completely renovated by the historical society after being struck by lightning in 1978.

The Affolter Cabin was constructed in 1860 by two Swiss brothers, Jacob and Frederick Affolter, near Haystack Mountain on Left Hand Creek near Longmont. Having failed at prospecting for gold, the brothers decided to farm, run dairy cattle, and sell supplies to miners and explorers. The cabin was moved to the park site in 1970.

The 1860 Hauck Milk House is a yellow sandstone building that originally stood on the farm of Robert and Ernestine Hauck. The structure, whose thick walls afforded good insulation, used spring water to cool dairy products and other perishable foods. It was moved stone by stone to the park and now utilizes water from the Denio-Taylor Mill Ditch. Examples of implements used by early farmers in the area are displayed in the milk house.

The 1873 Hubbard House is a frame cottage that was home to Royal and Adelaide Hubbard and their four children. When threatened with demolition to make way for a parking lot in 1971, the house was relocated adjacent to Old Mill Park.

The Billings Cabin was built in 1890 by George and Henrietta Billings as part of a hunting and fishing resort west of Lyons. When the City of Longmont created Buttonrock Dam, the logs were dismantled, numbered, and then reassembled in Old Mill Park in 1980.

The 1904 Victorian gazebo was moved to the park from the garden of the Sam Gildner home, and the Secor Centennial Garden was donated by Bill and Betty Jo Secor.

The east wall of the mill pond is the only remaining portion of the Longmont Flour Mill built by J. W. Denio in 1873. The mill's five-story plant was serviced by a railroad spur and powered for a time by a large mill wheel on the Denio-Taylor Mill Ditch. It served farmers until 1934, when it burned to the ground. In 1976, the City of Longmont provided funds for the creation of the mill pond, Denio-Taylor Mill Ditch, and mill wheel as part of a state centennial/national bicentennial project.

The St. Vrain Historical Society also was instrumental in creating the Pioneer Museum, which later became the Longmont Museum, operated by the City of Longmont (see separate listing). In addition, the organization saved the 1881 Old St. Stephen's Church, now leased as a gallery, and operates Hoverhome, a historic 1913–1914 country mansion, and the adjoining 1893 farmstead (see previous listing).

Old Mill Park, St. Vrain Historical Society, 237 Pratt St., P.O. Box 705, Longmont, CO 80502-0795. Phone: 303/776-1870. Hours: 8:30–dusk daily. Admission: free; group tours by appointment.

LOUISVILLE

History museum

LOUISVILLE HISTORICAL MUSEUM

The Louisville Historical Museum is a three-room museum located in a former grocery store on the main street of this former coal-mining community.

Louisville's past and the people who helped shape it are featured in the collection and exhibits, which include early photographs, clothing, telephones, books, and other historical materials ranging from an 1899 wedding certificate to equipment from the recently closed Steinbaugh Hardware Store.

Next door to the museum is the turn-of-the-twentieth-century three-room Tomeo House, which the City of Louisville purchased in 1983. Members of the Louisville Historical Commission refurbished the building and supplemented the Tomeo family's kitchen materials with period items such as china, furniture, dolls, and irons.

Louisville Historical Museum, 1001 Main St., Louisville, CO 80027. Phone: 303/665-9048. Hours: 10–3 Tues.–Thurs. Admission: free.

Children's museum

WORLD OF WONDER! CHILDREN'S MUSEUM

Interactive exhibits and play areas are the attractions at the World of Wonder! Children's Museum, a 6,000-square-foot facility that opened in Louisville in 1996.

Among the varied offerings are an arts-and-crafts room, large sandbox, music room, dance studio, puppet theater, game room, pirate ship, playhouse, and computers. In addition, children usually can interact with a traveling exhibition, such as the recent "A Maze of Rain Forests."

World of Wonder! Children's Museum, 1075 S. Boulder Rd., Suite 130, Louisville, CO 80027. Phone: 303/604-2424. Fax: 303/666-8376. Hours: 10–6 Tues.– Thurs. and Sat., 10–8 Fri., 10–2 Sun.; closed major holidays. Admission: adults, free; children 15 months–12 years, $5.99; school groups of 30 or more, $3.99 per student; other groups of 10 or more, $4.50 per person.

LOVELAND

History museum/art gallery

LOVELAND MUSEUM AND GALLERY

The Loveland Museum and Gallery is the cultural center of Loveland, a community that refers to itself as "A Work of Art."

The museum was the brainchild of Harold Dunning, an author, collector, curator, and mountain guide who began gathering pioneer artifacts and stories as early as 1919. The Loveland Museum has been operated by the City of Loveland since 1945. A larger facility was built in 1956, with the addition of an art gallery in 1970. The building's size was doubled to 26,000 square feet in 1992.

The museum's exhibits include historic period rooms, Mariano Medina's cabin, a topographic relief map of the Colorado–Big Thompson River Water Diversion Project, and such displays as "Life on Main Street," "Loveland's Great Western Sugar Factory," "Sweetheart Town, USA," and "Stone Age Fair." The art gallery features changing regional, national, and international art exhibitions.

Educational programs and classes, as well as special events such as concerts, performances, poetry readings, and demonstrations, take place throughout the year.

The museum also operates a one-room schoolhouse—Lone Tree School—in North Lake Park, where children can experience turn-of-the-twentieth-century school days.

Loveland Museum and Gallery, 503 N. Lincoln St., Loveland, CO 80537. Phone: 970/962-2410. Fax: 970/962-2910. Hours: 10–5 Tues., Wed., Fri.; 10–9 Thurs.; 10–5 Sat.; 12–4 Sun.; closed major holidays. Admission: free.

LUDLOW

Historic site

LUDLOW MASSACRE SITE

The coal-mining town of Ludlow, 14 miles northwest of Trinidad, was the site of the Ludlow Massacre. Twenty-one persons died during this 1913–1914 Colorado coal strike, which became a virtual civil war.

The strike, and the ensuing violence, took place during a period when miners—mainly immigrants who knew little English—were worked hard, paid little, subjected to dangerous working conditions, and generally taken advantage of by the mine owners, who refused to recognize the miners' labor union.

The strike began on September 6, 1913, when miners demanded, among other things, an eight-hour work day, a ten percent wage increase, pay for so-called "dead work" such as cleaning and timbering, and recognition of the United Mine Workers as their official bargaining agent.

When the mine owners refused, approximately 12,000 miners and their families moved out or were evicted from their company homes in many mining camps in the Walsenburg and Trinidad area. Tent cities were established at a half dozen sites in the region, one of the largest (some 900 miners and their families in about 275 tents) being outside the town of Ludlow.

Governor Elias M. Ammons declared martial law in the region and called out the state militia shortly after the strike began and violence broke out. Base camps for the militiamen were established near Walsenburg and Trinidad, with smaller camps at trouble spots. Troops patrolled the entire area, including Ludlow.

As the strike progressed, the situation became increasingly tense, with random rifle fire and dynamite explosions. To protect their families, many strikers dug caves beneath their tents. Meanwhile, many of the militiamen were replaced by guards paid by the state—and the mining companies.

By 1914, the shooting escalated. On April 19, officials were rebuffed in their efforts to arrest Louis Tikas, one of the strike leaders. The next day, three dynamite blasts were set off near the militia camp. Militiamen and hired guards responded with rifle and machine-gun fire, then attacked Ludlow's tent city, setting fire to the canvas dwellings. The charred bodies of two women and nine children later were found in one of the underground pits. An additional two children, seven miners, and one militia trooper were killed during the conflict.

The incident shocked the nation and incited the strikers, who marched on Forbes and burned it to the ground, killing several guards and nonstriking miners. Federal troops were called in to help the state militia bring peace to the mining fields. More than 400 strikers were indicted, as well as union leader John Lawson, who was convicted of murder (he was later freed when the verdict was set aside by the Colorado Supreme Court).

The labor dispute produced slightly better working conditions, hours, and pay but failed to achieve recognition for the United Mine Workers Union. Instead, a "company union" was established under the Rockefeller Plan (proposed by mine owner John D. Rockefeller), which hindered unionization of the mines and ultimately was outlawed.

The strike and violence focused public attention on working conditions in the mines and later influenced both the creation of the Colorado Industrial Commission, formed to mediate labor/management disputes, and passage of the state's first Workmen's Compensation Act.

Today, little remains of Ludlow save the ruins of structures and a memorial (said to be located over the hole where the two women and nine children died) commemorating the Ludlow Massacre.

Ludlow Massacre Site, 14 miles northwest of Trinidad. Contact: Trinidad History Museum, 300 E. Main St., Trinidad, CO 81082. Phone: 719/846-7217. Fax: 719/846-6872. E-mail: chsthmmanini@rmi.com. Website: www.trinidadco.com/htm. Alternate contact: Walsenburg Mining Museum, 110 5th St., Walsenburg, CO 81089. Phone: 719/738-1065. Fax: 719/738-2506. E-mail: esheldon@rmi.net.

LYONS

History museum

LYONS REDSTONE MUSEUM

The Lyons Redstone Museum is located in an 1881 restored schoolhouse saved from demolition by the Lyons Historical Society in 1977.

The 5,500-square-foot museum, which opened in 1979, features a slide show and an exhibit on Lyons history, as well as displays of various local artifacts, including a teller cage from an early bank, a re-created living room, a dentist's chair, a classroom, farming implements, tools, and historic photographs.

The Lyons Historical Society also provides drive-by tours of 1881–1917 sandstone buildings in the Lyons Historic District (see following listing).

Lyons Redstone Museum, Lyons Historical Society, 340 High St., P.O. Box 9, Lyons, CO 80540. Phones: 303/823-6692 and 303/823-5271. Fax: 303/443-

0084. Hours: June–Sept., 9:30–4:30 Mon.–Sat., 12:30–4:30 Sun.; closed remainder of the year. Admission: free.

Historic district

LYONS HISTORIC DISTRICT

The Lyons Historic District features 15 structures erected from 1881 to 1917 and built of red sandstone from local quarries. The Lyons Historical Society offers drive-by tours of the historic structures. Lyons sandstone, noted for its quality and distinctive red color, has been used in buildings throughout Colorado and in other states.

Lyons Historic District. Contact: Lyons Historical Society, 340 High St., P.O. Box 9, Lyons, CO 80540. Phones: 303/823-6692 and 303/823-5271. Fax: 303/443-0084.

MANASSA

Boxing museum

JACK DEMPSEY MUSEUM

Former heavyweight boxing champion Jack Dempsey—known as the "Manassa Mauler"—is honored at the Jack Dempsey Museum in his hometown of Manassa in the San Luis Valley.

The museum, which contains boxing gear, mementos, photographs, newspaper clippings, and other materials pertaining to Dempsey's career, is located in the one-room log cabin where he was born in 1895 and lived as a boy. The latest addition is a life-size bronze statue of the boxer by Robert Booth.

Dempsey, who began his boxing career fighting in mining camps, was the world heavyweight boxing champion in 1919–1926. He then became known for his vaudeville and motion-picture work, as well as ownership of the popular restaurant bearing his name in New York City. He died in 1983 at the age of 87.

Jack Dempsey Museum, 408 Main St., Manassa, CO 81141. Phone: 719/843-5207. Hours: Memorial Day–Sept., 9–5 Mon.–Sat. Admission: free.

MANITOU SPRINGS

Racing car museum

PIKES PEAK HILL CLIMB MUSEUM

The Pikes Peak Hill Climb to the top of the 14,110-foot mountain is the second oldest automobile race in the United States (the oldest is the Indianapolis 500). The annual race, which began in 1916, is now sponsored each year by the Pikes Peak Hill Climb Museum, located at the foot of Pikes Peak in Manitou Springs.

The 8,000-square-foot museum celebrates the history of the race and features race cars from 1920 to the present, trophies, Spencer Penrose's Pierce-Arrow race car, memorabilia, and an exhibit on the Unser family, including past winner Bobby Unser's race car.

Pikes Peak Hill Climb Museum, 135 Manitou Ave., Manitou Springs, CO 80829. Phone: 719/685-4400. Fax: 719/685-5885. E-mail: ppihc@usa.net. Website: www.ppihc.com. Hours: 9–5 Sat., 12–5 Sun.; extended hours in summer; closed major holidays. Admission: adults, $5; seniors, $3; children 13 and older, $2; children under 13, free.

Historic house/museums

MIRAMONT CASTLE MUSEUM

International Museum of Miniatures
Golden Circle Model Railroad Museum

Miramont Castle is a 46-room, 14,000-square-foot rambling structure built in 1895 as a private home and now operated as a museum by the Manitou Springs Historical Society to preserve the Victorian heritage of Manitou Springs and the Pikes Peak region.

Miramont was designed by Jean Baptiste Francolon, a French-born Catholic priest who commissioned Angus Gillis, a Scottish contractor, to build it. Father Francolon lived in the mansion with his widowed mother until 1904, when the building was purchased by the Sisters of Mercy as a sanitarium. In 1946, the building was converted to apartments. It became a museum in 1976.

Little of the original decor and only a few pieces of furniture have survived, but the historical society has overseen a representative restoration with furnishings and artifacts that once belonged to old families in the area.

The four-story castle, which was expanded in 1897, is a mixture of nine architectural styles—shingle-style Queen Anne, Romanesque, English Tudor, Flemish, domestic Elizabethan, Venetian ogee, Byzantine, Moorish, and half-timber Chateau.

Two mini-museums are part of the complex—the International Museum of Miniatures, containing the extensive collections of Doris

Crawford, and the Golden Circle Model Railroad Museum, housed in a separate building near the main structure. The property also features gardens, an eight-sided chapel, a conservatory (formerly a green-house), and the Queen's Parlor Tea Room, open from 11 to 4 in summer.

Miramont Castle Museum, Manitou Springs Historical Society, 9 Capitol Hill Ave., Manitou Springs, CO 80829. Phone: 719/685-1011. Fax: 719/685-1985. Hours: Jan.–Mar., 12–3 Tues.–Sun.; Apr.–day before Memorial Day, 11–4 Tues.–Sun.; Memorial Day–Labor Day, 10–5 daily; day after Labor Day–December, 11–4 Tues.–Sun; closed Easter, Thanksgiving, and Christmas. Admission: adults, $3; seniors, $2.50; children 6–11, $1; children under 6, free; adult groups of 20 or more, $2.50 per person, and senior groups of 20 or more, $2 per person.

Historic ruins/museums

MANITOU CLIFF DWELLINGS AND MUSEUMS

At the turn of the twentieth century, the State of Colorado and Colorado College moved Anasazi cliff-dwelling ruins and artifacts from McElmo Canyon in southwestern Colorado to the Manitou Springs vicinity as part of a Colorado College academic program.

The cliff dwellings, dating to the Great Pueblo Period of A.D. 1100–1300, were reassembled in Phantom Cliff Cañon, and the artifacts were made available for study at the college and opened to the public.

In 1906, however, the cliff dwellings became so popular that the college, not wanting to participate in the tourist business, sold the property to the Cliff Dwellings Ruins Corporation. The cliff dwellings and the first of two museums at the site were developed commercially as tourist attractions. A second museum was added in 1986 to display artifacts and present interpretive exhibits.

The two museums now feature early pottery tools, weapons, burial urns, and other artifacts of prehistoric Southwest Indian life, as well as educational exhibits on related topics.

The Pueblo, a three-story structure showcasing the architecture of today's Taos Pueblo Indians, also is open to visitors. In the summer, Native American dancers perform traditional dances at the site.

The cliff dwellings and museums, operated by Dontom Inc. since 1986, serve approximately 120,000 visitors each year.

Manitou Cliff Dwellings and Museums, U.S. Hwy. 24, P.O. Box 272, Manitou Springs, CO 80829. Phones: 719/685-5242 and 800/354-9971. Fax: 719/ 685-1562. Website: www.cliffdwellingsmuseum.com. Hours: June–Aug., 9–8 daily; May and Sept., 9–6 daily; Oct.–Apr., 9–5 daily; closed Thanksgiving and

Christmas. Admission: adults, $7; seniors, $6; children 7–11, $5; children under 7, free.

Historic railway

PIKES PEAK COG RAILWAY

For more than 100 years, the Pikes Peak Cog Railway has carried passengers from its historic Manitou Springs depot to the summit of the 14,110-foot mountain.

The nine-mile standard-gauge railway—the world's highest cog railway—has been in continuous operation since 1891. The Manitou & Pike's Peak Railway Company operates the cog railway eight times daily from late April to early November.

Modern Swiss-made trains now take passengers through a steep canyon and forested areas, then up above timberline to alpine tundra and on to the top of this country's best-known mountain. However, the railway still has on-site an original 1891 passenger car and an 1896 steam locomotive once used by the cog line.

Pikes Peak Cog Railway, Manitou & Pike's Peak Railway Co., 515 Ruxton Ave., P.O. Box 351, Manitou Springs, CO 80829. Phone: 719/685-5401. Fax: 719/685-9033. E-mail: cogtrain@mail.usa.net. Website: www.pikes-peak.com/pikespeak. Hours: late Apr.–early Nov., eight departures daily, from 8–5:20; closed remainder of the year. Round-trip ticket: adults, $23; children 5–11, $11; children under 5, free; groups of 15 or more, $22 per person.

Historic hotel

CLIFF HOUSE AT PIKES PEAK

The Cliff House at Pikes Peak, in Manitou Springs, opened in 1999 in a historic 1873 Victorian inn that later was expanded to become a 200-room hotel favored by tourists.

But the hotel's popularity faded in the 1960s as the public sought newer, more casual, and less expensive surroundings. In 1981, California developer James S. Morley converted the building into 42 apartments. However, the building was closed after a fire swept the fourth floor the following year. The structure stood vacant for 16 years.

The new hotel, with 57 rooms and suites, reopened in 1999, following a $9 million renovation. All the rooms feature Victorian decor, but none are alike in color, size, or shape. Seventeen of the suites are named for famous former guests, such as Clark Gable, F. W. Woolworth, J. Paul Getty, and Katherine Lee Bates, composer of "America the Beautiful."

Cliff House at Pikes Peak, 306 Canyon Ave., Manitou Springs, CO 80829. Phones: 719/685-3000 and 888/212-7000. E-mail: canon306@aol.com. Website: www.thecliffhouse.com. Hours: open 24 hours. Rates: vary with room and season.

Historic cemetery

CRYSTAL VALLEY CEMETERY

Many Manitou Springs pioneers are buried in Crystal Valley Cemetery, which is listed on the National Register of Historic Places.

In 1885, the city traded the land that served as its original cemetery to Dr. Isaac Davis for land that is now Crystal Valley Cemetery. Dr. Davis's mother was the first to be buried at the new site (her grave is marked with an 11-foot obelisk).

Others buried in the cemetery include Civil War general Charles Adams, who negotiated the release of the women and children from the Ute Indians in the Meeker Massacre of 1879; Inez Hunt, prominent children's book author; and Emma Crawford, concert pianist and spiritualist whose ghost allegedly haunts nearby Red Mountain, where she originally was buried.

Several noteworthy structures have been erected at the cemetery, including the turn-of-the-twentieth-century chapel and a 1938 stucco mausoleum, complete with furnishings, that took 14 years to build.

Crystal Valley Cemetery, 502 Plainview Pl., Manitou Springs, CO 80829. Phone: 719/685-4156. Hours: summer, 7:30–7:30 daily; winter, 8–5 daily.

Historic district

MANITOU SPRINGS HISTORIC DISTRICT

Manitou Springs became known in the late nineteenth century for its mineral water, touted as a remedy for almost any illness. Many of its springs still bubble, and samples of the "water cure" are available in some restaurants and stores. Walking tours of the naturally effervescent springs are still popular.

Today, Manitou Springs is mainly a tourist center and home to artists and craftspeople. Many Colorado Springs–area tourist attractions actually are located in Manitou Springs, including Miramont Castle, Manitou Cliff Dwellings and Museums, Cave of the Winds, Pikes Peak Hill Climb Museum, and Pikes Peak Cog Railway.

The Manitou Springs Historic District, which retains much of the city's early charm, was listed on the National Register of Historic Places in 1983. This old commercial district is bounded by El Paso Boulevard, Ruxton Avenue, U.S. Highway 24, and Iron Mountain Avenue.

In addition to the tourist attractions and historic early buildings, visitors will find antiques shops, galleries, restaurants, and an outdoor arcade in the downtown area.

Manitou Springs Historic District. Contact: Manitou Springs Chamber of Commerce, 354 Manitou Ave., Manitou Springs, CO 80829. Phones: 719/685-5089 and 800/642-2567. Fax: 719/685-0355.

MARBLE

History museum

MARBLE HISTORICAL SOCIETY MUSEUM

The history of Marble—once a major producer of marble for such structures as the Tomb of the Unknown Soldier, Lincoln Memorial, and Washington Monument—is traced at the Marble Historical Society Museum in this mountain town, a center for gold and silver mining in the 1880s, along the Crystal River.

The museum, which opened in 1979 in the town's 1910 schoolhouse, contains artifacts, records, and photographs relating to the town's history, geology, and industry, and tells the story of the damage wreaked on both the community and the marble mill by a 1941 mudslide.

Marble Historical Society Museum, 412 W. Main St., Marble, CO 81623. Phone: 970/963-0358. Hours: Memorial Day–Labor Day, 2–4 Sat.–Sun.; other times by appointment. Admission: free.

MAXEY

Historic ghost town

MAXEY GHOST TOWN

The plains town of Maxey, 18 miles northwest of Springfield in Baca County, was founded shortly after the turn of the twentieth century. By 1910, it had a post office, and by 1921 a church. But the little crossroads town was slowly deserted as ranches consolidated and residents moved away.

All that remains of Maxey is a stone church, a graveyard, and the foundations of the post office, general store, and several other buildings.

The church, which is being restored, was protected for many years by Jim McEndree, owner of the J–Lazy M Ranch, which covers much of the surrounding area. He and his workers fenced the church in and watched over the property, safeguarding it against grazing cattle and vandals. Earlier, Millie Ely erected a fence around the cemetery, and other Maxey residents planted irises, still visible, around it.

Maxey Ghost Town, 18 miles northwest of Springfield. Contact: Baca County Historical Museum, Baca County Historical Society, 741 Main St., Springfield, CO 81073. Phone: 719/523-6565.

MEEKER

History museum

WHITE RIVER MUSEUM

The White River Museum in Meeker occupies some of the original 1880 officers' quarters built by the army in the wake of the Meeker Massacre, in which Ute Indians killed Indian Agent Nathan C. Meeker and 10 others and kidnapped three women and two small children (see following listing). The massacre took place in 1879, when a party of Utes attacked the Indian agency in protest of efforts to turn them into farmers and make them give up their horses.

The army established a military post known as the Camp on White River at the present site of Meeker after rescuing the women and banishing the raiding Indians to reservations in southwestern Colorado and Utah.

The 5,000-square-foot museum, operated by the Rio Blanco County Historical Society, opened in 1956 in the original log building, which later was expanded to seven rooms. It contains collections and exhibits of Native American artifacts, period furniture, clothing, tools, stoves, musical instruments, school furnishings, photographs, and other items, many used by early settlers.

White River Museum, Rio Blanco County Historical Society, 565 Park St., P.O. Box 413, Meeker, CO 81641. Phone: 970/878-9982. Hours: mid-Apr. through Oct., 9–5 Mon.–Fri.; remainder of year, 11–3 Mon.–Fri.; closed major holidays, except Fourth of July. Admission: free.

Historic site

MEEKER MASSACRE SITE

During the 1879 Ute uprising now known as the Meeker Massacre, Indian Agent Nathan C. Meeker and 10 other settlers were killed at the White River Indian Agency. Mrs. Meeker, her daughter, and another woman with her two children were kidnapped during the raid.

Meeker, founder of the agricultural cooperative that later became the town of Greeley, wanted the Utes to give up their migratory hunting life and settle on farms. When he ordered some of the best horse pastures plowed under and an irrigation channel built through a field where the Utes raced their horses, the Indians rebelled.

Meeker called for army support. A detachment of troops, led by Major Thomas T. Thornburg, commandant of Fort Fred Steele in Wyoming, was on its way to the reservation when it was attacked. Thornburg and nine men were killed en route.

The Utes then turned on Meeker for calling the troops to the reservation. A small band of Utes set fire to the agency buildings, killed all the men, and kidnapped the three women and two children, who were held captive for nearly a month on Grand Mesa before being rescued.

After the uprising, all the Utes in Colorado were relocated—the Southern Utes to reservations in southwestern Colorado, and the Northern Utes to a reservation in Utah.

The Meeker Massacre occurred about three miles west of present-day Meeker, where a military camp was established and operated until 1883. When the post closed down, the buildings were sold to settlers. A roadside marker now indicates where the White River Indian Agency was and the massacre took place.

Meeker Massacre, 3 miles west of Meeker. Contact: White River Museum, Rio Blanco County Historical Society, 565 Park St., P.O. Box 413, Meeker, CO 81641. Phone: 970/878-9982.

Historic hotel

MEEKER HOTEL

The old Meeker Hotel, built in 1896, is still in operation on Meeker's Main Street. Most of its 24 rooms have been enlarged and modernized, but the hotel's decor, cafe, and restored lobby are clearly reminiscent of the past.

The mounted heads of more than 30 elk, buffalo, deer, and bighorn sheep overlook the lobby, which features exposed brick walls and oak floors. Newspaper accounts of Meeker's history are displayed on the walls. Theodore Roosevelt stayed at the hotel during a 1900 bear-hunting visit.

Meeker Hotel, 560 Main St., Meeker, CO 81641. Phone: 970/878-5255. Fax: 970/878-3412. Hours: open 24 hours. Rates: vary with room and season.

MESA VERDE

National park/archaeological museum/visitor center

MESA VERDE NATIONAL PARK

Chapin Mesa Archeological Museum
Far View Visitor Center

Mesa Verde National Park, the nation's first cultural park, is located in the southwestern corner of Colorado. It was created in 1906 to protect and preserve the cliff dwellings of the area's early inhabitants, the Anasazi (or "Ancient Ones"), sometimes called the Ancestral Pueblo People (the term preferred by their Pueblo descendants).

Mesa Verde National Park in southwestern Colorado was the nation's first cultural park and is one of the few places in the world where cliff dwellings are found. Courtesy Mesa Verde National Park.

The story of these early dwellers, who abandoned their homes in the steep cliffs sometime around A.D. 1300, is told at two locations in the park—Far View Visitor Center and Chapin Mesa Archeological Museum.

The visitor center, about 15 miles into the park, features approximately 30 displays on the site's history and historic jewelry, pottery, and baskets; the museum, 20 miles into the park, offers more than 40 exhibits—many containing artifacts representing daily life in, and the character of, this ancient culture.

The museum exhibits, some of which were developed in the early 1930s by the Civilian Conservation Corps, recently were renovated and updated. The exhibits include five miniature dioramas, among them a Pueblo III replica of the Spruce Tree House cliff dwelling. Other displays feature tools, basketry, pottery, and other artifacts relating to the cliff dwellers. Also on view are Native American beadwork and Navajo rugs.

Mesa Verde was one of the first national parks to have a museum. Mesa Verde's opened in 1917 in a log cabin built as a ranger station and storage shed. It became known as Fewkes Cabin because it contained many objects excavated by Dr. Jesse W. Fewkes, who conducted extensive archaeological work in the park between 1907 and 1922.

In 1925, the archaeological collections were transferred to the present 9,300-square-foot museum building, which opened to the public in 1926. The cabin was dismantled and reconstructed in 1930 to provide housing for seasonal employees. The oldest building in the park, it is now used as office space.

The museum and most of the stone structures in the park are National Historic Sites. The buildings were constructed in the late 1920s by park superintendent and architect Jesse Nusbaum. Work undertaken by the Civilian Conservation Corps from 1933–1942 resulted in the park's other structures and additions.

Mesa Verde National Park's main attractions are the ancient cliff dwellings and mesa ruins nearly 2,000 feet above the valley floor. The 80-square-mile park has approximately 600 cliff dwellings and nearly 4,000 surface sites, most of which are unexcavated and closed to the public.

Mesa Verde, one of the few places where cliff structures are found, became a World Heritage Cultural Site in 1978 and now attracts approximately 650,000 visitors annually. Once visitors pay the park entry fee, there is no charge for the visitor center, museum, or any of the surface ruin sites.

Five cliff dwellings are open to visitors in summer. Three of them, however, are accessible only by ranger-guided tours, which require tickets (obtainable at the visitor center for $1.75)—Cliff Palace, Balcony House, and Long House. The other two ruins—Spruce Tree House and Step House—are open to self-guided tours. Cliff Palace is the largest and most popular cliff dwelling. Spruce Tree House is closest to the museum.

During the winter (late October to early May, depending upon weather), all cliff dwellings are closed except Spruce Tree House, which is open year-round.

Far View Visitor Center, Mesa Verde National Park, Milepost 15, Ruins Rd., P.O. Box 8, Mesa Verde, CO 81330. Phone: 970/529-4465. Fax: 970/529-4637. Website: www.nps.gov/meve/. Hours: mid-Apr. through the first week in Nov., 8–5 daily; closed remainder of the year. Admission: free, but park admission is $10 per car, $25 per van, $200 per bus.

Chapin Mesa Archeological Museum, Mesa Verde National Park, Milepost 20, Ruins Rd., P.O. Box 8, Mesa Verde, CO 81330. Phone: 970/529-4465. Fax: 970/529-4637. Website: www.nps.gov/meve/. Hours: mid-Apr. through mid-Oct., 8–6:30 daily; remainder of the year, 8–5 daily. Admission: free, but park admission is $10 per car, $25 per van, $200 per bus.

MIDWAY

Historic ghost town

MIDWAY GHOST TOWN

Midway, located four miles north of Victor, was a shipping point for gold ore and coal, and a home and watering hole for miners in the Cripple Creek Mining District at the turn of the twentieth century.

Today, only a few miner's cabins and the ruins of the Grand View Saloon remain, but the 150-foot-deep glory hole, the largest mining hole in the district, can be seen at the top of Squaw Gulch, around the hill from Midway. The Kavanaugh Mill also is nearby.

Midway Ghost Town, 4 miles north of Victor. Contact: Victor Chamber of Commerce, P.O. Box 83, Victor, CO 80860. Phone: 719/689-3553.

MONTE VISTA

Visitor center

ALAMOSA/MONTE VISTA NATIONAL WILDLIFE REFUGE COMPLEX VISITOR CENTER

See description under Alamosa.

MONTEZUMA

Historic schoolhouse

MONTEZUMA SCHOOLHOUSE

An 1884 one-room schoolhouse, located on a hillside above 10,400 feet in the old silver-mining town of Montezuma, is operated as a historic site by the Summit Historical Society.

Montezuma Schoolhouse, Summit Historical Society, Montezuma, CO 80435. Contact: Summit Historical Society, P.O. Box 745, Breckenridge, CO 80424-0745. Phone: 970/453-9022. Fax: 970/453-8135. Hours: by appointment. Admission: donation requested.

MONTROSE

History museum

MONTROSE COUNTY HISTORICAL MUSEUM

The Montrose County Historical Museum, located in the 1912 former Denver & Rio Grande Railroad depot (listed on the National Register of Historic Places), focuses on pioneer life and the region's early inhabitants.

The museum, opened in 1974 in Montrose, tells the story of the settling of the Uncompahgre Valley, beginning with the Ute Indians, who roamed the area before prospectors came in search of gold and silver in the nearby San Juan Mountains.

Most of the collections and exhibits are devoted to farming and ranching in the area and feature agricultural equipment—horse-drawn farm implements, early tractors, grain reapers, potato planters, a threshing machine, a hay baler, and other pieces. The museum also contains Mormon scrapers and belly-dump wagons used to build roads and the Bureau of Land Reclamation's Gunnison Tunnel, as well as the original Barlow Sanderson stagecoach, which took passengers through the mountains to Ouray and Silverton; "Old Man Bosler's" ice wagon, which delivered ice to homemakers in early Montrose; and a Union Pacific caboose formerly used on the rail lines outside the depot.

Also on the site are two cabins—a one-room furnished homesteader's cabin and a sparsely furnished cowboy line cabin with dry sink and woodstove.

The museum building houses Native American artifacts, farming and mining equipment, tools, dolls, musical instruments, clothing, quilts, medical equipment, early newspapers, photographs, a re-created old-time country store, and a children's corner.

Montrose County Historical Museum, 21 N. Rio Grande St., P.O. Box 1882, Montrose, CO 81402. Phone: 970/249-2085 (summer) and 970/245-6135 (winter). Hours: mid-May through Sept., 9–5 Mon.–Sat.; closed remainder of the year. Admission: adults, $2.50; seniors, $2; children 5–12, $.50; children under 5, free.

Ethnic history/cultural museum

UTE INDIAN MUSEUM

The Ute Indian Museum in Montrose is devoted to the history and culture of the Ute tribes and the life of Chief Ouray, the peace-loving leader of the Southern Ute Indians, and his wife, Chipeta, who is buried on the grounds.

Ouray's adobe home, built by the U.S. government, burned in 1945, but the site is part of the museum's eight-and-a-half acres. Also located on the property is a marker honoring the Dominguez-Escalante Expedition of 1776.

The Utes lived in the mountains in summer and migrated to river valleys in winter. Colorado gradually consolidated Ute lands on the Western Slope, creating reservations in the southwestern corner of the state and moving the Uncompahgre and White River Utes to a reservation in Utah in 1880.

The 3,000-square-foot museum, founded by the Colorado Historical Society in 1956, recently has been renovated and expanded and now includes two galleries, classrooms, a gift shop, and the Montrose Visitor Information Center.

Among the exhibits are a Ute historical timeline; a Ute wickiup (dwelling) found near Cocherope Pass in Saguache County; dioramas showcasing Ute life and beliefs; an interactive computerized kiosk interpreting the Bear Dance, one of the oldest Ute ceremonies; and numerous photographs and artifacts, including dance skins, beadwork, feather bonnets, and leather garments, many of which belonged to Chief Ouray, Chipeta, and other noted Ute historical figures, such as Ignacio, Colorow, and Buckskin Charlie.

Many items in the Ute collection were purchased from Thomas McKee, a Montrose photographer who lived with the Utes, photographed them, and acquired various traditional and ceremonial objects.

Ute Indian Museum, 17253 Chipeta Dr., P.O. Box 1736, Montrose, CO 81402. Phone: 970/249-3098. Hours: Memorial Day–Labor Day, 9–5 Mon.–Sat., 11–4 Sun.; remainder of the year, 9:30–3:30 Mon. and Thurs.–Sat., 11–3:30 Sun.

Admission: adults, $2.50; seniors, $2; children 6–16, $1.50; children under 6, free.

National park/visitor center

BLACK CANYON OF THE GUNNISON NATIONAL PARK VISITOR CENTER

The history, flora and fauna, geology, and human exploration of the Black Canyon of the Gunnison are detailed in the national park's visitor center 15 miles east of Montrose. The canyon, formerly a national monument, became the nation's newest national park in 1999.

No canyon in North America equals the combined depth, narrowness, sheerness, and somber appearance of the Black Canyon of the Gunnison, which has been preserved in its wild state through this unique combination of geologic features.

The canyon, carved by the Gunnison River, is 53 miles long, but only 12 miles of the gorge lie within the Black Canyon of the Gunnison National Park, a National Park Service property administered through the adjacent Curecanti National Recreation Area. The steep-walled canyon varies in depth from 1,750 to 2,660 feet.

The visitor center is housed in a new log building opened in 1998. The exhibits provide a historical, geological, and ecological overview of the canyon area. The national park attracts more than 225,000 visitors annually.

Black Canyon of the Gunnison National Park, Colo. Hwy. 347, via U.S. Hwy. 50, 15 miles east of Montrose. Contact: Curecanti National Recreation Area, 102 Elk Creek, Gunnison, CO 81230. Phones: 970/249-1914 and 970/641-2337. Website: www.nps.gov/blca. Hours: Memorial Day–Labor Day, 8–6 daily; remainder of the year, 8:30–4 daily; closed New Year's Day, Thanksgiving, and Christmas. Admission: free, but park admission is $7 per car in Apr.–Oct.

MORRISON

History museum

MORRISON HERITAGE MUSEUM

Morrison's old-time businesses, families, and activities are featured at the Morrison Heritage Museum, located behind Town Hall in a building that formerly housed municipal offices and the police station.

The museum, which opened in the late 1970s, is operated by the Morrison branch of the Jefferson County Historical Society and the

Town of Morrison. It contains artifacts, photographs, and other historical materials from the area and presents special exhibits on such
topics as the Civilian Conservation Corps, which built Red Rocks
Amphitheater, and silent-movie star Pete Morrison, who was from
Morrison.

*Morrison Heritage Museum, 110½ Stone St., P.O. Box 564, Morrison CO 80465.
Phone: 303/697-1873. Fax: 303/697-8752. Hours: 1–3 Sat. and by appointment; closed major holidays. Admission: free.*

Natural history museum

MORRISON NATURAL HISTORY MUSEUM

Dinosaur fossils are the main attraction at the Morrison Natural
History Museum, located a short distance from Dinosaur Ridge, where
many of the bones were found.

Fossils include those discovered at Dinosaur Ridge in 1877 and
shipped off to the Peabody Museum of Natural History at Yale University. The discovery, which included the first *Stegosaurus* fossils, set off a
heated dinosaur-fossil hunt in the region.

In 1993, the Peabody Museum loaned a crate of the fossils to the
Morrison Museum, which will free the fossils from their matrix, create
plaster copies of them, and return the originals to Yale. Visitors to
the museum can observe the painstaking work of separating the 150-
million-year-old fossils from the surrounding rock.

Also on display are leg bones from an *Apatosaurus* (commonly known
as a *Brontosaurus*), a cast of the first dinosaur eggs ever found, a cast of a
row of teeth from a *Tyrannosaurus rex*, a leg bone from a young *Triceratops*, casts of dinosaur tracks, and various other dinosaur bones and
exhibits. In addition, the museum features live native reptiles, an
exhibit on deciphering animal tracks, and an outdoor pit of fossil fragments for children to identify.

The museum, which opened in 1990, is operated by the town of
Morrison.

*Morrison Museum of Natural History, 501 Colo. Hwy. 8, P.O. Box 564, Morrison,
CO 80465. Phone: 303/697-1873. Fax: 303/697-8752. Hours: 1–4 Wed.–
Sun.; closed major holidays. Admission: $1 per person; children 5 and under, free;
families, $2.50.*

Visitor center

DINOSAUR RIDGE VISITOR CENTER

Dinosaur Ridge near Morrison is where the bones of *Stegosaurus*, *Diplodocus*, *Apatosaurus*, and other dinosaurs were first discovered in 1877.

Since 1994, the Friends of Dinosaur Ridge have operated a small visitor center and offered guided and self-guided tours of the ridge. Sixteen interpretive signs describing fossil remains and other features are located along a one-mile stretch of Alameda Parkway, which traverses the site.

Many fossils are still embedded in the sandstone layers of the Morrison Formation on the west side of the ridge, and more than 300 footprints of Iguanodontids and ostrichlike carnivores are present in the Dakota Formation on the east side.

Dinosaur Ridge Visitor Center, 16831 W. Alameda Pkwy., Morrison, CO 80465. Phone: 303/697-3466. Fax: 303/697-8911. Hours: summer, 8–5 Mon.–Sat., 12–4 Sun.; winter, 9–4 Mon.–Sat, 12–4 Sun.; closed Thanksgiving, Christmas, and during deep snows. Admission: free, but guided tours cost $25 for up to 12 people, and $2 per person for groups of 13 or more.

Historic site/park

RED ROCKS PARK AND AMPHITHEATER

Red Rocks Park near Morrison is notable for both its jagged red rock formations, created 250–300 million years ago, and its 9,000-seat natural amphitheater built into the red sandstone hillside. The amphitheater hosts outstanding summer concerts by leading musical performers and holds Easter sunrise services in this spectacular outdoor setting.

The 640-acre park, operated by the Denver Parks and Recreation Department, was established in 1927, and the amphitheater was built by the Civilian Conservation Corps in 1936–1941.

Red Rocks Park and Amphitheater, 16351 County Rd. 93, Morrison, CO 80465. Phone: 303/697-8935. Alternate contact: Mountain Parks, Denver Parks and Recreation Dept., P.O. Box 1007, Morrison, CO 80465. Phone: 303/697-4545. Hours: 5 A.M.–11 P.M. Admission: free, but visitors must be out of park by 4 P.M. on concert days, or they will be charged for the event.

Historic fort replica/restaurant

THE FORT

The Fort restaurant in Morrison is housed in a replica of Bent's Old Fort, an 1833 adobe trading post near La Junta (see separate listing under La Junta).

The restaurant, opened in 1963 by Sam Arnold and his late wife, Carrie, has an early Colorado atmosphere, with employees dressed in frontier costumes, a menu featuring old western recipes for food and drink, and roving mandolin players on weekends.

The Fort, 19192 Colo. Hwy. 8 (just off U.S. Hwy. 285), Morrison, CO 80465. Phone: 303/697-4771. Fax: 303/697-4786. Hours: 5:30–10 Mon.–Fri., 5–10 Sat., 5–9 Sun.

MOSCA

National monument/visitor center

GREAT SAND DUNES NATIONAL MONUMENT VISITOR CENTER

The history and geology of the Great Sand Dunes National Monument near Mosca are the focus of exhibits at the park's visitor center.

The 38,000-acre national monument, opened in 1932 by the National Park Service, features approximately 40 square miles of sand dunes, some more than 700 feet high. The sand settles at the foot of the Sangre de Cristo Range because it is too heavy to rise with the winds that have carried it across the semi-arid floor of the San Luis Valley.

The national monument, which may become a national partk soon, also has a small museum that is not open to the public. It is essentially a storage area for historic documents, photographs, artifacts, and preserved mammals, birds, reptiles, and insects representative of the area.

Great Sand Dunes National Monument Visitor Center, 11999 Colo. Hwy. 150, Mosca, CO 81146. Phone: 719/378-2312. Fax: 719/378-2594. E-mail: patrick_myers@nps.gov. Hours: summer, 8:30–6 daily; winter, 8:30–4:30 daily; closed New Year's Day, Thanksgiving, and Christmas. Admission: free, but monument admission is $3 for adults (free for children 16 and under).

Historic ranch/hotel

INN AT ZAPATA RANCH

Two historic cattle ranches—Zapata and Medano—at the edge of the Great Sand Dunes National Monument near Mosca were founded in the 1860s and 1870s and combined into a single 100,000-acre ranch in 1912. They were operated together for 35 years before pieces were sold off and the properties separated. But the ranches were reunited in 1989 by the present owner, Rocky Mountain Bison Inc.

Since then, the historic San Luis Valley ranch has been restored. The Medano property remains a ranch, now supporting a herd of more than 2,000 bison. The Zapata property has become, for the most part, a hotel/retreat—the Inn at Zapata Ranch. But its future is now in doubt. In 1999, The Nature Conservancy of Colorado purchased the land, planning to turn it into a nature preserve.

Opened in 1990, the inn consists of 15 rooms in three buildings— the main building in the enlarged 1928 ranch house, the original 1880 bunkhouse, and a 1960s ranch house. The hotel also has an 18-hole championship golf course, restaurant, pool, spa, and health club.

Zapata Ranch, which is listed on the National Register of Historic Places, still retains a number of its early structures, including an 1878 stagecoach stop (now used as the golf-course superintendent's home) and four other buildings dating back to approximately 1880—a post office, currently used as a boiler room; blacksmith's shop, presently the laundry; cattle barn, converted into the sauna and massage area; and the bunkhouse, which houses inn guests.

In addition to watching bison graze near the golf course, golfers at the seventeenth tee can see a surviving structure from Mexican settlement days—a five-sided log structure believed to have been a Catholic church.

Inn at Zapata Ranch, 5303 Colo. Hwy. 150, P.O. Box 175, Mosca, CO 81146. Phones: 719/378-2356 and 800/284-9213. Fax: 719/378-2428. Hours: open 24 hours; closed Nov.–Mar. Rates: vary with room and season.

NATURITA

History museum

RIMROCKER HISTORICAL MUSEUM OF WEST MONTROSE COUNTY

The Rimrocker Historical Museum of West Montrose County in Naturita shares a 1920 schoolhouse (now the Community Building) with the local library and a community meeting room.

Opened by the historical society as part of the nation's bicentennial observance in 1976, the museum is devoted to area history and contains information and materials on mining, farming, ranching, and early life in west Montrose County.

Among the collections and exhibits are mining, farming, and ranching equipment, blacksmith's tools, household items, dolls, costumes, Native American artifacts, and materials related to the history of the Pion Colony (the Colorado Cooperative Company), which built the irrigation ditch to Tabequacke Park at the turn of the twentieth century.

Rimrocker Historical Museum of West Montrose County, Community Bldg., Town Park, Main St., Naturita CO 81422. (Postal address: P.O. Box 913, Nucla, CO 81424.) Phone: 970/865-2877. E-mail: cookib@aol.com. Hours: June–Labor Day, 2–5 Tues.–Sat.; remainder of the year by appointment. Admission: free.

NEDERLAND

History museum

NEDERLAND HISTORICAL MUSEUM

The Nederland Area Historical Society acquired and opened the 1930s Gillespie House in 1972 as the Nederland Historical Museum. The single-story structure, sometimes considered a miner's cabin, is furnished in keeping with the period.

In addition, the society recently leased the WPA-built county highway garage building in Nederland and is renovating the structure for a more comprehensive museum.

Nederland Historical Museum, Nederland Area Historical Society, Gillespie House, 200 N. Bridge St., P.O. Box 1252, Nederland, CO 80466. Phones: 303/258-0146 and 303/258-9204. Hours: by appointment only. Admission: free.

NEVADAVILLE

Historic ghost town

NEVADAVILLE GHOST TOWN

The gold-mining town of Nevadaville sprang up in Nevada Gulch about a mile southwest of Central City in 1860 shortly after John Gregory discovered gold at Mountain City (which later became part of Central City).

A year later, the mining camp boasted quartz mills, stores, hotels, tents, houses, hundreds of prospectors and miners, and a few families. In the ensuing years, some struck it rich as others toiled away in such mines as the Casey, Kansas, Ophir, and Hidden Treasure.

Nevadaville, which at various times was known as Nevada, Nevada City, and Bald Mountain, boomed in the 1860s and 1870s, suffered a setback in the 1893 silver crash, and bounced back in the late 1890s. Mining activity decreased after the turn of the twentieth century,

revived a bit before World War I and again in the 1930s, and then
ceased after World War II, when Nevadaville became a ghost town.

A few structures—some brick buildings and the ruins of the old
town hall—have survived, but the main attractions are the old cemetery
and the glory hole, which is 1,000 feet long and 300 feet deep. A number of summer cabins have been built in the area in recent years.

*Nevadaville Ghost Town, 1 mile southwest of Central City. Contact: Gilpin County
Chamber of Commerce, P.O. Box 488, Central City, CO 80427. Phone and fax:
303/582-5077.*

NEW CASTLE

History museum

NEW CASTLE HISTORICAL MUSEUM

The New Castle Historical Museum is housed in two buildings—the
former town hall and the original jail—both constructed at the turn of
the twentieth century.

The museum, which was opened in 1983 by the New Castle Historical Society, is devoted to area history and contains displays on sewing
machines, typewriters, blacksmith's tools, kitchen materials, hats, clothing, and photographs, as well as a replica of an early schoolroom.

*New Castle Historical Museum, New Castle Historical Society, 116 N. 4th St.,
P.O. Box 883, New Castle, CO 81647. Phone: 970/984-2116. Hours: Apr.–
Sept., 1–4 Wed.–Sat.; closed remainder of the year. Admission: donation requested.*

OPHIR

Historic ghost town

OPHIR GHOST TOWN

There are two Ophirs (named for the biblical site of King Solomon's
mines) about 14 miles south of Telluride in the San Juan Mountains.
Old Ophir was founded in the 1870s at the foot of the difficult but
much-traveled Ophir Pass; Ophir Loop, a railroad stop about two miles
to the west, followed several years later.

By the mid-1870s, Old Ophir, originally known as Howard's Fork,
had 200 residents, several mines, a stamp mill, and two areas for working free gold (loose gold not found in mines). Its mines, including the

What Cheer, Butterfly-Terrible, and Klondike, continued producing until the early 1900s, shipping out two railroad cars of ore daily.

Ophir Loop is best known for its railroad, an engineering marvel designed by Otto Mears that consists of three tiers of overlapping tracks and a 100-foot trestle, which still exists today.

Most of the surviving early structures are in Old Ophir, including the stamp mill, a hotel, and a number of cabins, some of which are still occupied.

Both Ophirs were plagued by fierce snowstorms and avalanches that buried buildings and made travel treacherous. An oft-repeated story concerns Sven Nilson, a conscientious mailman who carried mail over Ophir Pass from Silverton. He disappeared in a blizzard while delivering Christmas mail in 1883, but his body was not found until two years later, frozen in a snowbank with the mail still strapped to his back.

Ophir Ghost Town, 14 miles south of Telluride. Contact: Telluride Visitors Center, 666 W. Colorado Ave., P.O. Box 653, Telluride, CO 81435. Phones: 970/728-4431 and 800/525-3455. Fax: 970/728-6475.

OURAY

History museum

OURAY COUNTY HISTORICAL MUSEUM

The Ouray County Historical Museum, opened by the Ouray County Historical Society in 1971, is housed in the 1887 former St. Joseph Miners Hospital in Ouray. The museum contains 27 exhibits devoted to the history of the county, plus extensive collections covering a period from 1877 to the end of World War II.

Exhibits re-create a mine, assay office, blacksmith's shop, general store, and historic cabins. Also on display are collections of minerals, costumes, ranching materials, medical equipment, Native American artifacts, railroad objects, civic and school memorabilia, and historical photographs of the old mining area.

Periodically, the museum presents special exhibitions. Past offerings have highlighted June brides, veterans, quilts, crafts, and Christmas. The museum also offers walking and tin lizzie tours of historic buildings and houses in Ouray (walking tours cost $5 for one hour and $10 for two hours; auto tours are $10 for adults and $5 for children under 12).

Ouray County Historical Museum, Ouray County Historical Society, 420 6th Ave., P.O. Box 151, Ouray, CO 81427. Phone: 970/325-4576. Hours: summer,

9–4 daily; remainder of the year, 10–4 Sat.–Mon.; closed major holidays. Admission: adults, $3; children 6–12, $1; children under 6, free.

Historic mine

BACHELOR-SYRACUSE MINE

The Bachelor-Syracuse Mine near Ouray produced $90 million in silver, $8 million in gold, and $5 million in lead, zinc, and copper during its period of operation.

The mine was named for three bachelors (Armstrong, Sanders, and Hurlburt) who discovered silver in 1884 and then raised funds from investors in Syracuse, New York, for a tunnel enabling them to reach rich ore deposits at the bottom of the mine shaft.

Tours of the mine feature a 3,350-foot ride on a mine train called a "trammer." The train travels horizontally into Gold Hill, and a trained guide (frequently a former miner) explains where ore deposits were found and worked, what equipment was used, the role of explosives, and other aspects of mining.

Bachelor-Syracuse Mine, 1222 County Rd. 14, P.O. Box 380, Ouray, CO 81427. Phone: 970/325-0220. Fax: 970/325-4500. Hours: mid-May through mid-Sept., 10–5 daily; closed remainder of the year. Admission: adults, $10.95; seniors, $9.95; children 3–11, $5.95; children under 3, free.

Historic hotel

ST. ELMO HOTEL

Ouray's St. Elmo Hotel, originally a miners' hotel, was built in 1898 and has undergone substantial upgrading in recent years. Its most noteworthy feature is perhaps its resident ghost.

In 1920, so the story goes, Freddie Heit, son of the hotel's founder, shot himself in Room 5 after losing the hotel in a gambling bet and has been a benevolent ghost ever since; early on, guests claimed to hear mysterious footsteps and slamming drawers. Reports of Freddie's hauntings have virtually disappeared, but his picture still hangs in a stairwell leading to the hotel's Bon Ton Restaurant on the lower level.

The hotel originally had 24 small, spartan rooms, which have been converted into nine larger rooms filled with Victorian antiques. Room 5 is now a two-room suite.

St. Elmo Hotel, 426 Main St., P.O. Box 667, Ouray, CO 81427. Phone: 970/325-4951. Fax: 970/325-0348. Hours: open 24 hours. Rates: vary with room and season.

Historic hotel

BEAUMONT HOTEL

The 1886 Beaumont Hotel building, which has been closed since 1965, is about to come to life again in Ouray. The structure, listed on the National Register of Historic Places in 1973, was purchased in 1998 and is currently being restored.

The hotel was considered among the finest on the Western Slope in its heyday. Its ambience was French, its furnishings came from Marshall Field's in Chicago, and its dining-room staff were trained at the Brown Palace hotel in Denver.

The historic building and an adjoining commercial structure were purchased by High Peak Resources Inc., which is restoring the outside of the building and gutting and modernizing the dilapidated interior.

Beaumont Hotel, 5th Ave. and Main St., Ouray, CO 81427. Contact: Ouray Chamber Resort Assn., 1222 Main St., P.O. Box 145, Ouray, CO 81427. Phones: 970/325-4746 and 800/228-1876. Fax: 970/325-4868.

Historic district

OURAY HISTORIC DISTRICT

The Ouray Historic District encompasses almost the entire historic town site and reflects Ouray's importance as a supply center for the nearby San Juan Mountains mining regions from 1886 to 1915.

The small Victorian community, which calls itself "the Switzerland of the Rockies," is wedged into a corner of the Uncompahgre River Valley, with rock walls to the east and west, the cliff-hugging Million Dollar Highway snaking its way up Red Mountain Pass to the south, and popular geothermal hot-springs pools to the north.

The Ute Indians, including the town's namesake, Chief Ouray, spent much of their time in the area before gold and silver deposits were discovered in the surrounding mountains in the 1870s. More than 10,000 tunnels, cuts, and abandoned shafts from hard-rock mining days still can be seen within a 10-mile radius of Ouray.

The town, which became a National Historic District in 1983, has many carefully preserved buildings from the late nineteenth century, with brick Italianate structures dominating the commercial area and frame homes commanding overlooking hillsides.

Two buildings in the district are on the National Register of Historic Places—the Beaumont Hotel (see previous listing) and the Ouray

City Hall and Walsh Library. Among the other notable buildings are the Ouray County Courthouse, St. John's Episcopal Church, the Elks Lodge, First Presbyterian Church, St. Elmo Hotel (see separate listing), Western Hotel, and Wright Opera House. Historic houses include the Ashley, Hurlburt, King, Kullerstrand, Story, and Tanner homes. The Ouray County Historical Museum offers walking and tin lizzie tours of the historic structures.

Ouray Historic District. Contact: Ouray County Historical Museum, 420 6th Ave., P.O. Box 151, Ouray, CO 81427. Phone: 970/325-4576.

PAGOSA SPRINGS

History museum

SAN JUAN HISTORICAL SOCIETY MUSEUM

The early days of the Pagosa Springs area are featured in exhibits at the San Juan Historical Society Museum, which opened in 1970. The museum, housed in the old waterworks building in Pagosa Springs, contains items from early schoolrooms, a general store, a dentist's office, and a barbershop, as well as materials relating to lumbering and other aspects of community life.

San Juan Historical Society Museum, 96 Pagosa St., P.O. Box 1711, Pagosa Springs, CO 81147. Phone: 970/264-4424. Hours: Memorial Day–Labor Day, 9–5 Mon.– Fri., 9–1 Sat.; closed remainder of the year. Admission: adults, $2; children under 12, $1.

Art museum

FRED HARMAN ART MUSEUM

The former home of the late Fred Harman, noted artist, cartoonist, and creator of the *Red Ryder* and *Little Beaver* comics, is the site of the Fred Harman Art Museum in Pagosa Springs.

Opened in 1983, a year after Harman's death, the museum contains more than 2,000 items. They include more than 300 of his major oils and many other pen-and-ink works, as well as photographs, awards, firearms, and western memorabilia. Visitors can also see his studio. Harman was one of the founders of the Cowboy Artists of America.

Fred Harman Art Museum, 2560 W. U.S. Hwy. 160, P.O. Box 192, Pagosa Springs, CO 81147. Phone: 970/731-5785. Fax: 970/731-4832. E-mail: fharman@pagosa.net. Website: www.coloradodirectory.com/fredharmanmuseum.

Hours: Memorial Day–Labor Day, 10:30–5 Mon.–Sat., 12:30–4 Sun.; remainder of the year, 10:30–5 Mon.–Fri., except Feb.–Mar., when open by appointment only. Admission: adults, $2.50; students and children, $1; children under 6, $.50.

Historic site/visitor center

CHIMNEY ROCK ARCHAEOLOGICAL AREA VISITOR'S CENTER

One thousand years ago, as many as 2,000 Anasazi Indians inhabited the Chimney Rock Archaeological Area near Pagosa Springs. It is believed to have been the northernmost outpost of the Chaco Canyon Anasazi, who were concentrated mainly in New Mexico. The archaeological area is best known for its two towering chimneylike rock spires and large pueblo ruins below the ridge's summit.

In 1970, the federal government placed more than 3,600 acres at the site under the protection of the National Forest Service. Access to the restricted grounds now is possible only as part of Forest Service guided tours.

The 35-room Great House, Ridge House, Great Kiva, and some 200 other undisturbed structures are found within the 6 square miles that constitute the archaeological area, which is located in the San Juan–Rio Grande National Forests and the Southern Ute Indian Reservation. The architecture, pottery, and other artifacts from the site reveal the daily lives of the people who made Chimney Rock their home.

During summer, four tours are given daily. The 2.5-hour tours entail walks to two main sites and a Forest Service fire lookout. The archaeological area, which has a new visitor center with interpretive exhibits, is located 17 miles west of Pagosa Springs on U.S. Highway 160 and 3.5 miles south on U.S. Highway 151.

Chimney Rock Archaeological Area Visitor's Center, 3179 Colo. Hwy. 151, P.O. Box 310, Pagosa Springs, CO 81147. Phones: 970/264-2268 and 970/883-5359. Fax: 970/264-1538. E-mail: chimneyrock@chimneyrockco.org. Website: www.chimneyrockco.org. Hours: May 15–Sept. 30, visitor center open 9–4 daily, with guided tours at 9:30, 10:30, 1, and 2; closed remainder of the year. Admission: free. Guided tours: adults, $5; children 5–11, $2; children under 5, free.

Wildlife park/gallery

ROCKY MOUNTAIN WILDLIFE PARK

Live and mounted animals native to the region are on display at the Rocky Mountain Wildlife Park, which opened in 1985 five miles south of Pagosa Springs.

Inside the park building are 40 mounted animals; outside are nearly 20 live animals, including black and grizzly bears, mountain lions, bobcats, elk, mule deer, wolves, coyotes, and porcupines. Feedings usually take place at 4 P.M. in summer and 2 P.M. in winter.

The park building also houses the Rocky Mountain Wildlife Gallery, which features paintings and prints and can be visited free of charge.

Rocky Mountain Wildlife Park, 4821A U.S. Hwy. 84, Pagosa Springs, CO 81147. Phone and fax: 970/264-5546. Hours: May 15–Nov. 15, 9–6 daily; remainder of the year, 2–4 daily, except Wed. and Sun. Admission: adults, $5; children 3–12, $3; children under 3, free.

PALMER LAKE

History museum

VAILE HISTORICAL MUSEUM

The history of the town of Palmer Lake—and the lake itself—is the focus of the Vaile Historical Museum. Artifacts, photographs, and other historical materials pertaining to the area are on view at the museum, which opened in 1977 and is named for Lucretia Vaile, an early Palmer Lake settler.

Vaile Historical Museum, 66 Lower Glenway, P.O. Box 275, Palmer Lake, CO 80133. Phone: 719/481-2528. Hours: 2–4 Wed. and Sat.; closed national holidays. Admission: free.

PANDORA

Historic ghost town

PANDORA GHOST TOWN

Pandora, approximately one mile east of Telluride, was named for the Pandora Mine, discovered in 1875. But the town's primary income producer until the 1970s was the huge Smuggler-Union Mill, a flotation mill that processed ore from the Smuggler and Union Mines high in the surrounding mountains.

Aerial trams brought ore to the mill and transported workers and supplies to and from the mines, which had a total output of more than $50 million.

During its history, Pandora was the scene of snowslides, fires, and labor violence. The manager of the mines was murdered in 1902. The Western Federation of Miners, which had called a strike the year before to protest low wages, was blamed, but no one was convicted. In 1908, someone placed a bomb beneath the bed of the manager's replacement. The intended victim survived the assassination attempt only to commit suicide later on.

Several cabins and a number of ruins remain at the site of Pandora, a half mile north of Bridal Veil Falls, which cascades 365 feet down the side of a cliff.

Pandora Ghost Town, 1 mile east of Telluride. Contact: Telluride Historical Museum, 317 N. Fir St., P.O. Box 1597, Telluride, CO 81435. Phone and fax: 970/ 728-3344. E-mail: th/museum@infozone.org.

PAONIA

History museums

PAONIA MUSEUM AND BOWIE SCHOOLHOUSE MUSEUM

The North Fork Historic Preservation Society operates two adjacent museums—the Paonia Museum and the Bowie Schoolhouse Museum—in Paonia.

The historic schoolhouse, a late-nineteenth-century building that served children in the mining community of Bowie, was moved to its present site and opened as a museum in 1979. It has two classrooms, the original desks and potbellied stoves, and other materials from the period.

The Paonia Museum building, now adjacent to the schoolhouse, was moved from nearby Midway in 1995. The six-room structure was erected in 1904, used as a residence by teacher James Parks and his family, and later donated to the society for use as a museum. The museum is furnished as an early twentieth-century home and contains artifacts and photographs pertaining to schools and students; instruments used by early physicians; a telephone switchboard; and articles related to fruit growing and processing—Paonia's early primary industry.

Paonia Museum and Bowie Schoolhouse Museum, 1600 Colo. Hwy. 187, P.O. Box 622, Paonia, CO 81428. Phone: 970/527-3970. Hours: Apr.–Sept., 1–4 Tues., Thurs., and Sat.; closed remainder of the year, except by special arrangement. Admission: free.

PLATTEVILLE

History museum

PLATTEVILLE PIONEER MUSEUM

The Platteville Pioneer Museum uses artifacts, photographs, and other historical materials to trace the early history of the Platteville area. Opened in 1970, the museum, operated by the Platteville Historical Society, is located in the old library building. Among the objects on display are early branding irons, plows, clothing, kitchen utensils, photographs, and a wide variety of pioneer items.

Platteville Pioneer Museum, Platteville Historical Society, 502 Marion Ave., Platteville, CO 80651. Phone: 970/381-1105. Hours: 9–4 Wed. and 1–4 the fourth Sat. of each month. Admission: free.

Historic fort

FORT VASQUEZ MUSEUM

Fort Vasquez Museum is a reconstructed adobe fur-trading post built in about 1835 by mountain men Louis Vasquez and Andrew Sublette along the South Platte River near Platteville. It now is operated by the Colorado Historical Society.

The historic fort—about 100 feet square, with 12-foot-high walls—was an important trading center for Native Americans, who brought hides and pelts to the post in exchange for blankets, brass kettles, whiskey, silk handkerchiefs, and ivory combs. The compound boasted living quarters, a barn, storage rooms, and trade rooms. However, competing posts along the river forced Vasquez and Sublette to sell out in 1841, and the fort was abandoned a year later.

Over time, the adobe structure fell into ruin. By the 1930s, when the fort was largely reconstructed as a Works Progress Administration project, only small portions of the original walls remained. Excavations in the 1960s uncovered artifacts and additional information about the size and plan of the early trading post. The reconstruction was completed at this time.

Exhibits now re-create the fur-trading era and display Native American and other artifacts, as well as relay information about mountain and plains life during the first half of the nineteenth century. The reconstructed fort also has a museum store and a visitor information center that was built in 1964 and contains additional displays on the fur-trading period.

The fort was owned by Weld County until 1958, when it was deeded to the Colorado Historical Society.

Fort Vasquez Museum, 13412 U.S. Hwy. 85, Platteville, CO 80651. Phone: 970/785-2832. E-mail: susan@webaccess.net. Hours: Memorial Day–Labor Day, 9:30–4:30 Mon.–Sat., 1–4:30 Sun.; remainder of year, 9:30–4:30 Wed.–Sat., 1–4:30 Sun. Admission: free.

PONCHA SPRINGS

Historic hotel

JACKSON HOTEL

The Jackson Hotel in Poncha Springs has operated continuously as a hotel or bed-and-breakfast since 1878. In 1996, new owners purchased the building and began a three-year restoration that resulted in a western-style restaurant and hotel.

The hotel, which has 10 guest rooms, was once a stage stop between Aspen and New Mexico. Located five miles west of Salida, it is the oldest business in Chaffee County.

Native Americans were the first to inhabit what is now Poncha Springs, taking advantage of the healing properties of its warm waters. In the late nineteenth century, the town became a supply center for mining camps in the area, but fire destroyed most of the community in 1882. Poncha Springs later became a railroad junction and a miners' resort and health center.

Jackson Hotel, 6340 U.S. Hwy. 285, Poncha Springs, CO 81242. Phone: 719/ 539-4861. Fax: 719/539-2245. Hours: open 24 hours. Rates: vary with room and season.

PUEBLO

History museum

EL PUEBLO MUSEUM

A full-sized reproduction of the 1842 fur-trading post from which the city of Pueblo derives its name is part of the El Pueblo Museum, operated by the Colorado Historical Society.

The fort, consisting of an adobe quadrangle topped by two round bastions, was a crossroads for the Ute, Cheyenne, Arapaho, and Kiowa

Indians as well as mountain men, trappers, traders, and even Spanish soldiers.

Though trade with the Indians usually was friendly, an attack by a Ute band in 1854, and continued unrest along the Arkansas River, caused the fort to be abandoned the following year. Before disintegrating, the structure sheltered wandering travelers.

Although the fort's precise measurements were not preserved, the reproduction is based on surviving descriptions from books, letters, and diaries.

The El Pueblo Museum also includes exhibits on Native American, Mexican, and pioneer life, the trapping-and-trade era, ranching and agriculture, and industrial development by nineteenth-century immigrants on the Colorado frontier.

El Pueblo Museum, 324 W. 1st St., Pueblo, CO 81003. Phone and fax: 719/583-0453. Hours: 10–4:30 Mon.–Sat., 12–3 Sun.; closed New Year's Day and Christmas. Admission: adults, $2.50; seniors, $2; children 6–16, $2; children under 6, free.

History museum

PUEBLO COUNTY HISTORICAL SOCIETY MUSEUM

The history of the Pueblo area is told through collections and exhibits at the Pueblo County Historical Society Museum. The facility is located on the lower level of a historic former hotel now converted to public housing.

The 3,500-square-foot museum, which opened in 1986, features four exhibit rooms and the Edward H. Broadhead Library. Among the collections and exhibits are locally made saddles and related western objects; railroad furniture and artifacts; local baseball memorabilia; historical materials and prints from prominent families; Native American artifacts; and other displays related to area history.

Pueblo County Historical Society Museum, 212 S. Grand Ave., Pueblo, CO 81003. Phone: 719/543-6772. Hours: 1–4 Tues.–Sun.; closed major holidays. Admission: free.

Aviation museum

FRED E. WEISBROD/B-24 INTERNATIONAL MUSEUM

Twenty-five military aircraft, including a rare B-29 Superfortress bomber, are featured at the Fred E. Weisbrod/B-24 International Museum at Pueblo's municipal airport.

The museum, named for its founder, opened in 1972. In 1980, the B-24 Liberator bomber museum became part of the facility. The museum is owned by the City of Pueblo and operated by volunteer members of the Pueblo Historical Aircraft Society, many of whom are B-24 veterans.

Nearly 20,000 four-engine Liberator bombers were built during World War II, and they were flown by every Allied air force in every theater of war. The site of Pueblo's airport was a major B-24 training base. Today, only 13 Liberator planes are left in the world. Unfortunately, the museum does not possess one of the highly prized aircraft, but it does have an extensive historical exhibit on the B-24 bomber's wartime role. It also features displays of military uniforms, medals, equipment, and photographs.

Fred E. Weisbrod/B-24 International Museum, 31001 Magnuson Ave., Pueblo, CO 81001. Phone: 719/948-9219. Hours: 10–4 Mon.–Fri., 10–2 Sat., 1–4 Sun.; closed major holidays. Admission: free.

Firefighting museum

HOSE CO. NO. 3—A FIRE MUSEUM

Historical artifacts and other materials pertaining to firefighting in Pueblo and Colorado are the main attraction at the Hose Co. No. 3—A Fire Museum, housed in an 1881 fire station in Pueblo.

The station relied on horse-drawn firefighting equipment until 1914, when fire engines were first acquired. Visitors can still see where hay was lifted to the loft as horse feed, where early firemen slept and ate their meals, and the brass pole the firemen slid down when the fire alarm sounded.

The museum's collections include a beautifully restored 1850 hand-drawn fire-hose cart, a 1917 American La France fire truck, and such other firefighting equipment as leather and metal helmets, brass fire nozzles, wooden ladders, silver-plated fire chief's bugles, foam-making equipment, leather water buckets, and rescue and first-aid materials.

The museum is operated by the Colorado Fire Buffs Historical Society.

Hose Co. No. 3—A Fire Museum, 116 Broadway, Pueblo, CO 81004. Phone: 719/544-4548. Hours: by appointment. Admission: donation requested.

Mental health museum/historic building

COLORADO MENTAL HEALTH INSTITUTE AT PUEBLO MUSEUM

The history of the Colorado State Hospital (now the Colorado Mental Health Institute at Pueblo) from its inception in 1879 to the present is traced in the Colorado Mental Health Institute at Pueblo Museum.

The 4,600-square-foot facility, which opened in 1986, is housed in the former superintendent's residence on the institute's south campus. The Mediterranean-style house was built in 1883 and remodeled in the 1930s.

Most of the artifacts and exhibits are located in the former bedrooms; the basement contains the archives. The remainder of the house is used by hospital staff for meetings and other events.

Among the objects on display are early restraint devices for combative patients, a 6-foot-long electric wall clock from the early 1920s, and scrapbooks and personal memorabilia of the former superintendent, Dr. Zimmerman, and his family. The museum also features an exhibit on the hospital's dairy farm.

On the grounds is a former garage now filled with larger artifacts, mostly medical equipment too large for, or not ready for display in, the museum building; a 1934 playhouse with items donated by Dr. Frank Zimmerman's daughters; and a large courtyard with a rock and flower garden.

Colorado Mental Health Institute at Pueblo Museum, 13th and Francisco Sts., Pueblo, CO. (Postal address: 1600 W. 24th St., Pueblo, CO 81003.) Phone: 719/ 546-4168. Fax: 719/546-4484. Hours: by appointment. Admission: free.

Zoological park

PUEBLO ZOO

More than 300 animals are on display at the Pueblo Zoo, located on 25 acres in City Park. Owned by the city and operated by the Pueblo Zoological Society, the zoo was founded in 1903. It includes a historic district built in the 1930s and listed on the National Register of Historic Places.

Visitor favorites include Serengeti Safari's African lions; the Ecocenter rain forest, with its underwater view of penguins; and Johnson Station's kangaroos and emus.

A number of new attractions were introduced in 1998, including Asian Adventure, with black-crested macaques, Malayan sun bears, and a range of endangered Asian animals; a new panda exhibit; and a renovated display on maned wolves, featuring foxlike animals from the South American pampas.

Nearly $1.5 million has been spent on improvements and capital construction at the zoo since 1991, revitalizing its educational and recreational offerings. A $6.5-million renovation program is underway to update and improve the Animal House, Monkey Island and Mountain, Tropical Bird House, and bear pits. A natural history museum also is planned.

Pueblo Zoo, Pueblo City Park, 3455 Nuckolls Ave., Pueblo, CO 81005. Phone: 719/561-1452. Fax: 719/561-8686. Website: www.ruralnet.net/pueblo/zoo/. Hours: Memorial Day–Labor Day, 10–5 daily (10–8 on Fri.); remainder of the year, 9–4 daily; closed New Year's Day, Thanksgiving, and Christmas. Admission: adults, $4; children 13–18, $2; children 3–12, $1; children under 3, free.

Arts center and children's museum

SANGRE DE CRISTO ARTS AND CONFERENCE CENTER AND BUELL CHILDREN'S MUSEUM

The Sangre de Cristo Arts and Conference Center in Pueblo seeks to integrate arts into everyone's life by presenting exhibitions, programs, and services that educate, challenge, and meet the needs of the people of Pueblo and southern Colorado.

The 65,000-square-foot complex, opened in 1972, is owned and maintained by Pueblo County, which leases operation of the facilities to a nonprofit organization. It serves nearly 200,000 visitors annually.

The arts center has four galleries, one of which is home to the historically significant Francis King Collection of Western Art. The other three galleries present changing special exhibitions. The center also houses an interactive children's museum, as well as artist-in-residence studios in ceramics, photography, woodworking, and painting; classrooms and other instructional facilities for extensive arts education programs; two dance school studios and two resident dance companies; a 500-seat theater; a 7,000-square-foot conference center; and a patio/amphitheater for outdoor events.

The arts center currently occupies two buildings, but a third is being constructed for the children's museum, which is being expanded from 1,500 square feet to 12,000 square feet and renamed the Buell Children's Museum in recognition of a $1 million challenge grant from the Temple Hoyne Buell Foundation.

Sangre de Cristo Arts and Conference Center and Buell Children's Museum, 210 N. Santa Fe Ave., Pueblo, CO 81003. Phone: 719/543-0130. Fax: 719/543-0134. E-mail: artctr@ris.net. Website: www.chieftain.com/artscenter. Hours: 9–5 daily (galleries, 11–4); closed national holidays. Admission to arts center and galleries: free.

Art gallery

PUEBLO ART GUILD GALLERY

The Pueblo Art Guild was founded in 1959 and opened its gallery in 1963 to encourage and develop public appreciation of the arts and to provide exhibit space for amateur and professional artists.

Exhibitions by area artists are presented in the 2,400-square-foot gallery, and in the Sagebrush Gallery, which is used for shows and guild activities.

Special exhibitions are held throughout the year and include the Student Art Show, Spring Art Show, Rose Garden Show, Photography Show, Southwest Show, and Watercolor Show. The guild also offers monthly programming, including workshops, classes, and demonstrations of various media techniques.

Pueblo Art Guild Gallery, 1500 N. Santa Fe Ave., Pueblo, CO 81003. Phone: 719/543-2455. Gallery hours: 1–5 Tues.–Thurs. and Sat.–Sun.; closed major holidays. Admission: free.

Art gallery

FINE ART GALLERY AT THE UNIVERSITY OF SOUTHERN COLORADO

Exhibitions reflecting major cultural influences on the area are featured at the Fine Art Gallery at the University of Southern Colorado in Pueblo.

Approximately 10 shows—generally highlighting the work of Hispanic artists—are presented annually in the 2,200-square-foot gallery, which opened in 1970. Typically, half of the exhibitions are major shows by regional, national, and international artists; others include student, senior, and auction exhibitions.

Fine Art Gallery, University of Southern Colorado, Capps Capozzolo Center for Creative and Performing Arts, 2200 Bonforte Blvd., Pueblo, CO 81001. Phone: 719/549-2817. Fax: 719/549-2120. Hours: 10–5 Mon.–Fri. when classes are in session; closed most of summer and on major holidays. Admission: free.

Historic house museum

ROSEMOUNT MUSEUM

The splendor of the Victorian era is on display at the Rosemount Museum, a palatial 37-room mansion built in Pueblo in 1893 by John A. Thatcher, a successful merchant and banker. Thatcher named the house for his wife's favorite flower.

The 24,000-square-foot Richardsonian Romanesque mansion is constructed of pink rhyolite, contains most of its original furnishings and decorative arts, has an adjacent 6,000-square-foot carriage house whose lower level is now a cafe, and is surrounded by beautiful grounds.

The historic house still retains the original wall treatments; 10 fireplaces with marble, silver-plate, tile, and wood accents; Tiffany light fixtures of gold plate, brass, and silver; hand-decorated ceilings; an oak dining room table that seats 36; and elegant carved and inlaid furniture.

The mansion's third floor features another attraction—the artifacts and memorabilia collected by Andrew McClelland, Pueblo businessman and philanthropist, on a worldwide tour of 67 countries in 1904. The collection consists of urns, statues, pottery, paintings, an Egyptian mummy, and other materials.

The museum, opened in 1968, offers tours of the Victorian house.

Rosemount Museum, 419 W. 14th St., P.O. Box 5259, Pueblo, CO 81003. Phone: 719/545-5290. Fax: 719/545-5291. E-mail: Rosemnt@usa.net. Website: www.rosemount.org. Hours: June–Aug., 10–3:30 Tues.–Sat., 2–3:30 Sun.; remainder of the year, 1–3:30 Tues.–Sat., 2–3:30 Sun.; closed January and major holidays. Admission: adults, $5; seniors, $4; children 6–12, $2; children under 6, free; groups, $.50 discount per person.

Nature Center

GREENWAY AND NATURE CENTER OF PUEBLO

Max Watts Interpretive Center
Raptor Center of Pueblo

Educational, recreational, and conservation programs relating primarily to the environment and to natural and cultural history are offered at the 100-acre Greenway and Nature Center of Pueblo, located in beautiful Rock Canyon along the banks of the Arkansas River one mile west of Pueblo.

Opened in 1980 and managed by the University of Southern Colorado, the facility consists of the Max Watts Interpretive Center, the Raptor Center of Pueblo, a nature-center gift shop, and a restaurant. In addition, there are fishing and picnic areas, a playground, volleyball and horseshoe courts, xeriscape gardens, and more than 21 miles of walking, hiking, rollerblading, and biking trails (bicycle rentals are available).

The Max Watts Interpretive Center, attached to the nature center office/gift shop, is a new 1,200-square-foot multipurpose area with interactive exhibits, program/meeting spaces, and gift shop. The exhibits focus mainly on water, conservation, and the Arkansas River.

The Raptor Center provides care for injured birds of prey and emphasizes the importance of raptors and other wildlife through exhibits and programs. More than 130 wounded eagles, hawks, owls, and falcons are treated annually. At any given time, visitors can view one or more of these convalescent birds.

The nature center also offers nature trips, workshops, and talks; summer eco-camps for children; and environmental education programs on such topics as river life, birds of prey, and geology.

The Greenway Nature Center is one of the most popular facilities in the area, serving nearly 350,000 people annually.

Greenway and Nature Center of Pueblo, 5200 Nature Center Rd., Pueblo, CO 81003. Phone: 719/549-2414. Fax: 719/549-2547. Hours: grounds open from dawn until 10 P.M. daily; nature center, 9–5 Tues.–Sun.; center closed New Year's Day, Thanksgiving, and Christmas. Admission: free.

Historic district

UNION AVENUE HISTORIC DISTRICT

Pueblo's Union Avenue Historic District is a complex of turn-of-the-twentieth-century buildings that constituted the principal business district in south Pueblo from the 1890s to the 1930s. It is now a fashionable commercial area.

The historic district, listed on the National Register of Historic Places in 1982, is bounded roughly by Grand and Victoria avenues and Main and B streets.

Among the historic buildings are the 1881 Western National Bank Building and Old Dry Goods Building, 1883 Fresno Building and Holden Block, 1887 Graham-Westcott Building, 1889 Union Depot and Orman/Crook Building, 1891 McLaughlin Building and Anthony Building, 1893 Union Hall Complex, 1894 Turf Exchange, 1896 Tivoli Building and Center Building, 1904 Star Journal Building, 1910 Vail Hotel Building, 1917 City Hall, and 1919 Memorial Hall. The El Pueblo Museum (see separate listing), located next to old Fort Pueblo, is not far from the historic district.

Pueblo, on the banks of the Arkansas River, has been a historical crossroads from its earliest days. It was used as a camp by the Ute Indians even before Juan de Ulibarri, a Spaniard from Santa Fe, made the first recorded visit to the area in 1706.

It also is where Lieutenant Zebulon Pike built a log outpost during his 1806 exploration of the Arkansas River; where Major Stephen Long passed through during his 1820 expedition; and where Fort Pueblo was established as a trading post in 1842.

In the late 1850s, gold prospectors flocked to the Pueblo area. They were followed by the Denver & Rio Grande Railroad in 1872. The Colorado Coal & Iron Company (later the Colorado Fuel & Iron Company) opened its first blast furnace in 1881, and other companies built smelters in 1882 and 1888.

At the turn of the twentieth century, CF&I was the largest employer in Pueblo—a position it held until the 1980s, when an economic downturn caused it to cut back its steel production and work force. Since then, Pueblo has worked successfully to diversify and attract cleaner light industry.

Union Avenue Historic District. Contact: Historic Pueblo Business Center Assn., P.O. Box 5102, Pueblo, CO 81002. Phone: 719/543-5804. Fax: 719/542-5843.

RANGELY

History museum/park

RANGELY OUTDOOR MUSEUM

The Rangely Outdoor Museum, formerly the Rangely Museum, now occupies a five-acre site on the east side of town. The 1995 move permitted acquisition of a number of historic structures, including a 1940s oil-field camp house, a former oil company recreation hall, a 1931 schoolhouse, a turn-of-the-twentieth-century log cabin used as a school in the nearby mountains, and a 1920s homestead ranch house whose barn and other auxiliary structures will soon be added to the complex.

The museum's collections and displays cover three periods—the Native American and prehistoric natural history period (fossils, pictographs, tools, and other such materials), pioneer and early ranching period (barbed wire, harnesses, clothing, and household items), and energy-development period (oil-field structures, equipment, and related objects).

Rangely Outdoor Museum, 132 Main St., P.O. Box 131, Rangely, CO 81648. Phone: 970/675-2612. Hours: June–Aug., 10–4 daily; Apr.–May and Sept.– Oct., 10–4 Fri.–Sun.; closed remainder of the year. Admission: free.

RED MOUNTAIN

Historic ghost town

RED MOUNTAIN GHOST TOWN

Two early mining communities about 13 miles south of Ouray went by the name of Red Mountain—Red Mountain City and Red Mountain Town.

Red Mountain City was the largest mining camp in the Red Mountain Pass area in the 1880s, but its prosperity was short-lived. After just a few years, the miners moved over the pass to Red Mountain Town on the Silverton side. Most of Red Mountain City's surviving buildings were destroyed in a 1939 forest fire; only a few mining structures remained.

By the 1890s, Red Mountain Town was one of Colorado's most prosperous mining communities, with nearly 100 businesses and a population of approximately 10,000. Its production figures and the quality of its ores rivaled those of Leadville.

Rich ore was found in the area in the late 1870s, but the rush did not begin until the early 1880s. The National Belle Mine was followed by the Congress, Summit, Enterprise, and Yankee Girl. The latter was the most productive, operating on 12 levels and employing some 2,000 miners.

It has been estimated that $30 million in gold, silver, lead, zinc, and copper was taken from the Red Mountain and nearby Guston mines. In later years, extraction was made easier by the Treasury Tunnel, which drained water from mines as far away as Telluride. Parts of the tunnel were in use until recently.

Development of Red Mountain Town was hindered by fires, heavy winter snows and snowslides, and transportation problems. Otto Mears solved most of the transportation issues with his Million Dollar Highway and by completing a rail line from Silverton to Red Mountain Town by 1888.

Fires ravaged the community a number of times, the first in 1892. The town was rebuilt, but part of it burned to the ground several years later. A 1937 fire wiped out much of what remained, leaving only a few buildings and cabins, some of which still exist.

Red Mountain Ghost Town, 13 miles south of Ouray. Contact: Ouray Historical Society, 420 6th Ave., P.O. Box 151, Ouray, CO 81427. Phone: 970/325-4576.

REDSTONE

History museum

REDSTONE MUSEUM

A turn-of-the-twentieth-century log cabin that once served as the lamphouse for John Cleveland Osgood's coal mines is the home of the Redstone Museum. The structure, which now stands in a park along Redstone's historic main street, was relocated from Osgood's nearby model mining village.

The museum, opened in 1980, displays a collection of historical memorabilia, period costumes, mining artifacts, and historic photographs from the turn of the twentieth century to the 1950s.

Redstone Museum, Redstone Blvd., P.O. Box 425, Redstone, CO 81623. Phone: 970/963-9185. Hours: June–Sept., 10–5 daily; remainder of the year by appointment. Admission: free.

Historic building/hotel

REDSTONE INN

The Redstone Inn is an elegant hotel and restaurant located in a building originally erected by John Cleveland Osgood as a community hall and rooming house for bachelor coal miners in 1902.

The structure, which is listed on the National Register of Historic Places, was part of Osgood's model mining community, developed in hopes of avoiding labor problems. Osgood, the founder and president of Colorado Fuel & Iron Company, also established Redstone and started the company's coal mines and coke ovens in the Crystal River Valley.

The Tudor-style inn with the four-faced clock tower (a replica from a Dutch inn in Rotterdam) opened in the early 1980s and now has 35 rooms, a restaurant, bar, health spa, heated pool, and tennis courts.

Redstone Inn, 82 Redstone Blvd., Redstone, CO 81623. Phone and fax: 970/963-2526. Hours: open 24 hours. Rates: vary with room and season.

Historic building/bed-and-breakfast

REDSTONE CASTLE

Redstone Castle, formerly Cleveholm Manor, is a massive 24,000-square-foot structure built near Redstone in 1898–1902 by John Cleveland Osgood, founder of Colorado Fuel & Iron Company in Pueblo. The 42-room Victorian manor house has been operated as a bed-and-breakfast but its future is now clouded.

Osgood entertained such titans of the day as John D. Rockefeller, J. P. Morgan, Jay Gould, Theodore Roosevelt, and King Leopold of Belgium at the estate. The old mansion still boasts its solid mahogany woodwork, gold-leaf ceilings, silk brocade upholstery, red velvet walls, Tiffany chandeliers, marble and mahogany fireplaces, and Persian rugs.

In an attempt to avoid the labor problems afflicting other coal towns, Osgood tried to create a model coal-mining community in Redstone, one of 28 coal towns in the CF&I empire at the turn of the twentieth century. Attractive small houses were built for miners with families, and an upscale rooming house with a community hall was provided for single men. The latter is now the Redstone Inn, a distinctive Tudor-style hotel and restaurant (see previous listing). The miners, however, resented many of Osgood's rules and their loss of independence. Osgood later lost control of CF&I and the company's operations in Redstone.

Redstone Castle, listed on the National Register of Historic Places, opened as a bed-and-breakfast in 1986. In 1999, the castle was sold to a group of Denver and Dallas investors who planned to transform it into a hotel, conference center, and spa, but then put it up for sale.

Redstone Castle, 58 Redstone Blvd., Redstone, CO 81623. Phone: 970/963-3463. Fax: 970/704-1834. Hours: currently closed.

Historic districts

REDSTONE HISTORIC DISTRICT AND REDSTONE COKE OVEN HISTORIC DISTRICT

Redstone, located 12 miles up the Crystal River from Carbondale, has two historic districts, both of which sprang up during the coal-mining and -processing boom at the turn of the twentieth century.

The town of Redstone was founded by John Cleveland Osgood, president of Colorado Fuel & Iron Company. Osgood purchased coal claims and mined in the area, built coke ovens, and developed a model coal-mining village.

Redstone Historic District runs along the town's main street and the Crystal River from Hawk Creek to 226 Redstone Boulevard. This district consists mainly of refurbished miners' homes now used as summer retreats, and a number of art galleries and antiques shops along Redstone Boulevard. At the south end of town is the Redstone Inn, a hotel and restaurant built by Osgood in 1902 as a community hall and boardinghouse for single coal miners (see separate listing).

The Redstone Coke Oven Historic District marks the site of the coke ovens used to process coal in the area. The ovens, built in 1899, represent a type of industrial structure no longer in use and rapidly disappearing from the American West.

Redstone Historic District and Redstone Coke Oven Historic District. Contact: Redstone Historical Society, Redstone Blvd., P.O. Box 425, Redstone CO 81623. Phone: 979/963-9185.

RIFLE

History museum

RIFLE CREEK MUSEUM

Approximately 30 themed exhibits are presented at the Rifle Creek Museum, located in Rifle's former city hall. The 8,500-square-foot museum opened in 1967 and focuses on area history.

Exhibits, grouped by room, include an early general store, schoolroom, doctor's office, and dentist's office. One room contains Native American artifacts. Guided tours are offered.

Rifle Creek Museum, 337 East Ave., Rifle, CO 81650. Phone: 970/625-4862. Hours: May–Oct., 10–4 Mon.–Fri.; other times by appointment. Admission: adults, $2; seniors, $1.50; children 5–16, $1; children under 5, free.

ROCKY FORD

History museum

ROCKY FORD HISTORICAL MUSEUM

The Rocky Ford Historical Museum, located in the 1909 former Carnegie Public Library, focuses primarily on the history and archaeology of the Rocky Ford area.

The museum, which opened in 1941 and relocated to the old library building in 1976, contains exhibits and collections of artifacts, documents, and other materials from 1878 to the present. Topics include the Arkansas Valley Fair and Watermelon Day, the sugar and honey industries, everyday life of Rocky Ford residents, and the geology, anthropology, archaeology, and ethnology of the area.

Rocky Ford Historical Museum, 1005 Sycamore St., P.O. Box 835, Rocky Ford, CO 81067. Phone: 719/254-6737. Hours: mid-May through mid-Sept., 10–4 Tues.–Sat.; remainder of year by appointment. Admission: free.

ROMLEY

Historic ghost town

ROMLEY GHOST TOWN

Romley was one of three mining towns (the others being Hancock and St. Elmo) made prosperous by the Mary Murphy Mine, located 23 miles southwest of Buena Vista.

Romley was a shipping point for the silver-rich Mary Murphy Mine, named for a Denver nurse who treated one of the prospectors who discovered the mine.

The Mary Murphy, a mile from Romley, was established in the mid-1870s. Development of the mine—and Romley—was stimulated by the arrival of the Denver, South Park & Pacific Railroad and construction in 1883 of a 5,000-foot tramway that brought the ore down to the railroad.

The mine was sold to an English company after the turn of the twentieth century. Production peaked before World War I, though the mine operated intermittently until World War II. With the mine's closure, Romley's population rapidly declined, and the town was soon abandoned. However, a number of cabins and ruins of the schoolhouse still remain.

Romley Ghost Town, 23 miles southwest of Buena Vista. Contact: Greater Buena Vista Area Chamber of Commerce Visitors Center, 343 S. U.S. Hwy. 24, Buena Vista, CO 81214. Phone and fax: 719/395-6612.

RUSSELL GULCH

Historic ghost town

RUSSELL GULCH GHOST TOWN

Russell Gulch, located three miles southwest of Central City, is named for William Green Russell, who panned gold at the confluence of the South Platte River and Cherry Creek, then rushed to the mountains in 1859 when he heard of John Gregory's gold discoveries in Mountain City.

Russell and others began mining on a hillside several miles above the Gregory diggings. The new camp became known as Russell Gulch. By 1860, the mining community had a school and a church. Its population quickly peaked at 2,500 before the mines played out. Some mining continued into the twentieth century, but Russell Gulch became better known as a haunt of bootleggers, who produced and stored moonshine in deserted mine shafts during Prohibition.

A number of the early structures still stand, but the town's old school, church, and hotel are rapidly disintegrating.

Russell Gulch Ghost Town, 3 miles southwest of Central City. Contact: Gilpin County Chamber of Commerce, P.O. Box 488, Central City, CO 80427. Phone and fax: 303/582-5077.

SAGUACHE

History museum

SAGUACHE COUNTY MUSEUM

The Saguache County Museum occupies the old town jail and schoolhouse—a National Historic Site—along U.S. Highway 285 in Saguache. Established in 1959, the museum contains an assortment of historical materials, including an exceptional collection of arrowheads, and an Alferd E. Packer display in the jail cell where Packer was held briefly after his 1874 arrest for eating five of his companions during a winter trip through the nearby San Juan Mountains.

Packer escaped from the jail but later was captured, convicted, and sentenced to death. However, the verdict was declared unconstitutional on a technicality. Packer then was found guilty of manslaughter and sentenced to 45 years but was pardoned after serving only 5 years.

The museum also has 1920s and 1930s household materials and furnishings on display in the historic Hazard House near the main site.

Saguache County Museum, 405 8th St. (U.S. Hwy 285), P.O. Box 569, Saguache, CO 81149. Phone: 719/655-2557. Hours: Memorial Day–Labor Day, 10–5 daily; remainder of the year by appointment. Admission: adults, $2; children under 12, $.50.

ST. ELMO

Historic ghost town/historic district

ST. ELMO GHOST TOWN

St. Elmo, located 20 miles southwest of Buena Vista in Chaffee County, is one of Colorado's better-preserved ghost towns.

Originally called Forest City, St. Elmo began as a cluster of cabins in 1878. The town, incorporated in 1880, was the site of the productive Mary Murphy Mine and served as a supply, rail, and entertainment center for the mining area. During the boom years of the 1880s and 1890s, St. Elmo's population reached 3,000.

Much of the town—a National Historic District—is still intact despite an 1890 fire and includes the school, general store, post office, and various other false-fronted businesses and houses. St. Elmo also has acquired a few summer and year-round residents who have restored some of the old structures.

St. Elmo Ghost Town, 20 miles southwest of Buena Vista on County Rd. 162. Contact: Greater Buena Vista Area Chamber of Commerce Visitors Center, 343 S. U.S. Hwy. 24, Buena Vista, CO 81214. Phone and fax: 719/395-6612.

STS. JOHN

Historic ghost town

STS. JOHN GHOST TOWN

It was in Sts. John, one mile southwest of Montezuma in Summit County, that John Coley discovered silver in 1863. The town originally was known as Coleyville, but its name was changed to Sts. John by the Freemasons in 1867 in honor of their patron saints, John the Baptist and John the Evangelist.

The mining camp became a company town in 1872 when the Boston Silver Mining Association took over and built a comprehensive milling and smelting works. In succeeding years, it developed into one of the most completely company-owned towns in Colorado under the Boston Silver Company (later the Boston Mining Company). However, the town failed following the 1893 silver crash (although some intermittent mining was carried on in the area for years).

Sts. John was an unusual mining town in that it had a 350-volume library, no saloons, and an elegant mine superintendent's house with English furniture. The house still stands—without the furniture—but several boardinghouses and other structures are falling or in ruins, and the mill stack recently collapsed.

Sts. John Ghost Town, 1 mile southwest of Montezuma. Contact: Summit Historical Society, 309 N. Main St., P.O. Box 745, Breckenridge, CO 80424-0745. Phone: 970/453-9022. Fax: 970/453-8135.

SALIDA

History museum

SALIDA MUSEUM

The Salida Museum is a local history museum featuring artifacts and exhibits from the pioneer and mining days through the post–World War II era.

Founded in 1954, the 6,050-square-foot museum contains a wide variety of pioneer, mining, farming, ranching, and other implements; Native American artifacts; medical, dental, undertaking, industrial, and general-store equipment; and historical photographs.

The museum also owns a 365-foot-high smelter smokestack in Salida and a schoolhouse with original furnishings in Maysville.

Salida Museum, 406½ W. Rainbow Blvd., Salida, CO 81201. Phone: 719/539-4602. Hours: mid-May through mid-Sept., varies (call ahead); closed remainder of the year. Admission: adults, $1; children 6–12, $.50; children under 6, free.

Historic district

SALIDA DOWNTOWN HISTORIC DISTRICT

The Salida Downtown Historic District features a cluster of late-nineteenth-century buildings from its early mining and railroad days.

The historic district, one of the nation's largest, was listed on the National Register of Historic Places in 1984 and is bounded by the Arkansas River, the former narrow-gauge-railroad right-of-way, and Third and D streets.

Some of the district's historic buildings stand today because city officials and merchants required all downtown buildings to be constructed of brick after a disastrous fire in 1888. A few predate the fire.

Included among the historic brick structures are six colorful buildings on the south side of East First Street's 100 block—the 1886 Waggener Building, 1887 International Order of Odd Fellows Building, 1887 Bowne Block Building, late 1880s First Street Studio Building, 1890 First Street Cafe Building, and 1893 Salida Mail Building.

Salida Downtown Historic District. Contact: Heart of the Rockies Chamber of Commerce, 406 W. Rainbow Blvd., Salida, CO 81201. Phone: 719/539-2068. Fax: 719/539-7844.

SANFORD

Historic fort

PIKE'S STOCKADE

Pike's Stockade along the Conejos River near Sanford is a replica of the makeshift fort where Lieutenant Zebulon M. Pike and his men wintered during their ill-fated exploration of the San Luis Valley in 1806–1807.

It was here that Pike's party was arrested by Spanish soldiers for trespassing on Spanish-controlled lands. They were marched to, and imprisoned in, Santa Fe and Chihuahua, Mexico, before being released.

Pike's tales of the two cities and their need for all kinds of manufactured articles—which could be exchanged for furs and precious metals—fueled interest in what became the Santa Fe trade.

The stockade was reconstructed by the Colorado Historical Society from Pike's journal notes.

Pike's Stockade, Colo. Rte. Y, Sanford, CO 81151. (Contact: Fort Garland Museum, Hwys. 160 and 159, P.O. Box 368, Fort Garland, CO 81133.) Phone: 719/379-3512. Hours: Memorial Day–Labor Day, 10–5 daily; closed remainder of the year. Admission: free.

SAN LUIS

History/art museum

SAN LUIS MUSEUM AND CULTURAL CENTER

The San Luis Museum and Cultural Center in Colorado's oldest town houses Spanish colonial and post-colonial artifacts and Hispanic art. It also features indoor and outdoor theaters used for films, plays, pageants, festivals, and other special events.

Opened in 1980 by the town, the museum takes visitors through various historical eras in San Luis and adjacent Hispanic communities. On display are *santos*, wooden carvings of saints; *retablos*, religious paintings on wood; *bultos*, carved religious figures; and a replica of a chapel used by the Penitentes of the Hermandad, a Hispanic fraternal-religious brotherhood.

San Luis Museum and Cultural Center, 401 Church Place, P.O. Box 657, San Luis, CO 81152. Phone: 719/672-3611. Hours: Memorial Day–Sept., 10–4 daily; remainder of the year, 10–4 Mon.–Fri. Admission: adults, $1; children 5–12, $.50; children under 5, free.

Historic district

PLAZA DE SAN LUIS DE LA RIO CULEBRA HISTORIC DISTRICT

The Plaza de San Luis de la Rio Culebra Historic District includes the town and adjacent communal land of San Luis, a predominately Hispanic adobe community founded in 1851. It is the oldest town in Colorado.

The domed Capilla de Todos los Santos (Chapel of All Saints) on La Mesa de la Piedad y de la Misericordia (the Hill of Piety and Mercy) dominates the town. The Grotto of Our Lady of Guadalupe and the Spiritual Labyrinth of Prayer are also located on the mesa.

Leading up the steep incline are the Stations of the Cross Shrine, a series of bronze representations of the last hours of Christ's life, created by local sculptor Huberto Maestas. Fourteen stations are traditionally included; this series contains a fifteenth, representing the Resurrection.

Among the other sights in San Luis are the San Luis Museum and Cultural Center (see previous listing); the 1886 Sangre de Cristo Parish Church building, now a bed-and-breakfast; and the Knights of Columbus Education Building, which features exhibits on flora and fauna, ecology of the region, and Hispanic religious and cultural traditions of the area.

The historic district, established in 1978 and recently expanded, also includes La Vega, a 600-acre tract of land that is the only such remaining communal land in the nation.

Plaza de San Luis de la Rio Culebra Historic District. Contact: Town of San Luis, 408 Main St., P.O. Box 659, San Luis, CO 81152. Phone: 719/672-3321. Fax: 719/672-3553.

SILT

Historic park/living-history museum

SILT HISTORICAL PARK

The Silt Historical Park in Silt comprises a group of historic structures revealing how local people lived in the early twentieth century.

The park, developed and opened by the Silt Historical Society in 1983, includes a 1914 schoolhouse (moved from the Rifle Gap Dam area), a country store (reconstructed from a 1900 cabin), a blacksmith's shop (reconstructed from a 1932 cabin), a 1917 cow camp cabin (recycled from a honey extracting house), the 1914 Sallee family two-story hand-hewn log house, a two-room cabin containing a saloon and an office, and a building housing special exhibitions, a gift shop, and society offices. All have furnishings and artifacts.

The park also features several railroad cars (during Silt's early days cattle, sugar beets, and potatoes were shipped by rail from the area); horse-drawn farming, logging, and mining equipment; the Cactus Valley Ditch, a functioning irrigation ditch similar to those built by early settlers; and a collection of approximately 1,600 Native American artifacts found in the area.

Silt Historical Park, 707 Orchard St., P.O. Box 401, Silt, CO 81652, Phone: 970/ 876-5801. Hours: May–Oct., 10–3 Tues.–Sat.; closed remainder of the year. Admission: donation requested.

SILVER CLIFF

History museum

SILVER CLIFF MUSEUM

Two firefighting hose carts and a hook-and-ladder cart from the nineteenth century are among the items on display at the Silver Cliff Museum, housed in Silver Cliff's 1879 former firehouse and town hall.

Other collections and displays in the 2,500-square-foot municipal museum, which opened in 1959, include early clothes, furniture, household items, paintings, and photographs from the area, which was once a mining center.

Silver Cliff Museum, 610 Main St., P.O. Box 154, Silver Cliff, CO 81252. Phone and fax: 719/783-2615. Hours: Memorial Day–Labor Day, 10–4 Thurs.–Mon.; closed remainder of the year. Admission: adults, $2; children 6–13, $1; children under 6, free.

Wildlife refuge

MISSION: WOLF

Mission: Wolf is a 73-acre wolf refuge operated by Kent Weber and Tracy Brooks near Silver Cliff. It is open to the public. Large enclosures on the forested land house approximately 50 pure- and crossbred wolves, most of which were raised elsewhere and turned over to the sanctuary.

The refuge program emphasizes education. Weber and Brooks often travel to give talks to school and community groups and others about the wolves, pointing out that they cannot be domesticated.

Mission: Wolf, P.O. Box 211, Silver Cliff, CO 81249. Phone: 719/746-2919. Hours: 9 A.M.–sunset daily by appointment. Admission: free.

SILVER PLUME

Schoolhouse museum

GEORGE ROWE MUSEUM

The George Rowe Museum occupies an 1894 schoolhouse used to educate the children of Silver Plume until 1959.

The museum, named for its benefactor, was founded in 1960 by the People for Silver Plume, a nonprofit historical preservation group in the old silver-mining community.

In addition to a restored schoolroom, the museum contains numerous historical photographs and artifacts, including a hand-pump fire wagon purchased by the town after a major fire in 1884.

George Rowe Museum, 95 Main St., Silver Plume, CO 80476. Phone: 303/569-2562. Hours: Memorial Day–Labor Day, 10–4 daily; rest of Sept., 10–4 Sat.–Sun.; closed remainder of the year. Admission: adults, $2.50; seniors, $1.50; children 6–12, $.50; children under 6, free.

Historic building

SILVER PLUME DEPOT

The original Silver Plume Depot, built for the Colorado Central Railroad in 1884, is still in use as the Silver Plume terminal and ticket office for the Georgetown Loop Railroad, which travels between the two early mining communities in summer. A number of early steam engines and cars are on view in the adjacent rail yards.

Silver Plume Depot, 10 Mountain St., Silver Plume, CO 80476. (Contact: Georgetown Loop Railroad, 1106 Rose St., P.O. Box 217, Georgetown, CO 80444.) Phones: 303/670-1686 and 800/691-4386. Fax: 303/569-2894. Hours: Memorial Day weekend through the first weekend in Oct., 8:15–5:30 daily; closed remainder of the year. Admission: free.

Historic mine

LEBANON MINE

Production at the Lebanon Mine in Silver Plume peaked during the silver-mining boom of the 1870s and 1880s. The mine is now a tour site, part of the Georgetown Loop Railroad summer program.

Passengers riding the train between Georgetown and Silver Plume can stop (there is an additional charge) for a guided tour of the old silver mine and its support facilities, which include the mine manager's office, change room, blacksmith's shop, and toolshed.

The only way to access the mine is by train. The walking tour is a quarter of a mile and takes 1 hour and 20 minutes. Reservations are recommended.

Lebanon Mine Tour. (Contact: Georgetown Loop Railroad, 1106 Rose St., P.O. Box 217, Georgetown, CO 80444.) Phones: 303/670-1686 and 800/ 691-4386. Fax: 303/569-2894. Hours: Memorial Day weekend–Labor Day, varies with train arrivals. Admission: adults, $5; children 3–15, $3; children under 3, free.

Historic district

GEORGETOWN–SILVER PLUME HISTORIC DISTRICT

See description under Georgetown.

SILVERTON

History museum

SAN JUAN COUNTY HISTORICAL SOCIETY MUSEUM

The San Juan County Historical Society Museum, housed in the 1902 county jail building in Silverton, has more than three floors of exhibits on area history. The society also offers summer tours of the 1929 Mayflower Gold Mill (see separate listing).

In addition to the intact jail cells, the 2,000-square-foot museum, which opened in 1965, presents mineral, mining, and railroad exhibits. On the grounds are the old "Casey Jones" railbus, large mining machinery, and a 1912 miner's shack.

San Juan County Historical Society Museum, 1553 Greene St., P.O. Box 154, Silverton, CO 81433. Phones: 970/387-5838 and 970/387-5488. Hours: Memorial Day through mid-Oct., 9–5 daily; closed remainder of the year. Admission: adults, $2.50; seniors, $2; children under 13, free.

Railroad museum

D&SNG SILVERTON FREIGHT YARD MUSEUM

The Durango & Silverton Narrow Gauge Railroad, which carries tourists to and from Durango and Silverton during the summer, opened a second museum in 1999—the D&SNG Silverton Freight Yard Museum—near the line's terminal in Silverton.

The museum is devoted to the history of freight hauling in the old mining area and features early freight cars and examples of representative freight carried by the railroad, once part of the Denver & Rio Grande.

The Durango & Silverton Narrow Gauge Railroad Museum opened in the roundhouse adjacent to the Durango depot in 1998 (see listing under Durango).

D&SNG Silverton Freight Yard Museum, Durango & Silverton Narrow Gauge Railroad, 10th and Animas Sts., Silverton, CO 81433. Phone: 970/387-5416. Fax: 970/387-5594. Hours: May–Oct., 7:30–4:30 daily; closed remainder of the year. Admission: adults, $5; children 5–11, $2.50; children under 5, free. Museum admission also included in price of train tickets. Summer round-trip ticket: adults, $53; children 5–11, $27. Winter round-trip ticket: adults, $41.55; children 5–11, $20.80.

Historic mine

OLD HUNDRED GOLD MINE

Underground tours, mining equipment demonstrations, and gold panning are offered at the Old Hundred Gold Mine, five miles east of Silverton.

The gold mine, which also produced silver, copper, and other base metals, opened in 1903 and closed in 1973. It was reopened for tours in 1992.

A mine train takes tourists 1,600 feet into the hillside for a walking inspection and equipment demonstration. The one-hour tour is followed by gold panning and a look at early mining equipment outside the mine. Also visible from the site is a historic 1904 boardinghouse built at an elevation of 12,000 feet.

Old Hundred Gold Mine, 721 County Rd. 4-A (off Colo. Hwy. 110), Silverton, CO 81433. Phones: 970/387-5444 and 800/872-3009. Fax: 970/240-8597. Hours: May–Oct., 10–4 daily; closed remainder of the year. Admission: adults, $11.95; children 5–12, $5.95; children under 5, free.

Historic mill

MAYFLOWER GOLD MILL

The San Juan County Historical Society in Silverton offers tours of the 1929 Mayflower Gold Mill, which processed gold, silver, lead, zinc, and copper from the nearby mountains. It remained in operation until 1994.

The large mill, listed on the National Register of Historic Places, is one of the best surviving examples of a precious-metals working mill in the state. It still retains much of its milling equipment—original and more recent—as well as its aerial tram house and a three-story office building.

Located off Colorado Highway 110 near Silverton, the mill was built by the Shenandoah-Dives Mining Company. It was donated to the San Juan County Historical Society in 1995 by the Sunnyside Gold Corporation, a subsidiary of Echo Bay Mines.

Mayflower Gold Mill, 2 miles north of Silverton on Colo. Hwy. 110. (Contact: San Juan County Historical Society, P.O. Box 154, Silverton, CO 81433.) Phones: 970/387-0294 and 970/387-5488. Hours: Memorial Day–Labor Day, 10:30–3 daily; closed remainder of the year. Admission: adults, $8.50; seniors, $7.50; children 11–16, $4.50; children under 11, free; groups, $6.50 per person.

Historic hotel

GRAND IMPERIAL HOTEL

The Grand Imperial Hotel in Silverton was built during the silver-mining boom in 1881 and retains much of its early Victorian character.

The impressive lobby has fine leather couches, a pressed-tin ceiling, and a portrait of Lillian Russell over the piano. Many of the 38 rooms and suites have floral wallpaper, antique reproductions, and gravity-flush toilets.

The Gold King Dining Room is adjacent to the lobby. The Hub Saloon features a historic backbar with heavy cherry wood columns, intricate carvings, and even a bullet hole.

Grand Imperial Hotel, 1219 Greene St., P.O. Box 57, Silverton, CO 81433. Phone and fax: 970/387-5527. Hours: open 24 hours. Rates: vary with room and season.

Historic district

SILVERTON HISTORIC DISTRICT

The Silverton Historic District includes the old mining town of Silverton and a number of nearby mining-related facilities. It became a National Historic Landmark in 1961 and was listed on the National Register of Historic Places in 1966.

Silverton was originally known as Baker City, named for Charles Baker. Baker and his companions began prospecting in the Silverton area, near the center of the San Juan Mining District, in the 1860s. However, it was not until 1871 that the first profitable silver vein was discovered in Arrastra Gulch.

The Silverton Historic District's many late-nineteenth- and early-twentieth-century buildings reflect the prosperity enjoyed in one of Colorado's richest mineral-producing regions. Notable structures include the 1881 Grand Imperial Hotel (see previous listing) and 1902 county jail (now the San Juan County Historical Society).

The boundaries of the historic district were extended in 1997 to include the Shenandoah-Dives Mining Company's Mayflower Mill complex, a selective flotation mill with an aerial tram (see separate listing); Crooke's Polar Star Mill office/assay building from early mining days; an Animas Power and Water Company facility that diverted electrical power to mining and milling operations in the area; and Hillside Cemetery, where many of the early miners were buried.

Silverton Historic District. Contact: San Juan County Historical Society, P.O. Box 154, Silverton, CO 81433. Phone: 970/387-5488.

SNOWMASS VILLAGE

Arts center

ANDERSON RANCH ARTS CENTER

The Anderson Ranch Arts Center, a year-round arts community for artists of all abilities in Snowmass Village, presents exhibitions by emerging and established artists, including faculty, center residents, and visiting artists.

The center's roots go back to an informal arts program held in the historic log barns and ranch house of the Anderson family's sheep ranch in Brush Creek Valley, approximately 10 miles west of Aspen. Beginning in 1973, the center matured into a nationally recognized visual arts center emphasizing both crafts and fine arts.

Its diversified year-round program now offers summer workshops in ceramics, painting, printmaking, drawing, sculpture, furniture design, photography, and woodworking; digital imaging and creative studies; children's classes; field expeditions; public tours; lectures; exhibitions; and programs for visiting artists, artists-in-residence, and summer assistants.

The arts center has a print collection comprising works produced at the ranch by such noted artists as Peter Voukos and William Wiley.

Anderson Ranch Arts Center, 5232 Owl Creek Rd., P.O. Box 5598, Snowmass Village, CO 81615. Phone: 970/923-3181. Fax: 970/923-3871. Hours: 9–5 daily. Admission: free.

SPAR CITY

Historic ghost town

SPAR CITY GHOST TOWN

Spar City, a ghost town located 14 miles south of Creede, has had two incarnations—first as a boom-and-bust mining town and then as a summer vacation/fishing camp.

The site originally was named Fisher City after John Fisher, who found a rich float of silver and lead nearby in 1892. But other prospectors who rushed to the mining camp later that year changed the name to Spar City because of the area's large quantities of feldspar.

Though the Emma Mine looked promising, none of the mines produced sufficient profitable ore, and all were hurt by the 1893 silver crash. By the turn of the twentieth century, Spar City was nearly deserted.

One of the prospectors, Charles Brandt, stayed on and filed a homestead claim for the entire town in 1899. He became its sole owner for a number of years. In 1908, he started the Bird Creek Mine with the backing of Charles King of Hutchinson, Kansas, but the venture did not pay off. In 1913, King and a number of Kansas friends took over the town site and its ponds as a private summer vacation and fishing club. It was a move that saved most of Spar City's buildings, including the jail, hotel, saloon, dance hall, parlor house, and various businesses and log cabins. These cabins have been repaired and converted to private use over the years.

Spar City Ghost Town, 14 miles south of Creede. Contact: Creede Historical Society, Main St., P.O. Box 608, Creede, CO 81130. Phone: 719/658-2303.

SPRINGFIELD

History museum

BACA COUNTY HISTORICAL MUSEUM

The Baca County Historical Museum, operated by the Baca County Historical Society, occupies the old sheriff's quarters in the county courthouse in Springfield. Opened in the 1950s, the museum moved into the courthouse in 1993 and is devoted to the history of the area. Displays include early quilts, clothing, household items, military uniforms, arrowheads, and mounted animals.

Baca County Historical Museum, Baca County Historical Society, 741 Main St., Springfield, CO 81073. Phone: 719/523-6565. Hours: 9–3 Wed.; closed major holidays. Admission: free.

STEAMBOAT SPRINGS

History museum

TREAD OF PIONEERS MUSEUM

The history of ranching, skiing, and early settlement in Steamboat Springs is highlighted at the Tread of Pioneers Museum in this Western Slope community.

The museum, which opened in 1959, occupies three historic buildings (erected in 1900, 1911, and the 1920s)—one offering exhibit galleries and a gift shop, another for collections storage, and a third (newly acquired) containing a community meeting room, research center, and offices.

Exhibits focus on historic photographs, ranching, ski equipment, guns, Ute Indians, and period costumes, furniture, and rooms. The museum also has a large collection of Native American artifacts and is recording more than 100 oral histories.

Tread of Pioneers Museum, 800 Oak St., P.O. Box 772372, Steamboat Springs, CO 80477. Phone: 970/879-2214. Fax: 970/879-6109. E-mail: sbsmarty@juno.com. Hours: July–Sept., 11–5 daily; Apr.–June and Oct.–Nov., 11–5 Tues.–Sat; Dec.–Mar., 11–5 Mon.–Sat.; closed New Year's Day, Thanksgiving, Christmas, and one week in spring for cleaning. Admission: adults, $3; seniors, $2; children 6–12, $1; children under 6, free; groups of 10 or more, $10.

Arts center

ELEANOR BLISS CENTER FOR THE ARTS AT THE DEPOT

The Eleanor Bliss Center for the Arts at the Depot, located in the 1903 former Denver & Rio Grande Western Railroad Station in Steamboat Springs, features visual and performing arts programs. Offerings focus on dance, music, literature, and the visual arts.

The center, operated by the Steamboat Springs Arts Council, is named for art patron Eleanor Bliss, who led the fight to "Save the Depot" and rehabilitate the historic building, which had been condemned by the city in 1980. The structure now is listed on the National Register of Historic Places.

Changing exhibitions are presented in the center's art gallery and in the depot's former baggage room, which also serves as an auditorium and performance/class/meeting space.

Eleanor Bliss Center for the Arts at the Depot, Steamboat Springs Arts Council, 1001 13th St., P.O. Box 774284, Steamboat Springs, CO 80477. Phone: 970/ 879-9008. Fax: 970/879-4434. Hours: 9–5 Mon.–Fri.; closed major holidays. Admission free.

STERLING

History museum

OVERLAND TRAIL MUSEUM

The history of the nation's greatest migration of people—from the East to the goldfields and other opportunities of the West—is traced at the Overland Trail Museum in Sterling. The museum is located near this historic trail, which runs along the South Platte River. The route was first used by Native Americans and later by fur traders and explorers.

The museum's original building, a small stone structure, was erected in 1936 as a Works Progress Administration project. It replicates early fur-trading forts on the plains and features a massive fireplace built from petrified wood found in the area. The museum has since been expanded to nearly 15,000 square feet, and outbuildings have been moved to the site.

Over the years, the museum has evolved into a historical village that includes a one-room schoolhouse, a country church, a general store, a blacksmith's shop, a barn, and a shed housing farm machinery.

The Overland Trail Museum in Sterling. Courtesy Overland Trail Museum.

The two additions to the original museum have provided indoor exhibit space for pioneer artifacts, early firearms, turn-of-the-twentieth-century clothing, branding irons, barbed wire, dolls, toys, quilts, tools, household furnishings, and Native American artifacts. On display outdoors are a Concord stage and early farm machinery, some of it dating back to the homesteading days.

Overland Trail Museum, 21053 County Rd. 26.5 (I-76 and U.S. Hwy. 6 East), P.O. Box 4000, Sterling, CO 80751. Phone: 970/522-3895. Fax: 970/521-0632. E-mail: hagemeie@sterlingcolo.com. Hours: Apr.–Oct., 9–5 Mon.–Sat., 10–5 Sun.; remainder of the year, 10–4 Tues.–Sat.; closed New Year's Day, Thanksgiving, and Christmas. Admission: free.

STRASBURG

History museum/park

COMANCHE CROSSING MUSEUM

The Comanche Crossing Museum has seven buildings on 2.5 acres in Strasburg, where the Kansas Pacific Railroad laid the final tracks for the first continuous chain of railroad from the Atlantic to the Pacific in 1870. It was then possible to board a train in New York and travel all the way to San Francisco (the tracks joined at Promontory Point in Utah 15 months earlier only connected Omaha and Sacramento).

The museum, which opened in 1970, has four fully restored historic buildings and three display buildings. The historic structures include the 1891 Living Springs School, 1904 Wolf Creek School, 1910 Homestead House, and 1917 Union Pacific Depot.

Among the exhibits in the display buildings are a blacksmith's shop, cobbler shop, creamery, general store, beauty parlor, hat shop, telephone office, printing shop, barbershop, toy shop, and dress shop, as well as cattle equipment, railroad memorabilia, military uniforms, farm equipment, sewing machines, business machines, stoves, quilts, tools, Native American artifacts, a nineteenth-century windmill, and equipment from Strasburg's 1915 post office, 1916 soda fountain, and 1917 bank.

Comanche Crossing Museum, 56060 E. Colfax Ave., P.O. Box 647, Strasburg, CO 80136. Phone: 303/622-4690. Hours: June–Aug., 1–4 daily; closed remainder of the year. Admission: free.

TELLURIDE

History museum

TELLURIDE HISTORICAL MUSEUM

The history of San Miguel County from the early mining days to the current skiing boom is presented at the Telluride Historical Museum, housed in an 1893 former miners' hospital in Telluride. Founded in 1964 as the San Miguel Historical Society, the museum recently reopened after extensive renovation.

The museum features an 1890s bedroom and kitchen, boot shop, geology exhibit, tailor shop, mining exhibit, and displays of costumes, glass, Native American artifacts, fraternal lodge memorabilia, narrow-gauge railroad materials, clothing, toys, medical equipment, manuscripts, and historical photographs from 1875 to the present. It also contains author David Lavender's collected works and inventor L. L. Nunn's early alternating-current equipment.

Telluride Historical Museum, 317 N. Fir St., P.O. Box 1597, Telluride, CO 81435. Phone and fax: 970/728-3344. Website: www.telluridemuseum.com. E-mail: museum@rmi.net. Hours: 10–5 Mon.–Fri.; closed major holidays. Admission: adults, $4; seniors, $3; children under 12, $1.

Historic hotel

NEW SHERIDAN HOTEL

Telluride's historic Sheridan Hotel, built in 1891, became the New Sheridan Hotel in 1895, but it was not until nearly a century later that it was truly revamped and refurbished.

In 1994, the bunk beds, shared baths, and monthly ski/vacation rentals were replaced with luxury accommodations. The hotel now has 28 rooms and eight suites, as well as six two-bedroom suites in a separate building a block away. Surprisingly, however, eight single rooms still share baths.

The New Sheridan Bar looks much as it did when it opened in 1895, with a carved mahogany bar, wood paneling, ornate light fixtures, and room dividers with beveled lead-glass panels. But there is a new restaurant—the Chop House—plus an exercise room, rooftop hot tub, and mountain bikes for use by hotel guests.

In 1896, William Jennings Bryan delivered his famous "Cross of Gold" speech at the hotel during his presidential run. Once the center of Telluride's social life, the hotel now serves as a base for outdoor enthusiasts who enjoy skiing, hiking, biking, horseback riding, and river rafting.

New Sheridan Hotel, 231 W. Colorado Ave., P.O. Box 980, Telluride, CO 81435. Phones: 970/728-4351 and 800/200-1891. Fax: 970/728-5024. Hours: open 24 hours, but closed from mid-Oct. to mid-Nov. and mid-Apr. to mid-May. Rates: vary with room and season.

Historic district

TELLURIDE HISTORIC DISTRICT

The Telluride Historic District encompasses most of the original mining town, including approximately 300 buildings representative of western boomtown construction in the late nineteenth century.

Telluride got its start in 1875 when mining prospectors climbed into the box canyon along the San Miguel River and found rich deposits of gold and silver. Others rushed to the area and established such successful mines as the Liberty Bell, Union, Tomboy, Pandora, Gold King, and Smuggler.

Telluride, which had a reputation as a hell-raising mining town, prospered in the 1890s, when such buildings as the New Sheridan Hotel were erected. But at the turn of the twentieth century, the boom petered out. Mines began closing due to decreasing profits and labor problems. By 1930, most of the mines and banks had shut down.

Telluride was saved from abandonment when the Idarado Mining Company bought up the existing mines in 1953, connected them via a 350-mile network of tunnels, and mined millions of dollars of copper, lead, zinc, silver, and gold before closing in 1978.

It was during this period that the idea of creating a ski resort evolved. Ground was broken for the Telluride Ski Area in 1971. It was slow to take off but gradually became one of the leading skiing areas in the West. The superb snow conditions, 3,145-foot vertical drop of the ski slopes, and unsurpassed views of the jagged San Miguel Mountains attracted thousands of skiers to Telluride.

The burgeoning tourist business brought with it new hiking, mountain-biking, and jeep trails; bluegrass, jazz, film, and hang-gliding festivals; and development of the nearby Mountain Village megaresort with lodges, condos, homes, an 18-hole golf course, and a gondola connection to town.

Despite these developments, Telluride has managed to retain much of its Victorian charm. The downtown was declared a National Historic District in 1961, and an architectural review committee scrutinizes building plans to ensure that Telluride's basic character remains intact.

Telluride Historic District. Contact: Telluride Historical Museum, 317 N. Fir St., P.O. Box 1597, Telluride, CO 81435. Phone and fax: 970/728-3344. E-mail: museum@rmi.net. Website: www.telluridemuseum.com.

TINCUP

Historic ghost town

TINCUP GHOST TOWN

Tincup was one of Colorado's wildest and wickedest mining camps during the boom days of the late nineteenth century; now it is a quiet mining ghost town with an increasing summer population.

This Gunnison County community, located 26 miles north of Pitkin, was christened Tin Cup in 1860, when prospector Jim Taylor dipped his drinking cup into a mountain stream and found gold, but it was not until 20 years later that the Gold Cup and Jimmy Mack Mines went into full gold and silver production. The town, first known as Tin Cup Camp, became Virginia City when it incorporated in 1880, then reverted simply to Tin Cup (later Tincup).

By 1882, Tincup had 3,000 residents, 20 saloons, and four cemeteries. It also had eight marshals in rapid succession during the early lawless years. The first two were said to be controlled by criminal interests; most of the others either were shot, went insane, or became preachers. Only the eighth marshal managed to serve out his term.

Tincup became the biggest silver producer in the Gunnison area, and its population swelled to 6,000. However, the town's days as a major mining center were over by 1912, and mining activities and population steadily declined. The Gold Cup Mine closed in 1917, though it reopened for short periods until 1936.

Tincup became a ghost town, and most of its buildings disappeared. However, it experienced a summer revival in the 1950s after Denver radio personality Pete Smythe claimed his morning show originated from a mythical East Tin Cup. The town now has some old and newer log cabins, a church/community center, a general store, and a restaurant open during the summer.

Tincup Ghost Town, 26 miles north of Pitkin. Contact: Gunnison County Chamber of Commerce, 500 E. Tomichi Ave., P.O. Box 36, Gunnison, CO 81230. Phones: 970/641-1501 and 800/323-2453. Fax: 970/641-3467.

TOWAC

Historic site/ethnic history and cultural visitor center

UTE MOUNTAIN TRIBAL PARK

The Ute Mountain Tribal Park, established by the Utes to preserve the culture of the Anasazi, stretches over 125,000 acres for 25 miles along the Mancos River just south of Mesa Verde National Park.

Thousand-year-old cliff houses, kivas, storage rooms, and rock art of the area's early inhabitants can be seen in the undeveloped, rugged, and isolated backcountry. All visits are conducted via full- and half-day tours led by Ute guides. All tours must be arranged in advance at the visitor center. Schedules are affected by weather conditions, especially in winter.

Ute Mountain Tribal Park, Ute Mountain Visitor Center, P.O. Box 109, Towac, CO 81334. Phones: 970/565-3751, 970/749-1456, and 800/847-5485. E-mail: utepark@cone.net. Hours: Mar.–Oct., 8:30–4:30 daily by appointment; Nov.–Feb., 8–3 Wed.–Sat. by appointment. Tour cost: full day, $30 per person; half day, $17 per person; special rates for school groups and children.

TRINIDAD

History museum/historic houses and gardens

TRINIDAD HISTORY MUSEUM

    Santa Fe Trail Museum
    Baca House
    Bloom House
    Baca House and Bloom House Historic Gardens

The Trinidad History Museum is the umbrella name for a Colorado Historical Society–operated complex covering a city block in Trinidad. The facility includes a historical museum, two historic houses, and two historic gardens.

The complex, opened in 1961, overlooks the old Santa Fe Trail in the Corazón de Trinidad Historic District (see separate listing) and provides an authentic and effective setting for interpreting the area's cultural and ethnic legacies.

Trinidad was first settled by Hispanic farmers, then became a center for the cattle industry and later for coal mining. When the railroad was extended to Santa Fe in 1880, the days of trade and migration along the Santa Fe Trail, which passes through Trinidad, came to an end.

An exhibit area at the Santa Fe Trail Museum, part of the Trinidad History Museum, which also includes the Baca and Bloom historical houses and their adjoining gardens. Courtesy Colorado Historical Society.

The Trinidad History Museum consists of the Santa Fe Trail Museum, which occupies an 1869 adobe building that once housed the families of Baca farmhands and sheepherders; 1869 Baca House, a two-story territorial-style adobe house owned by Felipe Baca, a Hispanic businessman, rancher, and community leader; 1882 Bloom House, the three-story Victorian mansion of banker–cattle rancher Frank G. Bloom and family; and the gardens of the Baca and Bloom historic houses.

The Santa Fe Trail Museum—called the Pioneer Museum until 1998—features exhibits on the Santa Fe Trail and Trinidad's important role as a stop along it. The museum contains historical photographs, commercial goods, and family possessions pertaining to the lifeways of southeastern Colorado's early settlers. In the courtyard outside the building, freight wagons and buggies used to transport goods and people along mountain branches of the Santa Fe Trail are on display.

The Baca House was built by merchant John S. Hough in 1869 and purchased by the Baca family in 1873. The adobe dwelling reflects the eclectic mixture of Hispanic and Anglo furnishings typical of prosperous

Spanish-American families in the region. It has whitewashed walls, colorful Spanish textiles, and religious objects that contrast sharply with the ornately carved and upholstered furniture.

The interior of the Bloom House has been restored and furnished to reflect the fashion of the 1880s, with intricately patterned carpets and wallpapers, lace curtains, and an abundance of Victorian china and silver.

The grounds of the Bloom House have been redesigned as a Victorian garden with brick paths, a sundial, and a cast-iron fountain. The Baca House's garden contains a traditional outdoor oven, and vegetables and herbs typically grown for use in a nineteenth-century Hispanic home.

The complex property was acquired through the efforts of the Friends of Historical Trinidad and the Trinidad Historical Society and presented to the Colorado Historical Society in the early 1960s.

Trinidad History Museum, 300 E. Main St., Trinidad, CO 81082. Phone: 719/ 846-7217. Fax: 719/846-6872. Hours: May–Sept., 10–4 daily; remainder of the year by appointment. Admission: adults, $5; seniors, $4.50; children 6–16, $2.50; children under 6, free.

Art museum

A. R. MITCHELL MEMORIAL MUSEUM OF WESTERN ART

A prominent local artist is honored in the A. R. Mitchell Memorial Museum of Western Art in Trinidad.

Approximately 250 artworks by Arthur Roy Mitchell, a leading magazine illustrator in the 1930s and 1940s, can be seen at the museum, which opened in 1981 and moved to its present location in a former department store in 1991.

Western paintings by such other artists as Harvey Dunn, Harold von Schmidt, Nick Eggenhofer, Frank Street, Ned Jacob, Frank Hoffman, Grant Reynard, Paul Milosevich, Dave Powell, and Otto Kuhler are on display as well. Museum holdings also include the Aultman Collection of Photography, representing 106 years of photography by the family-owned studio begun by Oliver E. Aultman in 1889.

In addition, the museum has Mitchell's drawings, sketches, and personal papers; western memorabilia; Native American artifacts; and Hispanic religious folk art. It also presents changing temporary exhibitions.

A. R. Mitchell Memorial Museum of Western Art, 150 E. Main St., P.O. Box 95, Trinidad, CO 81082. Phone: 719/846-4224. Fax: 719/846-0690. Hours: Apr.– Sept., 10–4 Mon.–Sat.; other times by appointment. Admission: free.

Archaeology/natural history museum

LOUDEN-HENRITZE ARCHAEOLOGY MUSEUM AT TRINIDAD STATE JUNIOR COLLEGE

The geology, fossils, and archaeology of the Trinidad area are featured at the Louden-Henritze Archaeology Museum, located in the Freudenthal Memorial Library at Trinidad State Junior College in Trinidad.

Opened in 1954, the 2,400-square-foot museum has 26 display cases devoted to archaeology, geology, paleontology, Pleistocene fauna, rock art, projectile points, historical materials, and rotating exhibits.

Among the displays are specimens from early geological formations, plant and marine animal fossils, dinosaur tracks, and artifacts pertaining to the culture, food, and tools of prehistoric man found during excavations in the Trinidad area.

Louden-Henritze Archaeology Museum, Freudenthal Memorial Library, Trinidad State Junior College, 600 Prospect St., Trinidad, CO 81082. Phone: 719/846-5508. Fax: 719/846-5667. E-mail: loretta.martin@tsjc.ccoes.edu. Hours: 10–4 Mon.–Fri.; closed national holidays. Admission: free.

Children's museum

CHILDREN'S MUSEUM

The Children's Museum in Trinidad is located in the city's 1885 original municipal building, which once housed city offices, the police department and jail, and the firehouse. The building was converted into a museum by the Trinidad Junior Historical Society in 1981. Among the museum's displays are the old jail cells, a model railroad layout, a 1936 fire truck, and a replica of a one-room schoolhouse.

Children's Museum, Trinidad Junior Historical Society, 314 N. Commercial St., Trinidad, CO 81082. Phone: 719/846-7721. Hours: June–Aug., 12–4 Mon.–Fri.; other times by appointment. Admission: free.

Historic district

CORAZÓN DE TRINIDAD HISTORIC DISTRICT

Trinidad's historic old downtown, with its early brick streets and Victorian structures, was designated the Corazón de Trinidad Historic District and listed on the National Register of Historic Places in 1973.

Trinidad, initially a stop along the Santa Fe Trail, achieved its first permanent settlement in 1859. It then became a sheep- and cattle-raising center. With the discovery of coal and the arrival of the railroad, it underwent major expansion from 1880 to 1910. However, declining coal usage and the economic hardship of the Great Depression resulted in a dwindling population, a shrinking economy, and greater dependence upon tourism.

The historic district, bounded by Brown, Chestnut, Elm, Walnut, Third, Animas, First, and Nevada streets, contains many Victorian mansions, churches, and other structures from the turn of the twentieth century, including the Aaron House Synagogue, with its red domes and turrets, and the 1869 Baca House and 1882 Bloom House, both part of the Trinidad History Museum (see separate listing). The Santa Fe Trail Museum, the Victorian garden of the Bloom House, and the Hispanic garden of the Baca House also are part of the museum complex.

Two other museums—the A. R. Mitchell Memorial Museum of Western Art and the Children's Museum (see separate listings)—are in the historic district as well.

Corazón de Trinidad Historic District. Contact: Trinidad Chamber of Commerce, 309 N. Nevada Ave., Trinidad, CO 81082. Phone: 719/846-9285. Fax: 719/846-3545.

TURRET

Historic ghost town

TURRET GHOST TOWN

The gold- and copper-mining town of Turret, 13 miles north of Salida, was not established until 1897 and enjoyed only a short boom before sinking into a gradual decline. By the early 1940s, Turret, located in Cat Creek Valley on a spur of Turret Mountain, was a ghost town.

The Gold Bug, Vivandiere, Independence, and other mines were closed before 1920, and only a handful of people remained until World War II.

More than a dozen structures still can be seen among the town's rock formations.

Turret Ghost Town, 13 miles north of Salida. Contact: Heart of the Rockies Chamber of Commerce, 406 W. Rainbow Blvd., Salida, CO 81201. Phone: 719/539-2068. Fax: 719/539-7844.

TWIN LAKES

Visitor center

MT. ELBERT POWER PLANT VISITOR'S CENTER

The Mt. Elbert Power Plant at Twin Lakes is part of the Fryingpan-Arkansas Project, which diverts water from the western slope of the Continental Divide to the eastern slope for agricultural, industrial, and municipal use.

The value of a dam and reservoir at Twin Lakes, 14 miles south of Leadville on U.S. Highway 24, was recognized as early as 1879. But it was not until 1897 that the Twin Lakes Reservoir & Canal Company acquired the rights to build a reservoir, raising the lake levels with an earthen dam and dredging the channel between the two bodies of water.

The U.S. Bureau of Land Reclamation replaced the original dam in the late 1970s and opened the power plant and visitor center in 1980. The visitor center traces the history and explains the operation of the reservoir, power plant, and water system. It also features exhibits on the fish, animals, early trappers, and Native Americans of the lake area. Tours of the power plant are available.

Mt. Elbert Power Plant Visitor's Center, U.S. Bureau of Land Reclamation, Colo. Hwy. 82, Twin Lakes, CO. (Postal address: Granite Star Rte., Granite, CO 81228.) Phone: 719/486-2325. Fax: 719/486-3631. Hours: Memorial Day–Labor Day, 10–6 Mon.–Thurs., 9–6 Fri.–Sun.; closed remainder of the year. Admission: free.

Historic hotel

TWIN LAKES NORDIC INN

The Twin Lakes Nordic Inn, located in the resort community of Twin Lakes southeast of Mt. Elbert, occupies an 1879 hotel and former stage coach stop that became a brothel during the Depression.

The spartan facility operated from 1879 to 1903 as the Twin Lakes Hotel, then underwent a series of name changes under different owners before becoming the Twin Lakes Nordic Inn in 1986. It now has 13 rooms, some of which share baths, and a German-style restaurant.

Twin Lakes Nordic Inn, 6435 Colo. Hwy. 82, Twin Lakes, CO 81251. Phones: 719/ 486-1830 and 800/626-7812. Fax: 719/486-1830. Hours: open 24 hours; closed mid–Oct. to mid-Nov. and mid-Apr. to mid-May. Rates: vary with room and season.

U.S. AIR FORCE ACADEMY

Visitor center

Barry Goldwater Visitor Center at the U.S. Air Force Academy

Pictorial and audiovisual exhibits on cadet life and the history and programs of the U.S. Air Force Academy are available at the academy's Barry Goldwater Visitor Center near Colorado Springs.

The visitor center, which opened in 1961 and recently was renamed for the former senator and Air Force officer, also offers guided and self-guided tours of some of the training center's buildings, including the 17-spire Cadet Chapel, on this 18,500-acre campus, most of which is off-limits to visitors.

Barry Goldwater Visitor Center, U.S. Air Force Academy, 2346 Academy Dr., USAF Academy, CO 80840-9400. Phone: 719/333-7742. Fax: 719/333-4402. Hours: 9–5 daily. Admission: free.

Planetarium

Center for Educational Multimedia at the U.S. Air Force Academy

Public planetarium programs—as well as academic and military-training classes for cadets—are presented by the Center for Educational Multimedia at the U.S. Air Force Academy near Colorado Springs. The 150-seat planetarium, which opened to the public in 1959, uses a Digistar projection system for its sky shows.

Center for Educational Multimedia, U.S. Air Force Academy, 2120 Cadet Dr., 34ES/CEMM, USAF Academy, CO 80840-9400. Phone: 719/333-2779. Fax: 719/333-4281. Hours: Memorial Day–Labor Day, shows at 1, 2, and 3 Tues.– Fri., plus 6:30 or 7:30 on the third Fri. evening of each month; closed all major holidays except Memorial Day and Labor Day. Admission: free.

VAIL

Ski museum/hall of fame

Colorado Ski Museum–Ski Hall of Fame

The Colorado Ski Museum–Ski Hall of Fame in Vail traces the history of skiing in Colorado and honors those individuals who have made significant contributions to the development of the sport in the state.

The museum was founded in 1976; the hall of fame was established in 1977. A former telephone-company log building was the institution's home for 15 years before it moved into its present 3,000-square-foot quarters in the town's Transportation Center building.

The museum's galleries contain skiing artifacts, equipment, clothing, photographs, and videos covering more than 130 years of Colorado skiing. Exhibits focus on the 10th Mountain Division skiing troops, the development of Colorado ski areas, the World Alpine Ski Championships, the Forest Service, and the history of snowboarding. An 1860s–1990s timeline detailing the introduction and growth of skiing in the state is also on display.

The Colorado Ski Hall of Fame has inducted more than 110 pioneers, industry leaders, competitors, and other individuals influential in the sport. They are honored with plaques bearing their photographs and biographies.

Colorado Ski Museum–Ski Hall of Fame, 231 S. Frontage Rd. East, P.O. Box 1976, Vail, CO 81658. Phone: 970/476-1876. Fax: 970/476-1879. Hours: 10–5 Tues.–Sun.; closed major holidays and during May and Oct. Admission: free.

Botanic garden

Betty Ford Alpine Gardens

The highest public alpine garden in North America—and one of the highest in the world—is the Betty Ford Alpine Gardens, located in Gerald R. Ford Park at an elevation of 8,200 feet in Vail.

The garden, opened in 1987 by the Vail Alpine Garden Foundation, was named for the former First Lady in appreciation of her many contributions to the Vail Valley, where she and President Ford live during part of the year.

The Betty Ford Alpine Gardens consist of four smaller specialized gardens—the Alpine Display Garden, which features nearly 500 varieties of alpine and subalpine plants; the Perennial Garden, with 1,500 varieties of perennial flowers, shrubs, and trees; the Meditation Garden, where Rocky Mountain plantings are arranged according to oriental design principles to capture the spiritual aspects of gardens and mountains; and the Alpine Rock Garden, a collection of alpine and subalpine plants in varied mountain landscapes.

Free tours of the garden are given from early June through Labor Day and include a visit to an early schoolhouse, which was moved to the garden by the Eagle County Historical Society in the 1980s. The Vail Alpine Garden Foundation also provides school programs, lectures, workshops, wildflower field trips, and environmental education programs in the Vail and Eagle Valleys.

The garden is located near the Gerald R. Ford Amphitheater, site of numerous cultural programs presented by the Vail Valley Foundation and Bravo Colorado Music Festival, and the Manor Vail covered bridge.

Betty Ford Alpine Gardens, Gerald R. Ford Park, S. Frontage Rd., Vail, CO. (Contact: Vail Alpine Garden Foundation, 183 Gore Creek Dr., Vail, CO 81657. Phone: 970/476-0103. Fax: 970/476-8702.) Hours: sunrise to sunset daily. Admission: free.

VICKSBURG

Historic ghost town/museum

VICKSBURG GHOST TOWN

Traces of gold were found in Vicksburg, located 17 miles west of Granite, in the 1860s, but it was not until the 1880s that the mines became truly productive and the mining camp became a town with a school, hotels, and other features of a permanent community.

Vicksburg emerged as one of the three principal mining centers in Clear Creek Canyon (the others were Beaver City and, later, Winfield). But success did not last long, and Vicksburg gradually faded away after the turn of the twentieth century. However, trees planted along ditches on both sides of the main street still survive, as do several old cabins, one of which serves as a museum. A number of newer cabins have been added by summer residents.

Vicksburg, 17 miles west of Granite. Contact: Greater Leadville Area Chamber of Commerce, 809 Harrison Ave., P.O. Box 861, Leadville, CO 80461. Phones: 719/486-3900 and 800/933-3901. Fax: 719/486-8478.

VICTOR

History museum

VICTOR/LOWELL THOMAS MUSEUM

The Victor/Lowell Thomas Museum focuses on the history of Victor and mining in the area, as well as the life of world traveler, journalist, and author Lowell Thomas, who grew up and worked in the mining town.

Founded in 1960, the museum is housed in a building that was once a hotel and, later, a furniture store. It contains historical and mining exhibits, and memorabilia and materials relating to Thomas and his family.

Thomas, a leading radio newscaster and television host, traveled to distant places, gave lectures on his travels, made travelogues, and wrote books about his experiences. He headed the commission set up by President Woodrow Wilson to prepare a historical record of World War I, served as the voice of "Movietone News" in 1935–1952, and authored more than 50 books, some of them commentary, some of them tales of travel and adventure.

Victor/Lowell Thomas Museum, 3rd St. and Victor Ave., P.O. Box 191, Victor, CO 80860. Phones: 719/689-4022 and 303/889-0709. Hours: Memorial Day–Labor Day, 9–5 daily; closed remainder of the year. Admission: free.

Historic hotel

VICTOR HOTEL

The Victor Hotel in the historic mining town of Victor occupies a former bank building erected in 1899. The four-story structure, listed on the National Register of Historic Places, was purchased in 1991, renovated, and opened as a Victorian-period hotel the following year.

The renovation resulted in 30 guest rooms that blend exposed brick and original steam registers with modern conveniences such as private baths, phones, and cable television. The lobby features period decor and retains its original cage elevator.

Victor Hotel, 4th St. and Victor Ave., Victor, CO 80860. Phone: 719/689-3553. Fax: 719/689-3979. Hours: open 24 hours. Rates: vary with room and season.

Historic district

VICTOR DOWNTOWN HISTORIC DISTRICT

Sometimes called Colorado's "City of Gold," Victor boomed at about the same time as its neighbor, Cripple Creek, in the 1890s. Gold ore was found nearly everywhere. Later on, the streets were even paved with pieces of low-grade ore.

Most of the early gold mines, such as the Ajax, Independence, and Portland, have closed. Abandoned mines dot the landscape throughout the area. But gold mining still takes place around Victor. The largest operation, less than a mile from town, is the huge Cresson open-pit mine operated by the Cripple Creek and Victor Gold Mining Company.

Victor was founded in 1893. However, its hastily erected wooden shacks and other structures burned in a fire that swept the town in 1899. Brick buildings, many of which still stand, replaced the wooden structures. Victor's population grew to more than 12,000 by 1900.

The Victor Downtown Historic District, bounded roughly by Diamond Avenue and Second, Portland, and Fifth streets, contains many relatively unaltered and contiguous commercial, public, and religious buildings of late-nineteenth- and early-twentieth-century design. They formed the commercial core of this mining community, an important part of the Cripple Creek–Victor Gold Mining District.

Among the historic buildings are an 1899 former bank building now housing the Victor Hotel, and a turn-of-the-twentieth-century building that is now the Victor/Lowell Thomas Museum (see separate listings).

Victor Downtown Historic District. Contact: Victor Chamber of Commerce, P.O. Box 83, Victor CO 80860. Phone: 719/689-3553.

WALDEN

History museum

NORTH PARK PIONEER MUSEUM

The North Park Pioneer Museum opened in Walden in 1963 in a three-room ranch house built in 1882. Two expansions later, the museum now has 27 rooms of exhibits and collections.

The 5,600-square-foot museum contains a variety of historical artifacts, as well as early census, marriage, school, and brand records, and photographs tracing the development of the area.

Among the many pioneer items on display are a 1785 beaver trap, early snowshoes, an 1859 Sharps rifle, a horsehair mattress, a player piano, a horsehide coat, and a late-nineteenth-century buggy.

The museum also contains such diverse historical collections as early tools, clothes, shoes, hats, hair curlers, sewing machines, telephones, china, saddles, barbed wire, toys, school books, light fixtures, agricultural equipment, musical instruments, stereoscopes, postcards, washing machines, railroad equipment, and military uniforms.

Many of these objects are displayed in re-created historical rooms, such as a kitchen, school, country store, post office, laundry room, china room, railroad depot, and children's room.

A number of large items are on view outside the museum building, including wagons, a hay baler, a sagebrush grubber, and a coal cutter from an early mine in the area.

North Park Pioneer Museum, 365 Logan St., P.O. Box 678, Walden, CO 80480. Phone: 970/723-4711. Hours: mid-June to mid-Sept., 12–5 Tues.–Sun.; remainder of year by appointment. Admission: free.

WALDORF

Historic ghost town

WALDORF GHOST TOWN

At 11,666 feet in elevation, the mining town of Waldorf, nine miles southwest of Georgetown, once claimed to have the highest post office in the United States and the highest and most scenic railroad ride in the world.

It also had silver, first discovered in the Argentine Pass area in 1866. There already was a mill, a mining camp called Argentine, and a Georgetown-to-Montezuma stage stop located in Leavenworth Gulch on the way to the mountain pass when the town of Waldorf was founded at the site.

By 1905, Edward John Wilcox, a former Methodist minister, had acquired 65 mines in the area. But it was difficult to ship machinery in and ore out. So the following year, he built a railroad—the Argentine Central Railroad—to haul freight and tourists to and from Waldorf and nearly to the top of nearby Mount McClellan.

Everything went well at first, but the price of silver fell in 1907, and Wilcox sold the railroad the following year. The tourist business never took off, forcing the closure of the railroad in 1917. The tracks were removed in 1921.

Waldorf struggled to survive, with only intermittent mining operations on the side of Mount McClellan. But two fires in the 1950s dealt the town a death blow, leaving only a handful of deteriorating structures.

Waldorf Ghost Town, 9 miles southwest of Georgetown. Contact: Historic Georgetown Inc., 305 Argentine St., P.O. Box 667, Georgetown, CO 80444. Phone: 303/569-2840. Fax: 303/674-2625. E-mail: histgtwn@sprynet.com.

WALSENBURG

Mining museum

WALSENBURG MINING MUSEUM

The Walsenburg Mining Museum is one of two museums operated by the Huerfano County Historical Society, the other being the Fort Francisco Museum in La Veta (see separate listing under La Veta).

The mining museum, located in an 1896 former jail, was founded in 1987 and traces the history of the southern Colorado coal-mining industry. The collections and exhibits include mining equipment, miners' personal gear, mine records and maps, union items, historical photographs, and materials relating to coalfield wars and strikes.

Walsenburg Mining Museum, Huerfano County Historical Society, 110 5th St., Walsenburg, CO 81089. (Contact: Huerfano County Chamber of Commerce, 400 Main St., Walsenburg, CO 81089-2002.) Phones: 719/738-1065 and 719/738-1081. Fax: 719/738-2506. E-mail: esheldon@rmi.net. Hours: May–Oct., 9–4 Mon.–Fri., 12–5 Sat.; closed remainder of the year. Admission: adults, $2; seniors, $1; children under 12, $1.

WESTCLIFFE

Schoolhouse museum

WESTCLIFF SCHOOLHOUSE MUSEUM

A restored 1891 schoolhouse is the site of the Westcliff Schoolhouse Museum, which features a re-created one-room classroom from the late nineteenth century and historical photographs of the Westcliffe area.

The Westcliff (this is the town's original spelling) schoolhouse was built of local fieldstone and served local schoolchildren from 1891 to 1953. Since 1990, it has been a museum and community center. The building was listed on the National Register of Historic Places in 1989.

Westcliff Schoolhouse Museum, 302 S. 4th St., P.O. Box 466, Westcliffe, CO 81252. Phone: 719/783-9453. Hours: Memorial Day–Labor Day, 1–4 daily; other times by appointment. Admission: free.

WESTMINSTER

Horse museum/art gallery

ARABIAN HORSE TRUST MUSEUM

The Arabian Horse Trust, established in 1974, is a nonprofit foundation serving the Arabian horse industry by tracing the history of Arabian horses, providing educational programs, and conducting research in the field. The trust's headquarters in Westminster feature a museum, art gallery, library, and archives.

Among the items exhibited in the museum are noteworthy saddles, including the one given to President Dwight D. Eisenhower; bronze sculptures by prominent artists; and other materials pertaining to Arabian horses. Artwork depicting Arabian horses is displayed in the gallery.

Arabian Horse Trust Museum, 12000 Zuni St., Westminster, CO 80234. Phone: 303/450-4710. Hours: 8:30–4:30 Mon.–Fri.; closed major holidays. Admission: suggested donation of $3 per person and $10 per group.

Nature/butterfly/insect center

BUTTERFLY PAVILION AND INSECT CENTER

The Butterfly Pavilion and Insect Center in Westminster is one of only six butterfly houses in the nation. Opened in 1995 by the Rocky Mountain Butterfly Consortium, the 18,000-square-foot facility re-creates a tropical forest filled with more than 1,200 butterflies of 50 species. There is also an insect center introducing visitors to arthropods native to Colorado and to exotic species from around the world.

The butterfly pavilion covers 7,200 square feet and has more than 100 species of tropical and subtropical plants, which provide nectar and shelter for the butterflies. A 16,000-square-foot addition is under construction.

The nature center also has a working beehive; a cart on which insects may be examined—and sometimes touched; microscopes to view magnified arthropod parts, such as butterfly wings, spider legs, or tarantula fangs; and exhibits on the Atlantic and Pacific Oceans, including a pool filled with marine life that visitors can touch.

Butterfly Pavilion and Insect Center, 6262 W. 104th Ave., Westminster, CO 80020. Phone: 303/469-5441. Fax: 303/657-5944. Hours: 9–5 Tues.–Sun. Admission: adults, $6.50; seniors, $4.50; children 4–12, $3.50; children 3 and under, free.

Historic house

BOWLES HOUSE MUSEUM

The Bowles House Museum, operated by the Westminster Historical Society, is located in an 1876 Italianate building that was slated for destruction until a third-grade class from Vista Grande Elementary School launched a successful campaign to save it in 1981.

Since then, the house has been restored, transformed into a museum by the historical society, and listed on the National Register of Historic Places.

The house was erected by Edward Bowles, a freight handler who became Westminster's second homesteader in 1871 and lived in the house until his death in 1923. The building was abandoned in the late 1970s.

The museum opened in 1988 and now contains the restored living and dining rooms and six other rooms filled with photographs, clothing, furniture, kitchen utensils, books, and other historical materials from the early twentieth century. Westminster's first town hall—a small one-room structure—also has been moved to the site.

Bowles House Museum, Westminster Historical Society, 1924 W. 72nd Ave., Westminster, CO 80030. Phone: 303/430-7929. Hours: 10–4 Sat.; closed major holidays. Admission: adults, $1; children, $.50.

WHEAT RIDGE

Historic park/houses

WHEAT RIDGE HISTORIC PARK

Wheat Ridge Historic Park contains three types of early houses and the town's first post office.

The principal attraction is a sod house, built on the farm of James H. Baugh sometime before 1865. The house was constructed of 5,000 square feet of sod, cut in strips 30 inches wide and 6 inches deep. Listed on the National Register of Historic Places in 1973, the sod house was renovated into a museum as part of a community bicentennial project. Furnishings now reflect farm life in the 1880s and 1890s.

In 1892, Bert White bought 15 acres of the original 160-acre Baugh farm and constructed a brick bungalow just south of the sod house in the early 1900s. That five-room building also is part of the historical park.

Another early structure is a log cabin built sometime around 1863 by Henry Stevens, one of the first homesteaders in the Colorado Territory. The cabin was moved to Johnson Park in Wheat Ridge in 1959 and then relocated to its present site in 1985.

The fourth building at the historical park is Wheat Ridge's first post office, which was erected in 1913 and moved to the site in the early 1990s.

The park, established in 1975, is overseen by the Wheat Ridge Parks Department, and the museum is operated by the Wheat Ridge Historical Society.

Wheat Ridge Historic Park, 4610 Robb St., P.O. Box 1833, Wheat Ridge, CO 80034. Phone: 303/421-9111. Hours: 10–3 Wed.–Sat.; closed national holidays. Admission: donation requested.

Historic cemetery

MOUNT OLIVET CEMETERY

Mount Olivet Cemetery in Wheat Ridge opened in 1892 on the 440-acre farm of Joseph P. Machebeuf, Colorado's first Catholic bishop, who donated the land to the Denver Diocese as a Catholic burial ground.

Machebeuf arrived in Colorado from Santa Fe, New Mexico, in 1860, traveling from one mining camp to another and preaching the gospel before coming to Denver in 1862. He was made bishop in 1868. He is among the approximately 120,000 people interred at the cemetery, which now covers 393 acres.

Mount Olivet has nine mausoleums, among them a memorial to the Mother Cabrini Orphanage and a Pioneer Section, which includes some burial transplants from the old Mount Calvary Cemetery. The latest mausoleum is the converted 1969 chapel, which has four individual chapels.

Among those buried at the cemetery are Henrietta Dietemann and her son, Johnny, who was killed and scalped by Indians in Elbert County in 1868; William Gilpin, a member of the Fremont Expedition, who was appointed first governor of the Colorado Territory by Abraham Lincoln in 1861; John K. Mullen, who made Denver the flour-milling capital of the Rockies and became a leading philanthropist in the late nineteenth century; Horace A.W. and Elizabeth "Baby" Doe Tabor, who struck it rich in Leadville's silver mines, lost their fortune, and died virtually penniless; and John "Jack" Swigert, a former astronaut who was elected to the U.S. House of Representatives but died before taking office (his statue is in the U.S. Capitol's Statuary Hall).

Mount Olivet Cemetery, 12801 W. 44th Ave., Wheat Ridge, CO 80033. Phone: 303/424-7785. Fax: 303/424-5263. Hours: sunrise–sunset daily.

WINDSOR

Historic museum village

LAKEVIEW PIONEER VILLAGE

The Lakeview Pioneer Village in Windsor is a collection of five historic turn-of-the-twentieth-century buildings (an 1881 railroad depot, 1903 schoolhouse, 1904 shop that was formerly a creamery, 1906 town hall, and 1914 country church) and a 1991 re-creation of an early general store, all operated as a museum by the Windsor-Severance Historical Society. The museum opened in 1975.

The buildings contain artifacts and other historical materials pertaining to their original functions and to the history of the area. Visitors can arrange for a guided tour of the complex by contacting the local chamber of commerce.

Lakeview Pioneer Village, Windsor-Severance Historical Society, 116 5th St., Windsor, CO 80550. (Contact: Windsor Chamber of Commerce, 116 5th St., Windsor, CO 80550.) Phone: 970/686-7189. Hours: summer, 2–4 Tues., Thurs., and Sat.; winter, by appointment. Admission: free.

WINFIELD (Chaffee County)

Historic ghost town

WINFIELD GHOST TOWN

Winfield was one of seven mining camps in Clear Creek Canyon, 13 miles west of Granite in Chaffee County, in the 1860s and 1870s.

By 1890, Winfield was booming and boasted 1,500 residents. But after the silver crash of 1893, it was nearly deserted. The town experienced a brief revival in the early 1900s, when new companies began to work the old mines. The respite, however, was temporary, and Winfield was abandoned after World War I. A few of the old log cabins remain, supplemented by a number of newer summer cottages in the vicinity.

Winfield Ghost Town, 13 miles west of Granite. Contact: Greater Leadville Area Chamber of Commerce, 809 Harrison Ave., P.O. Box 861, Leadville, CO 80461. Phones: 719/486-3900 and 800/933-3901. Fax: 719/486-8478.

WINFIELD (Teller County)

Historic ghost town

WINFIELD GHOST TOWN

The base of mining millionaire Winfield Scott Stratton's operations was Winfield (sometimes called Stratton), five miles north of Victor in Teller County. Founded in 1900, Winfield was a company town with numerous brick buildings but no saloon or dance halls.

Stratton was a carpenter who drifted from one mining camp to another until he ended up in the Cripple Creek Mining District, where he discovered gold at the Independence Mine in 1891.

He made millions of dollars from his mines and other business deals, but he failed to find gold in Winfield.

Stratton died in 1902, but the town of Winfield survived until 1980, when a gold-leaching operator demolished most of the surviving buildings. Only a few weathered structures remain.

Winfield Ghost Town, 5 miles north of Victor. Contact: Victor Chamber of Commerce, P.O. Box 83, Victor, CO 80860. Phone: 719/689-3553.

WINTER PARK

Historic ranch

COZENS RANCH MUSEUM

The Cozens Ranch Museum between Winter Park and Fraser consists of a ranch house, stage stop, and post office constructed in 1874–1881 and now restored to reflect that period.

The structures were built by William Zane Cozens, who moved his family to Fraser Valley in 1874 after a career as sheriff in Central City. At its peak, the ranch covered more than 700 acres.

The Grand County Historical Association, which operates the Grand County Museum in Hot Sulphur Springs, restored and opened the ranch as a museum in 1990.

The 13-room ranch house, which was the residence of the Cozens family, contains some of the original wallpaper, carpets, furnishings, and family photographs. Each of the six upstairs bedrooms now interprets a different time period—for example, early settlement and development, and the time of frontier doctor Susan Anderson (called "Doc Susie") and President Dwight D. Eisenhower, who vacationed in Fraser Valley. The 1876 stage stop included a dining room. The post office was the first in Fraser Valley. The museum also has a full-size replica of the stagecoach that ran between Georgetown and Hot Sulphur Springs from 1876 to 1905.

Cozens Ranch Museum, 77849 U.S. Hwy. 40, Winter Park, CO 80482. (Contact: Grand County Historical Assn., P.O. Box 165, Hot Sulphur Springs, CO 80451.) Phone: 970/726-5488. Fax: 970/725-0129. E-mail: gcha@rkymtnhi.com. Website: www.grandcountymuseum.com. Hours: Memorial Day–Labor Day, 10–5 Mon.–Sat., 12–5 Sun.; remainder of the year, 11–4 Wed.–Sat., 12–4 Sun.; closed New Year's Day, Thanksgiving, and Christmas. Admission: adults, $4; seniors, $3; children 6–18, $2; children under 6, free; families, $10.

WOODLAND PARK

History museum

UTE PASS HISTORICAL SOCIETY MUSEUM

The Ute Pass Historical Society Museum in Woodland Park is seeking a permanent home. Meanwhile, it maintains a small changing exhibition and operates a bookstore in the Ute Pass Cultural Center. The Ute Pass area, which includes the U.S. Highway 24 corridor from Manitou Springs to the top of the pass west of Divide, follows the original trail of the Ute Indians.

The museum started out as the Pikes Peak Museum in Cascade, moved to Woodland Park in 1991, and then closed three years later to search for more adequate facilities.

The museum has an extensive collection of Ute Indian artifacts. Other collections include early agricultural equipment, ice-cutting equipment from the days when ice was cut from local ponds and shipped by rail, and materials relating to the interned Japanese Americans who worked the area's potato fields during World War II.

Ute Pass Historical Society Museum, Ute Pass Cultural Center, 720 W. Hwy. 24, P.O. Box 6875, Woodland Park, CO 80866. Phone: 719/686-1125. Hours: 9–12 Wed.; closed holidays. Admission: free.

WRAY

History museum

WRAY MUSEUM

The Wray Museum, located near the Colorado-Nebraska-Kansas line in Wray, is best known for its comprehensive exhibit—created by the Smithsonian Institution—on paleo-Indians. It also marks one of the oldest and largest communal bison-kill sites from the Stone Age.

In 1973, rancher Bob Jones, Jr., stumbled across some weathered bones while leveling a ridge on his property. Further investigation yielded more fossils and ancient spearheads.

The Smithsonian Institution was contacted, and a team headed by archaeologist Dennis Stanford was sent to investigate. Some 248 rare projectile points and 41,000 bones and bone fragments from 300 Ice Age bison were uncovered at the site. The animals are believed to have been hunted and killed by prehistoric Native Americans some 10,000 years ago.

After the 1973–1975 excavations, the spearheads and fossils were moved to the Smithsonian Institution in Washington. The Smithsonian later agreed to produce a permanent exhibit on the subject for the local museum. The exhibit, which re-creates a portion of the bone bed and features artifacts and photographs, opened in 1992 and is one of the few permanent Smithsonian exhibits outside the nation's capitol.

The 13,500-square-foot museum, opened in 1970 and housed in a former restaurant, has another noteworthy exhibit, this one dealing with the Battle of Beecher Island, which took place in 1868 on a small island in the Arikaree River approximately 15 miles south of present-day Wray (see separate listing under Beecher Island).

The museum also contains collections and exhibits highlighting textiles, art, Native American artifacts, big-game trophies, historical photographs, and other topics.

Wray Museum, 205 E. 3rd St., P.O. Box 161, Wray, CO 80758. Phone: 970/ 332-5063. Fax: 970/332-3137. E-mail: walborn@plains.net. Hours: 10–5 Tues.– Sat.; closed major holidays. Admission: adults, $1; children 12 and under, $.50.

YUMA

History museum

YUMA MUSEUM

The Yuma Museum near Lake Yuma traces the history of the area in its 3,200-square-foot facility and a two-room country schoolhouse moved to the site.

The museum, which opened in 1972, features dolls, farm tools, photographs, a buggy, a lumber wagon, a Congressional Medal of Honor received by resident George J. Shopp in the Civil War, a memorial plaque with the names of early settlers, and information and memorabilia pertaining to local families. A windmill, a railroad caboose, and a gazebo (actually a restored church bell tower) are displayed outdoors.

One room of the former Blach School, relocated from northeast of Yuma, has been restored as a schoolroom; the other room contains photographs, documents, genealogical materials, and old newspapers.

Yuma Museum, 306 S. Detroit St., P.O. Box 454, Yuma, CO 80759. Phone: 970/ 848-5430. Hours: summer, 1–5 Wed.–Sun.; winter, 8–11:30 Mon.–Fri.; closed holidays. Admission: free.

Appendix A

GEOGRAPHIC GUIDE BY REGION

NORTHEAST COLORADO

NORTHWEST COLORADO

Appendix B

TYPES OF MUSEUMS, HISTORIC SITES, AND RELATED FACILITIES

404 ♦ APPENDIX B

Selected Bibliography

Bancroft, Caroline, assisted by Daniel K. Peterson. *Unique Ghost Towns and Mountain Spots*. Boulder: Johnson Printing, 1997.

Bauer, Carolyn. *Colorado Ghost Towns*. Frederick, CO: Renaissance House, 1987.

Bauer, William H., J. L. Ozment, and J. H. Willard. *Colorado Postal History: The Post Offices*. Denver: J-B Publishing, 1971.

Benson, Maxine. *1001 Colorado Place Names*. Topeka: University Press of Kansas, 1994.

Brandes, T. Donald. *Military Posts of Colorado*. Fort Collins: Old Army Press, 1973.

Brown, Robert L. *Ghost Towns of the Colorado Rockies*. Caldwell, ID: Caxton Printers, 1990.

Caughey, Bruce, and Dean Winstanley. *The Colorado Guide*. 4th ed. Golden, CO: Fulcrum Publishing, 1997.

Colorado's Historic Sites and Museums. Frederick, CO: Renaissance House, 1989.

Colorado's Museums. Denver: Colorado-Wyoming Assn. of Museums, 1997.

Dallas, Sandra. *Colorado Ghost Towns and Mining Camps*. Norman: University of Oklahoma Press, 1985.

Directory of State Register Properties. Denver: Colorado Historical Society, 1997.

Eberhardt, Perry. *Ghosts of the Colorado Plains*. Athens: Swallow Press/Ohio University Press, 1985.

———. *Guide to the Colorado Ghost Towns and Mining Camps*. 4th ed. Athens: Swallow Press/Ohio University Press, 1997.

Florin, Lambert. *Ghost Towns of the Rockies*. New York: Promontory Press, 1987.

Gregory, Lee. *Colorado Scenic Guide: Northern Region*. 3rd ed. Boulder: Johnson Books, 1996.

———. *Colorado Scenic Guide: Southern Region*. 3rd ed. Boulder: Johnson Books, 1996.

Hughes, J. Donald. *American Indians in Colorado*. Boulder: Pruett Publishing, 1977.

Jessen, Kenneth. *Ghost Towns: Colorado Style*, vol. 1, *Northern Region*. Loveland, CO: J. V. Publications, 1998.

———. *Ghost Towns: Colorado Style*, vol. 2, *Central Region*. Loveland, CO: J. V. Publications, 1998.

Le Massena, Robert A. *Colorado's Mountain Railroads*. Denver: Sundance Publications, 1984.

Leonard, Stephen J., and Thomas J. Noel. *Denver: Mining Camp to Metropolis*. Niwot: University Press of Colorado, 1990.

McTighe, James. *Roadside History of Colorado*. Rev. ed. Boulder: Johnson Books, 1989.

Nall, Bruce, and Dick Kreck. *Colorado's Scenic Railroads*. Englewood, CO: Westcliffe Publishers, 1997.

Noel, Thomas J. *Buildings of Colorado*. New York: Oxford University Press, 1997.

———. *Colorado: A Liquid History and Tavern Guide to the Highest State*. Golden, CO: Fulcrum Publishing, 1999.

———. *Denver Landmarks and Historic Districts: A Pictorial Guide*. Niwot: University Press of Colorado, 1996.

Noel, Thomas J., Paul F. Mahoney, and Richard E. Stevens. *Historical Atlas of Colorado*. Norman: University of Oklahoma Press, 1993.

Rust, Mary Jane Massey. *Historic Hotels of the Rocky Mountains*. Niwot: Roberts Rinehart Publishers, 1997.

Ruth, Kent. *Landmarks of the West: A Guide to Historic Sites*. Rev. ed. Lincoln: University of Nebraska Press, 1986.

Ubbelohde, Carl, Maxine Bensen, and Duane A. Smith. *A Colorado History*. Rev. ed. Boulder: Pruett Publishing, 1976.

Wilkins, Tivis E. *Colorado Railroads: Chronological Development*. Boulder: Pruett Publishing, 1974.

Wolle, Muriel Sibell. *Stampede to Timberline*. Boulder: Muriel Sibell Wolle, 1957.

The WPA Guide to 1930s Colorado. Lawrence: University of Kansas Press, 1987.

Index

Rowe, George, Museum, 21, 351
Roxborough State Park, 18, 294–
   295; George T. O'Malley Visitors
   Center, 294–295; Persse House,
   294–295
Royal Gorge Bridge, 4, 19, 81
Russell Gulch ghost town, 344–345

Sagauche, 345
Saguache County Museum, 16, 345
St. Cajetan's Church. See Auraria
   Higher Education Center
St. Elizabeth's Church. See Auraria
   Higher Education Center
St. Elmo ghost town, 4, 19, 345–346
St. Elmo Hotel, 8, 324
St. Mary's Academy, 194; Coyle
   Gallery, 194
St. Vrain Historical Society, 297–
   299; Hoverhome 19, 297; Old
   Mill Park, 297–299
Sts. John ghost town, 4, 346
Salida, 347
Salida Downtown Historic District,
   347
Salida Museum, 347
Sand Creek Massacre, 22
Sanford, 347–348
Sangre de Cristo Arts Center and
   Conference Center, 6, 12, 16,
   335; Buell Children's Museum, 6,
   16, 21, 335
San Juan County Historical Society
   Museum, 7, 16, 352–354
San Juan Historical Society Mu-
   seum, 326
San Luis, 348–349
San Luis Museum and Cultural
   Center, 15, 348
San Rafael Historic District, 182
Santa Fe Trail Museum. See
   Trinidad History Museum
Sardy House, 5, 38
Schaefer, Dan, Visitors Center. See
   National Renewable Energy
   Laboratory
Schoolhouses, historic, 2, 9, 18, 20–

   21, 42–43, 205, 255–256, 314,
   329, 351, 375, 405
Schwayder Gallery. See University of
   Denver
Science museums and centers, 1, 12–
   14, 59–60, 134–137, 209–210,
   419. See also specific types
Sculpture parks, 1, 11–12, 194, 212,
   254, 419
Second Central School Building,
   20, 205
Shelby American Collection, 57
Silt, 349–350
Silt Historical Park, 349–350
Silver Cliff, 350
Silver Cliff Museum, 350
Silver Plume, 351–352
Silver Plume Depot, 351
Silver Plume Historic District. See
   Georgetown–Silver Plume
   Historic District
Silverton, 7–8, 352–355
Silverton Historic District, 354–355
Singer Gallery. See Mizel Arts Center
   of the Jewish Community Center
Skiing museums, 1, 15–16, 369–
   370, 419
Snowmass Village, 355
Sommers-Bausch Observatory. See
   University of Colorado at
   Boulder
South Central region, 3–4, 383–384
Southeast region, 6–7, 385
Southern Ute Indian Cultural
   Center Museum, 8, 15, 267–268
South Park City Museum, 4, 10, 204
South Platte Visitor Center. See U.S.
   Army Corps of Engineers
Southwest region, 7–8, 385
Space Exploration, Museum of. See
   May Natural History Museum
   and Museum of Space Explora-
   tion
Space museums. See Aviation and
   space museums
Spar City ghost town, 4, 19, 356
Springfield, 7, 356–357